Cont

D0434557

The *Michelin maps* you will need with this guide are :

PRINCIPAL SIGHTS

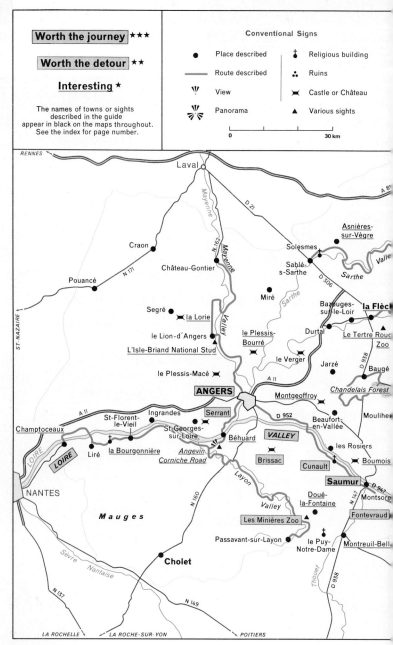

| Worth the journey ★★★ |
| Worth the detour ★★ |
| Interesting ★ |

The names of towns or sights described in the guide appear in black on the maps throughout. See the index for page number.

Conventional Signs

●	Place described	⊤	Religious building
—	Route described	∴	Ruins
ⱴ	View	⋈	Castle or Château
ⱴⱴ	Panorama	▲	Various sights

0 _____ 30 km

TOURISM IN THE LOIRE VALLEY...

To know the region more thoroughly study your

MICHELIN MAP

The symbols indicate:

☀	▬▬▬	Picturesque routes
	ⱴ Y	Panoramas, viewing points
▲ ⊤ ⋈		Interesting sites and monuments
▦ GR 3		Footpaths, State forests
▭ ● ⚑		Swimming pools, golf courses, etc.

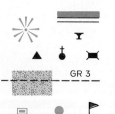

4

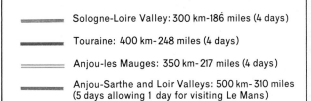

Sologne-Loire Valley: 300 km-186 miles (4 days)

Touraine: 400 km-248 miles (4 days)

Anjou-les Mauges: 350 km-217 miles (4 days)

Anjou-Sarthe and Loir Valleys: 500 km-310 miles
(5 days allowing 1 day for visiting Le Mans)

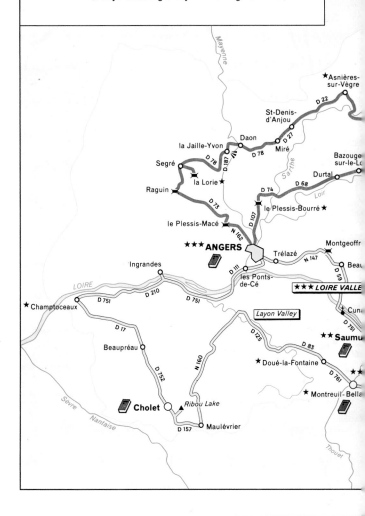

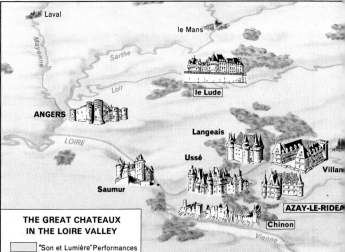

THE GREAT CHATEAUX
IN THE LOIRE VALLEY

"Son et Lumière" Performances

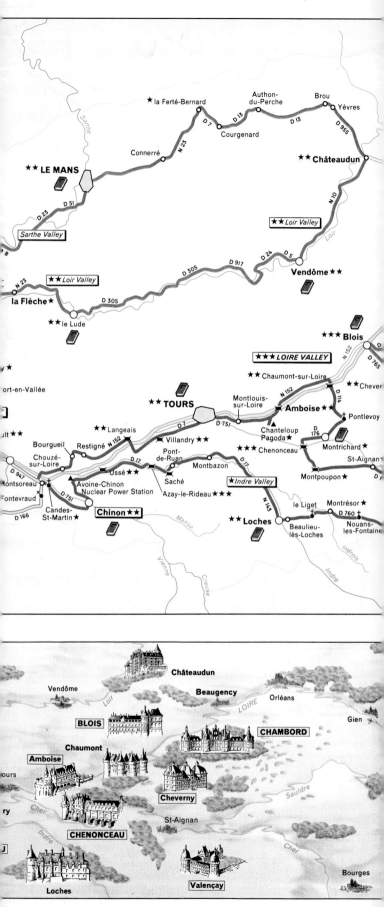

★ la Ferté-Bernard

Authon-du-Perche

Brou
○ Yèvres

D 7
D 13
D 13
D 955

Courgenard

Connerré
N 23

★★ **LE MANS**

★★ **Châteaudun**

D 23
D 51

N 10

Sarthe

Loir

★★ Loir Valley

Sarthe Valley

D 24
D 5

Vendôme ★★

N 23
★★ Loir Valley

D 917
D 305

la Flèche ★

D 305

★★ le Lude

★★★ **Blois**

Loir

N 152
D 765

★★★ *LOIRE VALLEY*

★★ Chaumont-sur-Loire
★★ Chever

ort-en-Vallée ★

★★ **TOURS**

Montlouis-sur-Loire

N 152

Amboise ★★

D 114

† Pontlevoy

★★ Langeais

D 7
D 751

Chanteloup Pagoda ★

D 176

★★ Villandry ★★

ult ★★

Bourgueil
Restigné
N 152

Chouzé-sur-Loire

Pont-de-Ruan

★★★ Chenonceau

Montrichard ★

D 947

Ussé ★★
D 17

Saché

Montbazon

D 17

St-Aignan ★

Montsoreau
D 751

Avoine-Chinon Nuclear Power Station

Azay-le-Rideau ★★★

Montpoupon ★

D ?

Fontevraud

★ *Indre Valley*

D 166

Candes-St-Martin ★

Chinon ★★

Manse

N 143

le Liget

Montrésor ★

Vienne

Creuse

★★ **Loches**

Beaulieu-lès-Loches

D 760 †

Nouans-les-Fontaine

Indrois

Indre

Châteaudun

Beaugency

Vendôme

Loir

LOIRE

Orléans

Gien

BLOIS

CHAMBORD

Chaumont

Amboise

ours

Cheverny

St-Aignan

Sauldre

CHENONCEAU

Cher

J

ry

Indre

Loches

Valençay

Cher

Bourges

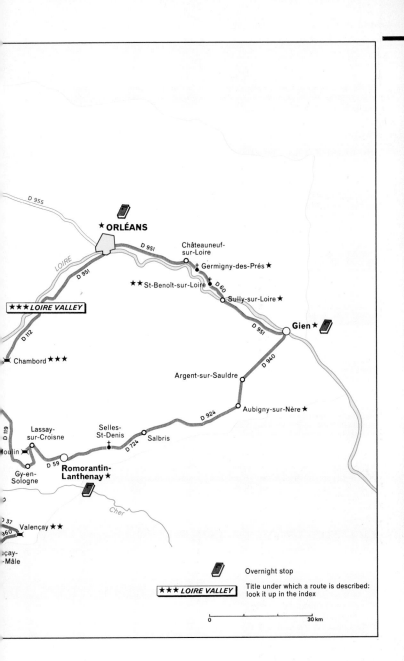

D 955

★ ORLÉANS

Châteauneuf-
sur-Loire

✝ Germigny-des-Prés ★

D 951

LOIRE

★★ St-Benoît-sur-Loire

D 60

Sully-sur-Loire ★

D 951

★★★ LOIRE VALLEY

D 112

Gien ★

D 951

D 940

Chambord ★★★

Argent-sur-Sauldre

D 924

Aubigny-sur-Nère ★

D 119

Lassay-
sur-Croisne

Selles-
St-Denis

Salbris

D 724

oulin

D 59

Gy-en-
Sologne

Romorantin-
Lanthenay ★

Cher

D 37

360

Valençay ★★

çay-
-Mâle

Overnight stop

★★★ LOIRE VALLEY   Title under which a route is described:
look it up in the index

0   30 km

(Photo S. Chirol)

Chenonceau Château

PLACES TO STAY

For names and addresses see the chapter Practical Information at the end of the guide.

The mention Facilities under the individual headings or after place names in the body of the guide refers to the information given on these pages.
The map below indicates towns selected for the accommodation and leisure facilities which they offer to the holidaymaker. To help you plan your route and choose your accommodation consult the following Michelin publications.

Accommodation

The **Michelin Red Guide France** of hotels and restaurants and the **Michelin Guide Camping Caravaning France** are annual publications which present a selection of hotels, restaurants and camping sites. The final choice is based on regular on-the-spot enquiries and visits. Both the hotels and camping sites are classified according to the standard of comfort of their amenities. Establishments which are notable for their setting, their décor, their quiet and secluded location and their warm welcome are distinguished by special symbols. The Michelin Red Guide France also gives the addresses and telephone numbers of the local Tourist Information Centres (Syndicat d'Initiative).

Youth hostels etc.

Several organisations cater for children, school groups and adults and offer courses at moderate prices: the Youth Hostel in Tours (Auberge de Jeunesse), the Vacances Familles d'Amboise Village, the Maison Rurale d'Education et d'Orientation.

Paying guests

One of the charms of this region is the wealth of châteaux and manor houses, often in quiet and attractive settings. Certain of these privately-owned mansions open their doors to paying guests, who have the pleasure of enjoying the gracious surroundings for a moderate cost. For their addresses and terms apply to the **Regional Tourist Committees**, to the **Tourist Information Centres** in Tours, Saumur, Chinon and Blois or to such organising bodies as **Château Accueil**.

Route planning, sports and recreation

The **Michelin 1/200 000 maps** in the series 🗺 to 🗺 and 🗺 to 🗺 cover the whole of France. Those which serve this guide are shown in the diagram on p 3. One glance will reveal the position of a place. In addition to information about the roads, the maps show beaches, bathing places on lakes and rivers, swimming pools, golf courses, race courses, gliding grounds, aerodromes, forest roads, long-distance footpaths, etc.

OUTDOOR ACTIVITIES

For names and addresses see the chapter Practical Information at the end of the guide.

Walking

There is a network of footpaths covering the area described in the guide. Topographical guides, published by the Fédération Française de la Randonnée Pédestre, show the routes of the long-distance footpaths (sentiers de grande randonnée – GR) and give good advice to walkers.
The **GR 3** which follows the Loire Valley passes through the Orléans, Russy and Chinon forests;
The **GR 3c** runs westwards across the Sologne from Gien to Mont-près-Chambord;
The **GR 31** runs from Mont-près-Chambord, on the southeast edge of the Boulogne Forest, south to Souesmes passing through the Sologne woods;
The **GR 32** passes though the Orléans Forest from north to south;
The **GR 335**, ''From the Loir to the Loire'', runs north-south between Lavardin and Vouvray;
The **GR 35** follows the Loir Valley;
The **GR 36**, the English Channel to the Pyrenees route, crosses the region between Le Mans and Montreuil-Bellay;
The **GR 46** follows the Indre Valley.

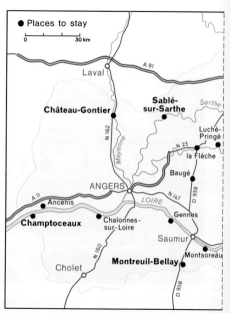

10

Riding and pony trekking

Noted for its studs and the National Riding School at St-Hilaire-St-Florent near Saumur, the region has numerous riding centres which are open to visitors. Some serve as an overnight halt for those on trekking holidays.
Trekking guides indicating the itineraries and overnight stops are published by regional and national associations.
Details of local equestrian centres are available from the Tourist Information Centres.

Cruising

In addition to the local sailing clubs centred on lakes, reservoirs and other stretches of water, the Loire basin offers opportunities for cruising enthusiasts to enjoy its waters. Pottering on the river is an original way to discover and appreciate to the full the beauty and calm of the riverside landscapes.
The **Maine** basin has good navigable stretches on the Oudon (downstream from Segré), on the Mayenne (downstream from Laval) and the Sarthe (downstream from Le Mans). Boats can be hired (no permit required) at Andouillé, Angers, Château-Gontier, Châteauneuf-sur-Sarthe, Chenillé-Changé, Grez-Neuville, Laval, Malicorne, Le Mans, Noyen-sur-Sarthe and Sablé.
The **Loire** offers similar opportunities as do the various canals (Briare and Loire lateral canals) starting from Châtillon-sur-Loire (Loiret), Montargis (Loiret) and Rogny-les-sept-écluses (Yonne).
For further information on cruising in the area apply to the Tourist Information Centres or to the Regional Tourist Committees.

Air trips

Throughout the year, weather permitting, it is possible to have a bird's eye view of the Loire Valley. Helicopters or small aircraft, such as the Cessna which has excellent visibility, fly over Chinon, Chambord, Chenonceau, Azay-le Rideau and the Valley of the Kings, starting from Tours-St-Symphorien, and over Amboise, Cheverny, Beaugency and the Sologne from Blois-le-Breuil. Other circuits, in accordance with the customer's wishes, are also possible.

Fishing

The swift or slow waters of the Loire Valley offer the fisherman various attractive possibilities.
Every type of authorised fishing is available: angling for gudgeon, roach and dace, or trying for pike or even the striped mullet which comes upstream as far as Amboise in summer, or catching the catfish, the tench and the carp in the holes in the Loire, the Indre and the Loir or in the pools in the Sologne which are also full of perch.
Trout can be found in the Creuse, the Sauldre, the streams of Anjou or the tributaries of the Loir while the Berry, Briare, or Orléans Canals contain eels and sometimes crayfish which can be caught with a dipping net.
Salmon and shad fishing require a flat-bottomed boat; the professionals have specialist equipment such as nets stretched across the river and held in place by poles fixed in the bed.

Regulations and open seasons. – Both differ according to whether the water is classed in the first category (salmon type fish) or in the second (non salmon type fish).
Salmon fishing is forbidden from 17 June to 28 February and is confined to the Loire.

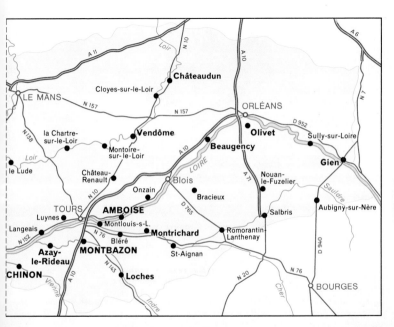

Useful tips. – It is best to observe the local, departmental and national regulations and to join a fishing association approved by the Préfet. The membership card, duly stamped, allows one three rods on second category water administered by a fishing association or one line on all public water.

Only one line is allowed on first category water and a supplementary stamp is required. Additional tax is payable on the right to cast, on fishing with nets and on fishing for salmon, etc.

On private property, where the fishing rights belong to the owner of the bank, this owner's permission must be obtained.

In the case of certain private lakes, which are excluded from the fishing legislation, the owner's permission (annual, monthly or daily permit) is the only formality required and can be granted at any time of the year.

Minimum size of catch. – The national regulations state that the fisherman must return to the water any fish which does not attain the minimum permitted length (40 cm for the pike, 35 cm for the sauger, 23 cm for the trout, 50 cm for the salmon, 9 cm for the crayfish).

Hunting

The Loire country is very popular for hunting as its varied terrain provides a diversity of sport: stalking, beating, coursing or shooting.

The plains of the Beauce and the meadows of Touraine and Anjou provide good feeding grounds for partridge, quail, thrush and lark. Hares find cover in the copses and the fields of maize and sugarbeet. Wild rabbits breed in the sterile marshland together with the partridge while the pheasant favours the watering places, particularly in the Cisse Valley.

Red deer and roe deer are to be found in the thick woods around Baugé, in the forests of Château-la-Vallière and Loches and around Valençay.

The wild boar favours the deep forest of Orléans and Amboise and the neighbourhood of Chambord.

The islands and banks of the Loire provide nests for teal and mallard.

The Sologne is a favourite haunt of game: duck, teal and woodcock on the lakes and rivers, pheasants by the roadside, wild boar in the marshy brakes and deer in the woods.

It is necessary to be affiliated to a private association or to a communal hunting society. Some bodies and private owners, however, issue permits for a single day only.

Cycling

The Fédération Française de Cyclotourisme and its departmental committees publishes a number of cycling tours of varying lengths.

Although the country is fairly level, the Indre Valley, the Sologne, the forest tracks and, above all, the banks of the Loire, particularly away from the main roads, are very attractive. The ever-changing scene and the rich heritage of the Loire Valley greatly add to the pleasure of a cycling tour.

Tourist routes

These routes, which are drawn up by the Regional Tourist Committees, recommend all the places described in this guide; there are regular coach tours of the châteaux.

*The current **Michelin Guide France***
offers a selection of pleasant, quiet and well situated
hotels. Each entry includes the facilities provided
(gardens, tennis courts, swimming pool and equipped beach)
and annual closure dates.

Also included is a selection of establishments recommended for their cuisine:
– well prepared meals at a moderate price, stars for good cooking.

*The current **Michelin Guide Camping Caravaning France***
indicates the facilities and recreational amenities offered
by each individual site.
Shops, bars, laundries, games room, tennis courts, miniature golf, children's play
area, swimming pool, paddling pool, etc.

Introduction
to the Tour

From Gien to the gates of Nantes the banks of the Loire and its tributaries offer an incomparable series of monuments rich in art and history which blend into the landscape. The gentle light which bathes the Loire Valley enhances the beauty of the Renaissance châteaux.

The neighbouring regions are also worth a visit: the Sologne, the Cher and Indre valleys, the endless plains of the Beauce, the green and sinuous valleys of the Loir, the Sarthe and the Mayenne but also the wooded country of Anjou. In between visiting the castles, the towns and the abbeys with their aura of medieval mysticism, one can enjoy the peace and beauty of the countryside in contrast to the bustle of the famous places. While the cultural and aesthetic pleasures are food for the soul, there is food for the body in the delicious cuisine of the Loire Valley, which is some of the finest in France and is accompanied by the excellent local wines which have an international reputation.

(© VU du CIEL by Alain Perceval®)

The Loire at Amboise

Times and charges for admission *to sights described in the guide are listed at the end of the guide.*

The sights are listed alphabetically in this section either under the place — town, village or area — in which they are situated or under their proper name.

Every sight for which there are times and charges is indicated by the symbol ⊙ in the margin in the main part of the guide.

DESCRIPTION OF THE REGION

GEOLOGICAL FORMATION

The Loire region is enclosed by the ancient crystalline masses of the Morvan, Armorican Massif and Massif Central and forms part of the Paris Basin.

In the Secondary Era the area invaded by the sea was covered by a soft, chalky deposit known as **tufa**, which is now exposed along the valley sides of the Loir, Cher, Indre and Vienne. A later deposit is the limestone of the sterile marshlands (**gâtines**) interspersed with tracts of sands and clays supporting forests and heathlands. Once the sea had retreated, great freshwater lakes deposited more limestone, the surface of which is often broken down into loess or silt. These areas are known as **champagnes** or *champeignes*.

During the Tertiary Era the folding of the Alpine mountain zone created the Massif Central, and rivers descending from this new watershed were often laden with sandy clays which when deposited gave areas such as the Sologne and the Forest of Orléans. Later subsidence in the west permitted the ingress of the **Faluns Sea** as far as Blois, Thouars and Preuilly-sur-Claise. This marine incursion created a series of shell marl beds *(falunières)* to be found on the borders of the Ste-Maure Plateau and the hills edging the Loire to the north. Rivers originally flowing northwards were attracted in a westerly direction by the sea, thus explaining the great change in the direction of the Loire at Orléans. The sea finally retreated for good leaving an undulating countryside with the river network the most important geographical feature. The alluvial silts (**varennes**) deposited by the Loire and its numerous tributaries were to add an extremely fertile light soil composed of coarse sand.

The limestone terraces which provided shelter and the naturally fertile soil attracted early human habitation, of which there are traces from the prehistoric era through the Gallo-Roman period (site of Cherré *p 120*) to the Middle Ages (Brain-sur-Allonnes *p 72*). This substratum is immediately reflected in the landscape: troglodyte dwellings in the limestone layers, vineyards on the slopes, cereals on the silt plateaux, vegetables in the alluvial silt; the marshy tracts of the Sologne were for many centuries untilled since they were unhealthy and unsuitable for any sort of culture.

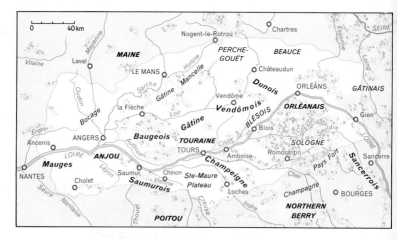

THE LANDSCAPE

The landscapes described by Du Bellay, Balzac, Alain-Fournier or Genevoix have not lost their essential characteristics but have been modified by post-war urbanisation and the growth of industrial and commercial estates on the outskirts of towns.

The garden of France. – From whatever direction one approaches the Loire region – across the immense plains of the Beauce, over the harsher Berry countryside or through the green wooded farmland *(bocage)* of the Gâtine Mancelle – one is always welcomed by the sight of vineyards, white houses and flowers.

For many foreigners this is perhaps one of the most typically French landscapes of all – a peaceful, moderate and gentle countryside.

But make no mistake, the "Garden of France" is not a sort of Eden full of fruit and flowers. The historian Michelet once described it as a "homespun cloak with golden fringes", meaning that the valleys – the golden fringes – in all their wonderful fertility, bordered plateaux whose harshness was only tempered by occasional fine forests.

Northern Berry. – This region lying between the Massif Central and the Loire country includes the **Pays Fort**, an area of clay soil sloping down towards the Sologne *(see Luçay-le-Mâle p 185)*. The melancholy atmosphere of the landscape is described by Alain Fournier in his novel *Le Grand Meaulnes*.

Between the Cher and the Indre is the **Champagne**, an area of limestone silt pockmarked with holes *(mardelles)*.

Orléanais and Blésois. – Below Gien the valley opens out, the hills are lower and a refreshing breeze makes the leaves tremble on the long lines of poplars and willows. This is the gateway to the Orléanais which covers the Beauce, the Loir Valley (ie the Dunois and Vendômois), the Sologne and Blésois (Blois region). In the vicinity of St-Benoît the valley, commonly known as the **Val**, is a series of meadows; beyond horticulture predominates with the growing of seedlings and rosebushes on the alluvial deposits known locally as *layes*. There is a proliferation of greenhouses, some with artificial heating. Orchards and vineyards flourish on the south facing slopes.

Touraine Landscape

From Orléans to Chaumont along its northern bank, the Loire eats into the **Beauce** limestone and then into the flinty chalkland and tufa. On the southern side the river laps the alluvial sands brought down by its own waters, and which, besides growing asparagus and early vegetables, are also covered in dense brushwood, where the kings of France once used to hunt. The great châteaux then begin: Blois, Chambord, Cheverny, Chaumont...

The **Beauce**, the granary of France, a treeless plain covered with a thin layer (2 m - 6 ft maximum) of fertile silt or loess, extends into the area between the Loire and Loir known as the Petite Beauce where silt tends to give way to clay in Marchenoir Forest. In the **Sologne** *(p 172)* and the **Forest of Orléans** meagre crops alternate with the pools and woodland.

Touraine. – The comfortable opulence of the **Loire Valley** delights the visitor already attracted by the luminous beauty of the light. The blue waters of the Loire, which flow slowly between golden sandbanks, have worn a course through the soft tufa chalk. Channels abandoned by the main river are divided into back-waters *(boires)* or occupied by tributary streams such as the Cher, Indre, Vienne *(p 92)* and Cisse.

From Amboise to Tours the flinty chalk soil of the valley slopes is clad with vineyards producing the well known Vouvray and Montlouis wines. **Troglodyte** houses have been carved out of the white tufa .

The **Véron** *(p 124),* lying between the Loire and the Vienne, is a patchwork of small fields and gardens bordered by rows of poplars.

The **Gâtine** of Touraine, between the Loir and Loire, was once a great forest; the area is now under cultivation, although large tracts of heath and woodland still exist: Chandelais and Bercé Forests.

The main features of the Touraine **Champeigne**, where the fields are studded with walnut trees, are the Forests of Brouard and Loches and the Montrésor Gâtine. The plateaux of Montrichard and Ste-Maure *(p 165)* are similar in many ways to the Champeigne.

Anjou. – Anjou like the Touraine has little physical unity but is typified more easily by the gentleness of its countryside, so lovingly described by the poet Du Bellay.

The north bank of the Loire consists of a fertile alluvial plain **(varenne de Bourgueil)** where spring vegetables flourish surrounded by the famous vineyards planted on the warm, dry gravels lying at the foot of the pine-covered hills. Between the Loire and the Authion, which is lined with willows, green pastures alternate with rich market gardens growing vegetables, flowers and fruit trees. The land below Angers is covered with vineyards especially the famous coulée de Serrant vineyard.

The pleasant **Saumurois**, which lies south of the Loire and extends from Fontevraud and Montsoreau to Doué-la-Fontaine and the Layon Valley *(p 112)* has three differing aspects: woods, plains and hillsides; the slopes are often clad with vineyards, which produce excellent wine including the white wine to which the town of Saumur has given its name. The many caves in the steep, tufa valley sides of the Loire around Chênehutte-les-Tuffeaux are now used for mushroom growing.

North of the river lies the sandy **Baugeois** *(p 59),* an area of woods (oak, pine and chestnut) and arable land.

Angers marks the border between the schist countryside of Black Anjou and the sharply contrasting limestone of White Anjou. The countryside is greener heralding an area of wooded farmland – le Bocage Segréen and the **Mauges** *(p 136)* – which is characterized by a patchwork of small fields surrounded by hedge-topped banks crisscrossed by deep lanes leading to small farmsteads. Around Angers nursery and market gardens specialize in flowers and seedlings.

Maine. – Only the southern part of this region is included in the guide.

The Lower Maine **(Bas-Maine)** otherwise known as Black Maine, is a region of sandstones, granites and schists and wooded farmland. Geographically this area is part of the Breton Armorican Massif. The Upper Maine **(Haut-Maine)**, covering the Sarthe and Huisne basins, is known as the White Maine because of its limestone soils.

THE ECONOMY

The bountiful Loire Valley assures a comfortable livelihood.

Activities of the past. – Many of the traditional local activities have disappeared: namely the growing of saffron in the Gâtinais; of anise, coriander and liquorice in Bourgueil; of madder; and the silk industry based on the mulberries and silk worms introduced to Touraine by Louis XI. The once familiar fields of hemp around Bréhémont and Béhuard, have dwindled in number as have the dependent ropeworkers.

Cottage industries have disappeared with the last of the local craftsmen, although Villaines is still a centre for wickerwork, but coopers, cartwrights and sabot makers are now few and far between. The flints of Meusnes and Villentrois are no longer used for the firearms industry.

Gone also are the blacksmiths' forges which were once so numerous on the forest outskirts. The coal of the Layon Basin is no longer mined.

The drastic decline in river traffic on the Loire has resulted in the closure of the boatyards at Angers and the sail-making factories at Ancenis. There is however still a demand for slates from Trélazé against fierce competition but the very fine white tufa stone from Bourré and Pontlevoy, which distinguishes the houses of Touraine, is no longer quarried.

Nowadays it is only in the museums that the old trades can be observed (flint stone museum at Meung-sur-Loire and Luçay-le-Mâle; slate museum at Trélazé).

Agriculture

Vines *(p 40)*, cereals and fodder crops are to be found nearly everywhere but it is the great variety of fruit and vegetables which most astonishes the visitor.

Fruit. – Ripening well in the local climate the succulent fruits of the region are renowned throughout France. Many have a noble pedigree: the *Reine-Claude* plums are named after Claude de France, the wife of François I, the *Bon-chrétien* pears originated from a cutting planted by St Francis of Paola *(p 183)* in Louis XI's orchard at Plessis-lès-Tours. They were introduced into Anjou by Jean Bourré, Louis XI's Finance Minister *(p 154)*. Rivalling the latter are the following varieties: *de Monsieur, William,* a speciality of Anjou, *Passe-Crassane* and *Beurré Hardy*.

Melons were introduced to the region by Charles VIII's Neapolitan gardener. Already in the 16C the variety and quality of the local fruit and vegetables was much praised by Ronsard among others. The walnut and chestnut trees of the plateaux yield oil and the much prized wood and the edible chestnuts, often roasted during evening gatherings.

Cultivation under glass, irrigation and new varieties have stimulated an agricultural revival. The Reinette apple from Le Mans has been supplanted by more prolific American varieties such as the Granny Smith or Golden Delicious.

Early vegetables. – Early vegetables are a speciality in the Loire Valley since, in general, they are ready two weeks before those of the Paris region. Asparagus from Vineuil and Contres, potatoes from Saumur, French beans from Touraine and artichokes from Angers are despatched to

(Photo J.-D. Sudres/Scope)

Rungis, the main Paris market. Mushrooms are one of the region's more unusual crops. They are grown in the former tufa quarries situated near Montrichard, Montoire, Tours and particularly in the Saumur area.

The Orléans region grows great quantities of lettuce, cucumbers and tomatoes, all in massive greenhouses.

Flowers and nursery gardens. – Pots of geraniums or begonias, borders of nasturtiums and climbing wistaria with its pale mauve clusters adorn the houses. The region of Orléans-la-Source, Olivet and Doué-la-Fontaine is famous for its roses and for its hydrangeas, geraniums and chrysanthemums which are grown under glass. Tulips, gladioli and lilies are grown (for bulbs) near Soings.

Nursery gardens proliferate on the alluvial soils of the Loire. The lighter soils of Véron, Bourgueil and the Angers district are suitable for the growing of artichokes, onions and garlic for seed stock. The medicinal plants that were cultivated in the Chemillé region during the phylloxera crisis are attracting re-newed interest.

Livestock

Cattle, sheep and pigs. – In the fodder growing areas *(champagnes* and *gâtines)* young dairy stock are reared inside while elsewhere beef and dairy cattle feed on the pastures of the Maine and Anjou valleys. The most popular breeds are the Normandy, Maine-Anjou and the Pie noire. Charolais cattle are fattened in the neighbourhood of Cholet. Milk production is concentrated in the valleys of Touraine, especially in the wooded farmland of Anjou and Les Mauges where the French Frisian-Pie Noire breed is favoured.

Sheep rearing is limited to the limestone plateaux of the Upper Maine where the black-faced *Bleu du Maine* prospers. Pigs are to be found everywhere but especially in Touraine, Maine and Anjou; the production of potted pork specialities – *rillettes* and *rillons* – is centred in Vouvray, Tours, Le Mans and Angers. The ever growing demand for the well known goats' cheeses has resulted in an increase in goat keeping.

Market days in the west country are colourful occasions: the liveliest are the pig markets in Craon and the calf sales in Château-Gontier and the cattle and goat sales in Chemillé and Cholet.

Poultry. – Poultry rearing (chicken farms at Loué in the Sarthe) has grown considerably; its development is linked to the food industry and the cooperatives which have greatly contributed to the agricultural revival which has taken place since the war.

Horses. – Numerous studs continue to rear for breeding and racing purposes while the finer arts and traditions of horsemanship are perpetuated by the National Riding School and *Cadre Noir* at St-Hilaire-St-Florent near Saumur. Many a small town still has its racecourse and local riding clubs and schools keep alive the interest in horses and horseriding and its ancillary crafts.

Industry

Although industry does not play a dominant role in the economy of the Loire Valley, recent growth is noticeable in the main towns and in the development of ancillary industries based on the processing of agricultural produce. With the exception of Châteaudun and Vendôme, the main industrial centres are to be found along the Loire at Gien, Sully, St-Denis-de-l'Hôtel, Orléans, Beaugency, Mer, Blois, Amboise, Tours and Angers. The new industry is therefore not concentrated in the main towns but helps to stimulate the economy in rural areas, eg. the region round Cholet. Michelin tyre factories have been set up at

Orléans, Tours and Cholet. Nuclear power stations are in operation at Avoine-Chinon, Belleville-sur-Loire, Dampierre-en-Burly and St-Laurent-des-Eaux.

Service industries

Insurance, mainly in Le Mans, conferences, a speciality of Tours and Orléans, and the great tourist potential are all factors in the attraction of investment into the region.

The cultural heritage, the forests, the 570 km - 354 miles of navigable water for leisure craft and the proliferation of leisure parks all play their part in the local economy.

MICHELIN GUIDES

The Red Guides (hotels and restaurants)
   Benelux — Deutschland — España Portugal —Main cities Europe — France — Great Britain and Ireland — Italia

The Green Guides (beautiful scenery, buildings and scenic routes)
   Austria — Canada — England: The West Country — Germany — Greece — Italy — New England —Portugal — Scotland — Spain — Switzerland London — New York City — Paris — Rome ... and 6 guides on France.

HISTORICAL TABLE AND NOTES
(Events of general historical import are printed in italics.)

The Bourbons (1589-1792)

1589-1610	*Henri IV.*
1589	Vendôme retaken by Henri IV.
1598	*Edict of Nantes.* Marriage of César de Vendôme *(Angers).*
1600	Henri IV marries Marie de' Medici.
1602	Maximilien de Béthune buys Sully.
1610-1643	*Louis XIII.*
1619	Marie de' Medici flees Blois.
1620	Building of the college by the Jesuits at La Flèche.
1626	Gaston d'Orléans, brother of Louis XIII, is granted the County of Blois.
1643-1715	*Louis XIV.*
1648-1653	*Civil war against Mazarin, The Fronde.*
1651	Anne of Austria, Mazarin and the young Louis XIV take refuge in Gien.
1669	Première of Molière's play *Monsieur de Pourceaugnac* at Chambord.
1685	*Revocation of the Edict of Nantes signed by Louis XIV at Fontainebleau.*
1715-1774	*Louis XV.*
1719	Voltaire exiled at Sully.
1756	Foundation of the Royal College of Surgeons at Tours.
1770	The duc de Choiseul in exile at Chanteloup.

The Revolution and First Empire (1789-1815)

1789	*Storming of the Bastille.*
1792	*Proclamation of the Republic.*
1793	*Execution of Louis XVI.* Vendean War.
	Fighting between the Republican "Blues" and Royalist "Whites". *(Cholet, Les Mauges).*
1803	Talleyrand purchases Valençay.
1804-1815	*First Empire under Napoleon Bonaparte.*
1808	Internment of Ferdinand VII, King of Spain, at Valençay.

Constitutional Monarchy and the Second Republic (1815-1852)

1814-1824	*Louis XVIII.*
1824-1830	*Charles X.*
1830-1848	*July Monarchy: Louis-Philippe.*
1832	The first steamboat on the Loire.
1832-1848	*Conquest of Algeria.*
1848	Internment of Abd El-Kader at Amboise.
1848-1852	*Second Republic. Louis Napoleon-Bonaparte, Prince-President.*

The Second Empire (1852-1870)

1852-1870	*Napoleon III as Emperor.*
1870-1871	*Franco-Prussian War.*
1870	Proclamation of the Third Republic on 4 September at the Town Hall in Paris.
	Frederick-Charles of Prussia at Azay-le-Rideau. Defence of Châteaudun.
	Tours becomes the headquarters of the Provisional Government.
1871	Battle of Loigny.

The Third Republic (1870-1940) and the Present day

1873	Amédée Bollée completes his first car, *l'Obéissante (Le Mans).*
1908	Wilbur Wright's early trials with his aeroplane.
1914-1918	*First World War.*
1919	*Treaty of Versailles.*
1923	The first Twenty-four hour race at Le Mans.
1936	Louis Renault establishes his first decentralised factory south of Le Mans.
1939-1945	*Second World War.*
1940	Defence of Saumur; historic meeting at Montoire.
1945	*Armistice of Rheims.*
1946	*Fourth Republic.*
1952	Inauguration of the *son et lumière* performances at Chambord.
1958	*Fifth Republic.*
1963	Opening of the Avoine-Chinon Nuclear Power Station, France's first nuclear power station.
1970	Founding of the University of Tours.
1974	The A 10 motorway links Tours and the capital.

THE RICH AND LENGTHY HISTORY OF THE LOIRE REGION

Antiquity and the Early Middle Ages

During the Iron Age a prosperous and powerful people, **the Cenomanni**, occupied a vast territory extending from Brittany to the Beauce and from Normandy to Aquitaine. They minted gold coins and put up a long resistance to both barbarian and Roman invaders. They reacted strongly to the invasion of Gaul and in 52 BC the **Carnutes**, who inhabited the country between Chartres and Orléans, gave the signal, at the instigation of the Druids, to raise a revolt against Caesar. It was savagely repressed but the following year Caesar had to put down another uprising by the Andes under their leader Dumnacos.

Peace was established under Augustus and a period of stability and prosperity began. Existing towns such as Angers, Le Mans, Tours and Orléans adapted to the Roman model with a forum, theatre, baths and public buildings. Many agricultural estates (villae) were created or extended as the commercial outlets developed. They reached their peak in 2C; by the end of 3C instability and danger were so rife that the city had been enclosed behind a wall.

At the same time Christianity was introduced by St Gatien, the first bishop of Tours; by the end of 4C it had overcome most opposition under **St Martin**, the greatest bishop of the Gauls (p 176), whose tomb later became a very important place of pilgrimage (St Martin's Day: 11 November).

In 5C the Loire country suffered several waves of invasion; in 451 Bishop Aignan held back the Huns outside Orléans while waiting for help. Franks and Visigoths fought for domination until Clovis was finally victorious in 507.

His successors' endless quarrels, which were recorded by Gregory of Tours, dominated the history of the region in 6C and 7C while St Martin's Abbey was establishing its reputation. In 732 the Saracens, who were pushing north from Spain, reached the Loire before they were repulsed by Charles Martel.

The order achieved by the Carolingians, which was marked by the activities of **Alcuin** and **Theodulf**, did not last. In the middle of 9C the Normans came up the river and ravaged the country on either side, particularly the monasteries (St Benoît, St Martin's). **Robert**, Count of Blois and Tours, defeated them but they continued their depredations until 911 when the Treaty of St-Clair-sur-Epte created the Duchy of Normandy. During this period of insecurity

Archives SNARK/Edimedia)

Alcuin and Rabanus Maurus
(National Library, Vienna)

the Robertian dynasty (the forerunner of the Capet dynasty) gained in power to the detriment of the last Carolingian kings. A new social order emerged which gave rise to feudalism.

Princely power

The weakness of the last Carolingian kings encouraged the independence of turbulent and ambitious feudal lords. Although Orléans was one of the favourite royal residences and the Orléans region was always Capet territory, Touraine, the county of Blois, Anjou and Maine became independent and rival principalities. This was the age of powerful barons, who raised armies and minted money. From Orléans to Angers every highpoint was crowned by an imposing castle, the stronghold of the local lord who was continually at war with his neighbours.

The counts of Blois faced a formidable enemy in the counts of Anjou, of whom the most famous was **Fulk Nerra** (p 47). He was a first class tactician; little by little he encircled Eudes II, Count of Blois, and seized part of his territory. His son, Geoffrey Martel continued the same policy; from his stronghold in Vendôme he wrested from the house of Blois the whole county of Tours. In 12C the county of Blois was dependent on Champagne which was then at the height of its power.

At the same period the counts of Anjou reached the height of their power under the Plantagenets (p 48); when Henri, Count of Anjou, became King Henry II of England in 1154 his kingdom stretched from the north of England to the Pyrenees. This formidable new power confronted the modest forces of the Kings of France but they did not quail under the threat of their powerful neighbours and skilfully took advantage of the quarrels which divided the Plantagenets.

In 1202 King John of England, known as John Lackland, lost all his continental possessions to Philippe Auguste (see p 89); the Loire country returned to the French sphere of interest.

In accordance with the wishes of his father, Louis VIII, when Louis IX came to the throne he granted Maine and Anjou as an apanage to his brother, Charles who abandoned his French provinces, including Provence, and tried to establish an Angevin kingdom in Naples, Sicily and the Near East, as did his successors. Nonetheless, Good **King René** (p 48), the last Duke of Anjou, earned himself a lasting place in popular tradition.

The Cradle of Feudalism

Feudalism is the sort of society which flourished in France in 11C and 12C in the region between the Seine and the Loire under the Capet monarchy.

The system is based on two elements: the fief and the lord. The **fief** is a ''beneficium'' (benefice) usually a grant of land made by a lord to a knight or other man who became his vassal.

The numerous conflicts of interest which arose from the system in practice produced a detailed code of behaviour embodying the rights of the parties. During 12C the services due were defined, such as the maximum number of days to be spent each year in military service or castle watch. Gradually the fiefs became hereditary and the lord retained only overall ownership. In the case of multiple vassalage, liege homage was paid to one lord and this was more binding than homage to any other.

An almost perfect hierarchical pyramid was created descending from the king to the mass of simple knights. The more important vassals had the right of appeal to the king in case of serious dispute with their suzerain; it was by this means that King John was deprived of his French fiefs by Philippe Auguste early in 13C *(p 89)*.

All the inhabitants of an estate were involved in the economic exploitation of the land; the estate had evolved from the Carolingian method of administration and was divided into two parts: the domain, which was kept by the lord for himself, and the holdings, which were let to the tenants in return for rent. The authority exercised by the lord over the people who lived on his estate derived from the royal prerogative of the monarch to command his subjects which passed into the hands of powerful lords who owned castles. This unlimited power enabled them to impose military service, various duties (road mending, transport, etc.) and taxes on their tenants.

Joan of Arc

The Hundred Years War (1337-1453)) brought back the English, who became masters of half the country and invested Orléans; if the town had surrendered, the whole of the rest of the kingdom would probably have passed into the enemy's hands. Then **Joan of Arc** appeared and proclaimed her intention of ''booting the English out of France''; national pride was awakened. The shepherdress from Domrémy persuaded Charles VII to give her a command *(p 90)*. With her little army she entered beleaguered Orléans, stormed the English strongholds and freed the city *(p 148)*. The fleeing enemy was beaten on the Loire, at Jargeau, and in the Beauce, at Patay, in spite of the betrayal of Compiègne and the stake at Rouen, the enemy's total defeat was assured.

16C: Royal munificence and religious tumult

The 16C was inaugurated with a firework display, an explosion of the new ideas in art and architecture produced by the Renaissance which ushered in one of the liveliest periods in the history of the Loire country.

The Renaissance. – The University of Orléans with its long-established reputation attracted a number of **humanists**: Nicolas Béraud, Étienne Dolet, Pierre de l'Estoille, Anne du Bourg. The world of ideas was greatly extended by the invention of printing – the first printing press in the Loire Valley was set up in Angers in 1477 – which made learning and culture more accessible. In the middle of the century the **Pleiade** was formed in the Loire Valley and attracted the best local talent *(p 30)*.

By choosing Touraine as their favourite place of residence the kings made a significant contribution to the artistic revival of the region. This chief instigators of the great French Renaissance were **Charles VIII** and particularly **Louis XII** and **François I**, who had all travelled in Italy; they transformed the Loire Valley into a vast building site where the new aesthetic ideals flourished: at Amboise, Blois and especially Chambord.

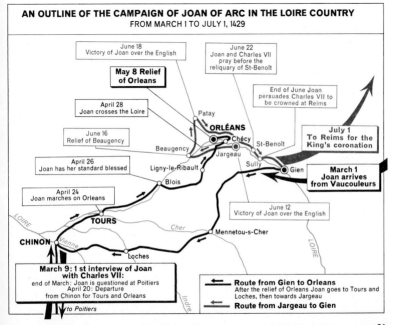

AN OUTLINE OF THE CAMPAIGN OF JOAN OF ARC IN THE LOIRE COUNTRY
FROM MARCH 1 TO JULY 1, 1429

The great lords and financiers followed suit and built themselves most elegant houses (Azay-le-Rideau, Chenonceau) while graceful mansions were erected in the towns.

The Renaissance was the expression of a new way of thinking which re-defined man's place in the world and presented a radically different view from that which had been held in the past.; this gave rise to the desire for harmony and the cult of beauty in all fields: poetry, music, architecture as an expression of nature shaped by man, etc.

Religious tumult. – The Renaissance excited not only intellectual activity but also the need for a moral and religious revival. Despite several local experiments (e.g. Le Mans), the Roman Church did not succeed in satisfying these aspirations. Naturally the ideas of **Luther** and **Calvin** (who was in Orléans between 1528 and 1533) were well received in cultivated circles. In 1540 the Church responded with repression; several reformers died at the stake but the reform movement continued to grow; nor was support confined

(Photo Explorer Archives)

François I in 1525 by Jean Clouet
(Louvre Museum)

to the elite but extended to the mass of the people, craftsmen and tradesmen. The dispute between Protestants and Roman Catholics inevitably led to armed conflict. In 1560 the **Amboise Conspiracy** *(p 44)* failed disastrously and ended in bloodshed. Catherine de' Medici tried to promote conciliation by issuing edicts of tolerance but in April 1562 the Huguenots rose up and committed many acts of vandalism in the towns: damaging places of worship and destroying statues, tombs and relics.

The Roman Catholics under Montpensier and Guise regained the upper hand and exacted a terrible vengeance, particularly in Angers *(p 49)*. From 1563 to 1567 there was relative peace but in 1568 the armed struggle broke out anew; the Catholic and Protestant armies, the latter under Condé and Coligny, caused waves of bloodshed. In Orléans the **feast of St Bartholomew** was celebrated with thousands of deaths. During the last quarter of the century the Reformed Churches were much weaker and **Henri III's** struggle with the Catholic League came to the fore. In 1576 Touraine, Anjou and Berry were granted to François d'Alençon, the king's brother and head of the League, as a conciliatory gesture but the Guises would not compromise and conspired against the king who, seeing no other solution, had them assassinated at Blois in December 1588 *(p 64)*. The population divided into Royalists and Leaguers, who were powerful in the Loire region. Henri III, who had been forced to withdraw to Tours, allied himself with Henry of Navarre and was marching on Paris when he himself was assassinated on 2 August 1589.

It took Henri IV nearly ten years to restore peace to the region. The brilliant period in the history of the Loire Valley, which coincided with the last years of the Valois dynasty, ended in tragedy.

17C and 18C: Peace is restored

The Loire country ceased to be at the centre of political and religious ferment. There were indeed a few alarms during the minority of Louis XIII and the Fronde, caused by the indefatigable conspirator, Gaston d'Orléans *(p 64)*. Order was however restored under Louis XIV. Centralisation under the crown stifled any sign of autonomy: the districts of Orléans and Tours were administered by energetic treasury officials while the towns lost the right to self-government.

In the religious domain the Roman Catholic Church re-established itself: convents and seminaries grew in number, the old monastic foundations underwent reform and the suppression of sorcery (in Loudun) went hand in hand with the rise in the intellectual level of the clergy. Protestantism had a struggle to survive, except in Saumur owing to the Academy *(p 166)*, and was dealt a devastating blow by the **Revocation of the Edict of Nantes** in 1685.

A developing economy. – Human enterprise benefited from the general stability. Agriculture developed slowly: cereals in the Beauce, raw materials for textiles (wool, linen, hemp), market gardening and fruit growing and wine making in the Loire Valley were a considerable source of wealth while cattle raising remained weak. Rural crafts played an important role together with urban manufacturing: hemp cloth round Cholet, cheesecloth in the district of Le Mans, sheeting in Touraine and Anjou, bonnets in Orléanais. The silk weavers of Tours achieved a firm reputation *(p 177)*.

Nevertheless in 18C, except for sheets from Laval and Cholet, the textile industry went into decline. Orléans, the warehouse of the Loire, specialised in sugar refining and the finished product was distributed throughout the kingdom. The Loire, under the control of the "community of merchants" *(p 121)*, was the main axis for trade and carried a great deal of traffic which was increased by the opening of the Briare Canal from the Loire to the Seine and the canal from Orléans to Montargis in 17C. Wine from Touraine and Anjou, wool from the Berry, iron from the Massif Central, coal from the Forez, wheat from the Beauce, cloth from Touraine and cargoes from exotic countries, everything travelled by water. On the eve of the Revolution these activities were in decline but the region had about two million inhabitants and several real towns: Orléans (pop 40 000), Angers (pop 30 000), Tours (pop 20 000) and Le Mans (pop 17 000).

The Revolution

Touraine and Orléanais accepted the Revolution but Maine and Anjou rose in revolt.

Social Conflict. – At first it was social conflict in which the country peasants were opposed to the towns people and the weavers from the villages. The towns people, who had been won over by the new ideas, were enthusiastic about the new political order while the peasants became more and more disillusioned, From 1791-2 the new fiscal regime did nothing to relieve the countryside; the sale of national assets was almost exclusively of advantage to the towns people. Religious reform upset parish life and the administrative reforms provoked criticism and discontent because they favoured the towns people. The national guards in their blue uniform were more and more disliked: they were sent out from the towns to compel compliance with the revolutionary decisions if necessary by force. The decree imposing mass conscription in March 1793 was seen as an unacceptable provocation in the country and the peasants rose in a body. Les Mauges in particular was immediately in the forefront of the battle *(p 136)*.

The Vendean War. – The Angevin rebels organised themselves and appointed leaders from among their number, countrymen like **Stofflet** and **Cathelineau** or noblemen like **Bonchamps**. For four months the **Vendean armies** won several important engagements in support of the Church and the king; they captured Cholet, Saumur and then Angers. The Convention replied by sending in several army units. The royalist Whites were severely defeated at Cholet on 17 October by General Kléber and General Marceau and had to retreat *(p 93)*. As they fled they were pitilessly massacred and the remnants of the "great Catholic and royal army" were exterminated in the Savenay Marshes beyond Nantes.

By way of reprisal against the local population the Convention appointed General Turreau in January 1794 to "clean up" the country. From February to May his **"infernal columns"** converged on the centre, killing women and children and setting fire to the villages.

The Chouans. – The war was followed by sporadic outbursts of guerilla activity: daring exploits, ambushes and even assassinations. Jean **Cottereau**, also known as Jean Chouan was the leading figure who gave his name to the movement. The country people maintained a relentless resistance. At the end of August a faint peace-making gesture was made under the authority of General **Hoche**. Charette and Stofflet, who continued the struggle, were arrested and shot in February and March 1796. The Vendean insurrection came to an end under the Consulate. The war left in its train much ruin and formidable bitterness which was revealed later in the very rigid political attitudes of the people of Maine and Anjou.

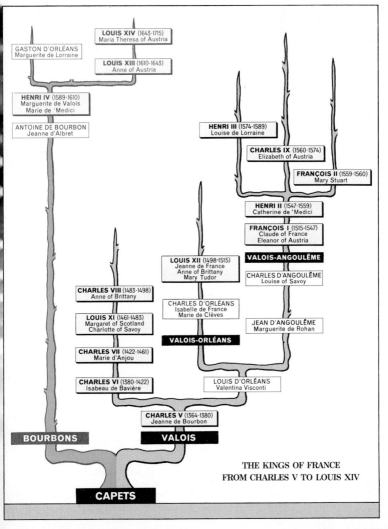

THE KINGS OF FRANCE
FROM CHARLES V TO LOUIS XIV

October 1870 - January 1871. – After the fall of the Empire, France recovered its balance under the stimulus of Gambetta who arrived in Tours by balloon on 9 October. The Bavarians who were victorious at Artenay, had already captured Orléans (11 October) and indicated that they would link up with the Prussian army at Versailles via the Beauce. Châteaudun put up a heroic resistance for ten hours on 18 and 19 October and was bombarded and set on fire in reprisal *(p 78)*.

The army of the Loire was formed under the command of **General d'Aurelle de Paladines**; two corps, the 15th and 16th (Chanzy), formed in the Salbris camp, set out from Blois for Orléans. The engagement took place at Marchenoir and then at Coulmiers on 9 November: the French were victorious and General von der Thann was forced to evacuate Orléans. Meanwhile the 18th and 20th corps tried to check the advance of the Duke of Mecklenburg on Le Mans and Tours but they were beaten on 28 November at Beaune-la-Rolande by Prince Frederick-Charles who had hastened south from Metz. On 2 December the 16th and 17th corps were defeated at Patay and Loigny where the Zouaves under Lt Col de Charette, the grand nephew of the Famous Vendéan, fought with distinction. Although cut in two the first army of the Loire survived. Orléans had to be abandoned while the government retreated to Bordeaux (8 December).

A second Loire army was formed under **General Chanzy**; it resisted every enemy attack and then retrenched on the Loir. On 19 December the Prussians captured Château-Renault and two days later arrived in front of Tours but did not besiege the town. The decisive battle was fought between 10 and 12 January on Auvours plateau east of Le Mans. Chanzy was forced to retreat towards Laval; Tours was occupied and Prince Frederick-Charles took up residence at Azay-le-Rideau *(p 57)*. The armistice was signed on 28 January 1871.

1917-18. – The Americans set up their headquarters in Tours while the first "Sammies" disembarked at St-Nazaire and were billeted along the Loire.

1940-44. – On **10 June 1940** the French Government moved to Tours and Cangé Château, on the southeast edge of the town, became the temporary residence of the President of the Republic. On 13 the Franco-British Supreme Council met in Tours; at Cangé the Council of Ministers decided to transfer the government to Bordeaux. During that week of tragedy the bridges over the Loire were machine-gunned and bombarded; floods of refugees choked the roads. The towns were badly damaged. 2 000 cadets from the Cavalry School at Saumur excelled themselves by holding up the German advance for two days along a 25 km - 15 mile front *(p 167)*. On 24 October 1940 Marshal Pétain met Hitler at **Montoire**, and agreed to his demands; collaboration was born. The Gestapo in Angers established a reign of terror in the region. The Resistance was born in 1941; the information and sabotage networks, the underground forces and the escape agents (the demarkation line followed the River Cher and ran between Tours and Loches) hampered the movements of the occupying forces who responded with torture, deportation and summary execution. In 1944 numbers of civilians were massacred by the Germans at St-Symphorien and Maille. The liberation was however drawing nearer; in August and September the American army and the forces of the Resistance achieved control of the area with heavy losses.

BIRTH AND EVOLUTION OF THE CHÂTEAUX

The first châteaux (5C to 10C). – In the Merovingian period the country was protected by isolated strongholds; some had evolved from Gallo-Roman "villas" (country estates) which had been fortified; others were built on high ground (Loches, Chinon). Generally they covered a fairly large area and served several purposes: residence of important people, place of worship, a place for minting money, an agricultural centre and a place of refuge for the population. This type of stronghold continued under the Carolingians but the growing insecurity in the second half of 9C introduced a wave of fortification in an attempt to counter the Norman menace. The early castles, which were built in haste, rested on a mound of earth surrounded by a wooden palissade; sometimes a central tower was erected as an observation post. The structure contained very little masonry. Until 10C castle building was a prerogative of the king but thereafter the right was usurped by powerful lords; small strongholds proliferated under the designation "towers", the keep had been invented.

The mott castle (11C). – The mott was a man-made mound of earth on which was erected a square wooden tower, the **keep**. An earth bank protected by a ditch supported the perimeter fence, which consisted of a wooden palisade and enclosed an area large enough to contain the people of the neighbourhood. The keep was built either as the last place of refuge or at the weakest point in the perimeter fence; some castles had more than one mott. In several of the Angevin castles built by Fulk Nerra *(p 47)* the keep protected a residential building erected at the end of a promontory, as at Langeais, Blois and Loches, which are typical of the Carolingian tradition.

The stone castle (12-13C). – By 11C some castles had defensive works built of stone. The keep was still the strongest point and took the form of a massive quadrangular structure. The keep at Loches, Langeais, Montbazon, Chinon (Coudray) and Beaugency are remarkable examples of 11C architecture.

The 12C keep overlooked a courtyard which was enclosed by a stone **curtain wall**, gradually reinforced by turrets and towers. Within its precincts each castle comprised private apartments, a great hall, one or more chapels, soldiers' barracks, lodgings for the household staff and other buildings such as barns, stables, storerooms, kitchens etc.

The tendency grew to re-arrange the buildings more compactly within a smaller precinct. The keep comprised a storeroom on the ground floor, a great hall on the first and living rooms on the upper floors. The compact shape and the height of the walls made it difficult to besiege and only a few men were required for its defence.

In 13C, under the influence of the crusades and improvements in the art of attack, important innovations appeared. Castles were designed by experts to be even more compact with multiple defensive features so that no point was unprotected. The curtain wall bristled with huge towers and the keep was neatly incorporated into the overall design. A circular plan was adopted for the towers and keep; the walls were splayed at the base; the depth and width of the moat were greatly increased. Sometimes a lower outer rampart was built to reinforce the main rampart; the intervening strip of level ground was called the lists. Improvements were made to the arrangements for launching missiles: new types of loophole (in cross or stirrup shape), stone machicolations, platforms, bratticing etc. The 13C castle, which was more functional and had a pronounced military character, could be built anywhere even in open country. At the same time a desire for indoor comfort began to express itself in tapestries and draperies and furniture (chests and beds) which made the rooms pleasanter to live in than they had been in the past.

The late medieval castle. − In 14C and 15C castle building the accent moved from defence to comfort and decoration. The living quarters were more extensive; large windows to let in the light and new rooms (state bedrooms, dressing rooms and lavatories) appeared; decoration became an important feature.

In the military sphere there were no innovations, only minor improvements. The keep merged with the living quarters and was surmounted by a watch tower; sometimes the keep was suppressed altogether and the living quarters took the form of a rectangular block defended by huge corner towers. The entrance was flanked by two semi-circular towers and protected by a barbican (a gateway flanked by towers) or by a separate fort. The top of the curtain wall was raised to the height of the towers which were crowned by a double row of crenellations. In 15C the towers were capped by pointed, pepperpot roofs.

Other fortified building. − Churches and monasteries, which were places of sanctuary and therefore targets of war, were not excluded from the fortification movement, especially during the Hundred Years War. The towns and some of the villages also turned their attention to defence and built ramparts round the residential districts. In 1398, 1399 and 1401 Charles VI issued letters and ordinances enjoining the owners of fortresses and citizens to see that their fortifications were in good order.

From the end of 13C fortified houses were built in the country districts by the lords of the manor; they had no military significance but are similar in appearance to the smaller châteaux.

The Renaissance château. − In 16C military elements were abandoned in the search for comfort and aesthetic taste: moats, keeps and turrets appeared only as decorative features as at Chambord, Azay-le-Rideau and Chenonceau. The spacious attics were lit by great dormer windows in the steep pitched roofs. The windows were very large. The spiral turret stairs were replaced with stairs that rose in straight flights in line with the centre of the main façade beneath coffered ceilings. The gallery − a new feature imported from Italy at the end of 15C − lent a touch of elegance to the main courtyard.

Whereas the old fortified castle had been built on a hill, the new château was sited in a valley or beside a river where it was reflected in the water. The idea was that the building should harmonise with its natural surroundings, although these were shaped and transfigured by man's hand; the gardens, which were laid out like a jewel casket, were an integral part of the design. Only the chapel continued to be built in the traditional style with ogee vaulting and Flamboyant decoration.

The Classical style, which dominated 17C and 18C, introduced a rigorous sense of proportion. The château became a country house set in a beautiful garden (Cheverny and Ménars).

Cheverny − Armoury

The siege. – The attacker's first task was to besiege the enemy stronghold. The defences he constructed (moat, stockade, towers, forts or blockhouses) were intended both to prevent a possible sortie by the besieged and to counter an attack from a relief army. In the great sieges it was a veritable fortified town encircling the place. In order to make a breach in the defences of the besieged place the attacker used mines, slings and battering rams. For this he had special- ist troops who were experts in siege operations.

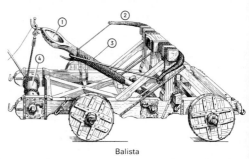

Undermining. – When the ground was suitable the attackers would dig tunnels under the ramparts and cur- tain walls. The cavity was shored up with wooden props which were set on fire when the attackers with- drew; the tunnel and the wall above then collapsed. The defenders would res- pond by digging another gal- lery intersecting the first and

Balista

The projectile is placed in ① and launched by the action of the spring ② on the release of the lever ③, which has been drawn back by the winch ④.

the combatants would fight underground. When they could no longer defend the breaches, the besieged withdrew to the keep.

Projectiles. – The machines used for launching projectiles worked on a spring or a counter balance. The most usual were the ballista, the cross-bow mounted on a tower, the trebuchet, the mangonel and the stone sling.

The large **mangonels** could launch stones of over 100 kg - 20lbs up to 200 m - 654 ft using an average trajectory. These rocks could smash the merlons, shake the walls or enlarge the breaches made by the battering ram.

Other projectiles were used: grape shot, incendiary arrows (Greek fire), flaming faggots and even carrion to spread dis- ease. The cross-bow fired shafts 5 m - 16 ft long which could fell a whole file of soldiers.

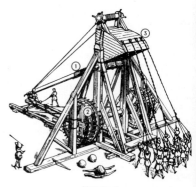

The siege tower. – This was the most highly developed weapon of attack. It was built of wood – the Middle Ages had marvellous carpenters – and covered with hide; it was about 50 m - 160 ft tall and could shelter hundreds of men.

To advance it to the foot of a wall it was necessary to fill in a section of moat and build a wooden slip way. The huge struc- ture was placed on rollers and moved with hoisting gear.

Mangonel

The lever ① is brought to ground level by the winch ②. When it is released it returns sharply to the perpendicular by the action of the counterweight ③ and the men pulling on the ropes. The projectile is launched by the catapult at the end of the lever.

The battering ram. – The ram comple- mented the work of the projectiles. It was manned by a hundred soldiers who main- tained the to-and-fro movement of the beam. For breaking down gates there was a smaller version which could be man- œuvred by a dozen strong men. The force of the large rams was very great; to cushion the blow the defenders would try to interpose bales of wool. The ram was protected by a stout wooden shield covered with hide which the defenders tried to pierce with stones and flaming faggots.

The assault. – The siege towers were equipped with draw-bridges which were let down on to the ramparts so that the soldiers could flood over the curtain walls while others rushed in through the breaches. Scaling ladders were erected against the walls. The more agile men threw grappling irons over the battlements and hauled themselves up hand over hand by rope. The defenders unleashed a hail of arrows and projectiles and tried to cut the ropes or throw down the ladders. Boiling pitch and quicklime were poured on the heads of the assault troops.

If the attackers succeeded in breaching the walls they still had to capture a succession of individual defences (gates, towers and keep). A determined defence could hold out for a long time by means of narrow twisting stairs, false entrances, traps, chicanes, loopholes and internal machicolations.

The era of the cannon. – The bombard increased in effectiveness. Towards the middle of 15C under the influence of the Bureau brothers, the French royal artillery became the best in the world. No fortress could withstand it. In one year Charles VII recaptured from the English sixty places which had resisted sieges of from four to ten months. Siege technique was altered and adapted. The place being besieged was encircled by a ring of fortified camps linked to one another by trenches. The artillery was then drawn up into position and the gunners were protected behind a bank or stockade. The firing rate was not very high and the aim was even less accurate. The defenders also used artillery and would make sorties to spike the enemy's guns. Military architecture was completely transformed; towers were replaced by low thick bastions and the curtain walls were built less high but up to 12 m - 40 ft thick. This new system of defences was brought to perfection by Vauban.

MEDIEVAL CHATEAU LIFE

One Living Room. – In 10C and 11C life in a castle was crude. The whole family lived, ate and slept in the same room on the first floor of the keep. Furniture was rare and tableware rudimentary.

A lonely life. – The owner of a castle had to be self-sufficient and lived in a climate of insecurity. When the lord was out hunting or fighting his neighbours or off on a crusade, his lady administered his affairs.

MEDIEVAL PALACE LIFE

The Great Hall. – In 13C living quarters began to improve. In the Near East the crusaders experienced a comfortable way of life and acquired a taste for it. In future public and private life were conducted in separate rooms. The most handsome room in the castle was the Great Hall; here the lord held audience and dispensed justice; feasts and banquets took place in it. The earlier loopholes were replaced by windows, fitted with panes and shutters. The walls were hung with paintings and tapestries, the floor tiles were covered with rush mats or carpets on which one could sit or lie; flowers and greenery were strewn on the floor and, in summer, in the fireplaces.

The bedchamber. – The bedchamber, which was the focus of a couple's private life, opened off the Great Hall. Except in royal or princely households, a married couple slept in the same room. The furnishings grew richer; the bed was set on a dais and surrounded with rich curtains; there were Venetian mirrors, tapestries, costly drapes, benches with backs, a princely chair, a praying-desk, library steps and cushions, a dresser, a table, chests, a cupboard. To entertain the ladies there was an aviary, often a parrot.
Mourning lasted for fifteen days during which the ladies hung their rooms with black and stayed in bed with the shutters closed. For a birth the shutters were also closed; the room was lit with candles and decorated with flowers and the most precious objects which were set on the dresser.
Near to the bedchamber there was a study which was also used for private audiences, a Council chamber and an oratory or chapel. A special room was set aside for the guards. In the larger houses there was also a state room where the ceremonial clothes were on display. After making his first toilette in his bedchamber among the close members of his household, the prince would take his place on the bed in the reception room and finish his dressing among a different company. This practice evolved into the solemn "levers" of Louis XIV.

Food. – The meals were gargantuan but the fare was good. When eaten in private the meals were served in the bedchamber or in the Great Hall. Before and after the meal basins and ewers of scented water were provided for the diners to rinse their hands since fingers often took the place of forks. The plates were of silver. At banquets the diners sat along one side of a great table since the central area was used by the jugglers, acrobats and musicians who provided entertainment in the intervals.

Bathing and hygiene. – Near the bedchamber or in a separate building was the bath house. Until 14C bathing was the fashion in France. The common people used to go to the public baths once a week; the upper classes often took a daily bath. The bath house contained a sort of pool which was filled with warm water and a chamber for the steam bath and massage. A barber or a chambermaid was in attendance for it was the fashion to be clean shaven. In the absence of a bath house, baths were taken in a tub made of wood or bronze or silver. Often people took supper together while bathing. Before a meal guests would be offered a bath. Men and women bathed together without being thought immoral.
These habits of cleanliness disappeared from the Renaissance until the Revolution. The preachers inveighed against the communal baths which they asserted had become places of debauch. In 13C there were 26 public baths in Paris; in Louis XIV's reign there were only two.
In other respects medieval castles were well enough provided with conveniences.

(Photo Edimedia)

Troubadours – Peterborough Psalter (1390)

Entertainment. – Castle life had always had plenty of idle hours and a variety of distractions had developed to fill them. Indoors there was chess, spillikins, dice, draughts and, from 14C, cards. Outdoors there was tennis, bowls and football, wrestling and archery. Hunting with hounds or hawks and tournaments and jousts were the great sports of the nobles. The women and children had dwarfs to entertain them; at court the jester was free to make fun of people even the king. There were frequent festivities. Performances of the Mystery plays, which sometimes lasted 25 days, were always a great success.

THE COURT IN THE LOIRE VALLEY

A Bourgeois Court. – The court resided regularly in the Loire Valley under Charles VII whose preference was for Chinon and Loches. These visits ended with the last of the Valois, Henri III. Owing to the straitened circumstances to which the King of France was reduced Charles VII's court was not brilliant; but the arrival of Joan of Arc in 1429 made the castle of Chinon for ever famous.

Louis XI disliked pomp and circumstance. He installed his wife, Charlotte de Savoie, at Amboise but he himself rarely came there. He preferred his manor at Plessis-lès-Tours where he lived in fear of an attempt on his life. His only interests were hunting and dogs.

The Queen's court consisted on fifteen ladies in waiting, twelve women of the bedchamber and 100 officers in charge of various functions including the saddler, the librarian, the doctor, the chaplain and the lute player. The budget amounted only to 37 000 *livres,* of which 800 *livres* were spent on minor pleasures: materials for needlework and embroidery, books, parchments and illuminating. Charlotte was a serious woman and a great reader; her library contained 100

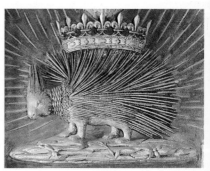

(Photo Pix)

Porcupine (Louis XII)
Cominus et eminus

volumes, a vast total for that time. They were works of piety and morality and books on history, botany and domestic science. A few lighter works, such as the *Tales of Boccaccio,* relieved this solemnity. In fact, compared with Charles the Bold, the royal lifestyle seemed homely rather than princely.

A Luxurious Court. – With the accession of Charles VIII, "the King of Amboise", at the end of the 15C, the taste for luxury appeared. Furnishings became rich: there were in the castle 220 Persian, Turkish and Syrian carpets, 45 beds, 60 chests, 60 tables, an incredible number of Flemish and Parisian tapestries, numerous works of art from Italy and sumptuous silverware. A magnificent aviary contained rare birds. Lions and wild boars, which were made to fight with huge mastiffs, were kept in a menagerie. The armoury contained a fine collection of armour, the battle axes of Clovis, St Louis and Du Guesclin.

A Gallant Court. – Louis XII, who was frugal, was the bourgeois "King of Blois". But under François I (1515-47) the French court became a school of elegance, taste and culture.

The Cavalier King invited men of science, poets and artists to his court. Women, who until then had been relegated to the Queen's service and treated like pupils in a girl's school, played an effective part; the King made them the leaders of a new society. He expected them to dress perfectly and he gave them clothes which showed off their beauty: he would spend 200 000 *livres* at a time on fabrics and finery.

The King also took care that these ladies were treated with courtesy and respect. A gentleman who had permitted himself to speak slightingly of them escaped the supreme penalty only by flight – "So great", says a contemporary historian, "was the King's anger, he swore that whoever reflected on the honour of these ladies would be hanged." A code of courtesy was established and the court set an example of good manners.

The festivals given by François I at Amboise, where he spent his childhood and the first years of his reign, were of unprecedented brilliance. Weddings, baptisms and the visits of princes were

(Photo Pix)

Salamander (François I)
Nutrisco et extinguo.

sumptuously celebrated. Sometimes the festivities took place in the country as on the occasion when the reconstruction of a siege was organised; a temporary town was built to be defended by the Duke of Alençon while the King led the assault and capture. To increase the sense of realism, the mortars fired large balls. Hunting, however, had pride of place; 125 people were employed in keeping the hounds at a cost of 18 000 *livres* per year while 50 looked after the hawks at a cost of 36 000 *livres.*

The Last Valois. – Under Henri II and his sons, Blois remained the habitual seat of the court when it was not at the Louvre. It was Henri III who drew up the first code of etiquette and introduced the title "His Majesty", taken from the Roman Emperors. The Queen Mother and the Queen had about 100 ladies in waiting. Catherine de' Medici also had her famous "Flying Squad" of pretty girls, who kept her informed and assisted her intrigues. About 100 pages acted as messengers. In addition there were 76 gentlemen servants, 51 clerks, 23 doctors and 50 chambermaids. The King's suite included 200 gentlemen in waiting and over 1 000 archers and Swiss guards. There was a multitude of servants. Princes of the Blood and great lords also had their households. Thus, from the time of François I, about 15 000 people surrounded the King; when the court moved, 12 000 horses were needed. By comparison in 16C only 25 French towns had more than 10 000 inhabitants.

QUEENS AND GREAT LADIES

The official position enjoyed by women at court around the King, often enabled them to play an important if not always a useful part in the political affairs of the country. It also enabled them to protect and develop the arts.

Agnès Sorel *(p 115)* adorned the court of Charles VII at Chinon and at Loches. She gave the King good advice and reminded him of the urgent problems facing the country after the Hundred Years War (1337-1453), while the queen, Marie d'Anjou, moped in her castle.

Louise de Savoie, the mother of François I, had a great devotion to St Francis of Paola. Only this piety, mingled with the superstitions of her astrologer, Cornelius Agrippa, restrained her ambition. She lived only for the accession of her son to the throne and for the disruption of the plans of Anne of Brittany by making him marry Claude, the daughter of Louis XII.

There were many women in the love life of François I including Françoise de Chateaubriant and the **Duchess of Étampes**, who ruled his court until his death.

Diane de Poitiers *(p 85)*, the famous favourite of Henri II, was a robust and hardy woman. She retained her energy, both physical and mental, well into old age, to the amazement of her contemporaries. She made important decisions of policy, negotiated with the Protestants, traded in Spanish prisoners, distributed honours and magistracies and, to the great humiliation of the queen, saw to the education of the royal children. Such was her personality that almost every artist of the period painted her portrait.

The foreign beauty of **Mary Stuart**, the hapless wife of the young King François II, who died at 17 after a few months' reign, threw a brief lustre over the court in the middle of the 16C. She is recalled in a drawing by Clouet and some verses by Ronsard.

A different type altogether, brown and swarthy, was **Marguerite de Valois**, the famous Queen Margot, sister of François II, Charles IX and of Henri III. Her bold eyes, her exuberance and her amorous escapades caused much worry to her mother, Catherine de' Medici. Her marriage to the future King Henri IV did little to tame her and was moreover annulled.

Catherine de' Medici *(p 86)* had married the Dauphin Henri in 1533 and was a figure at court for 55 years under 5 kings. Although eclipsed for a while by the beautiful Diane de Poitiers, she took her revenge on the death of Henri II by taking over Chenonceau.

With the accession of Charles IX, after the brief reign of François II, she became regent and tried to maintain the authority of the monarchy during the Wars of Religion by manoeuvring skilfully between the Guises and the Bourbons and using diplomacy, marriage alliances and family intrigue. Under Henri III her influence steadily diminished.

FAMOUS NAMES FROM THE LOIRE VALLEY

LITERATURE

The balance and clarity of the French language first found expression in the Loire Valley; its peaceful landscapes have fostered many French writers.

Middle Ages. – In 6C under the influence of St Martin Tours became a centre of great learning: Bishop **Gregory of Tours** wrote the first history of the Gauls in his Historia Francorum and Alcuin of York founded a famous school of calligraphy at the behest of Charlemagne while in 11C in the Latin poems of **Baudri de Bourgueil** art came under the influence of courtly life. At the beginning of 13C Orléans witnessed the impact of the popular and lyrical language of the Romance of the Rose, a didactic poem by two successive authors – the mannered **Guillaume de Lorris**, who wrote the first 4 000 lines, and the realist **Jean de Meung**, who added the final 18 000. The poem was widely translated and exercised immense influence throughout Europe. **Charles d'Orléans** (1391-1465) discovered his poetic gifts in an English prison. He was a patron of the arts and author of several short but graceful poems; at his court in Blois he organised poetic jousts. In 1457 **Villon** was the winner.

Hitherto a princely pastime, poetry in the hands of Good King René of Anjou became an aristocratic and even mannered work of art. In Angers **Jean Michel** , who was a doctor and a man of letters, produced his monumental Mystery of the Passion; its 65 000 lines took four days to perform.

Renaissance and Humanism. – When the vicissitudes of the Hundred Years War obliged the French court to move from Paris to Touraine, new universities were founded in Orléans (1305) and Angers (1364). They very soon attracted a vast body of students and became important centres in the study of European humanism. Among those who came to study and to teach were Erasmus and William Bude, Melchior Wolmar a Hellenist from Swabia and the reformers Calvin and Théodore de Bèze; **Étienne Dolet**, a native of Orléans, preached his atheist doctrines for which he was hung and burned in Paris.

(Archives SNARK/Edimedia)

Rabelais
(Condé Museum, Chantilly)

Rabelais (1494-1553), who was born near Chinon, was surely the most popular native of Touraine. After studying in Angers, he became a learned Benedictine and then a famous doctor. In the adventures of Gargantua and Pantagruel *(see p 89)* he expressed his ideas on education, religion and philosophy. He was very attached to his native country and made it the setting for the Picrocholine war in his books *(see p 93)*. His comic and realistic style, his extraordinarily rich vocabulary and his universal curiosity made him the first prose writer of his period.

The Pleiades (La Pléiade). — A group of seven poets, named after the constellation Taurus, founded a new school in the Loire Valley which was to dominate 16C poetry; their aim was to develop and cultivate their own language through imitation of Horace and the ancients. Their undoubted leader was **Ronsard**, the prince of Poets from near Vendôme *(p 156)* but it was **Joachim du Bellay** *(p 114)* from Anjou who wrote the manifesto of the group, the Defence and Illustration of the French Language, which was published in 1549. The other members of the group were Jean-Antoine de **Baif** from La Flèche, Jean Dorat, Étienne Jodelle, Marot and Pontus de Tyard who all held the position of Court Poet; their subjects were nature, women, their native country and its special quality, *"la douceur angevine"*.

Classicism and the Age of Enlightenment. — At the end of the Wars of Religion, when the king and the court returned north to the Ile-de-France, literature became more serious and philosophical. The **Marquis of Racan** composed verses beside the Loir; **Théophraste Renaudot**, the father of journalism, was born in Loudun in 1586; the Protestant Academy in Saumur supported the first works of **René Descartes**. In the following century, **Néricault-Destouches**, from Touraine, followed in Molière's footsteps with his comedies of character; Voltaire stayed at Sully; Rousseau, whose companion was a servant girl from Orléans, Thérèse Levasseur, lived at Chenonceau; Beaumarchais, who wrote The Barber of Seville, settled at Vouvray and visited the Duc de Choiseul in exile at Chanteloup.

Romanticism. — The pamphleteer **Paul-Louis Courier** (1772-1825) and the song writer **Béranger** (1780-1857), who were active during the second Bourbon restoration, were both sceptical and witty and liberal in politics. **Alfred de Vigny** (1797-1863), a native of Loches who became a soldier and a poet, painted an idyllic picture of Touraine in his novel, *Cinq-Mars*. The greatest literary genius of Touraine was **Honoré de Balzac** (1799-1850). He was born in Tours and brought up in Vendôme; he loved the Loire Valley and used it as a frame for the numerous portraits that he penned in his vast work, *The Human Comedy (p 159)*.

Contemporary writers. — The poet, **Charles Péguy**, who was born in Orléans, wrote about Joan of Arc and his beloved Beauce *(p 151)*. **Marcel Proust** *(p 109)* also returned to the Beauce in his novel *Remembrance of things past*. Another poet, **Max Jacob** (1876-1944), spent many years in work and meditation at the abbey of St-Benoît-sur-Loire.
The Sologne calls to mind the young novelist, **Alain-Fournier**, and his famous work, *Le Grand Meaulnes (The Lost Domain)*. The character of Raboliot the poacher is a picturesque evocation of his native country by the author **Maurice Genevoix** (1890-1980), a member of the Academy. **Georges Bernanos** (1888-1948), an original Catholic writer, is buried at Pellevoisin. The humourist **Georges Courteline** (1858-1929) was born in Touraine which was also the retreat of several writers of international reputation: Maeterlinck (Nobel prize in 1911) at Coudray-Montpensier *(p 93);* Anatole France (Nobel prize in 1921) at La Béchellerie; Bergson (Nobel prize in 1927) at La Gaudinière. **René Benjamin** (1885-1948) settled in Touraine where he wrote *The Prodigious Life of Balzac* and his novels about life in the region.
Angers was the home of **René Bazin** (1853-1932), a Catholic novelist, who was greatly attached to the traditional virtues and his home ground, and of his great nephew, **Hervé Bazin,** whose violent attacks on conventional values were directly inspired by his home town.

FINE ARTS

Clément Janequin (1480-1565), a master of religious and secular music, became an Angevin by adoption and was for many years head of the Angers Cathedral Choir School. **Jean Clouet** from Flanders, who was attached to Louis XII and François I, and his son **François,** who was born in Tours, drew some very fine portraits.
In 19C the sculptor and engraver, **David d'Angers** (1788-1856), achieved fame through his hundreds of medallions which record the profiles of the celebrities of his period.

Painters	Sculptors
Jean Fouquet (c1420-80). Portraitist and miniaturist, born in Tours; his backgrounds evoke the Loire Valley.	**Michel Colombe** (c1430-1514?). Head of an important studio in Tours; he combined Gothic tradition with Italian novelty.
The Master of Moulins (late 15C). His charm and purity of line are characteristic of the French school.	**Fra Giocondo** (c1433-1515). Famous monk from Verona, humanist and engineer who settled in Amboise in 1499.
Identified with Jean Perréal (c1455-1530).	**Guido Mazzoni** (c1450-1518). An Italian, known as Il Paganino, who specialised in terracotta.
Jean Bourdichon (c1457-1521). Miniaturist who painted Anne of Brittany, with a facile and seductive style.	**Domenico da Cortona** (1470-1549). Italian architect, called Il Boccadoro (Golden Mouth), in France since 1495.
Leonardo da Vinci (1452-1519). Invited to settle in the Loire Valley from 1516 by François I; died in Amboise.	**The Justes** (16C). Florentine family descended from Antoine Juste (1479-1519) who was naturalised in 1513 and settled in Tours in 1515.
François Clouet (1520-72). Born in Tours, he became portrait painter to the Valois kings. His work shows subtlety and penetration.	**Girolamo della Robbia** (1488-1566). Arrived in the Orléans region from Florence in 1518 and produced terracotta medallions.
Jean Mosnier (1600-56). Interior decorator and author of religious works. Worked mainly at Cheverny and Beauregard and also in the neighbourhood.	**Michel Bourdin** (1585-1645). From Orléans; a realist in style.

SCIENCE

The Royal School of Surgery, now the Faculty of Medecine and Pharmacy, was founded in Tours in 1756. It was also in Tours that **Bretonneau** (1778-1862) taught and conducted his research on infectious diseases; his work was brilliantly continued by his pupils **Trousseau** and **Velpeau**. Denis Papin (1647-1714), physicist and inventor, was born near Blois. A more fortunate physicist was **Charles** (1746-1823), born in Beaugency, who collaborated with the Montgolfier brothers and in 1783 made the first ascension in a hydrogen aircraft in Paris.

THE INHABITANTS OF THE LOIRE VALLEY

The character of the people in the Loire Valley is apparently best illustrated by the following legend which is current in Touraine. The holy relics of St Martin were being carried from Auxerre to Tours. The route was crowded with invalids and cripples who were instantly cured as the relics passed by. Two poor cripples who lived on alms suddenly heard the terrible news – terrible because for them it meant ruin. To escape the miracle which threatened them, they fled as fast as their poor limbs would carry them but they were too slow; the procession overtook them and they were cured. They had to abandon their crutches and begging bowl and work for their living. There was no point in lamenting their lot; it was better to profit from their cure. They went off along the banks of the Loire, praising the Lord and his saint with such enthusiasm that they were able to found a rich chapel and a village Chapelle-sur-Loire near Langeais.

The region where the "best French" is spoken. – Since the Loire Valley was the cradle of France, it is here that old France is recalled in the old sayings which have shaped the French language. It is in this region, so it is said, that the best French is spoken. This does not mean that one hears nothing but the best literary expressions; the local dialect is as unintelligible to the untuned ear as any other.

Fun and games. – The young people of the Loire Valley meet at the patronal festivals, the "assemblies" where a special platform is set up for dancing. In the past at the major festivals servants put themselves up for hire and accepted a coin *(le denier à Dieu)* from their new master to seal the contract.
In the fishermen's taverns on the banks of the Loire the old men still play *alouette* or *bigaille,* two games inherited from the boatmen which require 48 cards; declarations are made by signs.
There are about 500 clubs in the Loire Valley, from Bourgueil to Angers, where bowls **(boules de fort)** are played. The bowls are hollow on one side and weighted on the other; the ground is marked out in squares and surrounded by a raised edge. The bowls describe a skilfully judged curve before coming to rest near the jack *(maître),* the small white ball which is the target.

Festivals. – Mid-summer harvest, threshing and grape-picking are celebrated in a lively manner in the Loire Valley with huge meals and generous supplies of wine. Rabelais greeted the local wine as the "good September brew".

RURAL ARCHITECTURE

The various types of local houses to be found in the Loire Valley are determined by local building materials, local needs and customs.

On the plateaux and in the wooded plains. – In the **Beauce**, a wheat-growing plain, the farms are built round a closed courtyard with an imposing entrance. In the towns the houses are rough cast and roofed with flat tiles.
In the **Dunois** and the **Vendômois** the houses are decorated with a chequered pattern of alternate stone and flint. The long low cottages of the **Sologne** are roofed with thatch or flat tiles; the older houses are built of timber frames filled with cob while the more modern are of brick.

On the plateaux between the Cher, the Indre and the Vienne the country houses are often surrounded by clumps of walnut or chestnut trees. Flat tiles predominate in the country while slates are more common in town. The big house in any locality is usually recognisable by its hipped roof. Between the Sologne and the Loire one often sees red brick buildings with white tufa facings.
In **Anjou** there are two distinct types of building: those constructed of limestone in White Anjou in the east and those constructed of schist in Black Anjou in the wooded farmland: the Mauges, Craonnais and Segréen. The fine blue-black slates are found throughout the province except in the Mauges. In **Maine** the houses are built of limestone in White Maine on the River Sarthe and of granite or schist in Black Maine in the Mayenne Valley.

(after photo Arthaud)
Cottage in the Loire Valley

In the river valleys. – In the valleys of the Loire and its tributaries the typical vine-grower's house consists of the living quarters, the storeroom and the stable under one roof with an external oven and an outside stair beneath which is the entrance to the cellar.
A peculiarity of the valleys is the **troglodyte dwelling** which is hollowed out of the limestone tufa and has a chimney protruding at ground level. Often decorated with flowers and trellises and sheltered from the wind, it is cool in summer and warm in winter.

The practical information chapter,
at the end of the guide, regroups

– a list of the local or national organizations
supplying additional information
– a section on times and charges.

ART

ABC OF ARCHITECTURE

To assist readers unfamiliar with the terminology employed in architecture, we describe below the most commonly used terms, which we hope will make their visits to ecclesiastical, military and civil buildings more interesting.

Ecclesiastical architecture

illustration I

Ground plan. – The more usual Catholic form is based on the outline of a cross with the two arms of the cross forming the transept: ① Porch – ② Narthex – ③ Side aisles (sometimes double) – ④ Bay (transverse section of the nave between 2 pillars) – ⑤ Side chapel (often predates the church) – ⑥ Transept crossing – ⑦ Arms of the transept, sometimes with a side doorway – ⑧ Chancel, nearly always facing east towards Jerusalem; the chancel often vast in size was reserved for the monks in abbatial churches – ⑨ High altar – ⑩ Ambulatory: in pilgrimage churches the aisles were extended round the chancel, forming the ambulatory, to allow the faithful to file past the relics – ⑪ Radiating or apsidal chapel – ⑫ Axial chapel. In churches which are not dedicated to the Virgin this chapel, in the main axis of the building is often consecrated to the Virgin (Lady Chapel) – ⑬ Transept chapel.

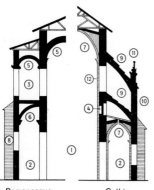

Romanesque   Gothic

◄ illustration II

Cross-section: ① Nave – ② Aisle – ③ Tribune or Gallery – ④ Triforium – ⑤ Barrel vault – ⑥ Half-barrel vault – ⑦ Pointed vault – ⑧ Buttress – ⑨ Flying buttress – ⑩ Pier of a flying buttress – ⑪ Pinnacle – ⑫ Clerestory window.

illustration III ▶

Gothic cathedral: ① Porch – ② Gallery – ③ Rose window – ④ Belfry (sometimes with a spire) – ⑤ Gargoyle acting as a waterspout for the roof gutter – ⑥ Buttress – ⑦ Pier of a flying buttress (abutment) – ⑧ Flight or span of flying buttress – ⑨ Double-course flying buttress – ⑩ Pinnacle – ⑪ Side chapel – ⑫ Radiating or apsidal chapel – ⑬ Clerestory windows – ⑭ Side doorway – ⑮ Gable – ⑯ Pinnacle – ⑰ Spire over the transept crossing.

illustration IV

Groined vaulting:
① Main arch – ② Groin
③ Transverse arch

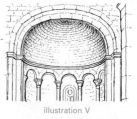

illustration V

Oven vault:
termination of a barrel
vaulted nave

illustration VI

Lierne and tierceron vaulting:
① Diagonal – ② Lierne
③ Tierceron – ④ Pendant
⑤ Corbel

illustration VII

Quadripartite vaulting:
① Diagonal – ② Transverse
③ Stringer – ④ Flying buttress
⑤ Keystone

▼ illustration VIII

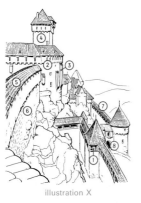

Doorway: ① Archivolt. Depending on the architectural style of the building this can be rounded, pointed, basket-handled, ogee or even adorned by a gable – ② Arching, covings (with string courses, mouldings, carvings or adorned with statues). Recessed arches or orders form the archivolt – ③ Tympanum – ④ Lintel – ⑤ Archshafts – ⑥ Embrasures. Arch shafts, splaying sometimes adorned with statues or columns – ⑦ Pier (often adorned by a statue) – ⑧ Hinges and other ironwork.

illustration IX ▶

Arches and pillars: ① Ribs or ribbed vaulting – ② Abacus – ③ Capital – ④ Shaft – ⑤ Base – ⑥ Engaged column – ⑦ Pier of arch wall – ⑧ Lintel – ⑨ Discharging or relieving arch – ⑩ Frieze.

Military architecture

illustration X

Fortified enclosure: ① Hoarding (projecting timber gallery) – ② Machicolations (corbelled crenellations) – ③ Barbican – ④ Keep or donjon – ⑤ Covered watchpath – ⑥ Curtain wall – ⑦ Outer curtain wall – ⑧ Postern.

illustration XI

Towers and curtain walls: ① Hoarding – ② Crenellations – ③ Merlon – ④ Loophole or arrow slit – ⑤ Curtain wall – ⑥ Bridge or drawbridge.

◀ illustration XII

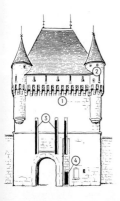

Fortified gatehouse: ① Machicolations – ② Watch turrets or bartizan – ③ Slots for the arms of the drawbridge – ④ Postern.

illustration XIII ▶

Star fortress: ① Entrance – ② Drawbridge – ③ Glacis – ④ Ravelin or half-moon – ⑤ Moat – ⑥ Bastion – ⑦ Watch turret – ⑧ Town – ⑨ Assembly area.

GLOSSARY OF ARCHITECTURAL TERMS USED IN THE GUIDE

Aisle: illustration I.
Altarpiece: illustration XVII.
Ambulatory: illustration I.
Apse: illustration I.
Apsidal chapel: illustration I.
Arcade: a range of arches within a larger arch.
Archivolt: illustration VIII.
Atlantes: supports in the form of carved male figures.
Axial or Lady Chapel: illustration I.
Bailey: open space or court of stone-built castle.
Barrel vaulting: illustration II.
Bartizan: a battlemented parapet.
Basket-handled arch: depressed arch common to late medieval and Renaissance architecture.
Bastion: illustration XIII.
Bay: illustration I.
Bracket: small supporting piece of stone or timber to carry a beam or cornice.
Brattice: a temporary wooden gallery or parapet for use during a siege.
Buttress: illustration II.
Capital: illustration IX.
Caryatids: supports in the form of carved female figures.
Cheekpiece: illustration XVIII.
Chevet: French term for the altar end of a church; illustration I.
Chi Rho: monogram of Christ comprising the Greek letters X and P.
Clamp: metal clamp joining two pieces of stone.
Coffered ceiling: vault or ceiling decorated with sunken panels.
Corbel: see bracket; illustration VI.
Crypt: underground chamber or chapel.
Curtain wall: illustration X.
Diagonal ribs: illustrations VI and VII.
Embrasure: splay of window or door; illustration VIII.
Entablature: that part of an order above the column comprising the architrave, frieze and cornice.
Flamboyant: latest phase (15C) of French Gothic architecture; name taken from the undulating (flame-like) lines of the window tracery.
Fresco: mural paintings executed on wet plaster.
Gable: triangular upper portion of a wall to carry a pitched roof; illustration III.
Gallery: illustration II.
Gargoyle: illustration III.
Groined vaulting: illustration IV.
Hypocaust: underground heating duct.
Keel vaulting: resembling an inverted ship's hull.
Keep: illustration X.
Keystone: middle and topmost stone in an arch or vault; illustration VII.
Lancet arch: arch with a pointed head.
Lancet window: high and narrow window terminating in a lancet arch.
Lavabo or lavatory: a trough for washing the hands in a monastery.
Lintel: illustration VIII.
Lists: a space enclosed by palisades in which jousting took place.
Machicolations: illustration X.
Mandorla: almond-shaped.
Misericord: illustration XVIII.
Moat: ditch generally water-filled.
Mullion: vertical post dividing a window.
Narthex: vestibule or portico at the west end of some early Christian churches.
Niello: inlaid enamel work.
Nimbus: halo.
Oculus: round window.
Organ case and loft: illustration XIV.
Oven vaulting: illustration V
Parapet walk: see sentry walk; illustration X.
Parclose screen: screen separating a chapel or the choir from the rest of the church; illustration XVIII.
Pepperpot roof: conical in shape.
Peristyle: a range of columns surrounding or on the façade of a building.
Phylactery: an inscribed scroll; an amulet.
Pier: illustration VIII.
Pietà: Italian term designating the Virgin Mary with the dead Christ on her knees.
Pilaster: engaged rectangular column.
Pinnacle: illustrations II and III.
Porch: covered area before the entrance to a building.
Postern: illustrations X and XII.
Rib vaulting: illustrations VI and VII.
Recessed tomb: funerary niche.
Retable: illustration XVII.
Rood beam: illustration XVI.
Rood loft or screen: illustration XV.
Rose window: illustration XVII.
Sentry walk: illustration X.
Spire: illustration III.
Stalls: illustration XVIII.

Telamones: supports in the form of carved male figures.

Torus: large convex moulding semicircular in shape at the base of a column or pedestal.

Tracery: intersecting stone ribwork in the upper part of a window.

Transept: illustration I.

Triforium: illustration II.

Triptych: three panels hinged together, chiefly used as an altarpiece.

Tunnel vaulting: see barrel vaulting.

Twinned: columns or pilasters grouped in twos.

Voussoir: wedge-shaped stone forming part of an arch or vault; illustration XIII.

Wall walk: see sentry walk; illustration X.

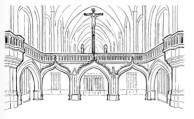

illustration XIV	illustration XV

Rood screen. – This replaces the rood beam in larger churches, and may be used for preaching and reading of the Epistles and Gospel. From the 17C onwards many disappeared as they tended to hide the altar.

Rood beam. – This extends across the chancel arch and carries a Crucifix flanked by statues of the Virgin and St John and sometimes other personages from the Calvary.

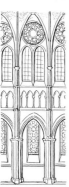
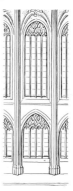
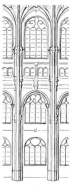

illustration XVI	illustration XVII	illustration XVIII
Organ	**Altar with retable or altarpiece**	**Stalls**
⑤ great organ case	① retable or altarpiece	① high back
② little organ case	② predella	② elbow rest
③ caryatids	③ crowning piece – ④ altar table	③ cheekpiece
④ loft	⑤ altar front	④ misericord

Romanesque, Gothic and Renaissance elevations

11C-12C	13C	Late 13C-14C	15C	16C
Romanesque	Lancet Gothic	Rayonnant Gothic	Flamboyant Gothic	Renaissance

RELIGIOUS ARCHITECTURE

Romanesque art (11-12C)

Orléanais. − The church in Germigny-des-Prés, which dates from the Carolingian period, and the Benedictine basilica of St Benedict are remarkable.
There are two fine churches in the Cher Valley in St-Aignan and Selles.

Touraine. − Various influences from Poitou are evident: apses with column buttresses, domed transepts, doorways without pediments.
The belltowers are unusual: square or octagonal with spires surrounded at the base by turrets.

Anjou. − The Angevin buildings are clustered in the region round Baugé and Saumur. Cunault church shows the influence of Poitou in the ogive vaulted nave buttressed by high aisles with groined vaulting. The domes roofing the nave of the abbey church at Fontevraud and the absence of aisles are features of the Aquitaine school.

Romanesque doorway
Saumur − St Peter's Church

From Romanesque to Gothic

The **Plantagenet style**, which is also known as **Angevin**, takes its name from Henry Plantagenet *(p 48)*. It is a transitional style which reached the height of its popularity early in 13C and had been abandoned before its end.

Angevin vaulting. − In ordinary Gothic vaulting all the keystones are at the same level but in Plantagenet architecture the vaulting is curved so that the central keystone was about 3 m - 10 ft higher than the supporting arches; the best example is St Maurice's Cathedral in Angers.
At the end of 12C the Angevin vaulting grew lighter; slimmer and more numerous ribs sprang from slender round columns. Early in 13C the high lierne vaulting was decorated with elegant sculptures.
The Plantagenet style spread from the Loire Valley into the Vendée, Poitou, Saintonge and the Garonne Valley. At the end of 13C it was introduced by Charles of Anjou to southern Italy.

Angevin vaulting

Mid 12C	Late 12C	Early 13C
St Maurice's Cathedral, Angers		Chancel of St Sergius' in Angers

Gothic art (12-15C)

Gothic art is characterised by the use of intersecting vaults and the pointed arch. The triforium, which originally was blind, is pierced by apertures which eventually give place to high windows *(illustrations p 35)*. The tall, slender columns, which were topped by capitals supporting the vaulting, were at first cylindrical but were later flanked by engaged columns.
In the final development the capitals were abandoned and the roof ribs descended directly into the columns.
The **Flamboyant style** follows this pattern; the diagonal ribs are supplemented by other, purely decorative, ribs, called liernes and tiercerons *(illustrations p 35)*.
The Flamboyant style (15C) of architecture is to be found in the façade of Holy Trinity in Vendôme and of St-Gatien in Tours, in Notre-Dame de Cléry and in the Sainte-Chapelle at Châteaudun.

Renaissance and Classical Styles (16-17-18C)

Italian influence is strong in the decoration of churches in the **Renaissance** period: basket-handle or round-headed arches, numerous recesses for statues. Montrésor church and the chapels at Ussé, Champigny-sur-Veude and La Bourgonnière are of particular interest.
In the **Classical** period (17-18C) religious architecture strove for a majestic effect: superimposed Greek orders, pediments over doorways, domes and flanking vaulting. The church of Notre-Dame-des-Ardilliers in Saumur has a huge dome; St Vincent's in Blois is dominated by a scrolled pediment.

SECULAR ARCHITECTURE

Gothic Period

In addition to the castles built for the Dukes of Anjou, such as Saumur, manor houses and mansions were constructed in 14C for merchants who had grown rich through trade. The 15C saw a proliferation in the lively ornate Gothic style of châteaux built of brick with white stone facings, such as the château at Lassay, of manor houses such as Le Clos-Lucé near Amboise, of town mansions with projecting stair turrets and high dormers, and of half-timbered houses. The finest examples of Gothic houses are to be found in Le Mans, Chinon and Tours.

Gardens. — Monastic gardens, such as those belonging to the abbeys in Bourgueil, Marmoutier and Cormery, consisted of an orchard, a vegetable patch with a fish pond and a medicinal herb garden. In 15C they were succeeded by square flower beds which were created by King René at his manor houses in Anjou and by Louis XI at Plessis-lès-Tours. A fresh note was introduced with shady arbours and fountains where the paths intersected; entertainment was provided by animals at liberty or kept in menageries or aviaries.

Renaissance Period

Before the wars in Italy, Italian artists had been made welcome at the French court and the court of Anjou; Louis XI and King René had employed sculptors and medallion makers such as Francesco Laurana, Niccolo Spinelli and Jean Candida. The Renaissance did not spring into being at the wave of a magic wand at the end of the Italian campaigns.

New blood, however, was imported into local art by the arrival of artists from Naples in 1495 at the behest of Charles VIII.

At Amboise and Chaumont and even at Chenonceau, Azay or Chambord, the châteaux still looked like fortresses but the machicolations assumed a decorative role. Large windows flanked by pilasters appeared in the façades which were decorated with medallions; the steep roofs were decorated with lofty dormers and carved chimneys. The Italian influence is most apparent in the low relief ornamentation. At Chambord and Le Lude the décor was refined under the influence of local masters such as Pierre Trinqueau.

The Italian style is most obvious in the exterior of the François I wing at Blois where Il Boccadoro copied Bramante's invention, the rhythmic façade which was composed of alternating windows and niches separated by pilasters. Later, as in Beaugency town hall, came semicircular arches and superimposed orders, then the domes and pavilions which mark the birth of Classical architecture.

The Italians created new types of staircases: two spirals intertwined as at Chambord or straight flights of steps beneath coffered ceilings as at Chenonceau, Azay-le-Rideau and Poncé. The Renaissance also inspired a number of town halls — Orléans, Beaugency, Loches — and several private houses — Hôtel Toutin in Orléans, Hôtel Gouin in Tours and the Hôtel Pincé in Angers.

Renaissance decoration

Azay-le-Rideau Château
Grand staircase frieze

① Shell — ② Urn
③ Scroll — ④ Dragon
⑤ Putto — ⑥ Cupid
⑦ Horn of plenty
⑧ Satyr

Gardens. — In his enthusiasm for Neapolitan gardens, Charles VIII brought with him from his kingdom in Sicily a gardener called **Dom Pacello de Mercogliano,** a Neapolitan monk, who laid out the gardens at Amboise and Blois; Louis XII entrusted him with the royal vegetable plot at Château-Gaillard near Amboise.

Pacello popularised the use of ornate flowerbeds bordered with yew and fountains with sculpted basins. The gardens of Chenonceau and Villandry (p 189) give a good idea of his style.

The extraordinary vegetable garden at Villandry, which is laid out in a decorative pattern in the style popular during the Renaissance, still has certain traditional medieval and monastic features; the rose trees, planted in a symmetrical pattern, symbolise the monks, each digging in his own plot.

Classical Period (17-18C)

Following the removal of the court to the Ile-de-France, architecture in the Loire Valley went into decline. Handsome buildings were still constructed but the designers came from Paris.

In the more austere climate of 17C the pompous style of the Sun King displaced the graceful fantasy of the Renaissance and the picturesque asymmetry of the medieval buildings. The fashion was for pediments, domes (Cheverny Château p 89) and the Greek orders (Gaston d'Orléans wing of Blois Château). Tower structures were abandoned in favour of rectangular pavilions containing huge rooms with monumental chimneys decorated with caryatids and painted ceilings with exposed beams; the pavilions were covered with steep roofs in the French style.

There was a new wave of château building — Ménars, Montgeoffroy — but the main legacy of the 18C is in the towns. Great terraces were built in Orléans, Tours and Saumur with long perspectives aligned on the axis of magnificent bridges which had level roadways.

STAINED GLASS

A **stained glass window** is made up of pieces of coloured glass fixed with lead to an iron frame. The perpendicular divisions of a window are called **lights**. Metal oxides were added to the constituent materials of white glass to give a wide range of colours. Details were often drawn in with dark paint and fixed by firing.

Varied and surprising effects were obtained by altering the length of firing and by the impurities in the oxides and defects in the glass. The earliest stained glass windows were made in 10C but none has survived.

12-13C. – The colours were intense and brilliant with blues and reds predominating; the glass and leading were thick and smoothed down with a plane; the subject matter was naive and confined to superimposed medallions.

The Cistericans favoured grisaille windows which were composed of clear to greenish glass with foliage designs on a cross-hatched background which gives a greyish (**grisaille**) effect.

14-15C. – The master-glaziers discovered how to make a golden yellow; lighter colours were developed, the leading became less heavy as it was no longer produced by hand, the glass was thinner and the windows larger. Gothic canopies appeared over the human figures.

16C. – Windows became delicately coloured pictures in thick lead frames, often copied from Renaissance canvases with strict attention to detail and perspective; there are examples at Champigny-sur-Veude, Montrésor and Sully-sur-Loire.

(Photo Pélissier / Vloo)

13C stained glass window (detail)
Angers Cathedral

17-18-19C. – Traditional stained glass was often replaced by vitrified enamel or painted glass without lead surrounds. In Orléans Cathedral there are windows with white diamond panes and gold bands (17C) and some 19C windows depicting Joan of Arc.

20C. – The need to restore or replace old glass stimulated a revival of interest in the art of stained glass. Representational or abstract compositions of great variety emerged from the workshops of the painter-glaziers: Max Ingrand, Alfred Manessier and Jean Le Moal.

MURAL PAINTINGS AND FRESCOES

In the Middle Ages the interiors of ecclesiastical buildings were decorated with paintings, motifs or edifying scenes. A school of mural painting akin to the one in Poitou developed in the valleys of the Loire and its tributaries. The remaining works of this school are well preserved owing to the mild climate and the relative lack of humidity. The paintings of the Loire region are recognizable by the weak matt colours against light backgrounds. The style is livelier and less formalized than in Burgundy or the Massif Central while the composition is more sober than in Poitou. Two techniques were employed: **fresco work**, which was done with watercolours on fresh plaster thus eliminating any retouching, and **mural painting**, where the colours were applied to a dry surface and which was therefore less durable.

Romanesque Period. – The art of fresco work with its Byzantine origins was adopted by the Benedictines of Monte Cassino in Italy, who in turn transmitted the art to the monks of Cluny in Burgundy. The latter used this art form in their abbeys and priories whence it spread throughout the whole country.

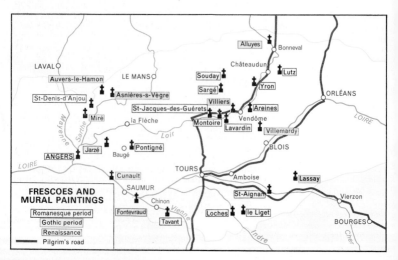

FRESCOES AND
MURAL PAINTINGS

Romanesque period
Gothic period
Renaissance
Pilgrim's road

The technique. — The fresco technique was the one most commonly used, although beards and eyes were often added when the plaster was dry so that they are usually no longer visible. The figures, drawn in red ochre, were sometimes highlighted with touches of black, green and the sky blue so characteristic of the region.

The subject matter. — The subjects, which were often inspired by smaller scale works, were intended to instruct the faithful in the truths of religion and also to instil a fear of sin and Hell. The most common theme for the oven vaulting was Christ the King enthroned, majestic and severe; the reverse of the façade often carried the Last Judgment; the walls depicted schemes from the New Testament while the Saints and Apostles adorned the pillars. Other frequently portrayed subjects are the Contest between the Vices and the Virtues and the Labours of the Months.

The most interesting examples. — Good examples of fresco painting are found throughout the Loir Valley in Areines, Souday, St-Jacques-des-Guérets, Lavardin and especially St-Gilles Chapel in Montoire. There is also a fine work in St-Aignan in the Cher Valley. The crypt of Tavant Church in the Vienne Valley is decorated with lively paintings of high quality.

In Anjou a man called Fulk seems to have supervised the decoration of the cloisters in St Aubin's Abbey in Angers. His realistic style, although slightly stilted in the drawing, seems to spring from the Poitou school. More characteristic of the Loire Valley are the Virgin and Christ the King from Pontigné in the Baugé region.

Gothic Period. — It was not until the 15C and the end of the Hundred Years War that new compositions were produced which remained in fashion until the mid 16C. These were more truly mural paintings than frescoes and new subjects were added to the traditional repertoire; a gigantic St Christopher often appeared at the entrance to a church *(p 45)* while the legend of the Three Living and Three Dead, represented by three proud huntsmen meeting three skeletons, symbolized the brevity and vanity of human life.

The most interesting examples. — In the Loire Valley such paintings are to be found in Alluyes, Lassay and Villiers. Two compositions with strange iconography adorn the neighbouring churches in Asnières-sur-Vègre and Auvers-le-Hamon.

Renaissance. — In 16C paintings in churches became rarer. There are however two surviving examples from this period: The Entombment in Jarzé church and the paintings in the Chapter House of Fontevraud Abbey.

GEMMAIL

Gemmail is a modern art medium consisting of assembling particles of coloured glass over an artificial light source. The inventor of this art form was **Jean Crotti** (1878-1958) *(p 179)*. The Malherbe-Navarre brothers, an interior decorator and a physicist, provided the technical expertise; they discovered a bonding agent which did not affect the constituent elements.

TAPESTRIES FROM THE LOIRE WORKSHOPS

Hanging tapestries, which had been in existence since 8C to exclude draughts or divide up great chambers, became very popular in 14C. The weavers worked from cartoons or preparatory sketches using wool woven with silk, gold or silver threads on horizontal (low warp — *basse-lisse)* or vertical (high warp — *haute-lisse)* looms.

Religious tapestries. — Owing to their value tapestries were used as investments or diplomatic gifts; as well as those commissioned for châteaux or even specific rooms some were hung in churches or even in the streets. The most famous is the 14C Apocalypse tapestry *(p 49)*.

Mille-fleurs. — The *mille-fleurs* (thousand flowers) ta-pestries evoke late medieval scenes — showing an ideal-ized life of enticing gardens, tournaments and hunting — against a green, blue or pink background strewn with flowers and plants and small animals. These are tradition-ally attributed to the Loire Valley workshops (*c*1500). Good examples exist in Sau-mur, Langeais and Ahgers.

Renaissance to 20C. — Paintings replace cartoons and finer weaving tech-niques and materials render greater detail possible. The number of colours multiplies and panels are surrounded by borders. In 18C the art of portraiture is introduced into tapestry work.

Jean Lurçat *(p 53)* recom-mended natural dyes. Con-temporary weavers experi-ment with new techniques and three dimensional ef-fects.

(Photo Musées d'Angers/© A.D.A.G.P. 1987)

Le Chant du Monde — Jean Lurçat. 1958
(Angers — Jean Lurçat Museum)

FOOD AND WINE

The Loire Valley is a region for good eating, cheerful drinking and calm digestion; it offers the visitor simple healthy cooking.
The following menu lists some of the local specialities and the best wines to accompany them.

Menu

HORS-D'ŒUVRE

Vouvray - Sancerre
Les rillons de Touraine.
Les rillettes du Mans, de Tours ou d'Angers.
Le boudin blanc bourré non de mie, mais de blanc de poulet.

POISSONS

Vouvray - Saumur - Montlouis - Sancerre - Rosés d'Anjou
Le brochet, le saumon, la carpe ou l'alose au beurre blanc.
La friture de Loire.
La brème farcie et surtout la matelote d'anguille au vin vieux.

VIANDES

Bourgueil - Chinon - Saumur-Champigny
Le gibier de Sologne.
Le carré ou la noisette de porc aux pruneaux.
Le cul-de-veau à l'angevine.
Le coq au vin du pays ou la fricassée de poulet.
Le chapon ou la poularde du Mans à la broche.

LÉGUMES

Les choux-verts au beurre.
Les asperges de Vineuil.
Les champignons farcis ou à la crème.
La salade à l'huile de noix.

FROMAGES

Bourgueil - Chinon
Crottins de Chavignol; Olivet à la cendre.
St-Benoît; Valençay; Selles-sur-Cher; Ste-Maure; Vendôme.
St-Paulin; crémets d'Anjou.

FRUITS

Les prunes et pruneaux de Tours, les melons de Tours.
Les fraises de Saumur, les abricots et les poires d'Angers.
Les Reinettes du Mans.

DESSERTS

Vouvray pétillant, Vouvray, Crémant de Loire
Saumur - Coteaux du Layon - Montlouis
Les macarons de Cormery.
Les chaussons aux pommes et toute la cohorte des cotignacs,
des confitures d'Orléans et des pâtisseries de Tours; les tartes des demoiselles Tatin.
Pour digérer:d'excellents marcs, des liqueurs de fruits dont Angers a le secret.

Hors-d'œuvre: various types of potted pork; sausage stuffed with chicken meat.

Fish: pike, salmon, carp or shad with butter sauce; small fried fish from the Loire; stuffed bream and eels simmered in wine with mushrooms, onions and prunes (in Anjou).

Main course: game from Sologne; pork with prunes; veal in a cream sauce made with white wine and brandy; casserole of chicken in a red wine sauce or in a white wine and cream sauce with onions and mushrooms; spit roasted capon or large hen.

Vegetables: green cabbage with butter; Vineuil asparagus; mushrooms stuffed or with a cream sauce; lettuce with walnut oil.

Cheese: St-Benoît, Vendôme and St-Paulin are made from cows' milk. Chavignol, Valençay, Selles-sur-Cher, Ste-Maure and crémets are made from goats' milk; the latter are small fresh cream cheeses; Olivet is factory-made with a coating of charcoal.

Fruit: plums and prunes from Tours; melons from Tours; Saumur strawberries; apricots and pears from Angers; Reinette apples from Le Mans.

Dessert: macaroons from Cormery; apple pastries; quince and apple jelly; preserves from Orléans and Tours pastries; caramelised apple turnovers.

Liqueurs: there are excellent marcs and fruit liqueurs, notably those from Angers.

Marcs: pure white spirit obtained from pressed grapes.

WINE

Local wines. — The best known white wines are from Vouvray, a dry, mellow wine with the flavour of ripe grapes, and Montlouis, with a delicate fruity flavour; both are made from the Chenin Blanc grape, known locally as the **Pineau de la Loire**.

The best known red wine, known as Breton, is made from the Cabernet Franc grape which came originally from Bordeaux and produces the fine, light wines of Bourgueil and those from Chinon which have a stronger bouquet; the same grape is used to make a dry rosé which has charm and nobility. Among the wines of Anjou are the Rouge de Cabernet and the Saumur-Champigny which have a fine ruby glow and the subtle taste of raspberries. The Cabernet de Saumur is an elegant dry rosé with a good flavour. Another red wine comes from the Breton vines grown on the Loudun slopes.

The wines of Sancerre, on the eastern fringe of the châteaux country, are made from the Sauvignon grape and are known for their "gun-flint" flavour.

Less famous wines are the *gris meuniers* from the Orléanais and the *gascon,* which are pale and have a low alcohol content.

The slopes of the Loir produce a dry white and an acid-tasting red which improve with keeping. A light and pleasant white wine is made from the Romorantin grape which is grown only in the Sologne. Loire wine has a delicate bouquet; it tastes of the grape and is not very intoxicating. The character of the region is most apparent in the wine cellars which are often old quarries hollowed out of the limestone slopes at road level. They are therefore easily accessible so that the owner can drive his vehicles straight in. The galleries often extend for several hundred yards. Some open out into chambers where local societies hold their meetings and festivities.

The wine cellars also witness the reunions of the wine producers' brotherhoods *(confréries vineuses)* which preserve the tradition of good wine in the Loire Valley and joyously initiate new members *(chevaliers)* to their brotherhoods: *Les Sacavins* in Angers, *les Entonneurs rabelaisiens* in Chinon, *la Chantepleure* in Vouvray and the *Coterie des Closiers de Montlouis.*

In the temple of Bacchus. — Behold the guest facing the barrels of the latest vintage, firmly fixed on their stands; they contain unsophisticated wine *(vin ordinaire)* which flows into the silver goblet when the plug is drawn. The owner fills the glasses and the ruby red nectar is held up to the light. The tumblers have no stem or foot so they cannot be set down until they are drained — *Nunc est bibendum* (now is the time to drink).

The wine is not to be swallowed in one draught but savoured first for its bouquet and then, after a knowing glance at one's neighbour, tasted in small sips. When the glass is empty, no words of appreciation are required, just a simple click of the tongue and the owner, his eyes shining, will say *"Ça se laisse boire...".*

From the huge pocket in his grey apron the owner produces an enormous key; the lock grates, the cellar is open. All round, projecting from recesses in the rock, are the coloured bottle tops: red, yellow, blue and white: full-bodied Sancerre; Vouvray which "rejoices the heart"; heady Montlouis, Chinon with its after taste of violets; Bourgueil with its hint of raspberries or wild strawberries and its Angevin brothers, sparkling Saumur, lively and spirited, white Saumur, dry and lively, wines from La Coulée de Serrant and the Layon. For the vintage years see the list printed in the current Michelin Red Guide France.

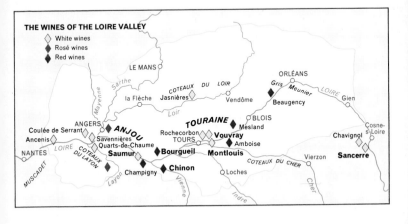

THE WINES OF THE LOIRE VALLEY

◇ White wines
◆ Rosé wines
◆ Red wines

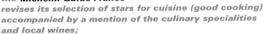

Key

Sights

★★★ **Worth a journey**
★★ **Worth a detour**
★ **Interesting**

**Sightseeing route with departure point indicated
on the road   in town**

		Castle, Château – Ruins
⊥	◎	Wayside cross or calvary – Fountain
		Panorama – View
		Lighthouse – Windmill
∪	☼	Dam – Factory or power station
☆	∪	Fort – Quarry
▲		Miscellaneous sights

Ecclesiastical building:
Catholic – Protestant

Building with main entrance

Ramparts – Tower

Gateway

Statue or small building

Gardens, parks, woods

B Letters giving the location
of a place on the town plan

Other symbols

Motorway (unclassified)

Interchange
complete, limited, number

Major through road

Dual carriageway

Stepped street – Footpath

Pedestrian street

Unsuitable for traffic

Pass – Altitude

Station – Coach station

Ferry services:
Passengers and cars
Passengers only

Airport

③ Reference number
common to town plans
and MICHELIN maps

Public building

Hospital – Covered market

Police station – Barracks

Cemetery

Synagogue

Racecourse – Golf course

Outdoor or indoor swimming pool

Skating rink – Viewing table

Pleasure boat harbour

Telecommunications tower or mast

Stadium – Water tower

Ferry (river and lake crossings)

Swing bridge

Main post office (with poste restante)

Tourist information centre

Car park

MICHELIN maps and town plans are north orientated.

Main shopping streets are printed in a different colour in the list of streets.

Town plans: roads most used by traffic and those on which guide listed sights stand are fully
drawn; the beginning only of lesser roads is indicated.
Local maps: only the primary and sightseeing routes are indicated.

Abbreviations

A	Local agricultural office (Chambre d'Agriculture)	J	Law Courts (Palais de Justice)	POL.	Police station
C	Chamber of Commerce (Chambre de Commerce)	M	Museum	T	Theatre
H	Town Hall (Hôtel de ville)	P	Préfecture Sous-préfecture	U	University

⊘ **Times and charges for admission are listed at the end of the guide**

The times indicated in this guide
when given with the distance allow one to enjoy the scenery
when given for sightseeing are intended to give an idea of the possible brevity
or length of a visit.

SIGHTS

listed alphabetically

Azay-le-Rideau Château mirrored in its moat

Michelin map 🆖 fold 16 or 🆖 fold 14 — Local map p 122 — Facilities

The town of Amboise, which lies on the south bank of the Loire below the proud remains of its castle, appears at its most picturesque when seen from the bridge or the north bank of the river.

★★ CHÂTEAU

Son et Lumière. — *See Practical Information at the end of the guide.*

The rock spur above the town, on which the château ruins stand, has been fortified since the Gallo-Roman period. Before long a bridge was built which brought in revenue from tolls on the passage of goods and increased the strategic importance of Amboise *(1)*.

For a period in the 11C there were two fortresses on the heights and one down in the town; all three were engaged in perpetual warfare. Eventually the Counts of Amboise gained the upper hand and held the domain until it was confiscated by Charles VII (1422-61).

The golden age of Amboise was the 15C when the château was enlarged and embellished by Louis XI and Charles VIII. Although the end of the century (1496) marks the beginning of Italian influence on French art, there is little to see at Amboise, since the new building was by then well advanced. The Italian style was to gain in popularity under Louis XII and flourish under François I.

Charles VIII's taste for luxury. — Charles VIII, who was born and grew up in the old castle, had since 1489 dreamed of enlarging and redecorating it in accordance with his taste for luxury.

Work began in 1492 and during the next five years two ranges of buildings were added to the older structure. Hundreds of workmen laboured uninterruptedly, if necessary by candle-light, to satisfy the king's desire to move into his new residence without delay. In the interim the king visited Italy where he was dazzled by the artistic standards and the luxurious life-style. He returned to France in 1495 laden with furniture, works of art, fabrics, etc. He also recruited to his service a team of scholars, architects, sculptors, decorators, gardeners and tailors... even a poultry breeder who had discovered the incubator.

Charles VIII was particularly impressed by the Italian gardens: "They lack only Adam and Eve, he wrote, to make an earthly paradise". On his return he instructed Pacello to design an ornamental garden on the terrace at Amboise. Among the architects whom he employed were Fra Giocondo and Il Boccadoro; the latter had worked at Blois and Chambord and on the Paris Town Hall.

A tragic death. — In the afternoon of 7 April 1498 Charles VIII was escorting the queen to watch a game of real tennis in the castle moat when they passed through a low doorway in the outer wall. Although not tall, the king hit his head on the lintel. Apparently unscathed, he chatted unconcernedly as the game progressed. Suddenly, however, he fell back unconscious. He was laid on a bed of straw in an evil-smelling chamber and such was the consternation caused by his collapse that he was left there until 11 o'clock in the evening when he died.

The whirl of gaiety under François I. — François d'Angoulême, the future François I, was only 7 when he came to Amboise with his mother, Louise de Savoie, and his sister, who was to become the famous and learned Margaret of Navarre. At Amboise, which Louis XII had appointed as his residence near to his own château at Blois, the young François, who was heir apparent to the throne, was given a thorough intellectual, sporting and military education. He continued to live at the château during the first three years of his reign and this was the most brilliant period in the life of Amboise. Magnificent festivities were organised to celebrate his engagement to Claude of France, his departure for Italy, the birth of the Dauphin, etc. Balls, tournaments, masquerades and wild beast fights followed one another in endless days given up to luxury and pleasure. A bevy of prostitutes was hired by the king to add to the enjoyment of the young noblemen of the court.

The wing of the château begun by Louis XII was completed by François I and his mother between 1517 and 1520 at a cost of 230 000 livres. Such was the king's passion for the arts that he invited Leonardo da Vinci to live at Le Clos-Lucé *(p 46)*. After 1519 he grew tired of Amboise and stayed there for only brief periods as for example on his return from captivity in Italy in 1526.

On 18 October 1534 Amboise was involved in the affair of the placards: a pamphlet inveighing against "the huge, horrible and unbearable abuses of the papal mass" was fixed to the door of the royal chamber. François I was furious and decided to take repressive measures; the religious quarrel became acrimonious.

François returned to Amboise on 8 December 1539 where he received his old adversary, Charles V, with great pomp and ceremony.

At the end of his life François preferred to live at Chambord or Fontainebleau.

Amboise Conspiracy (1560). — The conspiracy casts a bloody reflection on the château. In the turbulent years leading up to the Wars of Religion a Protestant, **La Renaudie**, gathered round him in Brittany a body of reformists who were to proceed to Blois in small groups to ask the young king for the freedom to practise their religion and also no doubt to try to lay hands on the Guises, the bitter enemies of the Huguenots.

---

(1) In the Middle Ages there were only seven bridges between Gien and Angers. Troops then moved very slowly and the possession or loss of a bridge had a great influence on operations. Towns at bridgeheads drew great profit from the passage of merchandise.

The plot was discovered and the court withdrew from Blois, which was indefensible, to Amboise where the king signed an edict of pacification in an attempt to calm things down. The conspirators, however, persisted and on 17 March they were arrested and killed as they arrived, including La Renaudie. The conspiracy was suppressed without mercy; some of the conspirators were hung from the balcony of the château, some from the battlements, others were thrown into the Loire in sacks, the noblemen were beheaded and quartered. In 1563 there was a truce followed by an Act of Toleration, signed at Amboise, which brought an end to the first war of religion; the country settled down to four years of peace.

Destruction. — Together with Blois, Amboise passed into the hands of Gaston d'Orléans, Louis XIII's brother and a great conspirator *(see Blois p 64)*; during one of his many rebellions, the château was captured by royalist troops and the outer fortifications were razed in 1631. It reverted to the crown and was used as a prison where Fouquet, his financial adviser, and the Duke of Lauzun, the lady-killer, were imprisoned by Louis XIV.

Later Napoleon granted the château to Roger Ducos, a former member of the Directory. As there were no subsidies for its upkeep, he had a large part of it demolished.

The château now belongs to the St-Louis Foundation which was set up by the Count of Paris to preserve the French national heritage.

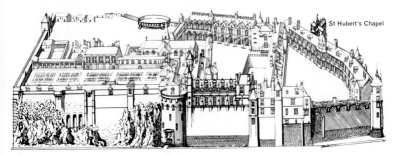

St Hubert's Chapel

Amboise Château in 16C
Only those parts shown in black are still extant.

⊙ TOUR *time: 3/4 hour*

Terrace. — You enter the château by a ramp which opens on to the terrace overlooking the river. From here there is a magnificent **view★★**, especially in the morning, of the lazy Loire and its verdant valley, the town's pointed roofs and walls. The Tour de l'Horloge is set above one of the town gates; to the west is silhouetted the Church of St-Denis with its squat bell-tower; and to the southeast Le Clos-Lucé can be seen.

In the time of Charles VIII the terrace was entirely surrounded by buildings. Festivals were held in this enclosed courtyard: tapestries adorned the walls, a sky blue awning showing the sun, the moon and the stars gave protection from the weather.

St-Hubert's Chapel (B E). — Curiously set astride the walls this jewel of Flamboyant Gothic architecture is all that remains of the buildings which once bordered the ramparts.

With pleasing proportions, finely sculpted decoration and crowned by a delicate spire, it is the work of Flemish masters who were brought to Amboise by Louis XI; they were also employed by Charles VIII before his admiration for Italian art began. Built in 1491 it was Anne of Brittany's oratory.

Before entering admire the Gothic door panels and the finely carved lintel: on the left **St Christopher** carries the Infant Christ while on the right **St Hubert**, the patron saint of hunting, looks at a cross which has appeared between the antlers of a stag.

King's Apartments (Logis du Roi). — This is the only part of the château which escaped demolition *(see illustration above)*. The Gothic Wing, built against the Minimes Tower — both built by Charles VIII — overlooks the Loire while the Renaissance wing, set at a right angle was constructed by Louis XII and raised by François I.

The tour includes a visit to the guardroom with its segmental ogive vaulting, the sentry walk with its beautiful view of the Loire, and several rooms furnished in the Gothic or Renaissance style and hung with lovely tapestries.

On the first floor the apartments arranged for Louis-Philippe contains Empire style furniture and portraits of the royal family by Winterhalter, the official painter.

In the Gothic Wing, the **Hall of States**, which was restored early this century, is a large room with ogive vaulting supported by a line of columns in the centre of the room. It was here that the Protestants headed by La Renaudie *(p 44)* were judged; most of them were then hung from the balcony, henceforth called "the Conspirators' Balcony". It was also the prison for nearly five years (1848-52) of the Algerian leader **Abd el-Kader**, the focus of resistance to French penetration of the Maghreb.

Minimes Tower (Tour des Minimes ou des Cavaliers). — This round tower is famous for its ramp which horsemen could ride up, assuring easy access for the provisioning of supplies. As in the Heurtault Tower on the south side of the château, the ramp spirals round an empty core which provides air and light. From the top, one overlooks the northern face of the castle and the Conspirators' Balcony and there is a fine extensive **view★★** of the Loire and its valley.

Gardens. — These pleasant gardens lie where parts of the château once stood. The bust of Leonardo da Vinci is on the site of the collegiate church, where he was buried.

★ LE CLOS-LUCÉ (B M¹) *tour: 1 hour*

A red brick manor house decorated with stone dressings, Le Clos-Lucé was acquired by Charles VIII in 1490. He had a small chapel built for his queen, Anne of Brittany. François I, Margaret of Navarre and their mother, the regent Louise de Savoie also resided here.

In 1516, François I invited **Leonardo da Vinci** to Amboise and lodged him at Le Clos-Lucé where the great Renaissance man lived until his death on 2 May 1519; he was 67.

While in residence he organised the court festivities, drew, studied a project for draining the Sologne and designed a palace for Louise de Savoie at Romorantin *(see p 158)*.

The tour includes Anne of Brittany's chapel, the great hall, restored to its 16C state, and the saloons with 18C wainscoting where Da Vinci most likely had his workshops.

On the first floor is the bedroom, restored and furnished, where Da Vinci died. In the basement, besides the kitchen with its huge chimney, is the **museum of da Vinci's "fabulous machines"** which displays a collection of models of the machines invented by the fertile genius of this polymath who was a painter, sculptor, musician, poet, architect, engineer and scholar, and was four centuries ahead of his time.

In the projection room a 56 minute film of the life of Leonardo da Vinci describes his talent as a painter, his re-

(Photo J.-L. Charmet/Explorer Archives)
Le Clos-Lucé
François I buying the Mona Lisa from Leonardo da Vinci

search on the human body and his speculations about the development of the foetus. It also shows the humanist who did not separate his scientific work from his spiritual reflections.

From the terrace near the Renaissance garden there is a view of Amboise Château which was connected to Le Clos-Lucé by an underground passage; the entrance can be seen in the museum. The park extends down to the river bank.

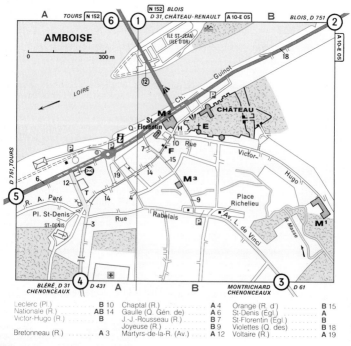

ADDITIONAL SIGHTS

Postal Museum (Musée de la Poste – B M³). – Installed in the Hôtel Joyeuse, an early 16C mansion, the museum has important collections on postmasters, messengers and their dispatches; uniforms, **badges**, a few coaches and motor vehicles. The two ground floor rooms depict the service in the early years when horses were used while the history of the letter post is traced on the first floor, and the maritime service on the second.

Town Hall Museum (Musée de l'hôtel de ville – B M²). – The former town hall, which was built early in 16C by Pierre Morin, Treasurer of France, and designed by Jacques Coqueau and Pierre Nepveu, the architects of Chambord and Chenonceau, now houses examples of the royal signature, a 14C Virgin and 19C paintings. Over the entrance door are two handsomely carved **dolphins**.

Clock Tower (Tour de l'Horloge – B F). – The tower, which is also known as the Amboise Belfry and was recently restored, was built in 15C at the expense of the inhabitants on the site of a town gateway called l'Amasse. The pedestrian street below is very busy in the summer season.

Nearby on the old town ramparts stands **St Florentine's Church** (B), built at the behest of Louis XI.

EXCURSION

★ **Chanteloup Pagoda.** – *3 km by ④ on the plan, D31 and signed road to the right. Description p 77.*

★★★ ANGERS
Pop 141 143

Michelin map 🔢 fold 20 and 🔢 fold 11 or 🔢🔢🔢 fold 31 – Local maps pp 126 and 138 See plan of built-up area in the current Michelin Guide France

The former capital of Anjou stands on the banks of the Maine, formed by the confluence of the Mayenne and the Sarthe, 8 km - 5 miles before joining the Loire. Today Angers is a lively town especially in the pedestrian precinct of the old town and along the Boulevard du Maréchal-Foch.

A flourishing trade is based on Anjou wines, liqueurs, fruit and vegetables, seeds, flowers, medicinal plants and other horticultural products. The Sacavins wine brotherhood *(p 144)* which was founded in 1905 organizes an autumn wine festival *(late September)*. There is an active electronics and car accessories industry.

The **Anjou Festival** *(p 194)*, with its many varied events (drama, music, dancing, poetry, art, etc), takes place throughout the Maine et Loire department and draws large crowds.

HISTORICAL NOTES

In the 1C BC Angers was at the centre of a community of hunters and fishermen. Their chief was Domnacus, who took to the heaths and forests and never submitted to the Romans who captured the city.

From Romans to Normans. – Angers-Juliomagus, the capital of the Andes tribe, covered 198 acres and flourished in 2C. Unfortunately few traces of this brilliant past have survived. In the Late Empire the city went into decline and was obliged to confine itself to a small area (22 acres) on a slope above the River Maine; under the combined effect of the German menace of invasion and general impoverishment the population decreased. Christianity, on the other hand, continued to make progress and in 453 a church council met in Angers. Bishop Thalaise was one of the important ecclesiastical figures of the period, a scholar who protected and defended his city.

Angers' religious rise was not affected by the bloody quarrels of the Merovingian succession; the abbeys of St Aubin and St Sergius were founded in the 6C and 7C and soon attracted new suburbs. Under the Carolingians the town recovered but was soon destabilised by the revolts of the nobility and the Norman invasions. In December 854 the Vikings pillaged Angers and withdrew. In 872 they returned and held the town for over a year. Charles the Bald, assisted by the Duke of Brittany, laid siege to the invaders and succeeded in dislodging them; a more or less legendary tradition says that Charles dug a canal intending to divert the waters of the Maine and when the Vikings realised that their ships would be grounded they fled in panic.

First House of Anjou (10-13C). – Under the early Counts, who were called Fulk, Angers enjoyed a particularly brilliant period.

The founders. – The weakness of the throne at the end of 9C gave rise to the emergence of independent principalities. The first Angevin dynasty was established in 898 by Fulk the Red, Viscount and then Count of Angers, a title which he handed down to his descendants.

Fulk II the Good extended his territory into Maine showing scant regard for the King of France, pale Louis IV of Outre-Mer, whom he openly despised, while Geoffrey I Grisegonelle exacted homage from the Count of Nantes. The Angevins also played a more subtle game manoeuvring between the Robertians (ancestors of the Capets), who were well established in the region, and the Carolingians whose power continued to wane.

Fulk Nerra and his successors. – The rise of the Angevin dynasty to the height of its power in 11C and 12C was due to exceptional political skill, uninhibited by any scruples, remarkable ability in warfare and a keen eye for alliances through marriage. **Fulk III Nerra** (987-1040) was the most formidable of this line of feudal giants. Disruptive and aggressive, he was always making war to extend his territory; one by one he obtained

Saintonge as fief of the Duke of Aquitaine, annexed the Mauges, extended his boundaries to Blois and Châteaudun, captured Langeais and Tours (he was expelled from the latter by Robert the Pious), intervened in the Vendômois, took Saumur etc. Ambitious, predatory, covetous, cruel and criminally violent, Fulk Nerra (the Black owing to his very dark complexion) was typical of the great feudal lord in the year 1000. From time to time he had sudden fits of Christian humility and penitence when he would shower gifts on churches and abbeys or take up the pilgrim's staff and depart for Jerusalem. He was also a great builder of castles, to protect his conquests, and of many religious institutions.

His son Geoffrey II (1040-60) continued his father's work consolidating the conquest of Maine and Touraine but he died without issue. The succession was divided between his two nephews who lost no time in quarrelling. Fulk IV finally gained the upper hand of Geoffrey III but at the cost of the Angevin possessions: the loss of Saintonge, Maine, the Gâtinais and he was too lazy to re-conquer the lost land. In 1092 his second wife, the young and beautiful Bertrade de Monfort, was seduced, abducted and married by King Philip I. For this scandalous behaviour the king was excommunicated *(p 60)*. The position was redressed by Geoffrey IV Martel, who was killed in 1106, and most of all by **Fulk V the Younger** (1109-31), who took advantage of Anglo-French rivalry and made judicious marriage alliances. He recovered Maine through his own marriage in 1109; two years later with the family's approval he married his two daughters to the kings of France and England. His greatest success was however the marriage in 1128 of his son Geoffrey to Mathilda of England, daughter and heir to Henry I and widow of the German emperor Henry V. His ultimate achievement concerned himself: in 1129, by then a widow, he married Melisand, daughter of Baldwin II and heir to the kingdom of Jerusalem. He founded a new Angevin dynasty in the Holy Land and consolidated the position of the Frankish kingdoms.

Geoffrey V (1131-51), known as Plantagenet because he wore a sprig of broom *(genêt)* in his hair, ruled with a rod of iron over "Great Anjou" (Anjou, Touraine and Maine) and tried to exercise his wife's rights over Normandy, which he annexed in 1144, and England, where Stephen of Blois had been king since 1135. Geoffrey died in 1151.

Plantagenets and Capets. — In 1152 **Henry Plantagenet**, son of Geoffrey *(p 129)* and Mathilda, married Eleanor of Aquitaine whom Louis VII had recently divorced. He already held Anjou, Maine, Touraine and Normandy; by his marriage he acquired Poitou, Perigord, Limousin, Angoumois, Saintonge, Gascony and suzerainty of the Auvergne and the County of Toulouse. In 1153 he forced Stephen of Blois to recognize him as his heir and the following year he succeeded him on the throne of England. He was now more powerful than his Capet rival. Henry II of England spent most of his time in France, usually at Angers. "He was a redhead, of medium height, with a square, leonine face and prominent eyes, which were candid and gentle when he was in a good humour but flashed fire when he was irritated. From morning to night he was involved in matters of state. He was always on the go and never sat down except to eat or ride a horse. When he was not handling a bow or a sword, he was closeted in Council or reading. None was more clever or eloquent than he; when he was free from his responsibilities he liked to engage in discussion with scholars". (M. Pacaut).

For the next fifty years there was war between the Plantagenets and the Capets. In the end it was the latter who were victorious: by relying on the subtleties of feudal law, they played upon the separatist tendencies of the individual provinces brought together in the Anglo-Angevin empire and the dissension that divided the Plantagenet family.

Philippe-Auguste inflicted a harsh blow when he captured the French territory of King John in 1205; this meant that Anjou and Touraine ceased to belong to the English crown but England and France continued to fight one another for supremacy until the end of the Hundred Years War.

Later Anjou Dynasty (13-15C). — During the regency of Blanche of Castille, Anjou was again lost as a result of the barons' revolt when Pierre de Dreux surrendered the province to Henry III. Taking advantage of a truce in 1231 Blanche and her son Louis began to build the impressive fortress of Angers.

Anjou returned to the Capet sphere of influence and in 1346 St Louis gave it, together with Maine, to his younger brother Charles as an apanage. In 1258 it was confirmed as a French possession by the Treaty of Paris. In 1360 Anjou was raised to a duchy by John the Good for his son Louis. From the 13C to the 15C Anjou was governed by the direct line of Capet princes and then by the Valois. The beginning and end of this period were marked by two brilliant figures, Charles I and King René.

Charles of Anjou. — Charles was an unusual personality — steeped in devotion and madly ambitious. At the request of the Pope, he conquered Sicily and the Kingdom of Naples and established his influence over the rest of the Italian peninsula. Heady with pride he dreamed of adding the Holy Land, Egypt and Constantinople to his conquests but the Sicilian Vespers returned him rudely to reality: on Easter Monday 1282 the Sicilians revolted and massacred 6000 Frenchmen of whom half were Angevins.

Good King René. — The last of the dukes was Good King René — titulary king of Sicily. He knew Latin, Greek, Italian, Hebrew and Catalan, painted and wrote poetry, played and composed music and was knowledgeable in mathematics, geology and law — one of the most cultivated minds of his day. He had the common touch and liked to talk to his subjects; he organised popular festivities and revived the old games of the age of chivalry. He loved flower gardens and introduced the carnation and the Provins rose. At twelve he married Isabelle de Lorraine and was devoted to her for thirty-three years until her death at 47 when he married Jeanne de Laval who was 21. Despite the odds, it was also a happy marriage. Towards the end of his life René accepted philosophically the annexation of Anjou by Louis XI. As he was also Count of Provence he left Angers which he had greatly enriched and ended his days in Aix at the age of 72 (1480).

During the period of the Duchy a university was founded in Angers which flourished with from 4000 to 5000 students from ten nations.

Henri IV to the present. — The Wars of Religion took on a bitter twist at Angers where there was a strong Calvinist church; on 14 October 1560 many people were attacked. Thereafter confrontations grew more frequent and in 1572 there was a massacre in the town.

It was in Angers Château that Henri IV finally brought the troubles of the League to an end in 1598 by promising his son César *(p 186)* to Françoise de Lorraine, daughter of the Duc de Mercoeur, the leader of the Catholic party. The marriage contract was signed on 5 April; the bride and groom were six and three years old. A week later the Edict of Nantes came into force; the Protestants had obtained freedom of worship. In 1652, although held by the forces of the Fronde, Angers had to submit to Mazarin; in 1657 the town lost its right to elect its local magistrates. After his arrest in Nantes, Louis XIV's Finance Minister, Fouquet, spent three weeks in the château in the Governor's apartments, guarded by d'Artagnan. By then the town had about 25 000 inhabitants and was slightly industrialised.

At the outbreak of the Revolution in 1789, Angers declared enthusiastically for the reformers. The cathedral was sacked and turned into a temple of Reason. In 1793 the defection of the Girondin administration allowed the Royalist Vendée party to capture the town between 20 June and 4 July. The Republicans lost no time in retaking it and the Terror claimed many victims.

In the early 19C Angers dozed until awakened by the arrival of the railway line from Paris to Nantes: the station was opened in 1849 by Louis-Napoleon. Modern development had begun and, apart from a pause early in this century, it has continued to increase during recent decades.

★★★ **CASTLE** (AZ)

time: 2 hours

Fulk's castle was rebuilt by St Louis between 1228 and 1238 and is a fine specimen of feudal architecture *(p 24)* in red schist and white stone. The moats are now laid out as gardens. The seventeen round towers, strung out over 1 km - 1/2 mile, are 40 to 50 m - 131 to 164 ft high. Formerly one or two storeys taller they were crowned with pepperpot roofs and machicolations. The towers were lowered to the level of the curtain walls under Henri III during the Wars of Religion. The original order had been to dismantle the fortress, but the governor simply decapitated the towers and laid out terraces and by the King's death most of the building was still intact.

(Photo Serge Chirol)

Angers Castle

From the top of the highest tower, the Mill Tower (**Tour du Moulin**), on the north corner, there are interesting **views★** over the town, the cathedral towers and St-Aubin, the banks of the Maine and the gardens laid out at the foot of the castle, and, in the castle precincts, the series of towers on the curtain wall, the careful design of the gardens punctuated with topiary arches, the chapel and the Royal Apartments (Logis Royal).

Continue by going round the **ramparts**, specially on the east side where a charming medieval garden is laid out with lavender, marguerites and hollyhocks growing in profusion, near vines like those which King René loved to plant.

★★★ **Apocalypse Tapestry.** — Sheltered in a specially designed building this particularly famous piece is the oldest and largest which has come down to us. It was made in Paris between 1373 and 1383 commissioned by Nicolas Bataille for Duke Louis I of Anjou from Hennequin of Bruges' cartoons based on an illuminated manuscript of King Charles V. It was used at the marriage of Louis II of Anjou to Yolande of Aragon in Arles in 1400 and then at religious festivals until the end of 18C when King René bequeathed it to the cathedral. It was later discarded as a piece of no value but restored between 1849 to 1870.

Originally 130 m - 426 ft long and 5 m - 16 1/2 ft high, it consisted of 6 sections of equal size, each with a major figure sitting under a canopy, their eyes turned towards two rows of 7 pictures, the alternating red and blue backgrounds of which form a chequered design. Two long borders represent the Sky, filled with angelic musicians, and the Earth, strewn with flowers (first part missing). The 76 pictures which have come down to us form a superb whole; the biblical text corresponding to each scene appears opposite the tapestries together with a reproduction of the reverse side.

One cannot remain unmoved by the scale of the work, the rigorous composition, as well as its great decorative value and purity of design. The tapestry closely follows the text of St John in the last book of the New Testament; to rekindle the hope of Christians shattered by the violent persecutions, the artist shows the victory of Christ in the form of prophetic visions and, after many ordeals, the triumph of his Church.

Chapel and Royal Apartments (Logis Royal). – These 15C buildings stand inside the enclosure. In the vast and light chapel, note the finely sculptured Gothic leaves of the door, the small separate ducal chapel with a fireplace, and on a keystone, the representation of the Anjou cross *(see p 58 at Baugé)*. The adjacent staircase, the work of King René, reaches the upper floor of the logis.

★★ **Mille-fleurs Tapestries.** – The **Passion Tapestry** is a series of four late 15C Flemish works (one is missing), which are wonderfully rich in colour. The hanging showing the Angels carrying the Instruments of the Passion, in spite of its religious theme, belongs to the group of *mille-fleurs* tapestries. Note the 16C **Lady at the Organ** and the fragment showing **Penthesilea,** the Queen of the Amazons, one of the Nine Heroines, women with chivalrous virtues.

(Photo Pix)

Angers – Passion Tapestry
Angel bearing Pilate's ewer

Governor's Lodging (Logis du Gouverneur). – This pleasant building modified in the 18C, half hidden between the east curtain wall against which it leans and the gardens, has a lovely collection upstairs of 15-18C **tapestries★**: Audenarde verdures (late 16C), Isaac and Jacob (early 16C), the Life of St Saturnin and the Legend of Samson (Brussels, 16C).

★★ **OLD TOWN** *time: about 2 1/2 hours*

Start from the château entrance and take the small Rue St-Aignan.

Crescent Mansion (Hôtel du Croissant) (AY B). – This 15C mansion, with mullion windows and accolade arches, housed the registrar of the Order of the Crescent (Ordre du Croissant), a military and religious chivalrous order founded by King René. The blazon on the façade bears the coat of arms of St Maurice, patron of the order, a 4C Christian legionary put to death because he refused to kill his co-religionists. Opposite stand picturesque timber-framed houses.

Continue to the St-Maurice Ascent, a long flight of stairs which leads to the cathedral square.

Fine view of the cathedral.

★★ **St-Maurice's Cathedral (Cathédrale St-Maurice – BY).** – This is a fine 12 and 13C building. The Calvary standing to the left of the façade is by David of Angers.

Façade. – It is surmounted by three towers, the central tower having been added in 16C. The **doorway** was damaged by the Protestants and the Revolutionaries, and in 18C by the canons, who removed the central pier and the lintel to make way for processions. Notice the fine statues on the splaying. The tympanum portrays Christ the King surrounded by the symbols of the Four Evangelists; the graceful folds of the garments show skilful carving.

Above at the third storey level are eight niches containing roughly carved bearded figures in 16C military uniforms, St Maurice and his companions.

Interior. – The single nave is roofed with one of the earliest examples of Gothic vaulting which originated in Anjou in the mid 12C. This transitional style known as Angevin or Plantagenet vaulting *(see illustrations p 36)* has the characteristic feature that the keystones of the diagonal (ogive) arches are at least 3 m - 10 ft above the keys of the transverse and stringer arches giving a more rounded or domical form. In Gothic vaulting all the keys are at roughly the same level. The vaulting of St Maurice covers the widest nave built at that time measuring 16.38 m - 64 ft across, whereas the usual width was from 9 to 12 m - 30 to 40 ft; the capitals in the nave and the brackets supporting the gallery with its wrought-iron balustrade are remarkably carved. The gallery is supported by a relieving arch at each bay. The Angevin vaulting in the transept is of a later period than that in the nave. The ribs are more numerous, lighter and more graceful. The evolution of this style was to continue along these lines.

ST MAURICE'S CATHEDRAL

0   30 m

N

BISHOP'S PALACE

CHANCEL

D
6   6
E
C

TRANSEPT
5
4   4
5

B
3
NAVE
2
★Treasury
1

Pl. Freppel

R. du Chanoine Urseau

A
Doorway

N.-D.- de Pitié Chapel

Pl. du Parvis St-Maurice

The chancel, finished in the late 13C, has the same Angevin vaulting as the transept. The 13C stained glass has particularly vivid blues and reds.

The church is majestically furnished: high 18C organ (A) supported by colossal telamones, monumental 19C pulpit (B), high altar (C) surmounted by marble columns supporting a canopy of gilded wood (18C), 18C carved stalls (D) in front of which is a marble statue of St Cecilia by David of Angers (E). The walls are hung with tapestries, mostly from Aubusson.

St-Maurice's **stained glass windows★★** allow one to follow the evolution of the art of the master glaziers from the 12C to the present day.

> *There is a detailed printed description of the windows in the church; they are best examined through binoculars.*

1 - St Catherine of Alexandria (12C).

2 - Dormition and Assumption of the Virgin (12C).

3 - The martyrdom of St Vincent of Spain (12C).

4 - Transept rose windows (15C): to the left Christ showing his wounds and to the right Christ in Majesty.

5 - North transept side windows (15C): St Rémi and Mary Magdalene.

6 - Chancel windows (13C) – from left to right: life of St Peter and St Eloi; St Christopher (16C); St Lawrence; the tree of Jesse; St Julian; the life of Christ, and lives of the Saints Maurille, Martin, Thomas of Canterbury and John the Baptist.

The modern windows of the chapel of Notre-Dame-de-Pitié and the south aisle bear witness to a revival of this art which had been in decline since the 16C.

★ **Treasury.** – Among the most interesting items are a green marble Roman bath which served as a baptismal font for the dukes of Anjou; a red porphyry urn given by King René; the carved wood reliquary shrine of Bishop Ulger (d. 1148) which was damaged during the Revolution; other reliquaries and gold and silver plate.

> *Walk past the Bishop's Palace to reach Rue de l'Oisellerie.*

At nos 5 and 7, there are two lovely half-timbered houses dating from the 16C.

> *Take the first road on the right.*

★ **Maison d'Adam** (BYZ D). – Picturesque 16C half-timbered house, with posts decorated with carved figures. It owes its name to the apple tree which appears to hold up the corner turret and was, until the Revolution, flanked by two statues of Adam and Eve. In 18C this house happened to be inhabited by a consulting judge called Michel Adam.

> *Continue along Rue Toussaint to no 33 bis.*

★ **David of Angers Gallery** (Galerie David d'Angers – BZ E). – The former 13C abbey church of All Saints (Toussaint) (restored) houses practically the complete collection of plaster casts donated by the sculptor David of Angers to his native town; its Plantagenet vaulting which collapsed in 1815 has been replaced by a vast iron-framed glass roof, so that the appearance of the exhibition is influenced by the weather; it is at its best on a fine day.

The well-displayed collection comprises monumental statues (King René, Gutenberg, Jean Bart whose bronze statue stands in Dunkerque), funerary monuments (e.g. of General Bonchamps whose tomb is in the church of St-Florent-le-Vieil *(p 163)*, busts of famous people of the time (Chateaubriand, Victor Hugo, Goethe, Balzac), and medallions in bronze of the artist's contemporaries.

In the chancel with its square east end lit by a rose added in 18C are exhibited terracotta studies, drawings and sketch book as well as the graceful *Young Greek Girl* which adorned Markos Botzaris's tomb. In a windowed recess stands the *Young Shepherd,* ideally placed against the greenery of the gardens of the modern public library.

To the south of the church are the 18C cloisters with two remaining galleries *(restored).*

> *Pass along the south side of the church to reach Logis Barrault.*

Logis Barrault (Fine Arts Museum – BZ M¹). – This beautiful late 15C residence was built by Olivier Barrault, the King's secretary, Treasurer to the Brittany States and Mayor of Angers. In 17C it was taken over by the seminary, whose pupils included Talleyrand, the future Bishop of Autun *(p 185).*

On the first floor is a beautiful collection of Medieval and Renaissance work: carved chests, statues (16C terracotta Virgin of Tremblay), enamels and ivories.

The second floor is devoted to paintings: lovely primitives, two remarkable small portraits of Charles IX as a young man and Catherine de' Medici after Clouet; 17C paintings (Philippe de Champaigne, Mignard) and above all the 18C French school (Chardin, Fragonard, Watteau, Boucher, Lancret, Greuze) together with sculptures by Lemoyne, Houdon and Falconet; and 19C works including sketches by David, Ingres, Géricault, Delacroix, landscapes by Corot and Jongkind; canvases by the local painters Lenepveu and Bodinier, and pastels (separate room) by Alexis Axilette, a native of the region, who was born at Durtal.

St-Aubin Tower (Tour) (BZ F). – 12C belfry of the former Abbey of St-Aubin, a wealthy Benedictine abbey founded in 6C. It took its name from St Aubin, Bishop of Angers (538-550), who was buried there. The monastery buildings now house the Préfecture.

★ **Préfecture** (BZ P). – On the left of the courtyard within the 17C buildings of the former St-Aubin's Abbey part of the cloister has been revealed: a **Romanesque arcade★★** with sculptures of remarkably delicate craftsmanship. The door with sculptured arching led to the chapter house; the arcades support a gallery from which those monks who had no voice in the chapter could listen to the proceedings; decorating the twin bay on the right of the door is a Virgin in Majesty with two censing angels while on the archivolt a multitude of angels bustle about; beneath this the scene of the Three Wise Men is painted: on the left Herod sends his men to massacre the innocents, while on the right the star guides the Wise Men. The last arcature on the right has the best preserved scene

ANGERS

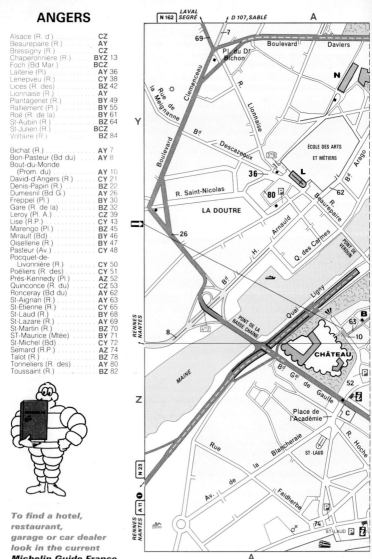

To find a hotel, restaurant, garage or car dealer look in the current **Michelin Guide France.**

of all in the centre the unequal combat between David armed with his sling and the giant Goliath in his coat of mail, is about to start; on the right the victorious David is cutting off the head of the vanquished and on the left he offers his trophy to King Saul.

Take Rue St-Martin to return to Place du Ralliement.

Lively **Place du Ralliement** (BY 55) is the centre of town, its shops dominated by the monumental façade of the theatre, adorned with columns and statues.

Take Rue Lenepveu then the first road on the left.

★ **Hôtel Pincé** (BY M²). — The Hôtel Pincé is a Renaissance mansion built for a Mayor of Angers and bequeathed to the town in 1861. It houses the **Turpin de Crissé Museum**, originally based on the fine personal collection of this local painter (1772-1859) who was chamberlain to the Empress Josephine and a member of the Institut de France. There are Greek and Etruscan vases on the ground floor and an Egyptian collection on the 1st floor. But the principal attraction is on the 2nd floor, a beautiful collection of ceramics, masks and Japanese engravings, the bequest of the Count of St Genys, nephew of Turpin de Crissé, as well as the Chinese collection (ceramics, bronzes, fabrics).

Make for Rue St-Laud.

St-Laud District. — The small Rue St-Laud (BY 68) is the axis of a pleasant pedestrian and shopping district, where several ancient façades can be seen: at no 21 Rue St-Laud (15C) and at no 9 Rue des Poëliers (16C) (CY 51).

Drive to the Church of St Sergius.

★ **Church of St Sergius** (St-Serge – CY). — Until 1802 it was the church of the Benedictine abbey of the same name founded in 7C. The 13C **chancel ★★** is remarkably wide, elegant and luminous, a perfect example of the Angevin style at its best, with its lierne vaulting descending in feathered clusters on to slender columns. The 15C nave, seems narrower because of its massive pillars; at the end the high windows are filled with graceful 15C stained glass depicting the Prophets (north side) and the Apostles (south side). On the rear wall of the chancel is a Flamboyant sacrarium where relics were kept.

Botanical Garden (Jardin des Plantes – CY). — There are beautiful trees and a pool in the lower part. A section reserved for succulent plants forms an exotic garden.

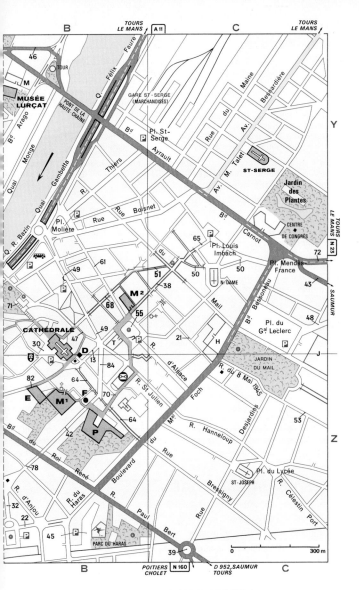

NORTH BANK OF THE RIVER MAINE *tour: 1 hour*

★★ **Lurçat Museum of Contemporary Tapestry** (ABY). – The museum is housed in the former **Hospital of St-John**★ (Ancien Hôpital St-Jean); it provided treatment and care for the sick from its foundation in 1174 by Etienne de Marçay, Seneschal of Henry II Plantagenet, until 1854.

Not only the large hospital ward, which is now the museum, is open but also the Romanesque **cloister** at the back, now festooned with creeper, and the 12C chapel with its interesting Baroque furnishings. To the west stands the **former granary** (**N**) (12C) with its twin bays.

The original and very beautiful **hospital ward** (12C) has three naves of equal height covered with graceful Angevin vaulting. On the right of the entrance is the former **dispensary**★ with its wooden panelling (1612) and a collection of pots, trivets, vessels and jars (17C to 19C). In the central recess stands a large pewter vessel (1720) containing an antidote to snake bites.

The room is hung with a series of Lurçat tapestries called **Le Chant du Monde** ★★ (The Song of the World). Jean Lurçat (1892-1966), who revived the art of tapestry, had discovered the Apocalypse Tapestry *(p 49)* in 1938 and been profoundly impressed by it. 19 years later he started the work displayed here, his masterpiece, a set of 10 compositions, some 80m-260 ft in length. There are notes in front of each tapestry explaining and interpreting Lurçat's work.

In addition to the paintings, ceramics and tapestries by Jean Lurçat (donated by Madame Lurçat), the collection contains other works from the period when the art of tapestry was being revived.

The majority of the nine rooms are used for temporary exhibitions.

★ **La Doutre** (AY). – The district "across the Maine" (d'outre Maine) has kept its old timber framed houses in good repair: in pretty Place de la Laiterie (**AY 36**), in Rue Beaurepaire which runs from the square to the bridge (N° 67, which is ornamented with statues and dates from 1582, was the house of the apothecary Simon Poisson) and along Rue des Tonneliers (**AY 80**).

Holy Trinity Church (**AY L**) is a 12C building with a 16C belfry.

EXCURSIONS

Les Ponts-de-Cé. − Pop 11 072. *7 km - 4 miles to the south by N 160.*
This is a straggling town about 2 miles long; its main street crosses a canal and several arms of the Loire, affording some fine views from the bridges. The history of this small town includes many bloody episodes. Under Charles IX 800 camp-followers were thrown into the Loire; when the château was taken from the Huguenots in 1562, any surviving defenders were treated to a similar fate. In 1793 numerous Vendeans were shot on the island that surrounds the château.
On the edge of the road, overlooking the Loire, stand the remains of a château (today the town hall), an ancient 15C fortress crowned with machicolations.

St-Aubin's Church. − This church, which was built in the Gothic style, has recently been restored after being gutted by fire in 1973. Some interesting items survived: altar pieces and statues (Christ in Captivity).

Trélazé. − Pop 11 067. *In the eastern suburbs, road to Saumur.*
Trélazé is famous for its slate which has been quarried since 12C. When the Loire was still a commercial highway, the blue-grey slates were carried upstream in boats to provide roofs for all the châteaux, manor houses and more modest residences which lined the banks of the river.

Slate Museum. − The museum, which is near a former quarry, presents the geological formation of slate, the old tools used in quarrying, the life of the men who worked in the quarries and the modern techniques.
There is a demonstration of old-style slate splitting given by former slatemen.

AREINES   Pop 908

Map ▣ fold 6 or ▨▨▨ fold 2 − 3 km - 2 miles east of Vendôme − Local map p 118

Areines, a village in the Loir plain, was an important town in the Roman era.

Church. − The plain façade is adorned by a 14C Virgin; the church itself is 12C. The interior is decorated with a group of **frescoes**, gracefully drawn and freshly tinted.
In the apse a majestic Christ is surrounded by evangelical symbols: the lion of St Mark, in stylised Byzantine manner; below are the Apostles with sky-blue haloes, typical of Loire Valley art *(p 39);* in the central window are warrior saints also with haloes.
The chancel vault shows the Lamb adored by angels; on the sides are the Annunciation and the Visitation, elegantly depicted, and the Nativity, partially effaced. The frescoes on the walls of the chancel seem to be of a later period: Marriage of the Virgin (right).

ARGENT-SUR-SAULDRE   Pop 2 687

Michelin map ▣▣ north of fold 11 or ▨▨▨ northwest of fold 19

Print works, clothing factories, potteries and dairies contribute to the commercial activity of this little town on the River Sauldre in the Sologne.

Château. − The 15C château has huge round towers; the park is open.

St-Andrew's Church. − The former château chapel has a stout porch-belfry. In the baptismal chapel there is a 16C group of the Trinity.

EXCURSIONS

★ **Étang du Puits, Cerdon.** − *27 km - 17 miles. Cross the Sauldre going northeast; turn left into D 176 between the river and the canal. After 6.5 km - 4 miles turn right.*

★ **Étang du Puits.** − The large and shining expanse of water covers 175 ha - 309 acres in the heart of an oak and pine forest; there is a fine view from the road along the retaining dyke. There are facilities for regattas as well as a beach, pedaloes, rowing boats and a playground. There is plentiful fishing for carp, bream and pike which can weigh up to 15 pounds. The reservoir feeds the Sauldre Canal which flows into the River Beuvron.

Continue round the reservoir on D 765 and then turn left into D 948.

Cerdon. − Pop 1 005. A peaceful, well-kept village in the Sologne. In the 15C church are several paintings and handsome modern stained glass in the chancel.

★ **Blancafort.** − *8 km - 5 miles southeast by D 8. Description p 63.*

ARVILLE   Pop 152

Michelin map ▣▣ southwest of fold 16 or ▨▨▨ fold 37 − Local map p 140

The D 921 running south from Le Gault-Perche gives a good view of the Templar commandery which later passed to the Knights of St John of Jerusalem. The ironstone building in its rural setting makes an attractive picture.

The Templars. − The order, which was both military and monastic, was founded in 1119 near the site of Solomon's Temple in Jerusalem. The members wore a white mantle bearing a red cross and were bound by their vows to defend the Holy City from the Moslems and protect all Christians making a pilgrimage to Jerusalem. To this end they built fortified commanderies on the main roads. A pilgrim would deposit a sum of money at his local commandery before setting out and in exchange for the receipt could draw the same sum on arrival in the Holy Land; thus the commanderies came to serve as banks in 13C.

The Templars lent money to the Popes and to kings and princes and grew rich and powerful. Early in 14C the order of Templars numbered 15 000 knights and 9 000 commanderies. It had its own judicial system, paid no tax and took its authority directly from the Pope. Such independence created many problems and brought about the order's downfall.

In 1307 Philip the Fair persuaded the Pope that the Templars should be brought to trial; he had every member of the order in France arrested on the same day. The Grand Master, Jacques de Molay and 140 knights were imprisoned in Chinon castle; the following year they were brought to Paris. A trial was held in which they were accused of denying Christ by spitting on the Cross in their initiation ceremonies; 54 of them, including Jacques de Molay were burned alive. It was a brutal punishment although the order had sometimes acted degenerately.

(after photo C. Breteau — Ed. Delmas)

Arville Commandery

The Commandery. — The 12C chapel is crowned by a gable belfry which is linked to a flint tower, once part of the town walls. The town gateway (late 15C) is decorated with two brick turrets with unusual conical roofs made of chestnut slats.

★ ASNIÈRES-SUR-VÈGRE   Pop 356

Michelin map 64 northwest of fold 2 or 232 fold 20

Asnières lies in an attractive setting, deep in the picturesque Vègre Valley. The D 190 from Poillé provides an attractive view over the old houses with their pitched roofs, the church and a mansion called the Cour d'Asnières.

Bridge. — This medieval hump-backed structure provides a charming **view★** of the river with water weed swaying smoothly in the current, of the old mill still in working order, in its setting of fine trees and of the elegant mansion with its turret and dormer windows on the right bank. Close to the mill stands a château known as the Moulin Vieux dating from the 17 and 18C.

Church. — The interior is decorated with Gothic **wall paintings★** — 13C in the nave and 15C in the chancel. The most famous, on the inside wall of the main façade, shows Hell. On the left Christ is preparing to release the souls trapped in Limbo by attacking the three-headed dog, Cerberus, with a lance; in the centre Leviathan is swallowing up the Damned; finally canine-headed demons are stirring a cauldron of the damned in which one can see the wimple of the lady of the manor and the bishop's mitre.

The walls of the nave and chancel evoke the New Testament cycle. The scenes on the north wall of the nave represent the Adoration of the Magi, Jesus' Presentation in the Temple and the Flight into Egypt. Note in the chancel a Baptism of Christ, a Flagellation and a Crucifixion.

Cour d'Asnières. — Standing a little to the south of the church is a large but elongated Gothic building, with attractively paired windows. It was here that the canons of Le Mans, the one time lords of Asnières, exercised their seigneurial rights, hence the name *cour* meaning court.

⊙Château de Verdelles. — *2.5 km - 1 1/2 miles by the D 190 in the direction of Poillé.*

This late 15C château has remained unaltered since its construction by Colas Le Clerc, Lord of Juigné. It marks the transition between the feudal castle and the stately home; four towers grouped closely together surround the central part of the château which has moulded windows. Admire the attractive suspended turret decorated with Gothic arcades.

★ AUBIGNY-SUR-NÈRE   Pop 5 693

Michelin map 65 fold 11 or 238 folds 18, 19
See town plan in the current Michelin Guide France

Aubigny, small yet animated, is a picturesque village on the River Nère which flows partly underground. Local activity centres on the fairs, the electric motor and lingerie factories and the sports ground.

The Stuart City. — In 1423 Charles VII gave Aubigny to a Scotsman, John Stuart, his ally against the English. He was succeeded by Beraut Stuart, who effected a reconciliation between Louis XI and his cousin, the future Louis XII, and then by Robert Stuart, known as the Marshal of Aubigny, who fought in Italy under François I.

Gentlemen and craftsmen from Scotland settled here. They established glassmaking and weaving using the white wool from the Sologne. Before the 19C the importance of cloth manufacture was so great that the town was known as Aubigny-les-Cardeux or the Carders' Aubigny. Rue des Foulons recalls the days when cloth was dressed by fulling in the waters of the Nère.

SIGHTS

★ **Old houses.** – A number of early 16C half-timbered houses have survived. The oaks used in their construction were given by Robert Stuart from the nearby Forest of Ivoy. There are several along Rue Cambournac and more in charming and busy Rue du Prieuré which is hung with shop signs from the Town Hall to the church. At the corner of Rue de l'Église and Rue du Bourg-Coutant stands the attractive **François I's house.** In the Rue du Bourg-Coutant, opposite the Maison St-Jean is the **Maison du Bailli★** with its carved beams. The tiny Rue du Charbon is also lined with half-timbered houses and the only 15C house to have survived the fire of 1512 stands in Rue du Pont-aux-Foulons.

St-Martin's Church. – At the entrance to the chancel two 17C painted statues represent a charming Virgin and Child and a dramatic Christ Reviled, while in the chancel a 16C stained glass window depicts the life of St Martin. In the third chapel to the right there is an admirable 17C wood *Pietà*.

Town Hall. – It is located in the former Stuart castle. The entrance gatehouse, dating from the time of Robert Stuart, is flanked by attractive brick bartizans; the keystone of the vault is emblazoned with the Stuart coat of arms. Pass into the charming but irregular courtyard with its mullioned windows and round or polygonal turreted staircases.

Duchess of Portsmouth's Park. – These gardens, still called the Grands Jardins, were laid out in the 17C and adorned with clipped hedges, arbours and fine trees. They are named after Charles II's favourite who lived at La Verrerie Château *(see below)*.

Ramparts. – The line of the old town wall, built originally by Philippe-Auguste, is marked by the streets enclosing the town centre and the three round towers overlooking the Mall which runs parallels to the Nère spanned by footbridges. There are views of the half-timbered houses and the small gardens.

EXCURSION

★ **Château de la Verrerie.** – *11 km - 7 miles southeast by D 89.*
This large isolated château near the Forest of Ivoy benefits from its lovely **setting★** beside a lake. It is believed that the château inspired Alain-Fournier for one of the episodes of his novel *Le Grand Meaulnes (p 30)*.
The château was originally built on a square plan around a courtyard; the oldest part was built by Charles VII. John Stuart received it from the French king at the same time as Aubigny. At the end of 15C Béraut Stuart began to build a château (residence and chapel) which was completed in the Renaissance period by his nephew, Robert, Marshal of Aubigny. Returned to the French in 1670, the château was given three years later, by Louis XIV to the Duchess of Portsmouth, Charles II's favourite.
To enter the courtyard pass through the gatehouse flanked by elegant bartizans. A graceful **Renaissance gallery★** in pink brick and white stone and built in 1525 by Robert Stuart, faces the entrance. Under the gallery are reproductions of frescoes from the first floor depicting the Stuarts. The 15C chapel, with its pointed spire was decorated with frescoes in 1525; note the carved wood tabernacle of the Renaissance period.
The visit includes the wing, behind the Renaissance gallery, added in the 19C. Its rooms are decorated with furnishings of the Renaissance to the Louis XVI period, silver, paintings and portraits. In the dining-room hang two large 18C tapestries from Beauvais; in the saloon a Renaissance cupboard contains four 15C alabaster weepers from Jean de Berry's tomb. In the boudoir is a collection of 19C dolls and their furnishings. The library contains memorabilia belonging to Melchior de Voguë (1829-1916). Archaeologist and diplomat he headed the excavations in Palestine and Syria.

AVOINE-CHINON Nuclear Power Station

Michelin map 🔢 fold 13 or 🔢 fold 34 (11 km - 7 miles northwest of Chinon)

Visitors' entrance near the Port-Boulet bridge.

Just below the confluence of the Indre and the Loire, on the south bank, the first French nuclear power station for producing electricity came on stream in 1963.
It was nicknamed the ball *(la boule)* and included in the Chinon A complex when two new generators – EDF 2 and EDF 3 – were built in 1965 and 1966. The original generator – EDF 1 – worked until 1973. Now part of the national industrial heritage, it has been converted into a **museum of the Nuclear Industry** which opened in 1986.
After visiting the control room and passing through the air-lock, one enters the domed containment building, an impressive moment, and sees the technicians painted in *trompe-l'œil* on the walls. The heat exchangers are a collection of vertical pipes which produce steam; splendidly lit, they look like organ pipes reaching to over 40 m - 130 ft high. The lift ascends to the reactor floor, 71 m - 233 ft above sea level; a TV camera in the reactor core relays its pictures in a giant **audio-visual film.** Four port-holes in the top of the containment building provide a view of the banks of the Loire and of the whole Avoine-Chinon site and its seven reactors. Three (Chinon A) belong to the Magnox type (natural uranium for the fuel, graphite for the moderator, carbon dioxide gas for the coolant); only EDF 3 is still generating electricity. The other four (Chinon B) belong to the pressurised water type and have a power output of 900 megawatts each.
The distinctive features of Chinon B are the four mechanical-draught cooling towers; less than 30 m - 98 ft high, they resemble huge circular parking lots and discharge their surplus steam over a wide area. They are an improvement on the huge concrete towers (120 m to 165 m - 394 ft to 541 ft) which are characteristic of the other nuclear power stations and discharge their steam high in the sky.
There are two other nuclear power stations in the Loire valley upstream from Avoine at **St-Laurent-des-Eaux** and **Dampierre-en-Burly**; both have information centres.

★ ★ AZAY-LE-RIDEAU Château

Michelin map 64 fold 14 or 232 fold 35 – Local map p 122 – Facilities – Photo p 43

Strategically sited at a bridging point on the Indre on the main road from Tours to Chinon, Azay was soon fortified. It is named after one of its lords, Ridel or Rideau d'Azay, who was knighted by Philippe-Auguste and built a strong castle.

The most tragic incident in its history was the massacre of 1418. When Charles VII was Dauphin he was insulted by the Burgundian guard as he passed through Azay. Instant reprisals followed. The town was seized and burnt and the Captain and his 350 soldiers were executed. Azay was called Azay-le-Brûlé (Azay the Burnt) until 18C.

A financier's creation (16C). – When it rose from its ruins Azay became the property of **Gilles Berthelot**, one of the great financiers of the time. He had the present delightful mansion built between 1518 and 1529. His wife, **Philippa Lesbahy**, directed the work, as Catherine Briçonnet had directed that of Chenonceau.

But under the monarchy, fortune's wheel turned quickly for financiers. The rich Semblançay ended his career on the gibbet at Montfaucon. Berthelot saw the fatal noose draw near, took fright, fled and later died in exile. François I confiscated Azay and gave it to the Captain of his Guard. In 19C one of the many subsequent owners undertook considerable restoration work and demolished the remains of the feudal fortress.

In 1870, when Prince Frederick-Charles of Prussia was staying in the château, one of the chandeliers crashed down on to the table. The Prince thought that his life was being threatened and Azay barely escaped further retribution. In 1905 the château was bought by the State for 200 000 francs.

★ ★ **Son et Lumière.** – See Practical Information at the end of the guide.

Enter from Rue de Pineau or Rue Balzac.

○ **TOUR** time : 3/4 hour

A tree-clad setting on the banks of the Indre provides the backdrop for the Château d'Azay, one of the gems of the Renaissance. Similar to Chenonceau, but less grandiose, its lines and dimensions suit the site so perfectly that it gives an unforgettable impression of elegance and harmony. Though Gothic in outline, Azay is modern in its bright appearance and its living accomodation. The medieval defences are purely symbolic and testify only to the high rank of the owners.

The massive towers of other days have given way to harmless turrets with graceful forms. Dormer windows spring from the corbelled sentry walk, the machicolations lend themselves to ornament and the moats are mere placid reflecting pools.

Partly built over the Indre, the château consists of two main wings at right angles. The decoration shows the influence of the buildings erected by François I at Blois: pilasters flank the windows, mouldings separate the storeys but here there is a strict symmetry throughout the design of the building.

The most remarkable part of the château is the great gable with double openings containing the **grand staircase**. At Blois the staircase is still spiral and projects from the façade; at Azay as at Chenonceau which was built a few years earlier, it is internal with a straight ramp.

The reflection in the water and the varnished wooden boats, specially built for the Son et Lumière show and moored at the water's edge, add to the gentle melancholy of the site and, together with the rows of houses and gardens along the River Indre, make excellent subjects for photographs.

ADDITIONAL SIGHT

St-Symphorien. – This curious 11C church, altered in the 12 and 16C, has a double gabled **façade★**. Embedded to the right are remains of the original 5 and 6C building: two rows of statuettes and diapered brickwork. To the left above the basket-handle arched porch, there is a Flamboyant window (restored) which dates from 16C.

EXCURSION

The Indre Valley from Azay to Pont-de-Ruan. – Round tour of 26 km - 16 miles east via D 17 and D 84 – about 2 hours.

Leave Azay going south by the bridge over the Indre which gives an attractive view of the château through the trees of the park.

Bear left immediately into D 17 and then right into D 57.

Villaines-les-Rochers. – Pop 939. Wickerwork has always been the mainstay of the village. In 19C Balzac wrote from the neighbouring Château de Saché: "We went to Villaines where the local baskets are made and bought some very attractive ones". The black and yellow osiers and the green rushes are cut in winter and steeped in water until May when they are stripped and woven. This craft is traditionally handed down from father to son who work in troglodyte workshops (several troglodyte houses can be seen).

The Villaines **Cooperative,** which was founded in 1849 by the parish priest, numbers about 80 families; a collective workshop has been set up which takes young trainees from the national school of osier culture and basket work at Fayl-Billot in Haute-Marne. The workshop can be visited and the craftsmen's work is on sale.

Return to D 17 by D217 which runs beside the River Villaine.

Saché. – *Description on p 159.*

Pont-de-Ruan. – Pop 510. A beautiful picture appears at the crossing of the Indre: two windmills, each on an island, set among trees. The site is described at length by Balzac in *Le Lys dans la Vallée.*

BAUGÉ

Pop 3 906

Michelin map 🔟 folds 2 and 12 or 🔢 fold 21

Baugé, a peaceful town with noble dwellings, is the capital and market town of the surrounding region, a countryside of heaths, forests and vast clearings. There is a good view of the town with its ruined walls from Rue Foulques-Nerra to the west.

Under the sign of the Cross of Anjou. – Baugé, which was founded in 1 000 by Fulk Nerra *(p 48),* became one of the favourite residences of Yolande of Aragon, Queen of Sicily, and her son, King René *(p 48),* in 15C. Yolande, who was a faithful supporter of Charles VII and Joan of Arc, repulsed the English from Anjou at the battle of Vieil-Baugé (1421) in which Sir Guérin de Fontaines distinguished himself at the head of the Angevins and some Scottish mercenaries.

René painted, wrote verses and hunted the wild boar in its lair *(bauge)* in the adjacent forests; he also prayed before the relic of the True Cross which was venerated at La Boissière Abbey *(p 69).*

Once Louis XI had gained possession of Anjou, Baugé went into decline: the saying ''I'll give you my rent from Baugé *(je vous baille ma rente de Baugé)''* means ''I can give you nothing''.

SIGHTS

Château. – This 15C building now serves as the town hall, tourist information centre and **museum** (collections of weapons, porcelain and old coins).

In 1455 King René himself supervised the building of the turrets, dormer windows, the oratory and the bartizan on the rear façade, where the master masons are portrayed. An ogee arched doorway gives access to the **spiral staircase** which terminates with a magnificent palm tree vault, decorated with the Anjou-Sicily coat of arms and other emblems: angels, tau crosses (T), symbols of the cross of Christ and stars which, in the Apocalypse, represent the souls of the blessed in eternity.

Chapel of the Daughters of the Heart of Mary (Chapelle des Filles du Cœur de Marie – B). – Formerly part of an 18C hospice, the chapel now houses a precious relic.

★★ **Cross of Anjou.** – The cross with two transoms (the upper one carried the inscription), which was also known as the Cross of Jerusalem, was venerated as a piece of the true cross by the Dukes of Anjou and in particular by King René. At the end of 15C after the Battle of Nancy in which René II Duke of Lorraine, a descendant of the Dukes of Anjou, beat Charles the Bold, the Lorraine troops adopted the Cross of Anjou as their own

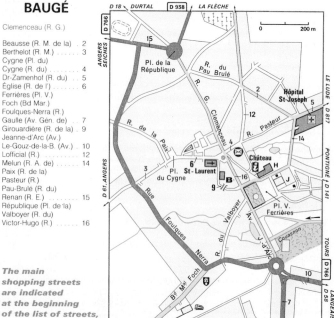

BAUGÉ

Clemenceau (R. G.)

Beausse (R. M. de la) . 2
Berthelot (R. M.) 3
Cygne (Pl. du)
Cygne (R. du) 4
Dr-Zamenhof (R. du) . 5
Église (R. de l') 6
Ferrières (Pl. V.)
Foch (Bd Mar.)
Foulques-Nerra (R.)
Gaulle (Av. Gén. de) ... 7
Girouardière (R. de la) . 9
Jeanne-d'Arc (Av.)
Le-Gouz-de-la-B. (Av.) . 10
Lofficial (R.) 12
Melun (R. A. de) 14
Paix (R. de la)
Pasteur (R.)
Pau-Brulé (R. du)
Renan (R. E.) 15
République (Pl. de la)
Valboyer (R. du)
Victor-Hugo (R.) 16

*The main
shopping streets
are indicated
at the beginning
of the list of streets,
which accompany
town plans.*

symbol in order to recognize one another in the mêlée and the cross became known henceforward as the Cross of Lorraine. It is supposed to be made from a piece of the true cross and brought back from the Holy Land after the crusade in 1241; it is a marvel of the goldsmith's craft, set with precious stones and fine pearls and was created at the end of 14C for Louis, first Duke of Anjou by his brother, Charles V's Parisian goldsmith. It is unusual in that it has a figure of Christ on both sides.

St-Joseph's Hospital (Hôpital St-Joseph). — The hospice, which was founded in 1643, is now run by the nuns of the St Joseph Order of Hospitallers.
The **dispensary★** with its original parquet floor and wall panelling displays a collection of herb jars which match the colours of the ceiling, glass and pewter vessels and 16-17C faience pots from Lyon and Narbonne with Italian or Hispano-Moresque decoration. It is best to visit on a bright day as the exhibits cannot be subjected to electric light. Across the corridor is the Chapel; the altarpiece with a gilt wood ciborium is 17C.

Hôtels. — The quiet streets of old Baugé are lined with noble mansions *(hôtels)* with high doorways: Rues de l'Église, de la Girouardière and Place du Cygne.

St-Laurent's Church. — 18C; the organ was restored in 1975.

EXCURSION

The Baugeois. — *Round tour of 38km - 24 miles — about 1 hour — local map p 59.*

> *Leave Baugé by D 141 going east along the Couasnon Valley.*

Dolmen de la Pierre Couverte. — About 3 km - 2 miles from Baugé branch off to the left taking the signposted path leading to the dolmen standing in a forest clearing *(1/2 hour on foot Rtn)*.

By car again, take D 141 towards Pontigné, with fine views to the right of the Couasnon Valley and the forested massif of Chandelais.

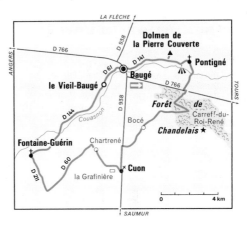

Pontigné. — Pop. 225. The **church**, dedicated to St Denis, whose effigy is above the Romanesque portal, is crowned by an unusual twisting spiral bell tower. Inside Angevin vaulting *(p 36)* covers the nave while the capitals of the transept sport monstrous heads and water leaf motifs; the charming central apse is supported by a complex network of radiating tori. In the apsidals 13-14C **mural paintings★** depict Christ the King and the Resurrection of Lazarus on one side and the Virgin Enthroned, surrounded by the Annunciation, the Nativity and the Adoration of the Shepherds on the other.

> *Follow the road behind the church and turn right on D 766.*

The road affords a fine view of the orchards in the valley.

> *Bear left and then turn right in the direction of Bocé.*

★ **Chandelais Forest** (Forêt de Chandelais). — This is a magnificent State owned property, covering 800 hectares - 2 000 acres. The splendid fully grown oak and beech trees are replanted every 210 years.

> *Follow the forest road to the central crossroads before turning right in the direction of Bocé. Then take D 939 to the left towards Cuon.*

Cuon. — Pop 413. Behind the church with the curious conical spire is a charming 15C manor house.
Opposite the church an old inn still bears the inscription "Au Soleil d'Or" (The Golden Sun) where travellers on foot or on horseback could find lodging.

> *From Cuon take the road to Chartrené.*

The wooded park on the left marks the site of the Château de la Grafinière.

> *Beyond Chartrené turn left to D 60. After 4.5 km - 3 miles follow D 211 to your right, crossing heaths and woodlands, to reach Fontaine-Guérin.*

Fontaine-Guérin. — Pop 579. The belfry of the much altered Romanesque **church** is crowned by a twisting spire.
Inside the 15C roof is decorated with 126 painted panels (15-16C) with secular themes. The D 211 towards St-Georges-du-Bois leads to an artificial lake with facilities for swimming, sail-boarding and picnicking.
A "Threshing Fête" with processions in traditional costume is held on the second Sunday in August.

> *Follow the Couasnon Valley, taking D 144 in the direction of Le Vieil-Baugé and passing within sight of ruins of the Château de la Tour du Pin.*

Le Vieil-Baugé. — Pop 1 104. Le Vieil-Baugé is the site of a battle in 1421 when the English were defeated by an Angevin army supported by Scottish mercenaries led by John, the Earl of Buchan. He was rewarded with the baton of High Constable of France.
The old village crowns a hilltop overlooking the valley of the Couasnon.

St-Symphorien, the church, has a slim spiral spire which leans owing to the internal wooden framework. The nave is partially 11C and the handsome **chancel★** is 13C with Angevin vaulting. The façade and the south transept are by the Angevin architect, Jean de Lespine, and date from the Renaissance.

BAZOUGES-SUR-LE-LOIR

Pop 1313

Michelin map 64 fold 2 or 232 fold 21

From the bridge there is a charming view★ of the river with its washing places, of the castle and the water mill, of the church and its tower in the square and the gardens mounting to the roofs of Bazouges.

Château. – The château of Bazouges, together with the castle water mill, was built on an attractive site on the banks of the Loir in 15C and 16C by the Champagne family, one of whom, Baudoin (Baldwin), was chamberlain to Louis XII and François I.
The entrance is flanked by two massive towers, with machicolations and pepper-pot turrets; one of them contains the 15C chapel which is decorated with Angevin vaulting and two old statues of St Barbara and St John. The guard room over the gateway leads to the sentry walk. Another more imposing guard room with a stone chimneypiece is on view as well as the 18C state rooms and the formal French park which is planted with cypresses and yew trees and surrounded by water.

Church. – The building dates from 12C. A solid tower rises above the crossing. The nave vaulting, which is made of oak shingles, is painted with 24 figures (12 Apostles and 12 angels) separated by trees each bearing an article from the Creed (early 16C).

BEAUFORT-EN-VALLÉE

Pop 4775

Michelin map 64 fold 12 or 232 folds 32, 33 – Local map p 127

Beaufort is set in the middle of the rich plains of the Anjou Valley. In 18-19C it was one of the largest manufacturers of sail cloth in France. The town is dominated by the ruins of the **château**, which was built in 14C by Guillaume Roger, Count of Beaufort and father of Pope Gregory XI. One of the towers was rebuilt in 15C by King René. From the top of the bluff on which the ruins stand there is a broad **view** of the surrounding country.
The **church**, which was largely restored in 19C, has a fine belfry built by Jean de Lespine and completed in 1542 over the 15C crossing. The interior contains a 17C Adoration of the Shepherds, a carved wooden altar (1617) and the earlier high altar, made of marble, which is now under the great window in the transept.

EXCURSION

Blou. – Pop 853. *16 km - 10 miles by N 147 towards Longué and D 206.*
The Romanesque **church** with its massive buttresses has curious 11C diapering on its north transept. A 13C belltower rises above the transept crossing.

★ BEAUGENCY

Pop 7339

Michelin map 64 fold 8 or 238 fold 4 – Local map p 123 – Facilities

Beaugency recalls the Middle Ages. It is best to enter the town from the south, crossing the River Loire by the age-old multi-arched bridge (attractive view). The oldest parts of the bridge date from 14C but there was a bridge before that because a toll was already in existence in 12C.

The Two Councils of Beaugency (12C). – Both councils were called to deal with the marital problems of Philippe I and Louis VII.
While visiting Fulk IV in Tours *(p 48)*, Philippe seduced the Countess Bertrade and repudiated Queen Bertha soon after. The king thought that he would easily obtain the annulment of his marriage by raising a vague claim of consanguinity but Pope Urban II refused him. The king persisted and was excommunicated so that he was unable to join the first Crusade (1099). Eventually the excommunication was lifted by the Council of Beaugency in 1104 and four years later the king died at peace with the church. He was buried according to his wishes at St-Benoît-sur-Loire.
Much more important was the council of 1152 which annulled the marriage of Louis VII and **Eleanor of Aquitaine.** The beautiful and seductive Eleanor, daughter and heir of the Duke of Aquitaine, had married Louis in 1137. For ten years the royal couple lived in perfect harmony, Eleanor exercising great influence on her husband. In 1147 they set out together on the crusade but once in Palestine their relationship deteriorated. Louis grew jealous of Eleanor's partiality for Raymond of Poitiers. They had a quarrel and returned to France separately. Divorce became inevitable and on 20 March 1152 the Council of Beaugency officially dissolved the union of Louis and Eleanor for prohibited kinship: both were descended from Robert the Pious.
Eleanor was not without suitors; almost immediately she married Henry Plantagenet *(p 48)*, the future king of England, so that her dowry, a large part of southwest France, passed to the English crown.
This event, one of the most important in the Middle Ages, was pregnant with consequences; it contained the pretext for many centuries of Anglo-French rivalry.

A disputed town. – Beaugency commanded the only bridge that crossed the Loire between Blois and Orléans before modern times. For this reason the town was often attacked *(see note 1 p 44)*. During the Hundred Years War (1337-1453) it fell into English hands four times: in 1356, 1412, 1421 and 1428. It was delivered by Joan of Arc in 1429.
The town was then caught up in the turmoil of the Wars of Religion (1562-98). Leaguers and Protestants held it by turns. At the time of the fire started by the Huguenots in 1567, the abbey was burnt down, the roof of Notre-Dame collapsed and so did that of the keep.
During the 1870-71 war against the Prussians there was fierce fighting not far from the town which was held by General Chanzy.

BEAUGENCY

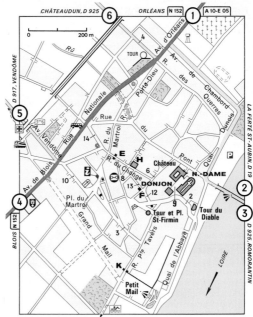

Cordonnerie
  (R. de la)   6
Maille-d'Or
  (R. de la)   10
Martroi (Pl. du)
Pont (R. du)

Abbaye (R. de l') 2
Bretonnerie
  (R. de la) 3
Châteaudun
  (R. de) 4
Dr-Hyvernaud (Pl.) 8
Dunois (Pl.) 9
Sirène
  (R. de la) 12
Traîneau (R. du) 13
Trois-Marchands
  (R. des) 14

*If you are puzzled
by an abbreviation
or a symbol
in the text
or on the maps,
look at the key
on p 42.*

SIGHTS

★ **Abbey Church (Église Notre-Dame).** — The Romanesque church was built in 12C as part of an abbey and has been restored. In the chancel a series of twinned arches alternates with the windows and larger arches; the huge round columns in the nave with their massive carved capitals represent the calm strength of the purest Romanesque art, despite the false wooden vaulting in the nave which was put up after the fire in 1567.
Near the church are the 18C buildings of the old abbey. At the bottom of the narrow Rue de l'Abbaye stands the **Devil's Tower** (Tour du Diable) which was part of the fortifications defending the bridgehead; in the Middle Ages the Loire flowed at its foot.
Place Dunois, the square in front of the abbey church and the keep, and **Place St-Firmin** make a picturesque combination, lit by old lanterns after dark.

★ **Keep (Donjon).** — This is a fine example of 11C military architecture. At this period, keeps were rectangular and buttressed; later they became circular. The interior is in ruins.

Château Dunois. — Formerly a medieval fortress, it was turned into a typical 15C residence, with mullion windows, a stair turret and an arcaded courtyard, by Dunois *(see p 78),* Lord of Beaugency.

★ **Orléans District Museum.** — The rooms of the Château Dunois now house a fine collection of furniture and costumes from the Orléans district. Traditional arts and crafts are evoked as well as souvenirs of local celebrities: Charles, the physician (1746-1823), Eugene Sue, writer (1804-57). From the loft one can see the 15C timberwork of the roof.

St-Firmin's Tower (Tour St-Firmin). — A street used to run under this tower, which is all that remains of a 16C church which was destroyed during the Revolution.

Templars' House (F). — Interesting Romanesque windows.

Town Hall (H). — From Place de la Poste one can admire the Renaissance façade. The Council Chamber on the first floor is hung with eight beautiful pieces of **embroidery**★, executed with incomparable skill. Four of them, depicting the four continents then known, are 17C; the others (gathering mistletoe and pagan sacrifices) are 18C. They belonged to the last but one Abbot of Notre-Dame, who came from a family of shipbuilders in Nantes, who had grown rich importing sugar cane from the Antilles; the sugar cane was shipped up the Loire and processed round Beaugency and Orléans.

Clock Tower (Tour de l'Horloge — E). — Originally the Exchange Tower, in 12C it became one of the gateways in the town wall.

Little Mall (Petit Mail). — It dominates the River Loire. Fine view of the valley.

Tavers Gateway (Porte Tavers — K). — Part of the old town walls.

BEAULIEU-LES-LOCHES
Pop 1 769

Michelin map 📖 fold 6 or 🗺🗺 fold 14

This old village contains the ruins of a famous abbey founded in 1004 by Fulk Nerra *(p 42),* who was buried there at his wish.
The **abbey church** is dominated by a majestic square Romanesque tower, surmounted by an octagonal spire. The arms of the transept also date from the Romanesque period but the nave and chancel were rebuilt in 15C after being destroyed by the English in 1412; beyond the chancel are a few traces of the original Romanesque apse. The interior is adorned with a 15C *Pietà,* some 18C terracotta statues in the chancel and some 17C portraits and a low relief carving of the last Supper in the sacristy.
A curious outdoor pulpit adjoins the old abbot's lodgings on the site of the old cloisters to the right of the church.
The former **Church of St-Laurent** has a Romanesque tower and curved Angevin vaulting.

BEAUNE-LA-ROLANDE

Michelin map 🗺 fold 11 or 🗺 fold 42

Beaune-la-Rolande in the Gâtinais takes its name from the River Rolande west of the town. It is a market town where sugarbeet and cereals have replaced saffron and vines.

Church. — The building is 15-16C with an elegant north side in the Renaissance style: pilasters with medallions, recesses, doorways with pediments decorated with busts. To the left is the gate to the former cemetery with an improving sentiment on the lintel. The aisles are almost as wide and high as the nave so that the building resembles the 'hall churches' of the late German Gothic period.

At the back of the left aisle there is a painting of the mystic marriage of St Catherine by Frederic Bazille who fell in the Battle of Beaune-la-Rolande in 1870. The last side chapel on the left contains a 17C gilt wood altar with panels depicting biblical scenes and a statue of St Vincent de Paul earlier than the stereotyped 19C representations.

★ BEAUREGARD Château

Map 🗺 north of fold 17 or 🗺 fold 15 (8 km - 5 miles northwest of Cour-Cheverny)

The château stands in a vast park laid out on geometric lines. Most of the building is early 17C but the central block, which has an arcaded gallery, is thoroughly 16C.

★★**Portrait Gallery.** — *Time: 3/4 hour.* Above the ground floor arcade is a gallery which was decorated for Paul Ardier, Lord of Beauregard at the beginning of 17C and Treasurer of the Exchequer under Louis XIII. The long room has retained its old Delft tiling depicting an army on the march: cavalry, artillery, infantry, musketry...; the panelling and the ceiling were painted by Pierre Mosnier.

The most interesting feature of the gallery is the collection of over 300 historical portraits. They are arranged in bays, each devoted to a different reign making a complete succession of monarchs from the first Valois, Philippe VI to Louis XIII. Round the portrait of each king are grouped the queen, the chief courtiers and important foreign contemporaries; thus, next to Louis XII are Isabella of Castille, her daughter Joan the Mad and Amerigo Vespucci, the Florentine explorer who gave his name to America. Each reign is complete with its dates and the king's emblem.

★**Cabinet des Grelots.** — This charming little room was fitted out towards the middle of 16C for Jean du Thiers, Secretary of State to Henri II and then Lord of Beauregard. His coat of arms, azure with three spherical gold bells *(grelots),* decorates the coffered ceiling; the bells reappear as a decorative motif on the oak panelling which lines the room and conceals the cupboards where the château archives are kept.

The huge 16C kitchen with two fireplaces is also on show.

★ BÉHUARD

Michelin map 🗺 fold 20 or 🗺 fold 31 — Local map p 126

Béhuard Island has accumulated round a rock on which stands the little church. The old village★ with its 15 and 16C houses makes a picturesque ensemble.

In the pagan era there was a shrine on the island dedicated to a marine goddess which was replaced in 5C by a small oratory where prayers were said for sailors "in peril on the Loire". In 15C Louis XI, who had been saved from a shipwreck by the intercession of the Virgin, built the present church which became an even more popular place of pilgrimage than in the past and was dedicated to the Virgin, the protector of travellers since she herself had experienced the dangers of travel during the Flight into Egypt.

Church (Eglise Notre-Dame). — The church, which is dedicated to the Virgin, faces the souvenir shop which stands on the site of the old **King's Lodging** (logis du roi) built in 15C, so it is said, for the visits of Louis XI; a small stairway leads to the church.

Part of the nave is composed of the island rock. Votive chains, presented by a lucky man who escaped from the barbarian galleys, hang in the chancel; the 16C stalls have delightfully malicious carved misericords. The statue of Our Lady of Béhuard stands in a niche in the chancel. The late 15C window of the Crucifixion in one of the aisles shows the donor, Louis XI *(left):* behind the entrance door there is an old medieval chest.

Walk. — It is worth exploring such an attractive site; a short path, the Calvary where religious ceremonies take place, leads down to the Loire and a broad sandy beach.

BELLEGARDE

Michelin map 🗺 fold 11 or 🗺 fold 42

The colour-washed houses of Bellegarde are grouped round a huge square and surrounded by rose nurseries, market gardens and wheat fields.

The town was called Choisy-aux-Loges until 1645 when it was bought by the Duke of Bellegarde. In 1692 it passed to Louis-Antoine de Pardaillan, **Duc d'Antin.**

Courtier and patron of the arts. — D'Antin was the legitimate son of Madame de Montespan and the Surveyor of the King. He was a model courtier; Voltaire wrote that he had a talent for flattery, not only in words but in actions. During a visit to Petit-Bourg Château, near Paris, Louis XIV complained about a row of chestnut trees which, although very fine from the garden, obscured the view from the royal apartments. D'Antin had the trees felled during the night and all trace of the work cleared away; on waking the King was astonished to find the view unobstructed.

D'Antin collected works of art and acted as a patron to artists. His mother was a frequent visitor at Bellegarde where he erected a series of brick buildings (1717-27).

SIGHTS

★ **Château.** – At the centre of this unusual and picturesque group of buildings stands the square keep, quartered with bartizans and cut off by a moat, which was built in 14C by Nicolas Braque, Finance Minister to Charles V.

The brick **pavilions** with stone dressings which surround the courtyard were built by D'Antin to house the château staff and his guests; from left to right they comprise the Steward's pavilion surmounted by a pinnacle turret, the Captain's massive round brick tower, the kitchen pavilion, the Salamandre pavilion, which houses the Town Hall and contains a salon with Regency wood panelling, and, on the other side of the gate, the Antin pavilion with a Mansard roof. A **rose garden** has been laid out round the moat.
A drive skirting the rose garden leads to the stables *(private property);* the pediment is decorated with three horses' heads sculpted by Coysevox.

Turn left to reach the church in Place du Marché.

Church. – The façade of this Romanesque building is a harmonious combination of proportion and decoration. Note the ornamentation of the central doorway: wreathed and ringed engaged piers support carved capitals depicting fantastic foliage and animals.

The nave contains a collection of 17C **paintings**: St Sebastian by Annibale Carrachi and St John the Baptist with the infant Louis XIV as St John by Mignard *(righthand wall)* and The Descent from the Cross by Lebrun *(righthand chapel);* Louise de la Vallière may have been the model for the two female characters in these pictures.

EXCURSION

Boiscommun. – Pop 810. *7.5 km - 5 miles northwest by D44.*
Of the castle only two towers and other ruins remain and these can be seen from the path which now follows the line of the former moat.
The **church** with its Romanesque doorway has a Gothic nave with a majestic elevation. It is relatively easy to discern the different periods of construction by looking at the changes in the capitals, the form of the high windows and openings of the triforium. At the end of the aisle, above the sacristy door, is a late 12C stained glass window showing the Virgin and Child. On leaving glance at the organ loft, ornamented with eight painted figures (16C) in costumes of the period; the figure of Roland is identified by the inscription.

★ BERCÉ Forest

Michelin map 🗒 fold 4 or 🗒🗒 folds 22, 23

Bercé Forest is all that remains of the great Le Mans Forest which used to extend from the River Sarthe to the River Loir; its foliage covers a fine plateau (5414 ha - 21 sq miles) incised by small valleys and natural springs.
The magnificent trees – robur-oaks which tower to over 45 m - 148 ft mixed with chestnuts and slim beeches – provide cover for a herd of deer.
In 16C Bercé Forest was crown property exploited for high quality oak. The trees, which were felled between 200 and 240 years old, yield a pale yellow wood with a fine grain much in demand in cabinet-making (veneers) and for export throughout Europe.

TOUR *time: 3/4 hour – 16 km - 10 miles from St-Hubert to La Futaie des Clos*

The trees which are destined to be felled are marked on the trunk; those with a number are to be retained.

Fontaine de la Coudre. – The spring, which is the source of the River Dinan, a tributary of the Loir, flows slowly under the tall oaks known as La Futaie des Forges.

★ **Sources de l'Hermitière.** – A deep valley thick with towering oaks and beeches hides the pure waters of these springs.

★ **Futaie des Clos.** – This is the finest stand of oaks in the forest. Two violent storms in 1967 caused great gaps among the trees. While some of the giant oaks (300 to 340 years old) are very decrepit, others are splendid specimens.

Park in the car park under the trees.

A path leads to the Boppe oak, or rather to its stump, protected by a roof, since the ancient tree was struck by lightning in 1934 at the venerable age of 262; its circumference was 4.77 m - 15 1/2 ft at 1.3 m - 4 ft from the ground. Its neighbour – Roulleau de la Roussière – still flourishes after 340 years; it is 43 m - 141 ft tall.

★ BLANCAFORT
Pop 1070

Michelin map 🗒 north of fold 11 or 🗒🗒 fold 19

This is a very picturesque and smart village clustered round the church which has an unusual belfry-porch.

★ **Château.** – The 15C château is built of red brick and has a uniform and rather plain façade. The courtyard which is flanked by two pavilions was added in 17C. The visit includes the library with its Regency panelling and the dining room with its walls covered in Flanders leather, painted, gilded and embossed; fine display of pewter.
The park provides a pleasant walk among the scroll-like flower beds laid out in the French style near the château or along woodland paths beside the river where the scents of the garden are strongest at dusk.

Blois is situated on the Loire between the Beauce to the north of the river and the Sologne to the south. It is the commercial centre of an agricultural region producing mainly wheat in the Beauce and in the valley wine, strawberries, vegetables and bulbs. First among the vegetables is the asparagus which was first cultivated at Vineuil and St-Claude in the Blois region; it has since spread to Contres in the south and into the Sologne where the soil is light.

Blois is built on the north bank of the Loire, on the hillside overlooking the river; many of the medieval streets still remain, steep and twisting and occasionally linked by flights of steps. The terracing of the houses produces the characteristic tricoloured harmony of Blois: white façades, blue slate roofs and red brick chimneys.

HISTORICAL NOTES

From the Counts of Blois to the Dukes of Orléans. — In the Middle Ages the Counts of Blois were powerful lords with two estates: Champagne and the region of Blois and Chartres. Despite the repeated attacks of their neighbours and rivals, the Counts of Anjou, particularly the mighty Fulk Nerra *(p 47)*, who whittled down their Blois domain, they founded a powerful dynasty.

The Count of Blois married the daughter of William the Conqueror and their son, Stephen, became king of England in 1135. At this period the House of Blois was in the ascendant under Thibaud IV. After his death in 1152, attention was concentrated on Champagne and the Loire land was somewhat abandoned together with England, where the Plantagenets took over in 1154 *(p 48)*.

In 1234 Louis IX bought a lease on the County of Blois from the Count of Champagne. In 1392 the last Count, Guy de Chatillon, sold the county to Louis, Duke of Orléans and brother of Charles VI. Thereafter the court of Orléans was held in Blois. Fifteen years later Louis of Orléans was assassinated in Paris on the orders of the Duke of Burgundy, John the Fearless. His widow, Valentine Visconti retired to Blois where she expressed her disillusion by carving on the walls: *Rien ne m'est plus, plus ne m'est rien* (Nothing means anything to me any more); she died inconsolable the following year.

A poet: Charles of Orléans (1391-1465). — Charles, the eldest son of Louis of Orléans, inherited the castle and spent some of his youth there. At fifteen he married the daughter of Charles VI, but she died in childbirth. At twenty he married again but soon departed to fight the English. He proved a poor general at the Battle of Agincourt where he was taken prisoner but his poetic gift helped him to survive twenty-five years of captivity in England. He returned to France in 1440 and being once more a widower he married, at the age of fifty, Marie de Clèves, who was then fourteen. The château of Blois was his favourite residence. He demolished part of the grim old fortress and built a more comfortable mansion. Charles formed a little court of artists and men of letters. Great joy came to him in old age: at seventy-one he had a son and heir, the future Louis XII.

The Golden Age of the Renaissance. — **Louis XII** was born at Blois in 1462 and succeded Charles VIII in 1498. Blois became the royal residence rather than Amboise. The King and his wife, **Anne of Brittany**, liked Blois and embarked on considerable improvements: the construction of a new wing and the laying out of huge terraced gardens, designed by the Italian gardener, Pacello, who also worked at Amboise. These gardens covered Place Victor-Hugo and extended towards the station. Queen Anne had a large suite (ladies-in-waiting, pages, equerries and guards) and lived in high style. She died on 9 January 1514; the king was soon married to a sixteen-years old English princess but he died on 1 January 1515 in Paris without a male heir. While at Blois he had drawn up the Customs of France, a code of law.

François I divided his time between Amboise and Blois. He commissioned the architect, Jacques Sourdeau to build a new wing at Blois; it is the most beautiful part of the château and bears the king's name. His wife, **Claude of France**, was the daughter of the dead king and was very attached to Blois, where she was brought up and where she died in 1524, barely twenty-five years old, having borne seven children in eight years. As François I was away fighting in Italy, her funeral was not held until November 1526. After that the king came to Blois no more.

Assassination of the Duke of Guise (1588). — The historical interest of the château reached its peak under **Henri III**. The States-General twice met at Blois. The first time was in 1576, when there was a demand for the suppression of the Protestant Church. In 1588 **Henri de Guise**, the Lieutenant-General of the kingdom and all powerful head of the League in Paris, supported by the King of Spain, forced Henri III to call a second meeting of the States-General, which was then the equivalent of Parliament. Five hundred deputies, nearly all supporters of Guise, attended. Guise expected them to depose the King. The latter, feeling himself to be on the brink of the abyss, could think of no other means than murder to get rid of his rival. The killing took place in the château itself, on the second floor *(see p 66)*. Relieved of the threat, Henry III exclaimed "Now, I am king!". Eight months later he himself succumbed to the dagger of Jacques Clement.

A conspirator: Gaston of Orléans (17C). — In 1617 **Marie de' Medici** was banished to Blois by her son, Louis XIII. A little court in exile grew up in the château; the leading figure was **Richelieu**, the queen mother's confidant and cardinal to be, but he became involved in intrigues and decided to flee to Luçon hoping for a more favourable occasion to pursue his ambition.

On 22 February 1619 the Queen Mother escaped; despite her size, she climbed down a rope ladder into the moat in the dark. After such a feat she and her son were reconciled... through the mediation of Richelieu!

In 1626 Louis XIII gave the county of Blois and the duchies of Orléans and Chartres to his brother, **Gaston of Orléans**, who was scheming against Cardinal Richelieu. Soon, however, he grew bored with his new estates and turned to conspiracy again but his inconstancy prevented him from carrying any project to its conclusion: one day he would talk of killing Richelieu, the next day he would be reconciled with him. He went into exile, he returned to France, started a new conspiracy and then left again. He was reconciled with the king in 1634 and was at last able to devote himself to his residence in Blois for which he had grandiose schemes. He sent for Mansart and commissioned a vast new building which would have entailed the destruction of the old château. Between 1635 and 1637 a new range of buildings was erected but then work had to stop owing to a lack of funds. The birth of the Dauphin released Richelieu from the need to humour the king's brother so the latter returned to his old ways. In 1642 he plunged into the plot hatched by the Duc de Bouillon and the Marquis de Cinq-Mars. He escaped conviction but was deprived of his claim to the throne. From 1650-53 he played an active part in the Fronde against Mazarin and was banished to his estates; after this further failure he finally settled down. He lived in the François I wing, embellishing his gardens, until he died, an exemplary death, in 1660, surrounded by his court.

★★★ CHÂTEAU time: 2 hours

Son et Lumière. – *See Practical Information at the end of the guide.*

Place du Château. –
This vast esplanade is the former "farm-yard" of the château. Slightly below, the terraced gardens offer a wide **view** over the roofs behind which can be seen the bridge over the Loire, and at the foot of the re-taining wall, an open square, Place Louis XII; to the right the spires of St-Nico-las' Church. Imme-diately on the left the cathedral with its Ren-aissance tower stands out.

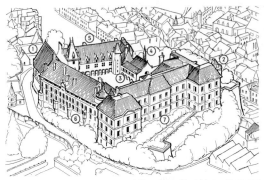

(after photo: Cie Aérienne Française)

Blois Château

Feudal Period:
① Chamber of the States General (13C)
② Foix Tower (13C)

Gothic-Renaissance Transitional Period:
③ Charles of Orléans Gallery (late 15C-early 16C)
④ St Calais Chapel (1498-1508)
⑤ Louis XII Wing (1498-1501)

Renaissance period:
⑥ François I Wing: Façade des Loges (1515-1524)

Classical period:
⑦ Gaston of Orléans Wing (1635-1638)

The **façade** of the châ-teau on the esplanade has two main parts: on the right the pointed gable of the Chamber of the States-General (1), relic of the former feu-dal castle (13C), and then the pretty build-ing of brick and stone erected by Louis XII (5). The latter building shows no symmetry and openings were still placed according to the amiable whims of the Middle Ages.

Two windows on the first floor have balconies. The one on the left opened from Louis XII's bedroom. His Minister, the Cardinal d'Amboise, lived in the nearby house, which was destroyed in June 1940 and has since been rebuilt with only moderate success. When the King and the Cardinal took the air on their balconies they could chat together. The great Flamboyant gateway is surmounted by an alcove containing a modern copy of an equestrian statue of Louis XII (copy executed in 1857 by Seurre). The window consoles are adorned with spirited carvings. The coarse humour of the period is sometimes displayed with great candour (first and fourth windows to the left of the gateway).

The inner courtyard. – Cross the courtyard to reach the delightful terrace (good **view** of St-Nicolas Church and the Loire) on which stands the **Foix Tower** (2) which formed part of the medieval wall.

Return to the courtyard which is lined with buildings from every period which, together, make up the château.

St-Calais Chapel (4). – Of the King's private chapel which was rebuilt by Louis XII, only the chancel remains. Mansart demolished the nave when he built the Gaston of Orléans Wing. The modern stained glass windows are by Max Ingrand.

Charles of Orléans Gallery (3). – Although called after Charles of Orléans this gallery probably dates from the Louis XII period. Until alterations were made in the 19C the gallery was twice its present length and connected the two wings at either end of the courtyard. Note the unusual basket-handle arches.

Louis XII Wing (5). – The corridor or gallery serving the various rooms in the wing marks a step forward in the search for more comfort and convenience. Originally rooms opened into one another. At each end of the wing a spiral staircase gave access to the different floors. The decoration is richer and Italianate panels of arabesques adorn the pillars.

François I Wing (6). – The building extends between the 17C Gaston of Orléans Wing and the 13C feudal hall, chamber of the States-General (1). Only fourteen years passed between the completion of the Louis XII Wing and the commencement of the

François I Wing, but the progress made was important. It meant the triumph of the Italian decorative style.

French originality, however, persisted in the general plan. The windows were made to correspond with the internal arrangement of the rooms, without regard for symmetry; they were sometimes close together, sometimes far apart; their mullions were sometimes double, sometimes single; and pilasters sometimes flanked the window openings, sometimes occupied the middle of the bay. A magnificent **staircase** was added to the façade and it was to be the first of a series. Since Mansart demolished part of the wing to make room for the Gaston of Orléans building, this staircase is no longer in the centre of the façade. It climbs spirally in an octagonal well, three faces of which are recessed in the building. This masterpiece of architecture and sculpture was evidently designed for great receptions. The well is open between the buttresses and forms a series of balconies from which members of the court could watch the arrival of important people.

Blois Château – François I Staircase

The decoration is varied and elaborate. The royal insignia *(p 28)* are used together with all the customary themes of the Renaissance *(p 37)*.

Gaston of Orléans Wing (7). – This range by François Mansart in the Classical style, is in sharp contrast to the rest of the building. Seen from the inner courtyard the comparison with the other façades is unfavourable. To judge Mansart's work fairly it must be seen from outside the château and imagined in the context of his original design. The proposed building would have occupied not only the site of the château but also the square and it would have been linked to the river by a series of terraces occupying the present station district.

Royal Apartments in the François I Wing. – The François I staircase climbs to the first floor where various rooms contain splendid fireplaces, tapestries, busts and portraits, furniture. The interior decoration was restored by Duban (19C). In the past the smoke from the fires, candles and torches soon blackened the décor.

First floor. – The most interesting room is that of Catherine de' Medici. It still has its 237 carved wood panels concealing secret cupboards which may have been used to hide poisons, jewels or State papers or may have been made in accordance with the practice of having wall cupboards in Italian style rooms. They were opened by pressing a pedal concealed in the skirting board.

Second floor. – This is the scene of the **murder of the Duke of Guise**. The rooms have been altered and the King's cabinet is now included in the Gaston of Orléans Wing. It is therefore, rather difficult to follow the phases of the assassination on the spot.

The plan below shows the lay-out of the rooms at the time of the murder. The account is taken from contemporary witnesses.

It is 23 December 1588 about 8 o'clock in the morning. Out of the 45 impoverished noblemen who are Henri III's men of action, 20 have been chosen to deal with the Duke; 8 of them with daggers hidden under their cloaks are waiting in the king's room, sitting on the chests and chatting about this and that. The 12 others, armed with swords, are in the old cabinet. Two priests are in the oratory of the new cabinet: the king is making them pray for the success of his enterprise.

The Duke of Guise is in the Council Room together with several important people. He has been up since 6 o'clock having spent the night with one of the ladies of the "flying squadron" *(p 28)* and is cold and hungry. First he warms himself at the fire and eats one one of the prunes in his comfit box. Then the Council started. Henri III's secretary tells Guise that the king would like to see him in the old cabinet. To reach this room, Guise has to go through the king's chamber because only two days previously the door between the Council Room and the cabinet had been walled up. The Duke enters the king's chamber and is greeted by the assassins. He turns left towards the corridor outside the cabinet. Guise opens the door and in the narrow passage sees the men waiting for him, sword in hand. He tries to retreat but is cut off by the eight men in the king's chamber. They fall upon their victim, seize him by his arms and legs and wrap his sword in his cloak. The Duke is very strong; he knocks down four of his assailants and wounds a fifth with

BLOIS CHÂTEAU : 2nd FLOOR IN 1588

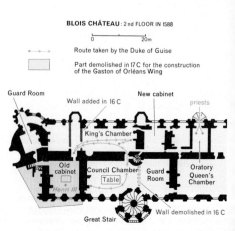

0   20m

← - - →   Route taken by the Duke of Guise

▨   Part demolished in 17 C for the construction of the Gaston of Orléans Wing

Guard Room   New cabinet

Wall added in 16 C   priests

King's Chamber

Old cabinet   Council Chamber   Guard Room   Oratory Queen's Chamber

Table

Henri III

Great Stair   Wall demolished in 16 C

his comfit box. He staggers to the door of the chamber and then collapses by the king's bed, riddled with stab wounds, murmuring "Miserere mei Deus". Henri III steps out from behind the tapestry where he has been hiding and walks up to his rival. Some men say he slapped his face crying "My God! isn't he big! he seems bigger now he is dead than when he was alive'. They went through the dead man's pockets and found a letter containing the phrase: "it costs 700 000 livres every month to sustain a civil war in France".

Afterwards Henri III went down to his mother, Catherine de' Medici, and told her joyfully: "I've lost my friend, the king of Paris is dead" — "God grant", his mother replied, "that you have not become king of nothing at all"; according to another version, she remained silent. With a quiet conscience, Henri went to hear mass in thanksgiving in St-Calais' Chapel.

The next day the duke's brother, the Cardinal de Lorraine, who had been imprisoned immediately after the murder, was also assassinated. His body was put with Guise's in a room in the château that cannot now be identified. Later they were burned and the ashes were thrown into the Loire. The queen mother did not long survive the drama but died about twelve days later.

Take the grand staircase down to the first floor and cross the Guard Room.

Chamber of the States General (Salle des États Généraux) (1). — This is the oldest (13C) part of the château, the feudal hall of the old castle of the Counts of Blois. From 1576 to 1588 the States-General, the French Parliament, used to convene in this hall. The twin barrel vaults are supported on a central row of columns.

Go out into the courtyard.

Archaeological Museum. — *Ground floor of François I Wing on the right of the grand staircase.* There is an **audio-visual presentation** on the château and a small archaeological museum displaying the Gallo-Roman remains discovered during recent excavations in Blois.

Robert-Houdin Gallery. — *Ground floor of François I Wing (entrance from the Archaeological Museum).*
The gallery is devoted to the famous local conjurer (1805-71), who was also scholar, writer and clockmaker. He invented electric clocks including the master clock (Horloge-mère - 1850) which was exhibited with the Mysterious Clock (Pendule mystérieuse - 1839), a fine piece with three main elements — moving hands, a dial and a glass column (a clock of this type can be seen at Cheverny Château).

★ **Fine Arts Museum.** — *First floor in Louis XII Wing.*
The main interest lies in the 16 and 17C paintings and portraits which are well hung: portraits of Marie de' Medici as the personification of France by Rubens, Gaston of Orléans, Anne of Austria and Louis XIV, as well as 17C Dutch and Flemish paintings. The chimney-pieces are marked with the arms of Louis XII and Anne of Brittany.

Façade des Loges and Gaston of Orléans Façade. — These two façades can best be seen at the beginning of the walk through Old Blois which is described below.

OLD BLOIS *time: 2 hours — route shown on plan on p 68*

★ **Anne of Brittany Pavilion** (Z B). — This graceful little building of stone and brick is now the Tourist Centre. Note the cable mouldings which emphasize the corners, and the openwork sculptured stone balustrade with the initials of Louis XII and Anne of Brittany, his wife. Originally the Pavilion was in the middle of the château gardens (the Avenue Jean-Laigret was later opened up) and the royal couple often went to say novenas in the small oratory, in order to have a son.

On the right along the Avenue Jean-Laigret, the Pavilion extends into a long half-timbered wing, also built under Louis XII and which was later used as an **orangery**.

Walk along the Place Victor-Hugo, which is lined on the north by the façade of the **Church of St-Vincent** (Z D) (17C) built in the style known as Jesuit, and on the south by the beautiful Façade des Loges of the château.

King's Garden (Jardin du Roi). — This small terraced garden, overlooking the Place Victor-Hugo, is all that remains of the vast château gardens, formerly directly accessible from the François I wing by a footbridge over the moat, and extending as far as the railway station. From near the balustrade there is an excellent **view**★ to the left over the high slate roof topping the Anne of Brittany Pavilion which was built in these gardens, as was the neighbouring orangery, and to the right over the Church of St-Vincent and the Place Victor-Hugo; in the background is the massive square silhouette of the Beauvoir tower, and to its right is the cathedral steeple; on the right runs the beautiful Façade des Loges or the François I Wing of the château, which the return angle of the Gaston d'Orléans wing is backed on to.

Façade des Loges. — The interior part of François I's first construction backed on to the feudal wall and had no outside view. This troubled the King and so he decided to add on against the outside of the ramparts a second building which would have a great many apertures. Since from here it is a sheer drop into the gully, the building had to be supported on a stone foundation.

The two storeys of *loges* and the upper gallery of this façade make it very different from other parts of the building. It somewhat resembles certain Italian palaces. But here again, the asymmetry of the windows, watchtowers, balconies, pilasters and the foundations, is very typically French.

There is an impressive row of gargoyles above the top floor of the *loges*.

Returning to Place des Lices, one can take in at a glance the majestic **Gaston of Orléans Façade** which overlooks the moat, its Classical style no longer comparing unfavourably with the gay and lively Renaissance façades.

BLOIS

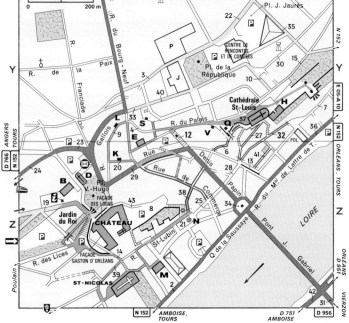

★ **St-Nicolas** (**Z**). – A beautiful building of the 12 and 13C, extremely homogeneous, the church was formerly part of the Benedictine Abbey of St-Laumer whose sober monastic buildings, in Classical style, extend to the Loire. Note the Benedictine plan (large chancel surrounded by an ambulatory and radiating chapels) and also the lovely historiated capitals in the chancel. To the left is a 15C altarpiece.

Jacobin Convent (**Z M**). – *Rue Anne-de-Bretagne.* The convent, which dates from 15C and 16C, houses a **Museum of Religious Art** *(first floor)* and a **Museum of Natural History** *(second floor);* both have fine exhibits well presented.

Louis XII Fountain (**Z N**). – This is a copy of the monument which was erected by Louis XII in the Flamboyant Gothic style; the original, which is badly damaged, is kept in the château.

Hôtel de la Chancellerie (**Z K**). – This late 16C mansion is one of the biggest in Blois. Behind the 17C carriage entrance note at the back of the courtyard the superb staircase with straight banisters.

Hôtel de Guise (**Y L**). – *At no 18 Rue Chemonton.* Renaissance building with windows surrounded by pilasters; the façade is decorated with a wide frieze of medallions.

★ **Hôtel d'Alluye** (**YZ E**). – *At no 8 Rue St-Honoré.* A fine private mansion built in 1508 for **Florimond Robertet**, Treasurer successively of Charles VIII, Louis XII and François I. When accompanying Charles VIII on his expedition to Naples, the financier took a liking to Italian art. Behind the façade of the mansion with its delicate Gothic Renaissance sculptures, a large **courtyard** opens up with pure Renaissance Italianate galleries. The building now houses the head office of a group of insurance companies founded in 1820.

Beauvoir Tower (**Y S**). – This ancient square keep (12C) of a fief was originally separated from that of the château, then redeemed in the 13C. Later the tower was integrated into the town's fortifications.
Old half-timbered façades line Rue Beauvoir (nos 5, 15 and 21), surrounding a 15C stone house (no 19).

Denis-Papin Steps (**ZY 12**). – At the top of the steps a long view suddenly opens up towards the south. Dominating the view is the statue of **Denis Papin**, recognized as the father of the steam machine. Born in Chitenay (12 km - 7 1/2 miles south of Blois) in 1647, he was forced into exile by the Revocation of the Edict of Nantes and published his memorandum on "How to soften bones and cook meat quickly and cheaply" in England; his "digester" known as Papin's cooking pot, thus became the forerunner of today's pressure cooker. In Germany under the patronage of the Landgrave of Hesse Papin discovered "a new way of raising water by the use of fire"; in 1706 in Kassel he carried out public tests demonstrating the motive power of steam. After the death of his patron, he died in poverty in 1714.

Maison des Acrobates (Y V). – *At no 3 Place St-Louis.*
This is a typical medieval house, with its half-timbered façade, its two corbelled storeys, and posts carved with acrobats, jugglers, etc.

St-Louis' Cathedral. – Built in the 16C and flanked by a high Renaissance tower with a lantern, the cathedral was almost entirely destroyed in 1678 by a hurricane. Thanks to the intervention of Colbert, whose wife was a native of Blois, it was rapidly reconstructed in the Gothic style. In the nave, above the large arches, one can still see the projecting stones which were to be sculptured like those in the bays of the chancel. The base of the tower (12C) is part of the original collegiate church built by St Solenne, bishop of Chartres in 5C, who taught Clovis his catechism and assisted at his baptism by St Remy.
The **crypt** *(entrance on the right of the chancel)* dates from 10C and was enlarged in 11C to accommodate the crowds of pilgrims; it was the largest of its day and contained the tomb of St Comblée.

Town Hall and gardens of the Bishop's palace (Y H). – *Access by the gate to the left of the cathedral.* Situated behind the cathedral, the town hall is in the former bishop's palace, built at the beginning of the 18C by Jacques-Jules Gabriel, father of the architect of Place de la Concorde in Paris.
Further towards the east, the gardens of the bishop's palace form a terrace overlooking the Loire, with a lovely **view★** (stand near the statue of Joan of Arc) over the river, its wooded slopes and the roofs of the town; to the south is the pinnacle of the Church of St-Saturnin, and to the right on the north bank, the pure spires of the Church of St-Nicolas. Lovely view also of the cathedral chevet.

Denis-Papin House (Y Q). – Also called Hôtel de Villebresme, this lovely Gothic house at the top of Rue Pierre-de-Blois spans the road with a timber framed footbridge.
At the bottom of Rue Pierre-de-Blois on the left a lovely Renaissance door stands out bearing the Latin inscription *"Usu vetera nova"* which can be translated "through use, the new becomes old" or on the contrary "the old becomes new again".
Go down Rue des Juifs: at no 3 is the 16-17C Hôtel de Condé, with its Classical courtyard. Lower down on the left, bordering a half-timbered house, is the crossroads of Rue des Papegaults (16C houses at nos 4, 10 and 14) and Rue du Puits-Châtel.

Rue du Puits-Châtel (Y 32). – Many interior courtyards are worth a glance through half open entrance doors.
At no 3 there is an outside staircase with a half-timbered balcony (16C); at no 5 the staircase turret is in stone and there are vaulted galleries and sculptured balconies on the landings (early 16C); next door at no 7 the Hôtel Sardini has a courtyard with Renaissance arcades and above the door of the staircase turret is Louis XII's porcupine.

ADDITIONAL SIGHTS

St-Saturnin Cloisters. – *Entrance indicated on the Quai Villebois-Mareuil.*
This former cemetery with timber-roofed galleries, was built under François I. It serves as a lapidary museum, containing fragments of sculptures from the houses of Blois destroyed in 1940.

Our Lady of the Trinity Basilica (N.-D. de la Trinité). – *Northeast of the plan. Take Rue du Prêche.*
This building designed by the architect Paul Rouvière, built between 1937 and 1949, has some fine stained glass and a Stations of the Cross sculptured out of cement by Lambert-Rucki. The 60 m - 200 ft high campanile affords an extensive view of the surrounding countryside *(240 steps)*. The carillon consists of 48 bells, the largest weighing over 5.3 tonnes - 5 tons. It is one of the best in Europe.

Poulain Chocolate Factory (Chocolaterie Poulain). – Auguste Poulain was born in 1825, the son of a modest farmer in the vicinity of Blois. While still very young he went to Paris and became an apprentice in a high-class grocery.
A few years later, he had saved enough to buy a shop in Blois and became a chocolate artisan, then opened his own factory in 1848.
Today Poulain Chocolate Factory produces 33 000 tons of chocolate a year and employs 900 people.

EXCURSIONS

★ **Ménars Château.** – *Description on p 139.*
Maves. – *19 km - 12 miles north by D 924 and D 112.* 15C pivotal windmill.

La BOISSIÈRE

Michelin map 🔢 south of fold 3 or 🔢🔢 fold 22

The name of La Boissière is linked with a precious relic: the Cross of Anjou *(p 58)*. The cross was brought from the Middle East in 13C by a crusader and given to the Cistercians at La Boissière who built a chapel for it. During the Hundred Years War the cross was kept in Angers Château. It returned to La Boissière in about 1456 and remained there until 1790 when it was transferred to Baugé.

La Boissière Abbey. – In 18C the abbey buildings were converted into a château. The 12C abbey church has been reduced to the chancel with an altarpiece and recumbent Gothic figures.

Chapel of the True Cross. – The 13C Gothic chapel *(restored)* stands on the road to Dénezé; the interior comprises three bays of Angevin vaulting.

BONNEVAL

Bonneval grew up in the Middle Ages round St-Florentin's monastery, a Benedictine abbey founded in 9C. The charming little town on the left bank of the Loir has retained some picturesque traces of the past: the old town walls reflected in the waters of the surrounding moat.

Former Abbey. — A specialist hospital, the Henri Ey psychiatric centre, now occupies the old abbey buildings. The beautiful 13C **fortified gateway★** with its pointed archway was integrated into the abbot's lodging, which was built by René d'Illiers, bishop of Chartres in the late 15C; it is an attractive building of chequered stonework, flanked by two machicolated towers and capped with pinnacled gables over the dormer windows. In front of the abbey stretches the **Grève,** a large shaded square beside the moat. For an attractive view of the old towers and the church spire reflected in the water of the moat go to the end of Rue des Fossés-St-Jacques to the west of the town.

Notre-Dame Church. — The early 13C church was built in the pure Gothic style; fine rose window above the flat chevet, woodwork and 17C statues.
From the nearby bridge, Rue de la Résistance, there is a picturesque view of the old town walls and the washing places at the water's edge.

St-Roch Gate and King's Tower (Porte St-Roch and Tour du Roi). — Several pointed arches mark the old houses which line the street, Rue St-Roch, which leads to St-Roch Gate with its two round towers. Beside it stands the King's Tower, the old keep, pierced by loopholes and capped with a pepperpot roof. This part of the town wall was built in 15C when the Mall Moat (Fossés du Mail) was dug to cut the town in two since the length of the walls made it difficult to defend.

Boisville Gate and Mill Bridge (Porte Boisville et pont du Moulin). — To the west of the town, between the railway and the by-pass, stands the Boisville Gate (13C), the only remaining part of the first town walls, which was reduced in 15C to less gigantic proportions.

EXCURSION

Alluyes. — Pop 626. *7 km - 5 miles northwest.*
Formerly one of the five baronies of Le Perche-Gouët *(p 152)*, Alluyes at the end of 15C belonged to Florimond Robertet *(p 68)*. All that is left of the old **castle** is the great round tower of the old keep and a fortified gate across the moat.
On the left bank of the river stands the **church** (15-16C); the south side presents a succession of pointed gables corresponding to the bays of the south aisle — a common architectural feature in this region. On the left wall of the nave are two Gothic murals depicting St Christopher and the Legend of the Three Living and the Three Dead *(p 39)*. On the left of the nave is a 16C Virgin bearing a representation of the Trinity on her breast and the arms of Florimond Robertet at her feet.

★ BOUMOIS Château

Boumois Château is hidden among the trees some 300 m - 330 yards from the D 952; the apparently feudal exterior of the 16C château conceals a graceful residence in the Flamboyant and Renaissance styles.
The drive leads to the main entrance; on the left stands a dovecot. A massive gate leads into the main courtyard which is protected by a fortified wall, formerly reinforced by a moat.
The house itself, which is late 15C, is flanked by two huge machicolated towers. The entrance to the stair turret in the inner courtyard is closed by an extraordinary wrought iron lock with detailed Renaissance motifs.
The tour passes through the great hall on the first floor (large collection of weapons, mainly 15 and 16C), a room with a wooden ceiling on the second floor, the parapet walk and the beautiful Flamboyant chapel with a pointed roof containing a marble effigy of Marguerite de Savoie and a Virgin by Salviati.

(after photo Karquel)

Boumois Château

The 17C dovecot is still equipped with its revolving ladder and 1800 nesting boxes. Aristide Dupetit-Thouars was born in Boumois in 1760; he died gloriously on the quarterdeck of his ship, the Tonnant, in the Battle of Aboukir in 1798 rather than haul down his flag.

---

*The **Maps**, **Red Guides** and **Green Guides** are complementary publications. Use them together.*

★ La BOURGONNIÈRE Chapel

Michelin map 📖 fold 18 or 📖 fold 29, 30 (9km - 6 miles southeast of Ancenis) — Local map p 126

South of D 751, between Bouzillé and Le Marillais, is the modest entrance to La Bourgonnière.

★ St-Saviour's Chapel. — Towers, turrets and buttresses adorn the chapel which is decorated with shells, the initials LC and tau-crosses (T) — all symbols of the Antonians, properly known as the Hospital Brothers of St Antony. The order was protected by Charles du Plessis and Louise de Montfaucon who had the sanctuary built between 1508 and 1523. The Antonians nursed people afflicted with ergotism, a violent fever, also known as St Antony's Fire since St Antony was invoked to relieve the suffering.

The beautiful doorway is surmounted by a lintel carved with foliage and horns of plenty. The door panels are marked with tau-crosses.

The star vaulting above the nave is ornamented with coats of arms and pendants. The oratory (right) contains a rare feudal bench decorated with 16C Italianate grotesques. Above the high altar is a remarkable statue of the Virgin, attributed to Michel Colombe, between St Sebastian and St Antony the Hermit.

The **altarpiece ★** (left), decorated with foliated scrolls and cherubs, as well as the central altarpiece, is probably the work of an Italian artist. There is a remarkable Christ in Majesty, clothed in a long tunic, crowned and nailed to a cross, against a painted background depicting the Angels bearing the instruments of the Passion, and Charlemagne and St Louis, the patrons of the donors.

BOURGUEIL   Pop 4 185

Michelin map 📖 fold 13 or 📖 fold 34 — Local map p 127

Bourgueil is well situated in a fertile region between the Loire and the Authion at the eastern end of the Anjou Valley where the hillsides are carpeted with vines. Ronsard was a frequent visitor and it was there that he met the "Marie" of his love songs. Nowadays the little town's renown derives from the full bodied red wines produced by the ancient Breton vines found only in that area. Rabelais mentions it in his works. A Wine Fair is held on the 1st Saturday in February.

Parish Church. — Illuminated by lancet windows, the large Gothic chancel is divided into three and covered with Angevin vaulting of equal height. Its width contrasts with the narrow and simple 11C Romanesque nave.

Halles. — Opposite the church backing on to the former Town Hall is the elegant marketplace with stone arcades where the Wine Fair is held during Easter weekend.

Abbey. — *East of the town on the road to Restigné.*

The abbey was founded at the end of 10C by the Benedictines and was one of the richest in Anjou. Its vineyards stretched over the entire hillside and its woods reached down to the Loire. In 13 and 14C it was fortified and surrounded by a moat. The elegant building by the roadside containing the **cellar** and **granary** dates from the same period; the gable is flanked by two turrets surmounted by an octagonal stone spire. The wine cellars were on the ground floor and the abbey's grain was stored on the floor above.

The tour includes the building constructed in 1739: 18C panelling in the dining room; wrought iron banisters; huge vaulted hall. The **museum** (first floor) displays a collection of costumes, bonnets and tools (early 20C).

Blue Windmill (Moulin bleu). — *2 km - 1 1/4 miles north.*

The windmill, which is built over a cellar, is of a similar type to the one at La Herpinière near Turquant *(p 145)*; the cap is mounted on a conical structure supported on a stone vault so that the cap can pivot to bring the sails into the wind. The miller manœuvres the cap by means of the tail or ladder which also serves as a counterweight to the sails, The sails have been restored according to a 15C model.

The tannin obtained from grinding the bark of the chestnut tree was used in the tanneries in Bourgueil.

There is a fine **view** down on to the vineyards of Bourgueil and south to the Loire Valley.

Cave touristique de la Dive Bouteille. — The cool chamber, hollowed out of the rock, contains a collection of old presses — one is 16C — and of photographs of the vineyard. Wine tasting.

EXCURSIONS

Restigné. — Pop 1 210. *5 km - 3 miles east by D 35.*
The wine-growing village lies just off the main road clustered round the **church.** The façade is decorated with a diaper pattern and the lintel of the south doorway is carved with fantastic beasts and Daniel in the lion's den. The Angevin Gothic chancel ending in a flat chevet, is similar to the one in Bourgueil; the key stones in the high vaults are decorated. The 11C nave is roofed with 15C timberwork; the beams are decorated with the heads of monsters.

Les Réaux. — *4 km - 2 1/2 miles south by D 749 and first right turning after the railway.*
In 17C the **château,** which dates from the late 15C, belonged to Tallement des Réaux, who wrote a chronicle, *Historiettes,* of early 17C French society. The charming château is surrounded by a moat and the entrance pavilion is flanked by two machicolated towers; the defensive features have however been subordinated to the decorative: chequer-work in brick and stone; gracefully carved ornamentation in the shell-shaped dormer windows, the salamander above the entrance; soldiers for weather vanes, etc.

Chouzé-sur-Loire. – Pop 2 075. *7 km - 4 miles south by D 749 and N 152.*
The attractive village on the north bank of the Loire was once a busy port; the deserted
dockside where the mooring rings are rusting and the **Nautical Museum** recall the past.
The charming 15C **manor house** in Rue de l'Église is where Marie d'Harcourt, wife of
Dunois, the famous bastard of Orléans *(p 78)*, died on 1 September 1464.

Varennes. – Pop 203. *15 km - 9 miles southwest by D 749 and N 152.*
From the old river port on the Loire there is a very attractive **view** of Montsoreau Château
(p 145). The towpath makes a pleasant walk on occasions.

Brain-sur-Allones. – Pop 1 708. *10 km - 6 miles west by D 35 and D 85 to the right.*
Excavations in a 14C house have discovered the medieval site of the Painted Cave (**Cave
Peinte**). Some beautiful faience tiles are displayed in the adjoining **museum**.

BREIL   Pop 303

Michelin map 64 fold 13 or 232 fold 34 (6 km - 3 1/2 miles southeast of Noyant)

The path to Breil through Baugeois Wood makes a pleasant walk.

Church. – The semi-circular apse and the tall stone spire above the nave make the
exterior Romanesque; fine Plantagenet vaulting *(see p 36)* in the chancel.

Le Lathan Château. – Facing the church is the château. The beautiful 17C park invites
admiration: neat hedges, a long green carpet trimmed with clipped yews followed by a
double row of lime trees.
The long water provides a fine perspective ending in the elegant 18C château.

★★ BRISSAC Château

Michelin map 64 fold 11 or 232 fold 32 – Local map p 127

The château is set in a fine park shaded by magnificent **cedar trees★**. The building is
unusual both for its height and for the juxtaposition of two buildings which were not
meant to stand side by side; the later building was supposed to replace the earlier.

The main façade is flanked by two
round towers with conical roofs,
ringed by graceful machicolations, traces of the medieval castle
which was built *c* 1455 by Pierre de
Brézé, minister to Charles VII and
Louis XI. The castle was bought by
René de Cossé in 1502 and severely damaged by the Wars of
Religion. René's grandson, **Charles
de Cossé**, Count of Brissac, was one
of the leaders of the League, the
catholic party which supported
the Guises *(see p 64)* in 16C; in
1594, as Governor of Paris, he
handed the keys of the city to
Henri IV who had just converted to
the Roman church and was
encamped outside the city; in gratitude the king raised him to a
dukedom. The new duke began to
rebuild his house to match his
elevated status; the work ceased
at his death in 1621 and the château was left in its present state.
The main façade between the
medieval towers is incomplete; it
consists of the central pavilion and
the left wing, abundantly ornamented with pilasters and statues
in niches. The right wing, which
would have replaced the Gothic
tower, was never built.

(Photo Hervé Boulé)

Brissac Château – Central Pavilion

TOUR *time : 1 hour*

The 17C French painted **ceilings** are
often embellished with sculptures; the walls are hung with superb tapestries and the
rooms are full of fine furniture. The grand salon is hung with Gobelins **tapestries** (18C) and
the crystal chandeliers are from Venice; the furniture is 18C as in the little salon. The
dining room contains some fine silverware.
The great gallery on the first floor presents the portraits of the Brissac line, including a
portrait of the famous widow Clicquot, a family relative. The stalls in the chapel are
heavily carved in the Italian Renaissance style. Tapestries hang in many of the rooms;
one depicting the story of Judith shows Louis XIII and his mother Marie de' Medici
reconciled... at least temporarily... after the battle of Ponts-de-Cé (1620).
On the second floor there is a delightful 17C-style theatre (restored), built in 1883 by the
Vicomtesse de Tredern, who had a true soprano voice.
North of Brissac on the road to Angers stands a handsome windmill.

BROU

Michelin map 🔲 fold 16 or 🔲 folds 37, 38.
Town plan in the Michelin Red Guide France

Although Brou was once a barony in Le Perche-Gouët, it is more characteristic of the Beauce; it is a market town centred on its market place where poultry and eggs are the main commerce. There are many old street names, unchanged since the Middle Ages.

Market Place (Place des Halles). — On the corner of Rue de la Tête-Noire stands an old house with jutting upper storeys, which dates from the early 16C; the timberwork is decorated with carved motifs.
In Rue des Changes near the market place there is another 16C house with a curved façade; the corner post bears the figures of St James and a pilgrim since Brou is on the route from Chartres to Santiago de Compostela in Spain.

EXCURSIONS

Yèvres. — Pop 1 458. *1.5 km - 1 mile by D 955, the road to Châteaudun.*
The **Church** dates mainly from 15C and 16C. The elegant Renaissance doorway is framed by carved pilasters (instruments of the Passion) and surmounted by a double pediment. The interior contains some remarkable Classical **woodwork★**: the pulpit which is decorated with effigies of the Virtues, the retable on the high altar, the altars in the side chapels and an eagle lectern. The door into the baptismal chapel is beautifully carved with scenes of the martyrdom of St Barbara and the baptism of Christ. There is a fine ceiling of carved wood and the cupboards in which the oil for Holy Unction is kept have been preserved. Behind the churchwardens' pew there is a collection of 18C and 19C vestments. The sacristy contains Louis XIII woodwork and collections of 18C and 19C sacred vessels.

Frazé. — *Description p 105.*

Tour of Le Perche-Gouët. — *Description p 152.*

BUEIL-EN-TOURAINE

Michelin map 🔲 fold 4 or 🔲 fold 23

Set above the valley of the River Long, Beuil-en-Touraine is the cradle of the Bueil family which has supplied France with an admiral, two marshals and a poet, Honorat de Bueil, Marquis de Racan *(see p 157).*
At the top of the hill there is a curious group of buildings formed by the juxtaposition of the Church of St Peter in Captivity (left) and the Collegiate Church of St Michael.

Church of St Peter in Captivity. — The church is built against a large but incomplete square tower; steps lead up to the door. Within there is a remarkable **font** in the Renaissance style: small statues of Christ and the Apostles in the panels. At the end of the nave there are traces of early 16C frescoes and old statues. Door into the collegiate church.

Collegiate Church of the Holy Innocents and St Michael. — The church was built by the Bueil family to contain their tombs. The recumbent figures of the Lords of Bueil and their ladies are laid in the recesses: the first wife (right) of John V of Bueil is wearing a headdress *(hennin)* and an emblazoned surcoat.

★ CANDES-ST-MARTIN

Michelin map 🔲 southwest of fold 13 or 🔲 fold 33 — Local map p 127

The village of Candes stands on the south bank of the Vienne at its confluence with the Loire; the church was built on the spot where St Martin died in 397 *(see p 176).*

★ Church. — The building was erected in the 12C and 13C and provided with defences in the 15C. The roadside façade is remarkable for its combination of military architecture and rich decoration. The vault of the porch is supported by a central pillar on to which the ribs fall in a cluster. The doorway is framed by sculptures (damaged).
Within, the nave is buttressed by aisles of the same height. The Angevin vaulting *(see p 36)* rests on soaring piers; the whole structure gives an impression of lightness. The nave was built at an angle to the older chancel.
On leaving the church look up at the west façade which is also fortified.
A narrow path on the right of the church leads to the top of the slope *(1/4 hour on foot Rtn)*; fine **view** of the rivers meeting.
Another walk via Rue St-Martin, below the church, and then Rue du Bas ends by a plaque showing the distances between the various ports on the Loire, recalling how much the river was used for transporting goods in former days.

Each year
*the **Michelin Guide France***
presents a multitude of up-to-date facts in a compact form.

Whether on a business trip, a weekend away from it all
or on holiday take the guide with you.

Chambord, which covers an area of 21,829 sq yards, is the largest of the Loire country châteaux. Its scale foreshadows Versailles. Its sudden appearance at the end of an avenue and the sight of its white mass gradually widening and becoming clearer in detail, make a deep impression, even more striking at sunset. To this must be added the fine structural unity of the building, the rich decoration it owes to the Renaissance, then at its height, and finally two marvellous features: the great staircase and the roof terrace.

(Photo Serge Chirol)

Chambord Château

HISTORICAL NOTES

Grandiose creation of François I (16C). – The Counts of Blois had built a small castle in this lonely corner of the Forest of Boulogne, which was excellent hunting country only four leagues from their capital. As a young man François I liked to hunt in the forest and in 1518 he ordered the old castle to be razed to the ground to make room for a sumptuous palace.

Several designs were proposed and no doubt Leonardo da Vinci, the King's guest at Le Clos-Lucé *(p 46)*, drew a plan which was made into a model by Il Boccadoro. In 1519 the surveyor, François de Pontbriant, who had worked at Loches and Amboise, took charge of the project. As the work progressed, the original plans were altered and large sums of money were swallowed up but the king did not stint. Even when the Treasury was empty and there was no money to pay the ransom for his two sons in Spain, when he was reduced to raiding the treasuries of the churches or to melting down his subjects' silver, the work went on. It suffered only one interruption, from 1524 to 1525 when the King was a prisoner after the Battle of Pavia. In his enthusiasm the King even proposed in 1527 to re-direct the course of the Loire so that it should flow in front of the château but the task would have been enormous and a smaller and closer river, the Cosson, was diverted instead.

By 1537 the major work was completed – the towers and body of the keep, the terraces; over 1800 men had been employed under the direction of Sourdeau and Trinqueau, master masons. Only the interior decoration was lacking. In 1538 the King decided to build a pavilion linked to the keep by a two storey building and a second symmetrical wing was added to the west side. In 1545 the royal pavilion was finished but François I, who till then had lived in the northeast tower, had little time to enjoy it as he died two years later. Henri II continued his father's work by building the west wing and the chapel tower while the curtain wall was completed. At his death in 1559 the château was still unfinished.

The château is a jewel of the Renaissance, the result of the "veritable mathematisation of architecture" (Jean Jacquart); it has 440 rooms, 365 windows, 13 main stairs and 70 backstairs.

Royal visits. – In 1539 the King was able to receive **Charles V** at Chambord. A group of young women dressed as Greek divinities went to meet the Emperor and strewed flowers at his feet. The visitor, charmed by this reception and amazed by the mansion, said to his host: "Chambord is a summary of human industry".

Henri II continued the building. It was at Chambord, in 1552, that the treaty with three German princes was signed, bringing the three bishoprics of Metz, Toul and Verdun to the French crown; it was ratified in 1648 by the Treaty of Westphalia. François II and Charles IX often came to hunt in the forest. Henri III and Henri IV hardly appeared at Chambord, but Louis XIII renewed the link.

The sport of kings. – The domain was rich in game and lent itself to hawking. At one time there were more than three hundred falcons. The royal packs received every attention and for breeding purposes, the best dogs were brought from the four corners of Europe to improve the strain. Hunting was the favourite medieval sport and princes were brought up to it from their earliest days. Louis XII took 5 m – 16 ft ditches in his stride. Despite his delicate constitution Charles IX used to hunt for as long as ten hours at a stretch, tiring in the process five horses and often spitting blood such were his exertions. He it was who accomplished the feat of stalking a stag without the help of the hounds.

La Grande Mademoiselle (17C). – Chambord was part of the county of Blois which Louis XIII granted to his brother, Gaston of Orléans *(p 64)*. One can be both a conspirator and a good father: Gaston's daughter, "La Grande Mademoiselle", relates that her favourite game as a child was to make her father go up and down one of the double spiral staircases while she passed him in the opposite direction, without ever meeting him.
Later, it was at Chambord that she declared her love to the Duke of Lauzun. She led him to a looking glass, breathed on it and traced the name of the irresistible charmer with her finger.

Louis XIV and Molière. – Under Louis XIV the property reverted to the crown. The King stayed at Chambord nine times between 1660 and 1685 and had considerable restoration work done.
Molière wrote *Monsieur de Pourceaugnac* at Chambord in a matter of a few days. At the first performance the King never smiled. Lully, who had written the music and was playing the role of apothecary, had an inspiration: he jumped feet first from the stage on the harpsichord and fell through it. The King burst out laughing and the play was saved.
Le Bourgeois Gentilhomme caused Molière renewed anguish. The King was icy at the first performance. The courtiers who were made fun of in the play were ready to be sarcastic. But after the second performance the King expressed his pleasure and the whole court changed their criticisms into compliments.

Maréchal de Saxe (18C). – Louis XV put the château at the disposal of his father-in-law, Stanislas Leszczynski, the deposed King of Poland. Then he presented the domain, with 40 000 livres revenue, to the Maréchal de Saxe as a reward for his victory at Fontenoy. Was this a coincidence or a piece of mischief by the son-in-law? Maurice de Saxe was the natural son of Auguste of Poland, the lucky rival of Stanislas and the man who drove him from the throne.
The luxury loving, proud and violent Marshal filled the château with life and excitement. To satisfy his taste for arms he found quarters there for two regiments of cavalry composed of Tartars, Wallachians and even Negroes, whom he brought from Martinique. These strange troops rode fiery horses from the Ukraine which were trained to assemble at the sound of a trumpet. The Marshal imposed iron discipline. For the least fault he hanged the culprits from the branches of an old elm. More by terror than by courtship Maurice de Saxe won the favours of a well known actress, Mme Favart, and compelled her to remain at Chambord. He re-erected Molière's stage for her amusement. Monsieur Favart played the triple role of director, author and consenting husband.
The Marshal died at fifty-four, killed, some said, in a duel by the Prince de Conti whose wife he had seduced. Others ascribed his death to a neglected chill. Vainglorious even in death, Maurice de Saxe had given orders that the six cannon he had placed in the main courtyard of the château should be fired every quarter of an hour for sixteen days as a sign of mourning.

From the Revolution to the Restoration. – After the Marshal's death the château was neglected and gradually fell into disrepair. What furniture was left was destroyed during the Revolution.
In 1809 Napoleon gave Chambord as an entailed estate to Marshal Berthier. Berthier sold the timber and left the estate unoccupied. After his death the Princess was authorized to sell it.
It was brought by public subscription in 1821 for the Duc de Bordeaux, heir to the throne and posthumous son of the Duc de Berry who had just been assassinated. Paul-Louis Courier *(p 30)* wrote such a trenchant pamphlet against the subscription that he was sentenced to two months in prison. He was so passionate in his politics that he even proposed that Chambord should be demolished.

The Affair of the White Flag (1871-73). – In 1871 Henri, Count of Chambord and, since the fall of Charles X in 1830, legitimate heir to the French throne, was close to achieving his purpose; it was in 1871, following the disruption of the war that the French elected a monarchist assembly in favour of the restoration of the monarchy.
The monarchists were, however, divided into two groups; the legitimists who supported the traditional monarchy and the Orléanists, more modern in their outlook, who upheld the principles of 1789. Eventually both parties agreed on the name of the heir: **Henri V**, the last of the Bourbon line. As he had always lived in exile for forty years, he was not aware of the realities of French politics when he returned to his native soil. He went to live at Chambord where on 5 July 1871 he proclaimed his convictions in a manifesto which ended with these words: "Henri V will not abandon the white flag of Henri IV".
The effect of this declaration on public opinion was a disaster: the royalists lost the partial elections. The Count of Chambord stubbornly refused to reconsider the matter and returned to Austria. Two years later in October 1873 a final attempt to compromise – a tricolour flag dotted with fleurs de lys – failed. The National Assembly accepted the situation and voted for the Republic. Henri did not succeed to the throne and died in 1883. Chambord Château, which had witnessed the final hours of the monarchy, passed to his nephew, the Duke of Parma. In 1932 his descendants sold it to the State for about 11 million francs.

⊙**TOUR**   *time: 1 1/2 hours*

★ **Son et Lumière.** − *See Practical Information at the end of the guide.*

Visitors enter through the Royal Gate (Porte Royale). It is advisable to obtain a plan of the château.

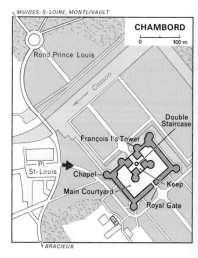

Although the ground plan of Chambord is feudal − a central **keep** with four towers, which is in itself a veritable castle, set in an enclosed precinct − the architecture is Renaissance and evokes no hint of war. The château is a royal palace built for pleasure. During the construction two wings were added, one containing the royal apartments and the other the chapel; the northwest façade is particularly impressive.

Chambord is the personal creation of François I. The name of the architect has not been recorded but the architecture seems to have been inspired by the spirit of Leonardo da Vinci who had been staying at the French court and died in the spring of 1519 when work on the château began. François I never saw the château finished; it was Henri II who raised the second storey of the chapel and Louis XIV who completed the building.

Main Courtyard. − From the entrance there is a fine view of the keep linked to the corner towers by two arcades surmounted by galleries. The two external spiral stairs in the north corners of the courtyard were added at the end of François I's reign.

Double Staircase. − The famous double staircase stands at the intersection of the cross formed by the four guard rooms. The two flights of steps spiral round one another from the ground floor to the roof terrace. The stonework at the centre and round the outside is pierced by many openings so that one can see from one flight across to the other and admire the splendid vaulting adorned with salamanders in the rooms which form a cross on the second floor. The pillars and capitals are beautifully decorated in the style of the early French Renaissance.

State Rooms. − The rooms on the ground floor and on the first floor have been restored and refurbished to evoke memories of the King and the many visitors to Chambord.

Ground floor: the Sun Room (Salle des Soleils) is named after the sunbursts decorating the shutters; the painting by Baron François Gérard shows the Recognition of the Duke of Anjou as King of Spain while the Brussels tapestry portrays the Call of Abraham. François I's Hunting Room is hung with a series of late 16C tapestries after cartoons by Laurent Guyot.

First floor: François I had his rooms in the north tower of the precinct wall; the chapel was symmetrically placed in the west tower. In the King's bedchamber the bed spread and hangings are of gold embroidered velvet (16C Italian); it was on one of the window panes that the King is supposed to have engraved a melancholy couplet: *Souvent femme varie, bien fol est qui s'y fie* (Woman often changes, he who trusts her is a fool). In François I's dressing room the salamander, the King's emblem, and the letter F alternate in the coffers of the barrel-vaulted ceiling; the room was used as an oratory by Queen Catherine Opalinska, wife of Stanislas Leszczynski. The Queen's Room in the François I Tower at the north corner of the keep, is hung with Paris tapestries relating the History of Constantine, after cartoons by Rubens.

The King's suite, which follows, is decorated with tapestries and historic portraits; the rooms in the centre of the northwest façade of the keep were furnished by Louis XIV. The Royal or State Bedchamber, which was used successively by Louis XIV, Stanislas Leszczynski and Marshal Saxe, was panelled in the Regency style in 1748 for the Marshal; the next room at the exact centre of the building has a remarkable view of the park. Marshal Saxe left his mark in the King's Guard Room in the form of a huge porcelain stove. The Dauphin's Suite in the East Tower, contains many mementoes of the Count of Chambord: paintings, the state bed presented by his supporters, statues of Henri IV and the Duke of Bordeaux, the first and last Counts of Chambord, as children, and a collection of miniature artillery given to the young Prince for his amusement and instruction; the cannon fired shot which could pierce a wall. Also on display is his third manifesto dated 5 July 1871 in which he declared "Henri V will not abandon the white flag of Henri IV".

Second floor: the rooms are devoted to hunting: weapons, trophies and other related items; among the tapestries there is the Story of Meleager after cartoons by Lebrun (F. Sommer Room) and the Story of Diana after cartoons by Toussaint Dubreuil (Diana Room).

Roof Terrace. − The terrace, a direct inspiration from Italy, is unique: a maze of lanterns, chimneys, stairs and dormer windows, all intricately carved and curiously decorated with a sort of mosaic of inset slates cut in various shapes − lozenges, circles and squares − in imitation of Italian marble. The stair continues above the terrace in a single spiral enclosed in a magnificent lantern 32 m - 105 ft high.

It was here that the court spent most of its time watching the start and return of the hunts, military reviews and exercises, tournaments and festivals. The thousands of nooks and crannies of the terrace invited the confidences, intrigues and assignations which played a great part in the life of that brilliant society. One of the terrace pavilions contains a permanent **exhibition** of 61 tableaux explaining the history of the château.

Park. — Since 1948 the park has been a national hunt reserve covering 5500 ha - 13591 acres of which 4500 ha - 11120 acres are forest; it is enclosed by a wall, the longest in France, 32 km - 20 miles long and pierced by six gates at the end of six beautiful rides. Walkers are admitted to a restricted area (520 ha - 250 acres) on the west side. Four observation hides have been built so that people can watch the herds of deer and sounders of wild boar browsing for food (before sunrise and after sunset).

★ CHAMPIGNY-SUR-VEUDE   Pop 950

Michelin map 🔢 fold 10 or 🔢🔢🔢 south of fold 34 (6 km - 4 miles north of Richelieu)

Champigny lies in the green Valley of the Veude and still has some 16C houses (Rue des Cloîtres and Route d'Assay). The most interesting sight, however, is the chapel, with its fine Renaissance windows, of the now vanished château.

★ **Sainte-Chapelle.** — The chapel, which is a remarkable example of Renaissance art at its height, was part of a castle built from 1508 to 1543 by Louis I and Louis II de Bourbon-Montpensier. The castle itself was later demolished on the orders of Cardinal Richelieu who felt that its magnificence outshone his nearby Château de Richelieu. Only outbuildings remain but even these give some idea of the size and splendour of the château that was pulled down. The Sainte-Chapelle, which owed its name to the portion of the True Cross which was kept there, was saved by the intervention of Pope Urban VIII.

Louis I of Bourbon, who had accompanied Charles VIII to Naples, wanted the chapel to be in the transitional Gothic-Renaissance style.

The peristyle, which was built later, is decidedly Italian in character: the detailed sculptured ornament is based on the insignia of Louis II of Bourbon and includes crowned and plain Ls, lances, pilgrims' staffs, flowers, fruit, etc. The porch has a coffered ceiling.

A fine wooden door dating from the 16C, carved with panels depicting the Cardinal Virtues, leads to the nave which has ogive vaulting with liernes and tiercerons. There also the visitor will see at prayer the figure of Henri de Bourbon, last Duke of Montpensier, carved by Simon Guillain at the beginning of the 17C.

★★ **Stained glass windows.** — Installed in the middle of the 16C, these windows are the chapel's most precious jewel. The windows all together form a remarkable example of Renaissance glasswork.

The subjects portrayed are: at the bottom — thirty-four portraits of the Bourbon-Montpensier House from the time of St Louis; above, the principal events in the life of St Louis; at the top — scenes from the Passion. The window in the centre of the chevet shows a moving representation of the Crucifixion. The vividness and delicate combination of colours throughout should be noticed, particularly the purplish blues with their bronze highlights which are beyond compare.

★ CHANTELOUP Pagoda

Map 🔢 fold 16 or 🔢🔢🔢 fold 14 (3 km - 2 miles south of Amboise) — Local map p 122

The pagoda stands on the edge of Amboise Forest, all that remains of the splendid château built by the **Duke of Choiseul**, one of Louis XV's ministers, in imitation of Versailles. It was later abandoned and demolished in 1823 by estate agents.

When Choiseul was exiled to his estates to please Madame du Barry, he turned Chanteloup into an intellectual and artistic centre. He commissioned the pagoda (1775-78) from the architect, Le Camus, as a memorial to his friends' loyalty. This unusual building looks somewhat out of place on the banks of the Loire but it shows how popular such "chinoiserie" was in 18C.

The **setting** ★ of the pagoda evokes the sumptuous surroundings of Choiseul's exile; there is a plan of the whole structure on the first floor of the building. The large fan-shaped pool, now over-grown, and the traces of the alleys in the park, which can be discerned from the balconies of the pagoda, help to resurrect the original design.

The pagoda is 44 m - 144 ft high and consists of seven storeys, each smaller than the one below.

From the top (149 steps) there is a fine **panorama** of the Loire Valley as far as Tours and of the Amboise Forest.

(after photo Yvonne Sauvageot)

Chanteloup Pagoda

77

CHÂTEAU-DU-LOIR   Pop 5891

Michelin map 🔟 fold 4 or 🔢 fold 23 – Local map p 120

The modern town has spread along the narrow valley of the River Yre but the old houses are clustered on the hill round the church.

St-Guingalois' Church. – In the chancel stands a huge terracotta *Pietà* by Barthélemy de Mello (17C): the Virgin's face is most expressive; the St Martin on horseback in the right aisle is by the same artist. In the left transept are two painted wooden panels by the Flemish Mannerist school depicting the Nativity (15C) and the Resurrection (late 15C). In the Romanesque crypt is a fine Christ Reviled in wood (16C).

Keep. – In the public gardens near the Town Hall stand the keep, all the remains of the medieval castle which gave the town its name. Beneath the keep were dungeons where many prisoners were kept temporarily on their way to the penal colony in Cayenne from the ports at Nantes or La Rochelle.

Plan your own itinerary by looking at the map of the principal sights (pp 4-6).

★★ CHÂTEAUDUN   Pop 16094

Michelin map 🔟 fold 17 or 🔢 fold 38 – Local map p 118 – Facilities

Châteaudun and its castle stand on a bluff, indented by narrow valleys called *cavées,* on the south bank of the Loir at the point where the Perche region joins the Beauce.

Fairs and Markets. – In 18 and 19C Châteaudun was an important centre for the grain trade. The farmers came in from the Beauce with samples of their harvest which was sold and delivered to the grain merchants; they then sold it on to the millers, cattle farmers and horse dealers.

On Thursdays the main square was a picturesque sight thronged with people conducting their business. Among the blue shirts, goffered bonnets, light carts and sheepdogs, move the porters, wearing the plaque, the sign of their function, which they have paid for in gold. Traders and farmers feast at the "Good Labourer" (Bon Laboureur) in Rue Gambetta where Zola went to observe them when he was writing his novel *The Earth* and tasted the local Beauce cheese accompanied by the traditional draught of beer.

The poppies of the Beauce are crushed in the presses to yield poppy seed oil. The sheep of the Beauce provide wool for the textile industry which is recalled in certain street names: Rue des Filoirs and Rue des Fouleries.

HISTORICAL NOTES

In 10C Châteaudun was seized by Thibaut the Trickster and so passed into the hands of the Counts of Blois. In 1392 the last of the Counts sold the counties of Blois and Dunois to Louis of Orléans, Charles VI's brother; Châteaudun passed by succession to Charles of Orléans, the poet, who offered it to his half-brother John, the Bastard of Orléans, whose descendants, the Orléans-Longueville family, owned Châteaudun until the end of 17C.

Birth of the Alexandrine. – It was at Châteaudun in 12C that the poet Lambert Licors was born. He was one of the authors of the Story of Alexander, a heroic poem inspired by the legend of Alexander the Great which was very popular in the Middle Ages. Its 22 000 lines were written in the heroic metre, with 12 feet to the line, which subsequently came to be known as the Alexandrine metre.

Dunois, the Bastard of Orléans (1402-56). – Handsome Dunois, the faithful companion of Joan of Arc, was the bastard son of Louis of Orléans and Mariette d'Enghien. He was brought up by Valentine Visconti, Louis of Orléans' wife, who loved him as much as her own children. From the age of 15 Dunois fought the English for several decades. In 1429 he rallied the army to the defence of Orléans and delivered Montargis. He took part in all the great events of Joan of Arc's career: Jargeau, Beaugency, Reims, Paris, etc. At the end of his life, crowned with honours, he founded the Sainte-Chapelle and in 1457 retired to Châteaudun where he received the poet François Villon.

Dunois was buried in the church of Notre-Dame de Cléry *(p 95)*. He was well educated and well read and Jean Cartier, the chronicler described him as "one of the best speakers of the French language".

A Financier. – Dodun, a native of the county of Dunois, started out with nothing and became Financial Controller under the Regency. In 1724 his portrait was painted by Rigaud; in 1727 Bullet built him a magnificent mansion in Rue de Richelieu in Paris; the château and the marquisate of Herbault came into his possession.

Dodun made up for his ill-gotten gains by acting with great generosity when Châteaudun burned down in 1723. His appeal to the King's Council produced funds for the reconstruction of the town and the work was directed by Jules Hardouin, nephew of Jules Hardouin-Mansart; he was responsible for the part of the town which is laid out on the grid system.

A Heroic Defence. – On 18 October 1870 the Prussians attacked Châteaudun with 24 cannon and 12000 men. Confronting them were only 300 national guards from the county of Dunois and 600 free fighters; although they held out all day behind their barricades, despite a heavy bombardement from midday to half past six, they were outnumbered and had to retreat. The Germans set fire to the town and 263 houses were destroyed. In recognition for services to France, Châteaudun received the Legion of Honour and adopted the motto "Extincta revivisco" (I rise again from the ashes).

★★ CHÂTEAU

time: 1 hour

Châteaudun is the first of the Loire châteaux on the road from Paris and stands on a bluff rising steeply above the River Loir (there is an excellent view from the north bank level with an old mill near the bridge). The buildings, which date from 12C and 16C, have been restored with care and taste and the rooms have been provided with furniture and hung with 17C and 18C tapestries. From the outside the château looks like an austere fortress but from the courtyard the buildings resemble a stately mansion.

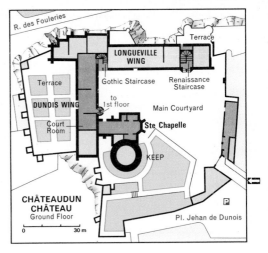

CHÂTEAUDUN CHÂTEAU
Ground Floor

The roofless keep, which is 31 m - 102 ft high, dates from 12C; it is one of the earliest round keeps, also one of the most impressive and best preserved.

The **basement rooms** which extend into the Dunois Wing are always open *(entrance at the bottom of the Gothic staircase)*. Two large adjoining rooms, beautifully decorated with palm tree vaulting, were the kitchens, with a double chimney extending the whole width of the room. The small rooms on the north side were occupied by the guards in charge of the exiguous prison cells, some of which have ogival vaulting.

Sainte-Chapelle. – Dunois was responsible for this graceful 15C building; it is flanked by a square belfry and two oratories and the chancel ends in a three sided apse. The upper chapel, which was provided for the servants, has a panelled wooden ceiling; the lower chapel has ogival vaulting.

The south oratory is decorated with a well preserved 15C mural of the Last Judgement. The charming collection of fifteen **statues★★** is an excellent example of the work produced in the workshops in the Loire Valley in the late 15C. Twelve of them are life-size and painted and date from the time of Dunois; they represent St Elizabeth, St Mary the Egyptian, deliciously clothed with her own hair, St Radegund with her sceptre, St Apollonia with a forceps gripping a tooth, St Barbara with her tower, St Geneviève, St Catherine holding the wheel and the sword that killed her, a Magdalen, St John the Baptist and St John the Evangelist, Dunois' patron saints, St Martha with a dragon at her feet and a majestic Virgin and Child; Mary was the patron saint of Marie d'Harcourt, Dunois' wife. The three smaller statues are of Dunois himself, St Francis and St Agnès and were added by François d'Orléans-Longueville and Agnès de Savoie, son and daughter-in-law of the Bastard.

Dunois Wing. – It was started in 1460 and is in the true Gothic tradition but the internal fittings suggest the desire for comfort which followed the Hundred Years War. In the huge living rooms, which are hung with tapestries, the massive overhead beams are exposed; the Court Room (Salle de Justice), where the Lord of the Manor gave judgment, was panelled in 17C and painted with the arms of Louis XIV when the king visited Châteaudun; it served as a revolutionary tribunal in 1793. On the top floor a vertiginous parapet walk beside the machicolations leads to the guard room.

Longueville Wing. – In completing his father's work, François I de Longueville had a staircase built in the Gothic style; it rises through three floors and opens on to the main courtyard through a double bay like an Italian loggia; the decoration is in the Flamboyant style. The design is in transition between the usual medieval turreted staircase of the Dunois Wing and the Renaissance at the east end of the Longueville Wing.

The Longueville Wing was built between 1511 and 1532 by François II de Longueville and then by his brother the Cardinal on foundations which date from the preceding century; it was never completed. At roof level an Italian cornice supports a Flamboyant balustrade. The staircase at the east end is richly decorated with Renaissance motifs in a Gothic setting. The rooms on the ground floor, including the Guard Room, are hung with tapestries. The huge chimney pieces in the grand salon on the first floor are in the Gothic or Renaissance style; the carved chests are 16C.

★ OLD TOWN (VIEILLE VILLE – A) *time: 1 1/2 hours*

Follow the route shown on the plan on p 80 on foot.

Rue du Château, which is lined by overhanging houses, opens into a charming little square with two old houses: the one with pilasters, beams and carved medallions is 16C, the other, much restored, is a corner house with a carved corner post showing the Virgin and St Anne (badly deteriorated).

Rue de la Cuirasserie, which contains a fine 16C house with a corner turret, opens into a square named after Cap-de-la-Madeleine, a town in the province of Quebec in Canada founded in 17C by a priest from Châteaudun. On the right is the work house (Hôtel-Dieu), founded in 1092 and modernised in 1762; on the left is the Law Court (Palais de Justice) housed in a former Augustinian Abbey, built in the Classical style.

CHÂTEAUDUN

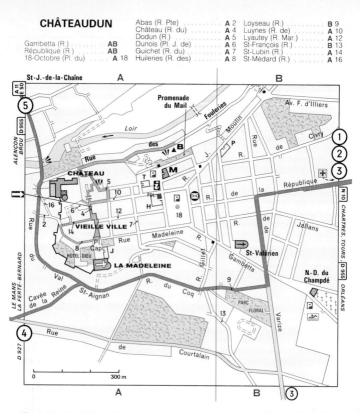

	Abas (R. Pte)	. . . .	**A** 2
	Château (R. du)	. . . .	**A** 4
	Dodun (R.)	. . . .	**A** 5
Gambetta (R.) . . . . **AB**	Dunois (Pl. J. de)	. . . . . .	**A** 6
République (R.) . . . . . . **AB**	Guichet (R. du)	. . . . . .	**A** 7
18-Octobre (Pl. du) . . . . **A** 18	Huileries (R. des)	. . . . . .	**A** 8

Loyseau (R.)	. . . .	**B** 9
Luynes (R. de)	. . . . . .	**A** 10
Lyautey (R. Mar.)	. . . . .	**A** 12
St-François (R.)	. . . . . .	**B** 13
St-Lubin (R.)	. . . .	**A** 14
St-Médard (R.)	. . . . . .	**A** 16

Rue des Fouleries (AB). — *Below the château on the bank south of the Loir.*
The many caves were used by the fullers in the treatment of skins. At no 35 the
Fuller's Caves **(Les Grottes du Foulon)** have been provided with lights and a commentary.

★ **Magdalen Church** (Église de la Madeleine — A). — The north façade is topped by pointed
gables, a common regional feature. The interior is vast; it was built in 12C to an
ambitious plan and never completed owing to a lack of funds. The south door,
overlooking a steep drop, is Romanesque with human figures and fantastic animals
carved over the arch.

Continue down Rue des Huileries to Rue de la Porte-d'Abas; on the left, near the ruins of
a Roman gate, stands the Porters' Lodge 16C (Loge aux Portiers) decorated with a
carefully restored statue of the Virgin.

Walk up Rue St-Lubin where a stream runs down the centre of the street to return to the
front of the château. Go through the arch at the beginning of Rue de Luynes and into
Impasse du Cloître St-Roch, then turn right into a narrow and winding street, Venelle des
Ribaudes, which opens into a small square on the edge of the bluff; from here there is a
pleasant view of the Loir and the river valley. On the right of the square stands a
15C house with a Flamboyant door and mullion windows.

Take Rue Dodun back to the château.

ADDITIONAL SIGHTS

St Valerian's Church (St-Valérien — B). — The church has a tall square tower and
crocketed spire; on the south side there is a fine Romanesque multifoil doorway.

Notre-Dame-du-Champdé Chapel (B). — All that remains of this chapel is a Flamboyant façade with finely worked ornamentation; a delicate balustrade is supported by sculpted consoles at the base of the gable which holds an effigy of the Virgin.

Mall Walk (Promenade du Mail — A). — The walk, which parallels the edge of the bluff
above the river valley, has been widened and turned into a public garden. The view★
extends westward across the Loir to the hills of the Perche region.

Museum (A M). — It is worth visiting for its remarkable collection of birds★ (stuffed) on the
first floor and its fine oriental porcelain, weapons and jewellery. A room on the ground
floor devoted to Egypt displays items from the royal tombs of the first two dynasties
(2955-2635 BC) discovered at Abydos by the Egyptologist Amelineau at the end of 19C.

Church of St John of the Chain (Église St-Jean-de-la-Chaîne). — *Exit* ⑤ *on the plan.*
In the suburb of St John on the north bank of the Loir stands an early 16C ogee arched
gate at the entrance to the churchyard. St John Church was built mainly in 15C but the
apses date from 11 and 12C.

From this side of the river there is a fine view of the north face of the château.

EXCURSION

Lutz-en-Dunois. — Pop 383. *7 km - 4 miles by* ②, *D 955; turn left after the aerodrome.*
Lutz has a charming Romanesque **church** with a low bell tower crowned by a saddleback
roof. The interior is decorated with 13C **murals** in red, yellow and ochre: Apostles and
Bishop Saints in the apse; on the walls of the nave: Christ's Entry into Jerusalem, the
Entombment, the Resurrection, the Descent into Purgatory.

CHÂTEAU-GONTIER

Michelin Map 🟦 fold 10 or 🟦🟦🟦 fold 19 — Local map p 138 — Facilities

The picturesque old town in the heart of Chouan country *(p 23, 137)* was founded in 11C by Fulk Nerra *(p 48)*. The old town with its narrow, winding streets is divided by the main street into two districts, one grouped round the Town Hall and the other round St John's Church.

Rue Trouvée on the east bank of the Mayenne was the birthplace of the Royalist leader, Mercier, son of an innkeeper, who was Cadoudal's best friend; he rose to the rank of general and field-marshal in the King's army in Brittany and was killed in 1801, at the age of 26, at the Battle of Loudéac.

The quays recall the days when Château-Gontier was a port on the river Mayenne which was canalised (boat trips and hire of house boats at the Relais nautique).

The calf sales, held on Thursdays, are among the largest in Europe.

SIGHTS

St John's Church (Église St-Jean — **A**). — The church was build in 11C of flint and red sandstone on land given by Fulk Nerra to Benedictines from Angers.

The **interior★** is remarkable for its forceful yet pure Romanesque style; the transept crossing is roofed by an unusual dome on pendentives ending in colonettes. Modern stained glass adorns the round-headed windows. The transepts are decorated with 12C frescoes: (left transept) creation of the birds, the domestic animals and Adam and Eve; God shows them the Tree of Good and Evil, the temptation of Eve who is expelled from the earthly Paradise; (chapel of St-Benoît) the three kings; (right transept) Noah building the Ark with a dragon on the prow; the dove appearing as the flood recedes. The beautiful crypt is roofed with groined vaulting supported on two rows of columns.

View point. — From under the elm trees on the terrace built on the old ramparts at the east end of the church there is a fine view of the river Mayenne.

World's End Walk (Promenade du Bout-du-Monde — **A**). — The path tumbles down through the gardens of the old priory towards the river which can be glimpsed at intervals.

Museum (**A M**). — Housed in a lovely 17C mansion, this museum contains a few fine paintings and sculptures as well as some Greco-Roman antiquities: a drawing by Le Brun of the battle between Constantine and Maxentius, canvases by the 17C Dutch school, an important 16C Italian painting of Cleopatra, a fine wooden **statue of St Martha** (15C French school) and a 14C marble Virgin.

Trinity Church (Église de la Trinité — **B**). — It was built in 17C as the chapel of the Ursuline convent. A statue of St Ursula adorns the pilastered façade. it was here that Lucrèce Mercier came to pray for her fiancé the Royalist leader Cadoudal; after his execution she became a nun in the convent.

Notre-Dame-du-Geneteil (**B E**). — This former college chapel was built of schist in the Romanesque style.

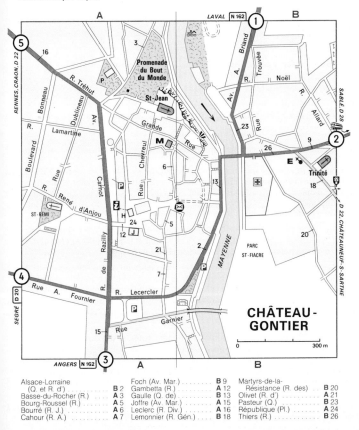

CHÂTEAU-GONTIER

CHÂTEAU-GONTIER

EXCURSIONS

La Maroutière Château. — *3 km - 2 miles by ③ on the plan.*
The château is set in a superb park containing one of the last private race courses; it is open only twice a year for horse racing.

St-Ouen Château. — *7 km - 4 1/2 miles by ④ on the plan, D 20 to Segré.*
Just before **Chemazé** this 15-16C château appears on the right of the road; the great square tower which contains the stairs bears a crown-like superstructure and the dormer windows are pedimented.

CHÂTEAU-LA-VALLIÈRE   Pop 1628

Michelin Map 🔢 northwest of fold 14 or 🔢🔢🔢 fold 22

This calm, small town ideal for tourists seeking a quiet haven is situated in a wooded region interspersed with many stretches of water.
Louise de la Baume le Blanc, better known as the Duchess of La Vallière, spent her childhood at La Vallière Manor, near the village of Reugny to the northeast of Tours.
Lady-in-waiting to Charles I of England's widow, Henrietta Maria, the gentle, gracious Louise captured the heart of the Sun King, Louis XIV, at Fontainebleau in 1662. She remained the royal mistress for five years before giving way to the haughty Mme de Montespan. Following her fall from favour, she retired to the Carmelite Convent in Rue St-Jacques in Paris and eventually took the black veil from the hands of the queen Maria-Theresa; the preacher was Bossuet. For the thirty-six years of her stay her piety, modesty and tolerance never failed her.

Happy Valley Lake (Étang du Val Joyeux). — This vast stretch of water *(bathing and sailing facilities)*, formed by the River Fare, lies in an attractive wooded setting. The nearby hill is crowned by a church.

Château-la-Vallière Forest. — The town is surrounded, except on the north side, by a vast forest of pines and oaks, interspersed with stretches of heath which covers about 3 000 ha - 11sq miles and is ideal for hunting.

EXCURSION

Vaujours Château. — *3.5 km - 2 miles by D 959 the Tours road, and afterwards D 34 to the right.*
The romantic ruins of this château are preceded by a fortified barbican and a rampart wall marked out at intervals by round towers; only one of the once battlemented towers stands in its entirety. The courtyard is bordered by the remains of the chapel and main building dating from the 15C. Louis XI came to the château several times to stay with his half-sister, Jeanne, the daughter of Charles VII and Agnès Sorel. Louise de La Vallière also held the title of the Duchess of Vaujours but only visited the château once in 1669.

*When looking for a pleasant, quiet and well situated hotel consult the current **Michelin Red Guide.***

CHÂTEAUNEUF-SUR-LOIRE   Pop 6029

Michelin map 🔢 fold 10 or 🔢🔢🔢 fold 41 or 🔢🔢🔢 fold 6

Châteauneuf has made good the damage caused by the bombardments that shattered the town in 1940.
On the site of the former fortified castle, where Charles IV the Fair died in 1328, Louis Phelypeaux de la Vrillière, Secretary of State to Louis XIV, built a small-scale imitation of Versailles. After the Revolution the château was sold to an architect from Orléans who had it demolished; only the domed rotunda, which is used as the Town Hall, the outbuildings and the pavilions in the forecourt remain.

Château. — The park is bordered by a moat; the western section is filled with water and crossed by a graceful stone footbridge. It is at its best at the end of May or in early June when the exotic plants and giant **rhododendrons** are in flower.

Loire Nautical Museum. — It is housed in the basement of the Rotunda, part of the 17C château *(walk anti-clockwise)* and displays engravings of the shipping on the Loire, navigational instruments, models, photographs of the ships and souvenirs of local traditions. Life in old Châteauneuf is presented in the kitchen of the château. The former stables, designed by Mansart, are now occupied by a documentation centre about the Loire and its ships.

St-Martial's Church. — The church was built late in 16C in the Gothic style but lost its nave in a fire in 1940; all that remains is a double arch through which the old market hall can be seen. Within stands the marble **mausoleum★** of Louis Phelypeaux de la Vrillière, Minister under Louis XIV, who died in 1681; it is an imposing Baroque monument, framed by two skeletons acting as caryatids, and was carved in Italy by a pupil of Bernini.

St Peter's Market Hall (Halle St-Pierre). — Next to the church stands the market hall, a picturesque building supported on wooden columns which was built in 1854.

82

EXCURSIONS

Fay-aux-Loges. – Pop 2 135. *9 km - 5 1/2 miles northwest by D 11.*
This little village on the banks of the Orléans Canal *(p 127)* has a handsome low **church** (11-13C). Although the vaulting is ogival the building gives the impression of a stout Romanesque church which is accentuated by the use of the hard Fay stone as a facing right up to the pyramidal spire. The modern stained glass blends well with the austere architecture.
The fortified house behind the church is the vicarage.

Combreux. – Pop 183. *13 km - 8 miles northeast by D 10 and then D 9.*
The town clusters picturesquely on the south bank of the Orléans Canal. On the north side of the town and the canal, east of D 9, stands the spectacular **château** (16-17C), built of brick with stone dressings and surrounded by a moat.
★ **Valley Lake** (Étang de la Vallée). – *2 km - 1 mile west.*
The reservoir which feeds the Orléans Canal is on the eastern fringe of the Orléans Forest in a wild setting of dense trees and tall reeds where ducks and moorhens cackle and quack.
Provision is made for fishermen and water sportsmen: bathing place; sailing and surf boarding are permitted.

CHÂTEAU-RENAULT
Pop 6 170

Michelin map 🔲 folds 5, 6 or 🔲 fold 1

Château-Renault was founded in 1066 by Renault, son of Geoffroi de Château-Gontier, on a tongue of land between the River Brenne and the River Gault at the point where they meet. In recent years the town has extended beyond its original confines. The main street runs in a large curve down to the river bank. The chemical and electronics industries have been added to the traditional activity of leather working.

Leather and Tanning Museum (M). – Housed in an old tannery, the museum displays the various stages in the traditional tanning process.

Château. – A 14C gate, surmounted by a hoarding (to enable the defenders to protect the entrance) leads in to the lime-planted terraces which offer an attractive **view**★ over the town.
The 12C **keep (B)** has been slighted; the old 17C château is now occupied by the Town Hall. The château belonged to the owners of the château in Châteaudun and then to two illustrious sailors: the Marquis of Château-Renault under Louis XIV and, under Louis XVI, the Count of Estaing who died on the guillotine in 1793.

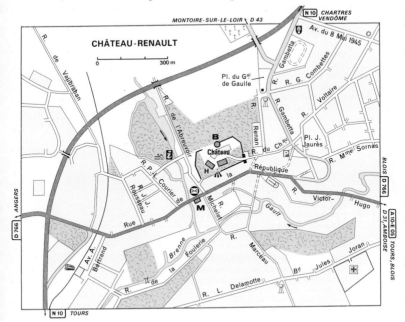

EXCURSION

St-Laurent-en-Gâtines. – Pop 546. *11 km - 7 miles west by D 766.*
At the roadside stands a massive building in brick and stone. Long known as "**la Grand' Maison**" (the Big House), it was formerly the residence of the abbots of Marmoutier, who owned the land of St-Laurent-en-Gâtines. It was built in 15C and converted into a church in 19C: a spire was raised on the polygonal tower which housed the stairs and two large Flamboyant windows were inserted on one side.

*The towns and sights described in this guide are shown in **black** on the maps.*

★★ CHAUMONT-SUR-LOIRE Château

Michelin map ⬚⬚ folds 16, 17 or ⬚⬚⬚ fold 14 — Local map p 123

The former fortress of Chaumont was demolished twice; it was rebuilt between 1465 and 1510 by Pierre d'Amboise, by the eldest of his seventeen children, Charles d'Amboise, and by his grandson, Charles II. The latter, thanks to his uncle, Cardinal Georges d'Amboise, who was in great favour with King Louis XII, became Grand Master of the King's Household, Marshal, Admiral of France and Lieutenant-General in Italy. In 1560 Catherine de' Medici, the widow of Henri II, acquired the castle only as a means of revenge against **Diane de Poitiers**, the mistress of the late King. The Queen compelled her rival to give up her favourite residence of Chenonceau in exchange for Chaumont. Diane de Poitiers never lived at Chaumont but retired to Anet where she died in 1566.

Catherine de' Medici's stay at Chaumont and the existence there of a room connected by a staircase with the top of a tower have given rise to conjecture. The room was said to be the study of **Ruggieri**, the Queen's Astrologer, and the tower, the observatory from which Catherine and her master plotter consulted the stars. It was apparently at Chaumont that Catherine read in the future the grim fate awaiting her three sons, François II, Charles IX, and Henri III and the accession of the Bourbons with Henri IV of Navarre.

Mass-produced medallions. — In the 18C one of the proprietors of the castle, Le Ray, Governor of the Invalides, hired the services of the famous Italian artist **Nini**, a glass engraver and potter for 1 200 *livres* a year, plus lodging and heating. Nini fitted out a workshop in the stables and an oven in a dovecot. With a hollow mould he reproduced many copies of medallions of more than a hundred famous people of the time, including Benjamin Franklin who spent some time at the château. Le Ray made a large profit from this new industrial method of portraiture.

19C. — Exiled from Paris by Napoleon, Madame de Staël spent some time in 1810 at Chaumont as a guest of Le Ray's son. She worked there, surrounded by her "court" which included Benjamin Constant and Madame Récamier. When her guests praised the landscape of the Loire, she replied sadly: "Yes, it's an admirable scene, but how much I prefer my gutter in the Rue du Bac."

In 1875 the castle was bought by Mlle Say, heiress to an industrial fortune, who soon became the Princess de Broglie; for Chaumont this was an era of luxury and magnificent festivities. Since 1938 Chaumont has belonged to the State.

⊙ TOUR OF THE CHÂTEAU *time: 3/4 hour*

Chaumont Château is as well sited as Amboise on the south bank of the Loire, overlooking the town and the river; the **view★** from the terrace is admirable. The feudal austerity of the buildings is softened by the Renaissance influences and complemented by the magnificent stables, a reminder of coaching days.

The park. — An uphill walk along a shady avenue giving glimpses of the Loire leads to the castle. This is a pleasant walk and will give an idea of the fine park with its centuries old cedars.

The building. — The outer west façade, which is the oldest, is severely military. Most of the windows that can be seen now did not exist originally. The two other façades, though they still have a feudal look, show the influence of the Renaissance.

At ground floor level there is a frieze bearing the interlaced Cs of Charles d'Amboise and his wife, Catherine, alternating with the rebus of the castle: a volcano or *chaud mont* (Chaumont). The emblem of Diane de Poitiers is carved in front of each machicolation: it consists of intertwined Ds or of the hunting horn, bow and quiver of Diana the Huntress.

Beyond the drawbridge, the entrance gate is adorned with the arms of France and the initials of Louis XII and Anne of Brittany on a field of fleurs de lys and ermin. The hat of the Cardinal d'Amboise is carved on the tower on the left, and the arms of Charles d'Amboise, Admiral and Marshal of France, on the right hand tower. These emblems are protected by small structures in a mixed Gothic and Italian Renaissance style. On entering the courtyard go first to the terrace. It was built in the 18C on the site of the north wing, which had been demolished by an owner who liked the view. A magnificent Loire landscape can be seen from it.

(Photo Hervé Boulé)

Chaumont Château
Spiral staircase

The apartments. — Note the room of two rivals Catherine de' Medici and Diane de Poitiers, Ruggieri's study and the Council Room, paved with Renaissance majolica tiles brought from Palermo in Sicily by the Princess de Broglie. They contain fine tapestries, good furniture and a collection of Nini's terracotta medallions.

The stables. — *About 50 m from the château.* Their size and appointments give an idea of the part played by horses in the lives of princely families.

Built in 1877 by the Prince de Broglie and lit by electricity in 1906, the stables were used until 1917, when the Prince went bankrupt and was forced to sell his horses.

In a corner of the stables note the double-roofed tower, the former dovecot, transformed into an oven for Nini *(see above)*, which later became the riding school for the children at the château.

Michelin map 🆔 fold 16 or 🆔 fold 14 (7 km - 4 1/2 miles east of Bléré) — Local map p 122

The beautiful château of Chenonceau *(1)* stretches across the River Cher in a perfect harmony of water, greenery, gardens and trees in a fine natural setting. To this perfection is added the elegance of the architecture, the interior decoration and magnificent furniture.

(Photo Mary Evans Picture Library/Explorer Archives)

View of Chenonceau in 1850 *(Lithograph by Leroy)*

The château shaped by women. — The first castle was built between 1513 and 1521 by Thomas **Bohier,** Collector of Taxes under Charles VIII, Louis XII and François I. Bohier's acquisition of Chenonceau and the château's frequent change of owner make up an eventful tale. For 400 years the women involved — wives, mistresses and queens — played the role of heroine, happy or sad.

Catherine Briçonnet, the Builder. — The Chenonceau estate, comprising a manor and a simple mill, belonged to the lords of Marques; they sold it in ruins to Bohier in 1499 but an heiress exercising her lineal right of redemption bought it back. Bohier however did not give up and patiently acquired all the adjoining fiefs and manors until the property was encircled. Eventually in 1512 Chenonceau was seized and put up for sale; Bohier bought it for 12 400 livres. Immediately he demolished all the old buildings except for the keep. As he was kept busy by his duties and often had to be with the army near Milan, he could not supervise the building of his new residence. It was his wife Catherine, from a family of great financiers in Touraine, who took charge and was the moving spirit. In the site chosen for the building and its simple plan one feels a feminine influence and an eye for convenience and comfort: the four rooms on each floor are arranged round a central hall and, another novelty, the stairs rise in a straight line.

The new building was completed in 1521 but Bohier and his wife had little time in which to enjoy it as they died in 1524 and 1526 respectively. A few years later, following the trial of Semblançay, Bohier's accounts were examined and he was shown to owe a large sum of money to the Treasury. In order to pay his father's debts, Antoine Bohier transferred the château in 1535 to François I who used it as a hunting lodge.

Diane de Poitiers, the everlasting beauty. — When Henri II came to the throne in 1547 he gave Chenonceau to Diane de Poitiers. She was twenty years older than he but very attractive. "I saw her" wrote a contemporary "at the age of 70 (in fact she died at 67) as beautiful to look at and as attractive as at thirty. She had a very white skin and wore nothing on her face". She was the widow of Louis de Brézé, for whom she had a splendid tomb built in Rouen Cathedral, and she always wore the colours of mourning: black and white. Her influence over Henri II was such that in addition to all the other favours she received, she made him wear mourning too, to the despair of the queen who was rejected and humiliated.

Diane was an able manager and intended to exploit her estate and her position; she took an interest in agriculture, in the sale of wine, in her financial income and in anything that earned money. She found an excellent source of revenue in the 20 livres tax on bells, of which she received a good share; Rabelais said "The king has hung all the bells of the kingdom round the neck of his mare". Diane was a woman of taste; she created a beautiful garden and had a bridge built linking the château with the north bank of the Cher.

Diane made provision for the future; the 1535 act by which Chenonceau became part of the royal estates was repealed and the château temporarily restored to Bohier but as he was in debt to the crown it was seized automatically and put up for auction; Diane had only to buy it officially and thus became the legal owner.

---

(1) The town of Chenonceau has an x but not the château.

Despite these precautions, when Henri II was killed in a tournament in 1559, Diane found herself face to face with Catherine de' Medici who was now regent. While her husband was alive the queen had been patient and dissembling and had accepted the situation, but now she wanted vengeance. Knowing that Diane was very attached to Chenonceau, she forced her to give up the property in exchange for Chaumont. After a brief attempt at resistance, Diane gave in, left the banks of the Cher and retired to Anet Château where she died seven years later.

Catherine de' Medici, the Magnificent. — With her love of the arts Catherine de' Medici also had a love of magnificence, and she satisfied both on a grand scale at Chenonceau. She had a park laid out, built a graceful two storey gallery on the bridge and added vast outbuildings.

Grand festivals were frequent and the people marvelled at them. One was given for the arrival of François II and Mary Stuart; another for Charles IX was even more brilliant. Young women disguised as mermaids welcomed the visitors from the moats along the avenue leading to the château. Their singing was matched by that of the nymphs emerging from the thickets. But the appearance of satyrs scattered the graceful chorus. Nothing was lacking from these festivities. There were banquets, dances, masquerades, fireworks and a naval battle on the Cher.

Henri III presided over a sylvan festival that cost 100 000 *livres* and made a sensation. "The most beautiful and virtuous ladies of the court", we are told, "appeared half naked, with their hair loose, like brides, and with the Queen's daughters, waited on the guests."

Louise de Lorraine, the Inconsolable (end of 16C). — Catherine bequeathed Chenonceau to her daughter-in-law, Louise de Lorraine, wife of Henri III. After the King's assassination by Jacques Clément, Louise retired to the château, put on white mourning according to royal custom and wore it to the end of her life; she was therefore known as the "White Queen" or the "White Lady". Her bedroom, her bed, her carpets and chairs were covered with black velvet, and the curtains were of black damask; crowns of thorns and Franciscan girdles were painted in white on black ceilings. For eleven years, faithful to the memory of her husband, Louise divided her time between prayer, needlework and reading.

Madame Dupin, an intellectual (18C). — From Louise de Lorraine Chenonceau passed to her niece, Françoise de Lorraine, wife of César de Vendôme, the son of Henri IV and Gabrielle d'Estrées who had themselves stayed at the château in 1598. In 1733 it became the property of Dupin, the farmer general who was the tax collector. Madame Dupin kept a salon which was attended by all the celebrities of the period. **Jean-Jacques Rousseau** was her son's tutor and it was for the benefit of this boy that he wrote his treatise on education, *Émile*. In the *Confessions* the philosopher wrote warmly of that happy time: "We had a good time in that beautiful place, we ate well, I became as fat as a monk".

Madame Dupin advanced into old age surrounded by the affection of the villagers so that the château survived the Revolution unscathed. At her wish she was buried in the park.

Madame Pelouze, Lover of Antiquity (19C). — In 1864 Madame Pelouze bought Chenonceau and made it her life's work to restore the château to its former glory. Catherine de' Medici had altered the main façade by doubling the windows and placing caryatids between them. The new openings were walled up and the caryatids were moved into the park. A building which had been added between the chapel and the library was removed. Madame Pelouze proceeded boldly with refurbishments in the debatable taste of the 19C.

The château now belongs to the Menier family.

⏱ **TOUR** *time: 2 hours*

Son et Lumière. — *See Practical Information at the end of the guide.*

Approach. — A magnificent avenue of plane trees leads to the château. The tourist who likes to indulge his fancy can try to imagine the entry of Charles IX, among mermaids, nymphs and satyrs. Standing back on the left, at the end of a path, you will see the caryatids moved from the façade by Mme Pelouze; the outbuildings erected to the plans of Philibert Delorme are on the right.

After crossing a drawbridge you reach a terrace surrounded by moats. To the left is Diane de Poitiers's Italian garden; to the right, that of Catherine de' Medici, bounded by the great trees in the park. On the terrace stands the keep of the original château remodelled by Bohier. Here you will read the initials "TBK" (Thomas Bohier and Katherine). You will find them again in the château, with the motto: *S'il vient à point, me souviendra*. The meaning of this motto is rather obscure. It may be: "If the building is finished it will preserve the memory of the man who built it."

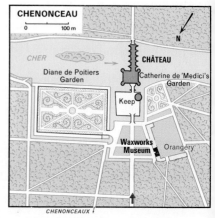

CHENONCEAU

0   100 m

CHER

Diane de Poitiers Garden

CHÂTEAU

Catherine de 'Medici's Garden

Keep

Waxworks Museum   Orangery

N

CHENONCEAUX

The château. — The château consists of a rectangular mansion with turrets at the corners. It stands on two piers of the former mill, resting on the bed of the Cher. The library and the chapel project on the left. Catherine de' Medici's two storeyed gallery stands on the bridge over the river. This building by Philibert Delorme has a classical simplicity contrasting with the rich, gay appearance given to the older portion by the sculptures on the balustrades, roof and dormer windows.

Ground floor. — The four main rooms lead off the hall. The former guardroom *(left)* is paved with majolica tiles and adorned with 16C Flemish tapestries; in the chapel is a 16C marble bas-relief of a Virgin and Child; the fireplace in Diane de Poitiers's bedroom was designed by Jean Goujon; pictures hang in Catherine de' Medici's Green Cabinet as well as an Oudenaarde tapestry.

The great gallery overlooking the Cher is 60 m - 197 ft long and has black and white chequered paving; incorporated in its ceiling is the ceiling of Louise de Lorraine's bedroom; during the first World War the gallery was converted into a military hospital and from 1940 to 1942 the demarcation line ran right through the middle.

In François I's bedroom hang paintings by Van Loo *(Three Graces),* Il Primaticcio *(Diane de Poitiers as the Huntress Diana),* and a handsome 15C Italian piece of furniture inlaid in ivory and mother of pearl is worth noting; in a salon with a magnificent French style ceiling are works by Rubens *(Jesus and St John),* Mignard, Nattier *(Mme Dupin)* and a portrait of Louis XIV by Rigaud, richly framed.

First floor. — One reaches it by a straight staircase, which at the time it was built was an innovation in France. From the vestibule, with its Oudenaarde tapestries depicting hunting scenes and Carrara marble statues of Roman emperors brought by Catherine de' Medici from Florence, walk through to Gabrielle d'Estrées' bedroom, the Royal, or Five Queens' Bedroom, the bedroom of Catherine de' Medici and finally to that of César de Vendôme. All the rooms are furnished and adorned with fine Gobelins tapestries.

A small convent for Capuchin nuns was installed in the attics, complete with a drawbridge which was raised at night to separate the nuns from the castle's other occupants.

Kitchens. — There is an attractive dresser and a series of brass containers.

Waxworks Museum. — The Dômes building, so called because of the shape of the roof, presents fifteen scenes evoking life in the château and the personalities connected with it.

The park. — The gardens and the banks of the Cher provide picturesque views of the château.

EXCURSION

Montlouis-sur-Loire along the Cher Valley. — *Round trip of 50 km - 31 miles — time: 1 3/4 hours.*

> *Leave Chenonceaux eastwards (direction Montrichard), immediately turn south across the Cher and take N 76 west towards Tours.*

Bléré. — Pop 4 060. Facilities. Place de la République at the entrance to Bléré was once a cemetery; the only monument now remaining was erected in 1526 and elegantly carved in the Italian style; it was the **funerary chapel** of Guillaume de Saigne, Treasurer of the Royal Artillery under François I.

Leugny Château. — This elegant château on the Cher was built by the architect Portier, a pupil of Gabriel, for himself. It is furnished in the Louis XVI style.

Véretz. — Pop 2 379. This smart little town nestles between the Cher and the hillside. It presents a charming picture from the north bank of the river: the houses and church lead the eye west to the tree-lined paths and terraces of the château. Among those who walked in the château park were the Abbé de Rancé (1626-1700) who reformed the Trappist order, the Abbé d'Effiat and Madame de Sévigné, the Princess de Conti and the Abbé de Grécourt who wrote light verse; Voltaire stayed at the Château de Véretz in his youth. In the village square stands a monument to **Paul-Louis Courier** (1772-1825), who spent his childhood near Luynes and served as an officer under the Empire. In 1816 he bought the Chavonnière estate with its large house on the Véretz plateau and made his home there with his young wife. From his country retreat he began to harass the government with caustic and witty pamphlets including the famous "A petty village tyrant under the Restoration". Despite his talent he was disliked for his quarrelsome and unbridled temper; on 10 April 1825 he was assassinated in the Larçay Forest in mysterious circumstances.

> *Take D 85 north across the River Cher to Montlouis.*

Montlouis-sur-Loire. — *Description p 142.*

> *Take D 751 east (direction Amboise) and turn right into D 40 to St-Martin-le-Beau.*

St-Martin-le-Beau. — Pop 2 051. The **church** has a finely sculpted Romanesque doorway.

> *Return to Chenonceaux by D 40.*

The times indicated in this guide

when given with the distance allow one to enjoy the scenery when given for sightseeing are intended to give an idea of the possible length or brevity of a visit.

★★ CHEVERNY Château

Michelin map 🔢 fold 17 or 🔢🔢🔢 fold 15

Not far from the châteaux of Blois and Chambord, Cheverny with its Classical white façade and slate roof, stands on the edge of the Sologne Forest.

Built without interruption between 1604 and 1634 by Count Henri Hurault de Cheverny, the château presents a rare unity of style in both its architecture and decoration. The symmetry and majesty of its façade are characteristic features of the Classical period. The interior is sumptuously decorated with furniture, sculpture, gilt, marble, multi-coloured panelling...

Son et Lumière. – *See Practical Information at the end of the guide.*

(Photo Hervé Boulé)

Cheverny Château

★★★ APARTMENTS *tour: 3/4 hour*

Grand Salon. – The ceiling of the Grand Salon on the ground floor is entirely covered, as is the wall panelling, with painted decoration enhanced with gilding. Among the paintings are a portrait of Cosimo de' Medici by Titian, a portrait of Jeanne d'Aragon from the School of Raphael and, on the chimneypiece, a portrait by Mignard of Marie-Johanne de Saumery, Countess of Cheverny.

Petit Salon. – The smaller salon, which follows, is hung with five 17C tapestries from Flanders after cartoons by Teniers. Both rooms contain Louis XIV and Louis XV period furnishings: Louis XV Chinese lacquered commode and Louis XV clock, decorated with bronzes by Caffieri.

Gallery. – It is furnished with magnificent Regency chairs and contains several paintings, including a canvas by François Clouet of Anne de Thou, Countess of Cheverny, a portrait of Jeanne d'Albret by Miguel Oñate and a self-portrait by Rigaud.

Salon. – This little salon is hung with 16, 17 and 18C paintings; the furniture includes a small gaming table incrusted with different types of Carrara marble.

Library. – The woodwork and the beautiful parquet floor are worthy of note; there are some very fine bindings too.

Dining-Room. – Across the hall is the dining-room which was refurbished in 19C when the passage and the chimney with the bust of Henri IV were installed. The room has retained its painted ceiling and small painted wall panels depicting the story of Don Quixote; both are by Jean Mosnier (1600-56), a native of Blois. The walls are covered with Cordoba leather embossed with the Hurault coat of arms.

Armoury. – The majestic great staircase rises in a straight flight to the armoury. The ceiling, the wainscotting and the shutters were painted by Mosnier, who also did the painting on the gilt wood chimneypiece, flanked by statues of Mercury and Venus. A collection of arms and armour from 15 and 16C is displayed on the walls as well as a tapestry from Paris (1610) showing the abduction of Helen.

King's Bedroom. – This is the most splendid room in the château. The ceiling is coffered in the Italian style, gilt and painted by Mosnier, as is the rich Renaissance chimneypiece, which is decorated with telamones, cherubs and plant motifs. The walls are hung with tapestries from the Paris workshops (1640) after Simon Vouet; beneath them are wainscots decorated with small pictures. The canopied bed is covered with Persian silk embroidered with flowers (1550).

The private apartments in the west wing are also open to the public.

The outbuildings. – There is **kennelling** for a pack of 70 hounds and the **trophy room** displays 2 000 deer antlers.

The château is still the home of the descendants of the Hurault de Cheverny family who have maintained the tradition of deer hunting; between autumn and Easter each year the hunt rides out in the surrounding woodland.

EXCURSION

⊙ **Troussay Château.** − *3.5 km - 2 miles west skirting the Cheverny park as far as D52; turn left and take the first right fork.*
This small Renaissance château was refurbished in the late 19C by the historian Louis de la Saussaye with furnishings from other now vanished historic buildings of the region: the stone carving of a porcupine, the emblem of Louis XII, on the rear façade and the beautiful **chapel door**★ carved with delicate scrolls. The tiles on the ground floor date from Louis XII's reign, the Renaissance windows came from the Guise mansion in Blois and the grisailles on the ceiling in the little salon are in the style of Jean Mosnier *(p 30)*. The outbuildings round the courtyard display a collection of agricultural implements and domestic equipment evoking life in the Sologne in times past.

★★ CHINON   Pop 8873

Michelin map 🔢 fold 9 or 🔢🔢🔢 fold 34 − Local maps p 92, 122 − Facilities

Chinon lies at the heart of a well known wine region and is surrounded by the fertile **Veron countryside** *(p 124)* and the beautiful **Chinon Forest**. To the tourist it looks like a medieval town dominated by the walls of its ruined castle which comes to life again each year during the **medieval market** *(see p 194)*.
Approach from the south for the best **view**★★ of the town and the castle brooding over the River Vienne.

Park in Quai Danton to inspect the castle in detail.

From the Quai the different parts of the castle are clearly visible: on the left − Coudray Fort; in the centre − the massive Middle Castle (Château du Milieu) extending to the narrow Clock Tower (Tour de l'Horloge) with its roof and machicolations; on the right − St George's Fort, now dismantled.
A walk along the banks of the Vienne is especially agreeable, particularly in the landscaped **English garden** (Jardin Anglais − **B**) where palm trees flourish in the mild climate of the Loire Valley.

Gargantua's Father. − François Rabelais (1494-1553) was born near Chinon at La Devinière *(see p 93)* and grew up in Chinon where his parents had a house in Rue de la Lamproie. He was the author of the spirited adventures of Pantagruel and his father Gargantua, two giants whose earthy realism always delights the reader. When Gargantua was born his first baby cry was for "A drink, a drink!"; fed on the milk of 17913 cows, he grew rapidly and "became fat in the face with about eighteen chins". The good-natured giants were fond of feasting and drinking and are freely invoked in the wine cellars of Chinon when the vintage is being tasted.

(Photo C. Rives/ C.E.D.R.I.)

River Vienne at Chinon

HISTORICAL NOTES

Chinon was originally a Gallo-Roman camp and then a fortress belonging to the Counts of Blois. In 11C it passed to their enemies, the Counts of Anjou, one of whom, Henry Plantagenet, built the major part of the present castle. In 1154 he became King of England but Chinon, at the heart of his continental possessions, was one of his favourite residences; he died there on 6 July 1189. It was during the Angevin period from 1154 to 1204 that Chinon thrived.

John Lackland, dispossessed vassal. − John, the youngest son of Henry II, inherited the Plantagenet empire on the death of his elder brother Richard the Lionheart, who was killed at Châlus in 1199. His deceitful character and his underhand plotting brought him many enemies. First he quarrelled with his nephew Arthur of Brittany who sought refuge at the French court. Then he abducted Isabelle d'Angoulême, the fiancée of the Count of La Marche, and married her at Chinon on 30 August 1200. Discontent with the behaviour of their overlord caused the knights of Poitou to appeal to the royal court in Paris. John refused to attend the hearing; he was condemned to forfeit his French fiefs.

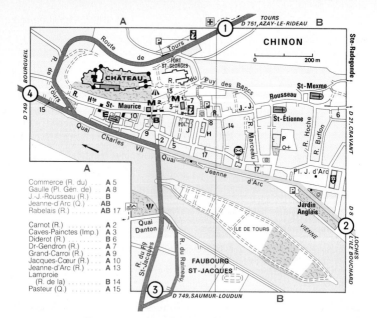

John was reduced to being King of England only and one by one Philippe Auguste captured all the former English strongholds in France; in 1205 Chinon passed to the French crown. John tried to fight back but in vain; after the truce of 26 October 1206 he was forced to give up. He sought, nonetheless, to gain his revenge and in 1213 he took part in the Anglo-German coalition against Philippe Auguste. He was defeated the following year by the future Louis VIII at the Battle of La Roche-aux-Moines near Angers. The French victory was confirmed by the Treaty of Chinon on 18 September 1214. John, who had alienated all the knights in his kingdom and fully deserved his nickname of Lackland, died two years later.

The Court of the "King of Bourges" (early 15C). − With the accession of **Charles VII** Chinon moved into the limelight. France was in a desperate situation. Henry VI, King of England, was also "King of Paris"; Charles VII was only "King of Bourges" when he established his little court at Chinon in 1427. The following year he called a meeting of the States-General of the central and southern provinces which had remained faithful to him. They voted 400 000 livres to organize the defence of Orléans, then besieged by the English *(p 147)*.

Joan of Arc at Chinon (1429). − Escorted by six men at arms, Joan travelled from Lorraine to Chinon, arriving on 6 March, without encountering any of the armed bands which were ravaging the country. The people took this for a clear sign of divine protection. Waiting to be received by Charles VII, Joan spent two days at an inn in the lower town, fasting and praying.

When the peasant girl of eighteen was admitted to the palace, an attempt was made to put her out of countenance. The great hall was lit by 50 torches; 300 gentlemen in rich apparel were assembled there. The King hid among the crowd. A courtier wore his robes.

Joan advanced shyly, immediately recognized the King and went straight to him. "Gentle Dauphin", she said − for Charles, not having been crowned, was only the Dauphin to her − "my name is Jehanne la Pucelle (Joan the Maid). The King of Heaven sends word by me that you will be anointed and crowned in the city of Reims, and you will be the Lieutenant of the King of Heaven, who is the King of France".

Charles was obsessed with doubts about his birth owing to the scandalous behaviour of his mother, Isabella of Bavaria. When the Maid said to him: "I tell you in the name of Our Lord Christ that you are the heir of France and the true son of the King", he was reassured and almost believed in the heroine's mission.

His advisers were more stubborn. The poor girl was made to appear before the court at Poitiers. A bench of doctors and matrons was to decide whether she was bewitched or inspired. For three weeks she was cross-examined. Her naïve replies, her swift repartee, her piety and her confidence in her heavenly mission convinced the most sceptical. She was recognized as the "Messenger of God". She returned to Chinon, where she was equipped and given armed men and left on 20 April 1429 to accomplish her miraculous and tragic destiny *(see map p 21)*.

★★OLD CHINON (VIEUX CHINON) *time: 3/4 hour*

Rue Haute St-Maurice (Rue Voltaire) (A)

Chinon was once surrounded by high walls which earned it the name Ville Fort (Fortified town); the old town with its pointed roofs and winding streets nestles between the quays on the River Vienne and the castle bluff. There are many medieval houses with picturesque details: half-timbered houses with carved beams, stone gables with corner turrets, mullioned windows and carved doorways.

Start from Place Charles-de-Gaulle.

Take **Rue Voltaire**, formerly called **Rue Haute St-Maurice**, which is the main axis of the old town.

ⓥ **Wine and Cooperage Museum (A M[1])**. — Housed in a wine cellar, the museum uses life-size automats and a recorded commentary to present the work of a vineyard, the wine-making process and the cooper's art.

In a righthand turning, Rue des Caves-Peintes, which leads up to the hillside, is the **Caves Peintes** where, according to Rabelais, Pantagruel drained many a glass of cool wine; the paintings have disappeared but since Rabelais' time these old quarries have always been devoted to the Sacred Bottle since it is here that the annual ceremony of the Entonneurs Rabelaisiens (the wine growers' brotherhood) is held.

No 19 Rue Voltaire is a 14C half-timbered house. Rue Jeanne-d'Arc, climbs steeply up to the castle; a plaque marks the **well** where, according to tradition, Joan of Arc placed her foot when she dismounted from her horse on arriving in Chinon.

Hôtel Torterue de Langardière (18C). — *Rue Jeanne-d'Arc.*
The Classical façade is enhanced by handsome wrought iron balconies.

★★ **Grand Carroi (A B)**. — *(carroi* = crossroads). *Facing no 44 turn left down Rue du Grand-Carroi.*
Despite its restricted size, which hardly merits such a grand name, this was the centre of the town in the Middle Ages, where Rue Haute St-Maurice, an old Gaulish road, intersected Rue du Grand-Carroi which led down to the bridge over the Vienne. This is the setting for the annual "Medieval Market" *(see p 194).*

The picturesque courtyards of the old houses are open to the public; the prettiest are not far from one another: No 30, called the Red House (**Maison Rouge** — 14C) is half-timbered with brick and an overhanging upper storey; another half-timbered house, no 45, is decorated with statues serving as columns; no 44, the States-General House (**Hôtel des États-Généraux**) is a handsome 15-16C brick building, which houses the Museum of Old Chinon, and the broad stone doorway of no 48, 17C Government House (**Hôtel du Gouvernement**), opens into a courtyard lined with graceful arcades.

Bailiff's Court (Palais du Bailliage). — *No 73 Rue Haute St-Maurice.*
Walk round into Rue Jacques-Cœur to admire the southern façade of this building which houses the Hostellerie Gargantua: the corbelled turret and the crocketed gable.

ⓥ **St-Maurice Church (12-16C) (A E)**. — The vaulting in the nave and the chancel are in the pure Angevin style.

Further west in **Rue Haute St-Maurice** is the **Bodard de la Jacopierre House** (no 81), a 15-16C building with a town gateway (15C) picked out in nails on the wooden façade; no 82 is a 16C building (**Hôtel des Eaux et Forêts**) with a corner turret and elegant dormer windows.

ⓥ **Museum of Old Chinon and of River Transport (A M[2])**. — The museum is housed in the States-General House, where Richard the Lionheart is said to have died in 1199 after being at the siege of Châlus in the Limousin, and where the States-General — the French Parliament — met in 1428 at the request of Charles VII to provide him with the money to continue the war against the English.

The ground floor exhibits are mainly concerned with folk art. There are beautiful rooms: the main hall on the first floor has a full portrait of Rabelais by Delacroix; and the second floor, where the roof is in the form of a ship's hull, contains the collections of a local historical society. There are also Joan of Arc's relics (1431) and St Mexme's cope brought back from the Holy Land during one of the Crusades, as well as Gothic chests and wooden statues of the Virgin.

There are various exhibits connected with the traffic on the Vienne and the Loire and models of the different kinds of vessels: flat-bottomed barges, lighters and expendable pine wood boats *(p 122).*

★★ **CASTLE** *time: 1 hour*

Son et Lumière. — *See Practical Information at the end of the guide.*

ⓥ It is best to approach the castle by the Route de Tours (D 751) which skirts the massive walls on the north side. Built on a spur overlooking the Vienne, this vast fortress (400 m by 70 m - 1312 ft by 230 ft) dates mostly from the reign of Henry II (12C). Abandoned by the court after the 15C and bought in 17C by Cardinal de Richelieu, the castle was dismantled little by little until Prosper Mérimée undertook to preserve it. The grandiose ruins evoke eight centuries of history.

It was composed of three sections separated by deep dry moats.

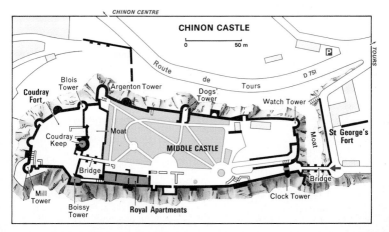

St George's Fort. – The eastern fort, which is now dismantled, protected the vulnerable side of the castle which was accessible from the plateau.

Middle Castle (Château du Milieu). – The entrance to the Middle Castle is across the moat and through the 14C Clock Tower (Tour de l'Horloge) which is unusually shallow (only 5 m - 16 ft deep). A bell, the Marie Javelle, which is dated 1399, sounds the hour from the lantern at the top of the tower. One is free to stroll in the gardens and explore the ruined towers; from the south curtain wall there is a very picturesque **view★★** of the slate roofs of Old Chinon, the Vienne and the river valley.

Coudray Fort. – West of the gardens another bridge crosses the moat to Coudray Fort on the point of the rock spur. Coudray keep (right) was built by Philippe Auguste early in 13C; the Templars *(see p 54)* were imprisoned here by Philip the Fair in 1308 and it was they who carved the famous graffiti on the north wall of the present entrance. Joan of Arc lodged on the first floor, now roofless, in 1429.

Royal Apartments (Logis royal). – Joan of Arc was received in the great hall on the first floor; it is now in ruins, only the fireplace remains. The ground floor rooms have been restored and house a museum: the guard room displays a large model of the whole castle as it was in 15C; in the kitchens there is a beautiful Aubusson tapestry (17C) depicting Joan of Arc recognizing the Dauphin; the family tree of the Capets, the Valois and the Plantagenets and a map of France in 1420 explain the position of the Dauphin Charles when Joan of Arc arrived. A small lapidary museum leads to the Boissy Tower (13C) where a beautiful vaulted chamber was used as a chapel.

ADDITIONAL SIGHTS

St Stephen's Church (St-Étienne – B). – Rebuilt in ten months by Philippe de Commines (*c* 1480), the church has a Flamboyant door carved with his coat of arms.

Rue Jean-Jacques-Rousseau (B). – Several picturesque medieval houses can be seen, especially nos 71 and 73 at the crossroads with Rue du Puy-des-Bancs.

St-Mexme (B). – Two imposing towers overlooking Place St-Mexme and the nave and the narthex are all that is left of this 10-11C church.

St Radegund's Chapel (B). – *Access on foot by the steep path which begins northeast of St Mexme's Church.*
The steep rise is bordered by troglodyte houses. In the 6C a pious hermit had his cell built in the cave. Radegund, the wife of King Chlotar I, came to consult the hermit about her intention to leave the court and found the convent of the Holy Cross (Ste-Croix) in Poitiers – the cell was later enlarged into a chapel where the hermit was buried. A Romanesque portal leads into the chapel. On the left is a Romanesque fresco depicting a Royal Hunt; on the right 17C paintings recount St Radegund's life. One can also visit the **cave** dwelling, adjoining the chapel, and the **museum**.

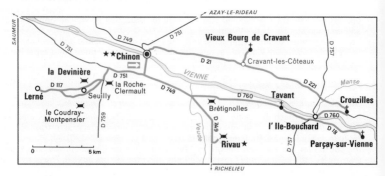

EXCURSIONS

Boat Trips. – *Excursions on the Loire and the Vienne leave from Chinon and Montsoreau. Time: about 2 hours.*

★ **Vienne Valley.** – Michelin map 67 folds 9, 10 or 232 folds 34, 35. *Round tour of 60 km - 38 miles – about 3 hours.*

Leave Chinon to the east by Rue Diderot and D21.

The road follows the chalky slope through the well-known vineyards of Cravant-les-Côteaux.

Vieux-Bourg de Cravant. – *1 km - 1/2 mile north of Cravant-les-Côteaux.*
The **church** of this old town is particularly interesting because of its age. The nave is a rare example of the Carolingian style (early 10C). The 11C south portal is adorned with a twisted fringe; just at the entrance to the chancel two rectangular pillars have been adorned with Merovingian interlacing. These pillars used to support the roof of the south portal. In the south chapel, added in the 15C, there are remains of a fresco (on the west wall) representing the chapel's donors; who probably were Georges de La Trémoille, Minister to Charles VII, Catherine de l'Ile-Bouchard, his wife, and their children. There is also a lapidary museum.

Follow D21 to Panzoult and then take D221 to Crouzilles.

Crouzilles. − Pop 453. Built in the 12C and covered with Angevin vaulting in 13C, the **church** is fascinating owing to the way in which the statues have been incorporated into the church's structure. The buttresses on either side of the Romanesque door have been carved with a niche to hold a statue; in the apse statues have been placed at the springing line of the vault: St Peter, the Virgin, St John, St Paul and in the southeast corner of the south transept the "beau Dieu de Crouzilles".

Take D 760 west to L'Ile-Bouchard.

L'Ile-Bouchard. − *Description p 108.*

The road passes in front of the church of St-Gilles, then crosses the Vienne to the other half of the town.

Take D 18 east to Parçay-sur-Vienne.

⊙**Parçay-sur-Vienne**. − Pop 1 538. This 12C **church** has a fine Romanesque doorway flanked by blind arcades. It is decorated with carved archivolts representing bearded faces, foliated scrolls and palmettes and the ensemble is adorned with a motif resembling fish scales. The capitals in the chancel are decorated with fantastic animals of amazing ugliness inspired by the Apocalypse of St John the Divine.

Return to L'Ile-Bouchard and take D 760 westwards along the south bank of the Vienne.

⊙**Tavant**. − Pop 218. This Romanesque **church** is of special interest owing to its 12C **frescoes**★ which adorn the vaulting, the apse and crypt. More marked in the crypt than in the church, the figures show a power of expression and a degree of realism extremely rare during the Romanesque period. Note the capitals in the chancel.

About 2 miles further on, beyond Sazilly, D 760 passes **Bretignolles Château** (left), a Louis XII style building with turrets.

Turn left into D 749.

★ **Rivau Château**. − *Description p 157.*

Return to Chinon by D 749 and ③ on the plan.

Rabelais Country. − *25 km - 15 miles by ③ on the plan. The road runs through a tunnel of enormous plane trees to St-Lazare; turn right into D 751, an old Roman road; after 3 km - 2 miles turn left into D 759; then turn right into D 24 and fork right into D 117.*

⊙**La Devinière**. − This house was the birthplace of **François Rabelais** (1494-1553). He was the son of a Chinon lawyer and after a studious childhood, he became a monk, fell in love with ancient Greek and studied the humanists. He transferred to the secular clergy, studied medicine at Montpellier and became a famous doctor, under the patronage of such great names as Cardinal Jean du Bellay and his brother the Governor of Piedmont; in 1551 the Cardinal obtained the living at Meudon for Rabelais.

With the publication of *Pantagruel* in 1532 Rabelais, the distinguished Hellenist, revealed the humourous side of his character by choosing burlesque farce and every kind of comedy to express his philosophy.

At La Devinière one sees Rabelais' room and a small museum illustrating his life and work; there is an interesting study on the origins of his hero Gargantua.

Return to D 117 going south.

On the opposite side of the valley stands the beautiful **Coudray-Montpensier Château** (15C) with its myriad roofs. In between lies **Seuilly-Côteaux**, a long straggling street of troglodyte houses.

It was in the abbey at Seuilly that Rabelais was educated; he used it as the setting for one of his characters in *Gargantua*.

Lerné. − Pop 338. Picturesque village built of yellow tufa.

In Rabelais' book this was the village from which the bakers *(fouaciers)* of a special sort of bread set out to sell their goods *(fouaces)* in Chinon market; it was a dispute between them and the shepherds from Seuilly that sparked off the comic Picrocholean War between Pichrocole, king of Lerné, an aggressive fighter, and Grandgousier, the wise prince of Seuilly, who was Gargantua's father.

Return to Chinon, taking D 224 which runs through Seuilly-Bourg at the bottom of the slope; near the road junction with D 749 (right) stands **La Roche-Clermault Château** which was taken by assault by Pichrocole and his men in Rabelais' story.

CHOLET

Pop 56 528

Michelin map 67 folds 5, 6 or 232 fold 30.
Town plan in Michelin Red Guide France

Cholet is a spacious modern town, which thrives on its various industries: textiles, shoes, fashion, plastic, electronics, agricultural machinery and a Michelin tyre factory. The town is surrounded by the pastures of Les Mauges *(p 136)* and is also an important cattle market.

Ravages of War. − There is scarcely a building in Cholet which dates from before the Revolution since the town suffered sorely in the Vendean wars *(p 23)*. At the beginning of the peasant insurrection the town was captured by the Whites (15 March 1793) who then regrouped before marching victoriously on Saumur and Angers. On 17 October Cholet was captured by Kléber after a bloody battle in which 40 000 Vendeans faced 25 000 Blues; the victor described it as a "battle between lions and tigers"; the dead numbered 10 000. On 10 March 1794 after hand to hand fighting in the streets Stofflet was victorious but a few days later the "infernal columns" under General Turreau put Cholet to fire and the sword. On 18 March Stofflet returned but was soon repulsed by General Cordelier; the town was left in ruins.

Cholet handkerchiefs. – Cholet has been involved in the cultivation of hemp and flax since 11C; spinning and weaving are long-established industries. In 16C the handkerchief was introduced into France from Italy; in 18C Cholet cloth was part of the cargo of manufactured goods which the ship owners of Nantes and La Rochelle traded on the coasts of Africa in exchange for slaves who were then sold in the West Indies; the money was spent on rum which was imported into France; this was the "triangular trade". Despite the devastation of the town in the revolutionary wars, Cholet was not destroyed; it re-established its crafts and tenaciously fostered the textile industry throughout the 19C. Cholet cloth, handkerchiefs and table linen are now well known; the locals have a particular affection for the traditional red handkerchief with a white border.

SIGHTS

★**History and Vendean War Museum.** – The ground floor is devoted to the old cloth-making technique (weaving loft, display of handkerchiefs); on the first floor the various aspects of the Vendean wars are illustrated: maps, souvenirs, paintings of the local leaders.

★**Fine Arts Museum.** – A handsome 19C house, set in its own grounds, provides an elegant setting for a collection of paintings by modern artists: Toulouse-Lautrec, Vuillard, Bonnard, Fernand Léger, Braque, Chagall, Matisse, Vasarely, Arp, etc.

Rue du Commerce. – A pedestrian precinct has been created in the town centre, Rue du Devau which becomes Rue du Commerce, where rare 18C wrought-iron balconies adorn the houses. On the south side of the street the **Mall Garden** makes a pleasant setting for the Law Courts.

EXCURSIONS

Ribou Leisure Park. – *5 km - 3 miles southeast by D 20.*
An artificial lake encircled by hills provides facilities for sports (boating, archery...).
★**La Goubaudière** Farm has been converted into a **Rural Museum** showing a typical late 19C interior of the Cholet region: furniture, everyday articles, collection of tools and agricultural machinery from 1900-50.

Beyond the Moulin-Ribou dam turn left into D 258 to La Tessoualle; there take D 157 east past Le Verdon Lake to Maulévrier.

Maulévrier Oriental Park. – The park was created between 1902 and 1910 by Marcel the architect who designed the oriental pavilion for a Paris Exhibition in 1900. Khmer sculptures and Bhuddist temples are enhanced by their agreable setting.

Coudray-Montbault Château. – *25 km - 15 1/2 miles east by N 160 and D 960.*
The moated 16C château with its two massive round towers of brick and stone and green lozenge decoration was built on the ruins of a 13C castle. A ruined chapel in the park contains a recumbent figure and an Entombment.

CINQ-MARS-LA-PILE   Pop 2 438
Michelin map 🔲 fold 14 or 🔲🔲🔲 fold 35 (5 km - 3 miles northeast of Langeais)

The place name is derived from a curious monument in the shape of a slim tower *(pile)*, dating from the Gallo-Roman period, which dominates the ridge east of the village. The structure is 5 m - 16 1/2 ft square and 30 m - 98 1/2 ft high and is topped by four small pyramids, one at each corner. It could be a funerary monument or a navigation light but it is most likely a mausoleum built in 2C AD.

Castle. – Two round towers (11 and 12C) on the hillside mark the site of the medieval castle where Henri d'Effiat, Marquis of Cinq-Mars, was born. He was the favourite of Louis XIII but was convicted of conspiring against Richelieu and beheaded in Lyon in 1642 at the age of 22.
Each tower contains three rooms one above the other roofed with eight-ribbed ogive vaulting. From the top there is an extensive view of the Loire Valley. The surrounding **park★** is particularly beautiful: here a romantic garden, there a complicated maze, elsewhere dense woodland. The bushes are clipped and the paths neatly edged but with a light touch that does not spoil the natural charm.

★ CLÉRY-ST-ANDRÉ   Pop 2 242
Michelin map 🔲 fold 8 or 🔲🔲🔲 fold 4 – Local map p 123

The present **church** had its origin in a humble chapel to which, in 1280, some ploughmen carried a statue of the Virgin found in a thicket. The cult of this statue spread throughout the district, and the chapel, being too small to accommodate the pilgrims, was transformed into a church served by a college of canons. This was destroyed in 1428 by the English commander Salisbury, on his march to Orléans. A **pilgrimage**, which is very popular, is held on 8 September and the following Sunday.
Charles VII and Dunois supplied the first funds for rebuilding, but the great benefactor of Cléry was **Louis XI**. During the siege of Dieppe, while still only the Dauphin, he made a vow: if he were victorious, he would give his weight in silver to Notre-Dame de Cléry. His prayer was answered and he kept his vow. When he became King, Louis XI dedicated himself to the Virgin and his attachment to Cléry was strengthened thereby. He was buried there by his wish and the building was completed by his son, Charles VIII.
The house (now a school) in which Louis XI stayed during his visits to Cléry is on the south side of the church opposite the transept entrance.

★ BASILICA   *time: 1/2 hour*

Notre-Dame de Cléry is a 15C building with the exception of its square tower abutting the north side of the church which is 14C and alone escaped destruction by the English. *Entrance in the transept.*
The interior of the church is austere yet elegant; it should be imagined in the warm light of its former stained glass windows and hung with tapestries.

The Tomb of Louis XI. – The tomb stands on the north side of the nave and is aligned with the Virgin's altar, so that it lies at an oblique angle to the axis of the church.
The marble statue of the King is the work of an Orléans sculptor, Bourdin (1622). It took the place of the original bronze statue melted down by the Huguenots.

Louis XI's Vault. – Louis XI's bones and those of his wife, Charlotte de Savoie, are still in the vault which opens on to the nave near the tomb. The two skulls, sawn open for embalming, are in a glass case. Note the decorative mourning band *(litre - see p 34)* which runs round the vaulting.
Tanguy de Châtel, who was killed during a siege while saving the life of Louis XI, is buried under a flagstone alongside the royal vault. Further to the right another stone covers the urn containing the heart of Charles VIII. The inscription on this urn is repeated on the nearest pillar.

★ **St James's Chapel.** – *South aisle.* This was built by Gilles de Pontbriand, Dean of the church, and his brother to serve as their tomb. The Gothic decoration is very rich. The vaulting is decorated with girdles, pilgrims' purses, for Cléry is on the pilgrimage route to St James's shrine in Santiago de Compostela, Spain. The walls are studded with ermines' tails and bridges (the arms of the Pontbriands). There are three fine statues of which two are of wood: St James in a pilgrim's cloak is 16C, St Sebastian is 17C, and the Virgin with the very delicate features is 16C and of stone. The Breton style wooden grille was offered by Louis XIII in 1622.

Dunois Chapel. – *From the St James's Chapel the second door to the left.* Dunois and his family lie here *(p 78)*. The church at Cléry was finished when this chapel was added (1464) so that the construction of the vaulting was complicated by the presence of a buttress.

Stalls. – These were presented by Henri II. Their seats are carved with human masks and the initials of the donor and his mistress, Diane de Poitiers (see cheekpieces – *see p 34* – of second row on the right).

Chancel. – On the modern high altar is a statue in wood of Notre-Dame de Cléry. In the central window a fine piece of 16C stained glass represents Henri III founding the Order of the Holy Spirit.

Sacristy and oratory of Louis XI. – In the second ambulatory bay on the right is the beautiful door to the sacristy, in pure Flamboyant style. Above it a small opening leads to an oratory *(spiral staircase in the sacristy)* from which Louis XI could follow the services.

CLOYES-SUR-LOIR   Pop 2 653

Michelin map 🔟 southwest of fold 17 or 🔢 fold 38 – Local map p 118 – Facilities

Cloyes, once a fortified town, bestrides a bend in the Loir on the southern edge of the Beauce; it was also a staging post on the pilgrim road to Santiago de Compostela. It is a welcoming town with several old houses and a church with a 15C belfry. In 1883 **Zola** stayed in Cloyes to study the local customs for his novel – *The Earth* – which is set in Cloyes and Romilly-sur-Aigre *(see below)*.

The Children's Crusade. – In 1212 a young shepherd from Cloyes, called Estienne, gathered a following of about 20 000 children on a pilgrimage to the Holy Land. Neither their parents nor their friends could deter them. The expedition was doomed to failure: some children died on the road, others perished at sea and a few were even sold to the Saracens.

Yron Chapel. – *1 km - 1/2 mile south on N 10 (direction Vendôme), then turn right into D 8¹; entrance in the garden of the old people's home.* The Romanesque chapel is decorated with well preserved **mural paintings** in red and ochre tones. Those in the nave are 12C and depict the Flagellation and the Offering of the Magi (left), Judas' Kiss and a priest (St Bernard) (right) and the Apostles (apse) below a delicate realisation of Christ in Majesty (14C).

EXCURSIONS

Montigny-le-Gannelon Château. – *2 km - 1 1/2 miles north by D 23. Description p 141.*

Aigre Valley. – *Round trip of 20 km - 12 1/2 miles. Leave Cloyes-sur-le-Loir by D 8 going east.* The road climbs on to a plateau overlooking (right) the Aigre Valley.

Romilly-sur-Aigre. – Pop 360. The quiet country village climbs the slope on the south bank of the Aigre. Above the village on the edge of the plateau *(D 8³ direction Ouzouer-le-Doyen)* stands an unusual church adjoining a fortified building. Romilly appears in **Zola's** novel *The Earth* under the name of Rognes; the big Beauceron farm described by Zola is probably based on La Touche about 500 m - 550 yards beyond the church.

Return through the village to D 8; turn right.

La Ferté-Villeneuil. – Pop 361. Drive through the village down to the banks of the Aigre where a fortified Romanesque church with a solid tower complements the charming scene.

Take the road back to Cloyes.

CORMERY
Pop 1 169

Michelin map no 64 fold 15 or 238 fold 15

Cormery, which is famous for its macaroons, is prettily sited beside the Indre with inns on either bank. Near the bridge, half-hidden under the weeping willows is an **old mill**; downstream the river feeds the ancient washing place.

Old Abbey. – The Benedictine Abbey, which was founded in 791, was suppressed a thousand years later in 1791; the buildings were confiscated and sold and mostly demolished. The few remains conjure up a picture of the complete abbey; the model shows it as it was in 14 and 15C.

Rue de l'Abbaye, which begins beside the Town Hall *(on N 143)* passes under a tall ruined tower, **St Paul's Tower,** the huge 11C belltower above the entrance to the church; note the Romanesque low-reliefs and the decorative effect below the upper windows. The **Prior's Lodging** at the foot of the tower is marked by an elegant staircase turret. In the street on the left are the arches of the **former refectory** (13C). Of the church itself nothing remains on the far side of the tower; the street follows the line of the nave. The graceful Gothic chapel (left) which was reserved for the Abbot was originally next to the apsidal chapel of the church and linked to the **Abbot's Lodging** which has a turret and a half-timbered penthouse.

⊙**Notre-Dame-du-Fougeray.** – The church of Our Lady of Fougeray, which dominates the valley, is a Romanesque building with elements typical of the Poitou region: a large apse with three apsidal chapels, storiated brackets, a frieze and a dome on pendentives over the transept crossing.

In the cemetery opposite the church there is an altar and a 12C lantern of the dead.

COURTANVAUX Château

Michelin map 64 fold 5 or 238 fold 1 (2 km - 1 1/4 miles northwest of Bessé-sur-Braye)

⊙The Gothic building sheltering in the valley was the seat of a marquisate held successively by the Louvois and Montesquiou families; one of the owners was Michel Le Tellier, Marquis de Louvois and Louis XIV's Minister for War.

In 1815, when Napoleon fell, the château came to life again after 150 years of neglect and became the residence of the Countess of Montesquiou who had been governess to the King of Rome, Napoleon's son by Marie-Louise.

An avenue of plane trees leads to the charming Renaissance gatehouse. The buildings have typical 15C and 16C features: tall roofs, mullioned windows and pointed dormer pediments. The courtyard is dominated by two terraces. The main block, called the "grand château", has a suite of four rooms (47 m - 154 ft long) on the first floor; they were re-decorated in 1882.

CRAON
Pop 5 021

Michelin map 63 fold 9 or 232 fold 18

Craon (pronounced Cran) is a quiet Angevin town on the River Oudon surrounded by woodland and pastures, devoted to arable farming and cattle raising. It is famous for its horses races (August and September). From the terrace behind the church there is a pleasant view of the town.

Craon was the birthplace of Volney (1757-1820), the philosopher, who enjoyed great fame in his lifetime.

⊙**Château.** – Built *c*1770 in the local white tufa, this elegant château has a curvilinear pediment and windows adorned with festoons characteristic of the Louis XVI period. The courtyard façade is in a severe neo-Classical style. Several 18C rooms with fine woodwork and Louis XVI furnishings are on show.

In the landscaped garden beside the Oudon there is an underground ice house, built in 19C. In winter it was filled with ice and packed snow to serve as a cold chamber for the preservation of food in the summer.

EXCURSIONS

⊙**Mortiercrolles Château.** – *11 km - 7 miles southeast by D25 and a path to the left.* This beautiful château was built in the late 15C by Pierre de Rohan, Marshal of Gié. A broad moat surrounds the long curtain wall with its four corner towers, which is guarded by a remarkable **gatehouse★** with alternating courses of brick and stone and fine machicolations in tufa. In the courtyard the building containing the main apartments (right) is decorated with superb dormer gables. At the rear of the courtyard an elegant chapel of brick with stone courses was re-roofed in 1969: note the beautiful Renaissance side door and the piscina adorned with beautiful shells.

La Frénouse. – *14 km - 9 miles northeast of Craon by N 171 and D 126.*
A driveway lined with giant statues leads to La Frénouse, an old farmhouse (restored), and to an unusual museum built of stone and mortar by Mr Tatin (1902-83) to display his paintings and ceramics. One can detect a Latin-American echo which reminded Mr Tatin of his childhood.

⊙**Robert Tatin Museum.** – The museum was created as a link between the East and West. A collection of structures is grouped round a pool; the walls are covered with drawings and the sculptures are like totems.

★★ CUNAULT Church

Michelin map 🔢 fold 12 or 🔢 fold 32 (12 km - 8 miles northwest of Saumur) — Local map p 127

Cunault Abbey was founded in 847 by monks from Noirmoutier fleeing from the Normans; in 862 they had to move from Cunault and take refuge further away in Tournus in Burgundy where they deposited the relics of St Philibert. Cunault therefore became a rich Benedictine priory dependent on Tournus Abbey. The monastic church is a beautiful Romanesque structure dating from 11-13C.

Tour. — The huge 11C belltower has been extended by a 15C stone spire; the broad façade is simply decorated with arches at the base and three windows above. In contrast the tympanum over the door is richly decorated with an Adoration of the Virgin in generous high relief. Gregorian chant.

Interior. — On entering one is struck by the size and height of the pillars. Cunault church was built in the regular Benedictine style to provide for the liturgical ceremonies (seven per day in the Rule of St Benedict) and for the crowds which attended the pilgrimage on 8 September. The ambulatory with its radiating chapels which circumscribed the chancel and the side aisles were broad enough to take the traditional processions and the raised chancel enabled the faithful to see the celebrant.

(Photo Cauchetier/Pix)

Cunault Church — Detail of the doorway

The empty church is now doubly impressive for its clean lines and for the rich decoration (11-12C) of the 223 **capitals**. Only two, at the entrance to the chancel, are visible without binoculars: (right) nine monks standing and (left) St Philibert welcoming a sinner. The ambulatory chapels contain (starting on the left) a 16C Pietà, a 16C ash vestment wardrobe (for stiff copes) and a rare 13C carved and painted **shrine** belonging to St Maxenceul who converted Cunault in 4C. In 15C the church was decorated with frescoes: a few fragments and a fine St Christopher remain. The four bells in the tower come from Constantine cathedral in Algeria. Opposite the church stands the prior's lodging, an attractive 16C house.

DAMPIERRE-EN-BURLY   Pop 909

Michelin map 🔢 fold 1 or 🔢 fold 7 (13 km - 8 miles west of Gien)

The flat tiled roofs of Dampierre present an attractive spectacle to anyone approaching from the west on D 952 from Ouzouer-sur-Loire; as the road crosses the tree-lined lake by a causeway, the ruins of a château come into view; beyond what remains of the towers and curtain wall of the castle rises the church tower.
In the square by the church stands one of the château gatehouses, an elegant early 17C building, in brick and stone, decorated with bossed pilasters beneath a pyramidal roof.

Nuclear Power Station. — *3 km - 2 miles south; signposted.*
The four gigantic cooling towers (165 m - 541 ft high and 135 m - 443 ft diameter at the base) rising out of the flat Loire Valley belong to the nuclear power station which, like those at Chinon *(p 56)* and St-Laurent-des-Eaux, uses the river to supply water to the cooling system. The Dampierre complex, which was commissioned in 1980 and 1981, consists of four production units with an output of 900 MW using enriched uranium in pressurized water reactors. The way in which the reactors work is described in the information centre.

DANGEAU   Pop 752

Michelin map 🔢 fold 17 or 🔢 fold 38 (9 km - 6 miles west of Bonneval)

The village square is bordered by old houses of brick and timber construction (15C).

St Peter's Church. — The church, which was built early in 12C by monks from Marmoutier, is a vast, well-arranged structure in a very pure Romanesque style. The buttresses and facings are of iron stone. The door in the south porch is decorated with scrolls and strange symbols carved on the lintel: the cross appears between the sun and the moon which have human faces, avarice is shown as a demon holding a purse, luxury as a female figure.
The wooden ceiling in the nave is supported on archaic pillars. There are several statues in the aisles: the two figures on horseback are typical of popular 15-17C religious art. The baptistry contains a marble triptych of the Passion and the Resurrection, dated 1536.

DESCARTES

Michelin map 68 fold 5

It was in Descartes, formerly known as La Haye, that **René Descartes** (1590-1650), the famous French philosopher, physicist and mathematician was baptised, although the family home was in the neighbouring town of Châtellerault. At the age of eight he was sent to the Jesuit College of Henri IV in La Flèche where he received a semi military education, before joining the army under the Prince of Nassau. While pursuing his military career, he travelled widely in Europe, devoting most of his time to study, and the pursuit of his life's mission as it was revealed to him on 10 November 1619. In 1629 he went again to Holland where he stayed for twenty years, studying at various universities and writing and publishing some of his most famous works. In 1649 he accepted an invitation to the Swedish royal court, where he died on 11 February 1650.

Cartesian thought. – In 1637 Descartes had *Discourse on Method* published. It was exceptionally written in French and not in Latin, the common language of all learned works. The *Discourse* has radically influenced modern philosophical thought – it introduced a new mentality and thus new problems.

Descartes explained how he was deceived by the knowledge he had received from education and books. He suggested the rejection of all accepted ideas and opinions – to doubt until convinced of the contrary by self-evident facts. He concluded his thought with: "... I who doubt, I who am deceived, at least while I doubt, I must exist and as doubting is thinking, it is indubitable that while I think I am".

Descartes Museum. – *29 Rue Descartes*. This house is where Descartes was born. Documents recounting his life and works are displayed.

EXCURSIONS

Balesmes. – *2 km - 1 mile to the northwest by D 750*. Standing amidst this charming village with its houses roofed in rose-coloured tiles, the church presents an attractive belfry over the transept crossing.

Les Ormes. – *7 km - 4 miles to the west on N 10*. The **château** gates border the road (as you leave the village by the north). A magnificent alley of chestnut and plane trees leads to the courtyard. The central building, an early 20C reconstruction, is linked to two 18C pavilions by means of single storey arcades with roof-top terraces. Two wings (18C) at right angles to the main front, face one another across the courtyard.

The former stables, known as **La Bergerie**, present a severe but striking Classical pediment on the other side of N 10.

Ferrière-Larçon. – *16 km - 10 miles to the east by D 100*.

Château du Châtellier. – Standing on a rocky outcrop, commanding the Brignon Valley, this castle (rebuilt 15 and 17C) has preserved some of its medieval fortifications: moats, drawbridges and to the east of its rampart, an imposing round keep with a spur.

Ferrière-Larçon. – Pop 348. The picturesque tile roofs of this village climb haphazardly up the valley slopes. The **church** is an interesting mixture of styles with a narrow Romanesque nave (12C) and a vast, luminous Gothic chancel (13C). The elegant Romanesque bell tower is capped by an octagonal stone spire with a pinnacle at each corner.

★ DOUÉ-LA-FONTAINE

Michelin map 67 fold 8 or 232 fold 32 – Local map p 113

Doué and its outskirts are built on a chalk plateau which is riddled with caves; some are old quarries, others were excavated to provide housing or storage, as a wine cellar or a stable. The caves are invisible from the street since they were not hollowed out of the hillside as in the valley of the Loire and its tributaries but were below ground level and opened laterally into a broad ditch forming a courtyard. Some are still in use but most were abandoned long since.

Doué still has a number of old houses with turrets and external stairs. The town's main activities are nursery gardening and rose growing; examples of these arts are on show in the **Rose Garden** (a public garden on the Soulanger road) and at the famous flower show, **Journées de la Rose**, which takes place each year in mid-July in the arena.

A windmill marks the entrance to Doué in the Saumur road, the lone survivor of the many that used to cover the region.

★★**Zoo (Parc zoologique des Minières).** – The zoo is situated on the western edge of Doué on the road to Cholet (D 960); the **setting★** is a series of old quarries, now overgrown. The tunnels, caverns and smaller cavities have been used to provide the animals with a natural outdoor habitat, to enable as much contact with the public as possible (in summer some of the monkeys roam freely while the macaws perch in the

(Photo Weyland)

Doué-la-Fontaine Zoological Park

trees). The way of life and the characteristics of the various creatures living in the zoo are explained on the notices. There are several threatened species which would not survive unless they were bred in captivity: snow panthers, Sumatra tigers, wolves, gibbons, the lemurian colobus and Andean condor. A quarry has been turned into a "Vulture Safari" where the visitor can walk among the birds of prey; the "Emu Safari" enables one to see these huge birds at close range. Nine families of monkeys roam freely on as many islands.

Arena. — In 15C an old quarry in the **Douces** district was transformed into an arena when terraces of seats were cut out of the solid rock. It is now used for theatrical and musical performances and the flower show *(p 98)*. Beneath the terraces are vast caves which were for a long time inhabited and kitchens and other rooms are still visible. Royalists were imprisoned here during the revolutionary wars.

Carolingian House (Maison Carolingienne). — *Boulevard du Docteur-Lionnet, on the southern outskirts of the town near the road to Argenton-Château (D 69).*
This 9C fortified dwelling was later transformed into a keep.

EXCURSIONS

Rochemenier troglodyte village (Village troglodytique de Rochemenier). — *6 km - 3 1/2 miles north by D 69 and D 177.* Two troglodyte farms, which were abandoned in the 1930s, are open to the public. The underground village, which extended over a large area, is now deserted and hidden by the new "aerial" houses in which the majority of the inhabitants live.

La Fosse troglodyte hamlet (Hameau troglodytique de la Fosse). — *5.5 km - 3 miles north by D 214.*
Excavations in 1979 revealed this fine example of a type of rural architecture which was formerly unappreciated; the hamlet used to house three families until it was abandoned in the 1940s.
Like the *bories* of Provence it shows how the peasants adapted to living underground. The various chambers were hollowed out below ground around a sunken courtyard, similar to the troglodyte dwellings in Tunisia; only the chimneys protruded above ground level. Ovens and chimneys were dug straight into the earth; so were stores for grain and vegetables.

Sculpted Cavern (Caverne sculptée). — *5.5 km - 3 miles north by D 69.*
This cave at **Dénezé-sous-Doué** is most unusual; its walls are carved with hundreds of grotesque figures. From the attitudes and dress and musical instruments the archaeologists have dated the carvings to 16C; they are probably the work of a secret society of stone masons and depict their initiation rites. The guides are ready to give a detailed explanation of the different scenes.

Coudray-Montbault Château. — *24 km - 15 miles west by D 960. Description p 94.*

DURTAL   Pop 3 240

Michelin map 64 fold 2 or 232 fold 20

Durtal is attractively sited in the shelter of its château on the Loir. The **Chambiers Forest** on the southern edge of the town provides 1 300 ha - 5 sq miles of walks among the oak and pine trees; broad rides radiate from the King's Table (table au roy). The race course is a popular meeting place for the sporting fraternity.

Château. — This lordly stronghold on the Loir belonged to François de Scepeaux, Marshal of Vieilleville, who was host to Henri II, Charles IX and Catherine de' Medici. It came through the Revolution relatively unscathed and is now a retirement home.
The six-storey keep and the round towers with machicolations and pepperpot roofs are 15 and 16C. The sentry walk provides a view of the Loire Valley and the Chambiers Forest. The main range and the other buildings are in the Louis XIII style. Note the tapered dormers framed with twisted columns in the courtyard. The tour of the interior includes the kitchens, the dungeons, the 15C round tower and the great hall which is decorated with frescoes.

Verron Gate. — This 15C gate flanked by two turrets is part of the original curtain wall of the castle.

Old Bridge. — View of the River Loir, the watermills, the pointed roofs of the town and a medieval round tower upstream.

★ La FERTÉ-BERNARD   Pop 9 797

Michelin map 60 fold 15 or 232 folds 11, 12 — Local map p 153

La Ferté-Bernard is a lively commercial town at the centre of an agricultural region. The old houses cluster round the Church of Our Lady of the Marshes. The lush pastures of the Huisne valley are watered by this river, its tributary the Même and several smaller streams.
The old fortified town, which grew up round the castle *(ferté)* was built on stilts in the middle of the marshes. It was distinguished by the name of the first feudal lord, Bernard, whose descendants held the domain until 14C. Under Louis XI it was the property of the Guise family; in 16C it enjoyed a period of economic prosperity which produced some remarkable buildings which contribute to the charm of the town. After taking the side of the League and being defeated by the troops of Henri IV, La Ferté was sold to Cardinal de Richelieu in 1642; his heirs held it until the Revolution.

La FERTÉ-BERNARD ★

La Ferté-Bernard was the birth place of the poet **R. Garnier** (1544-90); he wrote seven tragedies of which the best known, *The Jews,* echoes Corneille and foreshadows Racine. His play *Bradamante* is an early tragi-comedy while his modernism links him to Voltaire.

The lambs of La Ferté. — "It needs only two to strangle a wolf" so it was said. In 1590 the troops of Henri IV under the Prince de Conti were besieging La Ferté which was defended by the supporters of the League who were commanded by a descendant of the Emperor of Byzantium, Drago Comnenos.

As food was in short supply, Comnenos decided to get rid of the surplus population and expelled a number of women to fend for themselves to the great delight of the besiegers. Comnenos then disguised 200 of his ruffians as young women and expelled them. The besiegers approached with great expectations but when they came within range the "lambs" threw off their bonnets and petticoats and turned into hardened old troopers who put the credulous suitors to flight.

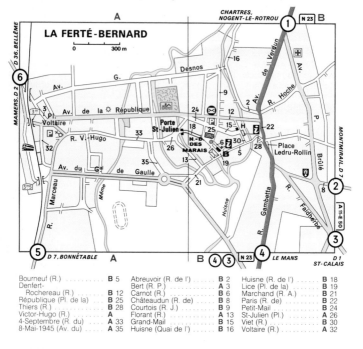

SIGHTS

★★ **Church of Our Lady of the Marshes** (Notre-Dame-des-Marais — B). — This magnificent building is a fine example of the Flamboyant style with early touches of the Renaissance. The nave and transept and the square tower were built between 1450 and 1500; from 1535 to 1544 Mathurin Delaborde worked on the church and between 1550 and 1590 the Viet brothers were in charge of the construction of the spacious chancel (completed in 1596); the ambulatory serves the radiating chapels which have galleries and flying buttresses and solid buttresses topped with crocketed pinnacles.

Exterior. — There are Renaissance motifs in the carved decoration of the chancel; the south side is ornamented with scroll work and busts of Roman emperors in the spandrels; there are niches in the buttresses. The low gallery is supported on a carved cornice of shells and busts in relief between the corbels. On the balustrade stand some unusual little statues of the King of France and his twelve peers etc; in the spaces are the words "Regina Coeli". The upper gallery spells out the letters of "Ave Regina Coelorum". The height of the chancel compared with the original tower on the lefthand side reveals the ambition of the plans drawn up in the late 16C.
The entrance is the Flamboyant south door.

Interior. — At the west end are the original Renaissance holy water stoups; the nave contains the organ pipes supported on a Flamboyant corbel.
The very elegant chancel consists of soaring arches, each one surmounted by a small statue on a dais, a light and simple Renaissance triforium and tall windows filled with light 16 and 17C glass.
The three **apsidal chapels**★ are of particular interest. The righthand chapel has an astonishing ceiling of ogive vaulting meeting in a crown-shaped pendant; the windows and the delicate carved cartouches and the stoup are all 16C. In the central chapel the spaces between the ribs are decorated with stalactites and honeycombs; the Renaissance window (left) shows the meal at Bethany with Mary Magdalene at Jesus' feet. The lefthand chapel has an unusual ceiling. The altarpiece in the side chapel on the left of the chancel shows the instruments of the Passion.

St Julian's Gate (Porte St-Julien — A). — The gate which is protected by two round towers and machicolations was built in 15C under Louis XI; the moat was fed by the River Huisne. There was a postern and a double gate for vehicles guarded by a portcullis and a drawbridge.

Regional Museum. – The eight rooms in St Julian's Gatehouse present collections of postcards of France, porcelain dolls with regional headdresses and a reconstruction in terracotta of craftsmen at work and of the interior of a house in the Sarthe region, with carvings, ceramics and pottery and mannequins dressed in late 19C costume.

Old Houses. – East of St Julian's Gate in Rue de l'Huisne are a few Renaissance houses (no 15 - telamon).
There are several old houses in Rue Carnot including a pilgrim inn (15C) on the road to Santiago de Compostela and a house (butcher's shop) decorated with painted telamones representing a pilgrim (ground floor) being stared at by a madman and a grimacing Moor and two people (first floor) stoning St Stephen.

Market (B B). – The market hall *(restored)* in Place de la Lice and Rue Carnot was built in 1535. The façade overlooking the square is decorated with Guise lions on each gable and an extensive tile roof pierced by dormers and supported by very fine woodwork.

Fountain. – The granite fountain (15C-16C) is fed by a spring in les Guillottières district which is channelled beneath the Huisne.

EXCURSIONS

Ceton Church. – *8 km - 5 miles northeast by D 153.*
St Peter's Church (recently restored) derives its importance from the Cluniac priory to which it belonged from 1090. The tower is Romanesque, the Gothic nave and chancel were built in 13-16C. Each bay in the side aisles has its own roof at right angles to the nave in the Percheron manner.
A touchingly naive 16C Entombment stands out in the interior among the fine statues.

Le Perche-Gouët Round Trip. – *Description p 152. From Ceton drive 5 km - 3 miles east to Les Etilleux.*

La FERTÉ-ST-AUBIN   Pop 5 498

Michelin map 🔢 fold 9 or 🔢🔢🔢 fold 5

The town extends north-south between the N 20 and the railway line. Smelting works, saw mills, garment factories and nursery gardens are among its commercial activities. The old district by the château has a few typical local houses: low, timber-framed with brick infill, huge roofs of flat tiles.

Château. – The château on the south bank of the Cosson was built in the middle of the 17C of brick with stone courses; it is connected with the life of the Marshal of La Ferté-Sennecterre. A moat surrounds the majestic pile.
The tour of the château can be rounded off with a visit to the **Horse Museum**.

St Aubin's Church. – 12-16C. The tall tower over the entrance dominates the Cosson Valley.

EXCURSION

Le Ciran Domain. – *7 km - 5 miles east; signpost on D 108.*
The domain is a stretch of typical Sologne country: forest, scrub, meadows, streams, pools. The château and the old storehouse contain a little **museum** devoted to the Sologne and its former way of life.

★ La FLÈCHE   Pop 16 241

Michelin map 🔢 fold 2 or 🔢🔢🔢 fold 21 – Local map p 120 – Facilities

This charming Angevin town, pleasantly situated on the banks of the Loir, is renowned for its *Prytanée,* a military college which has trained generations of officers.
Market town for the varied fruit produce from the Maine, La Flèche has recently experienced an industrial expansion with the building of several large factories, including the printing works of the paperback publishers *Livre de Poche.*
Students tend to group around the Henri IV Fountain (on the square of the same name); and yet a stroll along the Boulevard Latouche and Carmes Gardens is also pleasant.

Henri IV, the Gay Old Spark. – La Flèche was given as part of a dowry to Charles de Bourbon-Vendôme, the grandfather of Henri IV of Navarre, of "Paris is well worth a Mass" fame.
It was here that the young Prince Henri happily spent his childhood and where in 1604 he founded a Jesuit college, which was to become the *Prytanée.*

Cradle for Officers. – The Jesuit college grew rapidly and by 1625 there were 1 500 pupils. Full of their success, the good fathers started a dispute with the Governor of the town who wanted to prevent them fishing in their moat; the dispute became known as the "war of the frogs". Following the expulsion of the Jesuits from France in 1762, the college became a military school and then an imperial military academy *(prytanée)* in 1808. The pupils were nicknamed *"brutions"* owing to their lack of good manners but the college produced some famous people: Descartes, La Tour d'Auvergne, the Dupetit-Thouars and several generals and marshals: Davout, Junot, Jourdan, Bertrand, Gallieni.

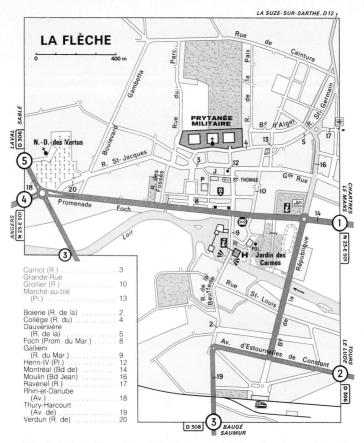

LA FLÈCHE

0   400 m

Missionaries in Canada. – Jérôme le Royer de la Dauversière, a native of La Flèche was one of the founders of Montreal. The paganism of the Canadian Indians moved him to create the "society of Our Lady for the conversion of the Savages" which started a little colony in 1642 which is now the capital of Quebec. In 1646 several Jesuit priests from La Flèche, working as missionaries in the Huron country, were martyred by the Iroquois Indians: Jogues, Lalemant and Brébeuf. Another old pupil of the college in La Flèche, **François de Montmorency-Laval**, became the first bishop of Nouvelle-France in 1674.

Unhappy exile. – Under the monarchy La Flèche was a peaceful town with nothing to offer by way of entertainment but a hairdresser's, two billiard halls and a café. **Gresset** (1709-77), the poet whose playful spirit produced the adventures of the parrot Vert-Vert, composed his heroic-comic masterpiece while in exile in La Flèche for indiscreet use of his tongue and his pen.

SIGHTS

★ Military College (Prytanée national militaire). – Essentially it is a school for the children of officers or civil servants who are working for the baccalauréat; they are selected after taking an entrance exam at the age of 15. The school also takes young students from any background, whose school record is acceptable, to prepare them for entrance to the national service academies *(grandes écoles);* there is a cavalry section. A monumental Baroque doorway, surmounted by a bust of Henri IV, marks the entrance to the former Jesuit college. It opens into the main courtyard, also known as the Austerlitz courtyard; at the far end stands a Louis XVI style house (1784) which is the commanding officer's residence. The school has an excellent library of some 45 000 volumes; some date from 15C.

★ St Louis's Chapel. – 1607-37. The chapel is in the Sebastopol Court where the architecture is austere. It is arranged in the typical Jesuit manner: nave bordered by side chapels, large galleries, plentiful light. The Baroque décor is impressive from the great retable on the high altar to the magnificent organ (1640) in its graceful loft. Set in an upper niche in the left transept is a heart-shaped lead gilt urn which contains the ashes of the hearts of Henri IV and Marie de' Medici.

Chapel of Our Lady of the Virtues (Notre-Dame-des-Vertus). – This is a charming Romanesque chapel with a semicircular arched doorway and oven-vaulted apses.
The wooden vaulting in the nave is completely decorated with 17C paintings (scrolls and medallions). The Renaissance **woodwork★** came originally from the chapel of Le Verger Château *(p 188);* note the "Muslim warrior" on the back of the main door; the panels are Renaissance. The carvings in the nave include medallions and religious attributes: the Last Supper near the pulpit.

Château des Carmes (H). – The 17C buildings erected on the ruins of a 15C fortress now house the Town Hall. The façade facing the Loir consists of a steep gable flanked by two machicolated turrets. The **Carmes Garden,** which is open to the public, reaches down to the river; from the bridge there is a fine view of the calm water reflecting the garden and the château.

EXCURSION

★ Le Tertre Rouge Zoo (Parc zoologique). − *5 km - 3 miles east. Leave La Flèche by ② on the plan and turn into D104; continue for 1 km - 1/2 mile after the third level crossing.*

The zoo covers 7 ha - 17 acres in a forest setting. There are mammals (wild animals, monkeys, deer, elephants, etc.), many birds, particularly birds of prey in a huge aviary, numerous reptiles in two vivariums (pythons, boas, crocodiles, tortoises, etc). The **Natural Science Museum** presents a diorama of the regional fauna. The 600 animals in the collection of the naturalist Jacques Bouillault can be seen in their natural postures in a reconstruction of their natural habitat.

★★ FONTEVRAUD-L'ABBAYE   Pop 1850

Michelin map 64 southwest of fold 13 or 232 fold 33 − Local map p 127

Fontevraud Abbey is on the borders of Anjou, Touraine and Poitou. Despite its deterioration it is the largest group of monastic buildings in France. There is a good view of the abbey from the Loudon road on the south side of the village.

Foundation (1101). − The order at Fontevraud was founded by **Robert d'Arbrissel** (c 1047-1117) who had been a hermit in the Mayenne Forest before being appointed by Urban II to preach in the West. With a group of disciples he chose this place to found a mixed community.

From the beginning the abbey was unique among religious houses in that it had five separate buildings accommodating monks (St-Jean-de-l'Habit), nuns (St Mary), lepers (St Lazarus), invalids (St Benedict) and fallen women (St Mary Magdalene).

Each body had its own church and cloister, its own refectory, kitchen and dormitory. Robert d'Arbrissel had ordained that the whole community should be directed by an Abbess chosen from among the widows; she was later designated as "Head and General of the Order" and this arrangement continued unaltered as long as the Abbey existed. In 1119 Pope Calixtus II came to bless the cemetery and consecrate the church.

The Order had dependent houses in England and Spain. The one at Amesbury was founded by Henry II in repentance for the murder of Thomas à Becket.

An Aristocratic Order. − The success of the new Order was immediate and it quickly took on an aristocratic character; the abbesses, who were members of noble families, procured rich gifts and powerful protection for the abbey. The Plantagenets showered it with wealth and elected to be buried in the abbey church. The abbey became a refuge for repudiated queens and daughters of royal or exalted families who, voluntarily or under compulsion, retired from the secular world. There were thirty-six abbesses, many of royal blood including five from the House of Bourbon, between 1115 and 1789. Louis XV entrusted the education of his four younger daughters to the Abbess of Fontevraud. There were periods of great laxity; to which the abbey was predisposed because of its recruitment and the fact that the monks were disinclined to obey a woman but an energetic abbess was always found to redress the situation. Marie de Bretagne (15C) was the first reforming abbess. Renée and Louise de Bourbon in 16 and in 17C Jeanne-Baptiste de Bourbon, daughter of Henri IV, and Madame de Montespan's sister, Gabrielle de Rochechouart-Mortemart, the "queen of the abbesses", made the abbey a spiritual and cultural centre of great renown.

In 18C Fontevraud owned 75 priories and about 100 estates; the community consisted of 100 nuns and 20 monks.

Plantagenet Tombs. − As a family the Plantagenets heaped wealth on the abbey and fifteen of them were buried in the abbey church. Henry II, his wife, Eleanor of Aquitaine and their son Richard the Lionheart are buried in the crypt. Later transfers to the crypt include the hearts of John Lackland and of his son Henry III, who rebuilt Westminster Abbey which in the 13C became the traditional burial place of English sovereigns.

Violation of the Abbey. − The Huguenots desecrated the abbey in 1561; in 1792 the Order was suppressed by the Revolutionaries who completely destroyed the monks' monastery in the following year.

In 1804 Napoleon converted the remaining buildings into a state prison which was closed only in 1963.

Cultural Vocation. − In 1975 the Abbey embarked on a new vocation as a **Centre Culturel de Rencontre** (Cultural Centre of the West) which conserves the buildings and organises concerts, spectacles, exhibitions, seminars and lectures. Since 1983 the activities of the FRAC (Regional Fund for Contemporary Art) have been housed at Fontevraud.

★★ ABBEY *time: 1 hour*

Among the buildings around the entrance court, most of which date from the 19C are, on the left, the vast 18C stables *(la fannerie)* and on the right, the 17 and 18C abbess's house adorned with garlands and low-reliefs.

★★ Abbey church. − This vast 12C church divided into storeys at the time it served as a prison has again found its original purity.

The wide nave with its delicately carved capitals is roofed by a series of domes, a characteristic of churches found in the southwest of France (Cahors, Périgueux, Angoulême, etc.). Fontevraud is the northernmost example of these curious domed churches and this can be explained by the important links between the Anjou and Aquitaine during the Plantagenet reign.

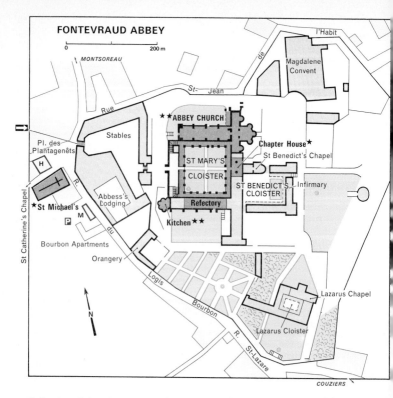

FONTEVRAUD ABBEY

0   200 m

Built several decades earlier than the nave, the transept and chancel resemble the Benedictine plan: an ambulatory and radiating chapels where the luminosity and repetition of vertical lines – slender columns, arcades, pillars – signify the aspiration to reach up to heaven.

In the south arm of the transept are the **Plantagenet tombs★**, polychrome recumbent figures representing Henry II, Count of Anjou and King of England *(p 48)*, his wife Eleanor of Aquitaine, who died at Fontevraud in 1204, their son Richard the Lionheart and lastly Isabella of Angoulême, second wife of their son, King John of England. In the 16C these recumbent figures were laid in the kings' cemetery *(cimetière des rois)* of which only the base still stands in the nave to the left of the chancel's entrance.

St Mary's Cloisters (Cloître Ste-Marie). – The cloisters in the nuns' convent have Renaissance vaulting except on the south side, which is still Gothic inspired.

A richly sculptured doorway in the east gallery, paved with the coat of arms of the Bourbons, opens into the **chapter house★** which is decorated with 16C mural paintings representing the abbesses.

St Benedict's Cloisters (Cloître St-Benoît). – Restored in parts (17-18C) the cloisters used to lead to the infirmary and housed the warming-room. The north wing includes the 12C St Benedict's Chapel.

Refectory. – This large hall (45 m - 148 ft long) with its Romanesque walls is roofed with Gothic vaulting which replaced a timber ceiling in 1515.

★★ Kitchen. – This is the only Romanesque kitchen which has been conserved over the centuries – despite its alterations. In many respects it resembles the kitchen at Glastonbury.

The technical skill of Magne, the architect backed by his artistic feeling combines to form a most intriguing building. The kitchen is roofed with overlapping stones and topped by a number of chimneys, inserted in 1904; built on an octagonal plan and capped by an octagonal hood, the building was originally flanked by eight apsidal chapels, three of which were destroyed in the 16C, when the kitchen was attached to the Refectory. The kitchen's large size can be explained by the great number of people it served and the large amount of smoked meat and fish (it was also used as a smoke room) consumed as part of the daily diet.

(Photo M. Guillard/Scope)

Fontevraud Abbey – Kitchen chimneys

ADDITIONAL SIGHTS

★ **St Michael's.** – A low lean-to gallery was built against the walls of this parish church in 18C, giving it an unexpected character and sheltering a beautiful 12C door with Romanesque paintings. Although the church was enlarged and remodelled in 13 and 15C, an inner arcade with small columns and typical Plantagenet style vaulting remain from the original Romanesque building.

The church contains numerous **works of art**★. The high altar of carved and gilded wood was made at the behest of the Abbess, Louise de Bourbon, in 1621 for the abbey church. In a north side chapel is a 15C wooden Crucifix simultaneously tormented and at peace, and an impressive 16C Crowning with Thorns by the pupils of Caravaggio. In a Crucifixion painted on wood in an archaic style by Étienne Dumonstier, the artist sought to portray the pitiful waste of the struggles between Catholics and Protestants by depicting the protagonists at the foot of the Cross. One can make out Catherine de' Medici as Mary Magdalene, Henri II as the soldier piercing the heart of Christ, and their three sons, François II, Charles IX and Henri III. Mary Stuart is the Holy Woman with a crown; the Virgin has the features of Elizabeth of Austria. The modest nun in the foreground is the Abbess, Louise de Bourbon who was host to Mary Stuart in 1548, Charles IX in 1564 and Catherine de' Medici in 1567.

St Catherine's Chapel. – This 13C chapel stands in what was originally the churchyard; it is crowned by a lantern of the dead.

★ FOUGÈRES-SUR-BIÈVRE Château

Michelin map 🆄 fold 17 or 🔢 fold 15 (8 km - 5 miles northwest of Contres)

In the charming village of Fougères, surrounded by nursery gardens and fields of asparagus, stands the austere yet noble north façade of the feudal looking château of Pierre de Refuge, Louis XI's Chancellor.

Without much difficulty you can pick out the moats, drawbridge, arrow slits – replaced in the 16C by windows – and the keep's battlements *(p 33)* which disappeared when the roof was added.

The building was begun in 1470. Already, twenty years before, Charles d'Orléans had pulled down the old fortified castle at Blois and built a more cheerful residence in its place. The builder of Fougères did not follow the new fashion. He built a true stronghold round the square 11C keep.

However, when completed by his son-in-law, Jean de Villebresme, the château acquired a certain grace: the east wing in the main court has a gallery of arcades with lovely dormer windows; the attractive turreted staircase in the northwest corner with its windows flanked by pilasters with Renaissance motifs; the large windows added in 18C to the south wing which made it ideal as a spinning mill in 19C.

The size of the rooms seen from within is impressive; so is the wooden roof-frame of the main building which is shaped like a ship's hull and the conical roof-frame of the towers.

EXCURSION

Roujoux Leisure Park. – *5 km - 3 miles east by D7 towards Fresnes.*
The home park of Roujoux Château, which was rebuilt by René de Maille in the reign of Louis XIII, has been arranged for leisure activities: open space, picnicking, games, mini-golf.
Inside the château there is an historical **museum** where puppets re-enact the life of the château since the coming of the Vikings.

FRAZÉ   Pop 481

Michelin map 🔟 fold 16 or 🔢 north of fold 37 (8 km - 5 miles northwest of Brou)

Frazé is a little village in the valley beside the River Foussarde. Its origins are Gallo-Roman; later it was fortified and surrounded by water. The square, Place de la Mairie, provides a charming view of both the church and the château.
Frazé is a good starting point for an excursion into the lush region of Le Perche-Gouët *(p 152)*.

Château. – The château was begun to a square plan in 1493 and protected by a moat and a pool; it was completed in 16 and 17C with the outbuildings which form an entrance porch.
The surviving buildings include a watch tower; two towers of which one stands alone and is decorated with machicolations and a moulding; a fort flanked by towers and ornamented with sculpted corbels; an interesting chapel with historiated ornaments. An old well, gardens, canals and terraces enhance the courtyard and the park.

Church. – There is an attractive Renaissance doorway supported by three telamones.

GREEN TOURIST GUIDES

Picturesque scenery, buildings
Attractive routes
Touring programmes
Plans of towns and buildings.

★ GERMIGNY-DES-PRÉS Church

Map 64 fold 10 or 238 fold 6 (4 km - 2 1/2 miles southeast of Châteauneuf-sur-Loire)

The little church in Germigny is a rare and precious example of Carolingian art; it is one of the oldest in France and can be compared with the imperial rotunda in Aix-la-Chapelle.

Theodulf, a clergyman at Charlemagne's court. – Theodulf was a Visigoth from Spain who came to Neustria after 782 and joined Charlemagne's erudite circle. Before 798 he became Bishop of Orleans and then Abbot of Micy and of St-Benoît-sur-Loire. He was a brilliant scholar, a poet steeped in the ancient culture and a weighty theologian; he was very active in his diocese, promoting schools and fostering study and the intellectual life.

He had a villa (country estate) not far from Fleury; Germigny Church is the oratory, all that now remains. The house was sumptuously decorated: murals representing the Earth and the World, marble floors and superb mosaics in the oratory which date from about 806.

On Charlemagne's death, Theodulf fell into disgrace, accused of plotting against Louis the Pious; he was deposed in 818 and exiled; he died in Angers in 821. His villa was set on fire and destroyed by the Normans in 9C. Much of the original rich decor was destroyed by Lisch's clumsy restoration in 19C.

(Photo M. Guillard/Scope)

Germigny-des-Prés Church – Apsidal mosaic

⊙TOUR time: 1/2 hour

The east apse – the only original remnant – has a remarkable **mosaic**★ ★ on the roof; it represents the Arc of the Covenant surmounted by two cherubim flanked by two archangels; between them appears the hand of God. The use of gold and silver in the design of the archangels links this mosaic to the Byzantine art of Ravenna. Other elements in the décor – the stucco blind arcades, the triumphal arch (destroyed) and the capitals – show the combination of several artistic influences: the Ommiads, the Mozarabs and the Lombards. The work was discovered under a thick layer of distemper in 1840 when some archaeologists saw children playing with cubes of coloured glass which they had found in the church and decided to investigate. The early church, built on the Greek cross plan, had four identical apses; the interior would have been sumptuously decorated with mosaics and stucco ornamentation and the floor paved with inlaid marble and porphyry. The altar is lit by a square lantern above the crossing fitted with panes of translucent alabaster (the technique for fitting glass panes was not then widespread). The present nave, which dates from 15C, has replaced the fourth apse.

★ GIEN   Pop 16 784

Michelin map 65 fold 2 or 238 fold 7 – Facilities

Built on a hill overlooking the north bank of the Loire, Gien, a small town with many flowers, is well known for its faience. It was bombed several times between 1940 and 1944, and it suffered considerable damage but its recovery was rapid. Respect for the traditional forms of regional architecture and a careful use of local materials have given the reconstructed quarters an original and attractive appearance. From the bridge there is a lovely **view**★ of the château, the houses along the quays and the Loire.

Gien is a very old town which grew up round a castle, said to have been built by Charlemagne. It was here in 1410 that the Armagnac faction was set up in support of Charles of Orléans against the Burgundians in the civil war which led up to the last episode in the Hundred Years War. Later **Anne de Beaujeu** (1460-1522), the Countess of Gien, has the château rebuilt.

GIEN

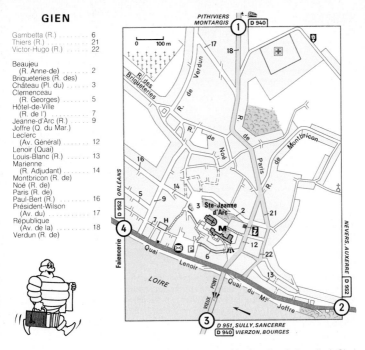

She was Louis XI's eldest daughter and 23 years old when her father died. She was appointed regent during the minority of her brother Charles VIII (1483-91), a position which she held with success and firmness, revealing qualities of great statesmanship; her authority was acknowledged by those around her.

In 1652 during the Fronde, the armed revolt mounted by the great princes (Condé, Beaufort and Madame de Longueville) against the king forced Anne of Austria, Mazarin and the young Louis XIV to flee from Paris; they took refuge in Gien while Turenne, at the head of the royal troops, defeated the enemy at Bléneau *(25 km - 15 1/2 miles east of Gien).*

SIGHTS

★★ **International Hunting Museum (Musée International de la Chasse — M).** — Gien Château on the eastern fringe of Orléans Forest and the Sologne, a region abounding in game, is an ideal setting for a hunting museum. The **château★** which dominates the town was built in 1484 of red brick with a slate roof. The decoration is restrained: a pattern of contrasting dark bricks and bands of white stone and a few stair turrets.

The rooms of the château with their beamed ceilings and fine chimneypieces make a worthy setting for the exhibition of fine art inspired by hunting: tapestries, porcelain, cut glass, paintings etc. The other displays are devoted to the weapons and techniques used in hunting since the prehistoric era: powder flasks, strip cartoons, porcelain plates and jugs, decorated pipes, hunting knives, fashion plates, chimney plaques, crossbows, harquebuses, pistols and guns with detailed ornamentation.

Hunting scenes depict mythological and Christian legends: Diana surprised in her bath by Acteon whom she turned into a stag which was devoured by her own dogs; numerous portrayals of the legend of St Hubert *(p 45)*. There are displays on the fashioning of a gun flint and the making of a pistol with Damascene decoration; the falconry gallery explains the significance of the different coloured hoods; beneath its superb roof the great hall is devoted to the work of François Desportes (1661-1743), a great animal painter attached to Louis XIV: another room contains the uncluttered art of Florentin Brigaud (1886-1958), a sculptor and engraver of animals. The Daghilhon-Pujol Room displays a collection of jacket buttons decorated with hunting motifs. The trophy room contains the 500 antlers given to the museum by the great hunter, Claude Hettier de Boislambert.

From the château terrace there is an extensive **view★** of the River Loire and the slate roofs of the town, reconstructed in the traditional style with pointed gables and diaper patterning in the brickwork.

On the north side of the château stands the **Church of St Joan of Arc;** it was rebuilt in brick in 1954 adjoining the 15C belltower which is all that remains of the collegiate church founded by Anne de Beaujeu. The slender round pillars of the interior create an atmosphere conducive to meditation such as is found in Romanesque churches.

Porcelain Factory (Faïencerie). — *West of the town (exit ④ on the plan). Access by Quai or Rue Paul-Bert.*

When the factory was founded in 1821 Gien was chosen because it was near the deposits of clay and sand needed for the paste, had plentiful supplies of wood to fire the kilns and the Loire provided transport of the finished product. Gien was well known for its dinner services and objets d'art when at the end of 19C it developed a new technique called Gien blue *(bleu de Gien)* which produced a deep blue glaze enhanced with golden yellow decoration. As well as continuing the old expensive handmade pieces, the factory produces modern services at reasonable prices. An old paste store has been converted into a small **museum** displaying old pieces; some of the very large ones were made for the Universal Exhibition in 1900. There is also a display of current production.

GIZEUX

On the east side of the village stands the **church** which contains 17C tombs of the Du Bellay family. On the right are two kneeling figures in white marble: René du Bellay (d. 1611) in armour and his wife Marie, in an open-necked dress and bonnet. On the left is Martin du Bellay, their son, and his wife, both wearing ruffles.

EXCURSION

Vernantes. – *12 km - 7 1/2 miles west by D215 and D206.*
Vernoil. – Pop 1 368. The **church** has a massive belltower. Enter the priory yard (right) to see the solid octagonal turret and mullioned windows of the old prior's lodging.
Take D58 west.

Vernantes. – Pop 1 743. A 12C tower capped by a stone spire marks the site of the **church**; only the chancel is still standing. The nave destroyed by lightning in 19C has been replaced by a simple porch. A new church has been built on the other side of the square.

GUÉ-PÉAN Château

Michelin map 🗺 fold 17 or 🗺 fold 15 (13 km - 8 miles east of Montrichard)

Gué-Péan Château is isolated in a quiet wooded valley; there is a riding stables in the outbuildings and a picnic area in the grounds. The château was built as a country house in 16 and 17C but the plan is that of a feudal castle: three ranges of buildings round a closed courtyard with a huge round tower at each corner, surrounded by a dry moat and reached by a stone bridge. The detail is more decorative: the tallest tower (the other three were never completed) is capped with a bell-shaped roof and delicate machicolations; the other buildings, with arcades and elegant windows flanked by pilasters, are roofed in the French manner.

Interior. – Rooms furnished in the style of Louis XV and Louis XVI are hung with tapestries and paintings; Germain Pilon designed the Renaissance chimneypiece in the Grand Salon. The library houses autographs and historic souvenirs. Access to the sentry walk.

L'ILE-BOUCHARD

Michelin map 🗺 north of fold 4 or 🗺 folds 34, 35 – Local map p 92

Formerly one of the ports on the River Vienne, the ancient settlement of L'Ile-Bouchard derives its name from the midstream island where in 9C the first known lord, Bouchard, is said to have built a fortress which was destroyed in the 17C. The estate was bought by Cardinal Richelieu and belonged to his descendants until 1789.

St Leonard's Priory (Prieuré de St-Léonard). – *South of the town, signposted.*
The priory church stood on the lower slopes of the valley; little now remains standing: 11C Romanesque apse in white tufa, an ambulatory and radiating chapels. The arcades were reinforced by additional arches a century later.
The historiated **capitals★** *(left to right)* represent:
1st pillar, Annunciation and Visitation, Nativity, Adoration of the Shepherds, Adoration of the Three Wise Men;
2nd pillar, Circumcision, Massacre of the Innocents, Flight into Egypt, Jesus in the midst of the doctors;
3rd pillar, Judas' Kiss, Crucifixion, Last Supper;
4th pillar, Jesus' Entry into Jerusalem, Descent into Hell, Beheading of St John the Baptist.

St Maurice's Church. – The octagonal tower, which dated from 1480, is capped by an openwork stone spire. The main building is in the transitional Flamboyant-Renaissance style and supported on pilasters decorated with Renaissance medallions. The very beautiful early 16C bishop's **throne★** in the chancel is adorned with most graceful Renaissance carvings portraying the Annunciation, the Nativity and the Flight into Egypt; the sculptors are shown on the cheek pieces *(p 34).*

Beside the church stands a charming early 17C manor house with pedimented dormers.

St Giles' Church (St-Gilles). – On the north bank of the Vienne, beside the D760, stands this 11C church which was enlarged (nave) in 12C and altered again (chancel) in 15C. The two attractive Romanesque doorways have no tympanum but are decorated with remarkable plants and geometric figures. The dome on squinches over the transept crossing supports a Romanesque tower.

(Photo M. Guillard/Scope)
St Maurice's Church. – Bishop's throne (detail)

ILLIERS-COMBRAY Pop 3 453

Michelin map 60 fold 17 or 237 south of fold 26

Illiers, on the upper reaches of the River Loir, is a market town serving both the Beauce and the Perche regions.

"Combray". – It was under this name that **Marcel Proust** (1871-1922) portrayed Illiers in his novel *Remembrance of Things Past* in which he analysed his feelings and those of the people he had known.
Marcel Proust spent his holidays in Illiers where his father Dr Proust had been born; it was in his Aunt Léonie's room that he tasted the madeleine cakes which, many years later, were to resurrect such a volume of memories.
In town one can recognise the bourgeois district – *le côté de chez Swann* – facing the rich wheat fields of the Beauce and the aristocratic district – *le côté de Guermantes* – drawn to the Perche region and its horses. In the novel the Loir becomes the Vivonne.

SIGHTS

Aunt Léonie's House. – *4 Rue du Docteur-Proust.*
The house of Madame Amiot, Proust's aunt, is now a **museum** devoted to the life, the work and the acquaintance of the writer.

Catelan Meadow (Pré Catelan). – *South of the town on D 149.*
The landscaped gardens, which include a "serpentine", a dovecot, a pavilion and a few fine trees, make a pleasant walk beside the Loir. This little garden is evoked by Proust in *Jean Santeuil.*

Information in this guide is based on tourist data provided at the time of going to press. Improved facilities and changes in the cost of living make alterations inevitable: we hope our readers will bear with us.

★ INDROIS Valley

Michelin map 64 folds 16, 17 or 238 folds 13 to 15

The River Indrois winds its picturesque way westwards through the clay and chalk of the Montrésor marshland *(gâtine)* to join the Indre. Its course is lined by willows, alders and poplars and lush green meadows. The sunny slopes are planted with fruit trees, in orchards or espaliers, and a few vines.

FROM NOUANS-LES-FONTAINES TO AZAY-SUR-INDRE

33 km - 20 miles – about 2 hours

Nouans-les-Fontaines. – Pop 883. The 13C church harbours a masterpiece of primitive art: the **Deposition★★** or *Pietà of Nouans* (behind the high altar) by Jean Fouquet. The vast painting on wood (2.36 m by 1.47 m - 6 3/4 ft by 3 1/2 ft) is one of the finest late 15C French works. The deliberately neutral colours employed, the resigned expressions of the figures, and their majestic attitudes make this a moving composition.

Coulangé. – At the entrance of this pleasant hamlet stands (right) the bell tower of the former parish church (12C). On the opposite bank of the river a round tower and part of a wall are all that remain of the fortifications which once protected the former Benedictine abbey of Villeloin.

★**Montrésor.** – *Description p 143.*

Beyond Montrésor the D 10 offers scenic views of the lake at Chemillé-sur-Indrois and the country east of Genillé.

Genillé. – Pop 1 420. The houses climb up from the river to the late 15C château with its angle towers and dovecot. Dominated outside by its belfry the interior of the church possesses a 16C Gothic chancel.

St-Quentin-sur-Indrois. – Pop 425. The town occupies one of the best sites in the valley.

East of the village the road (D 10) offers a fine view south of Loches Forest before joining the course of the River Indre at Azay-sur-Indre.

Azay-sur-Indre. – *Description p 117.*

INGRANDES Pop 1 450

Michelin map 63 fold 19 or 232 fold 30 – Local map p 126

In 17C and 18C Ingrandes was a major port on the River Loire. From the south bank of the river one can see the low walls which protect the town when the river is in spate.
Its position just south of the Breton border made it an important centre for smuggling salt. Anjou was subject to the salt tax *(gabelle)* which was particularly unpopular since salt was the only means of preserving food; Brittany was exempt.

Church. – The church was designed in 1956 in the regional style. It is built of granite with a slate belltower; the modern stained glass windows were made by the Ateliers Loire after cartoons by Bertrand.

INGRANDES

EXCURSION

Champtocé-sur-Loire. – Pop 1 233. *6 km - 4 miles east on N 23.*
On the northeast side of the town stand the ruins of the castle of **Gilles de Rais** (1404-40), a sinister personality who may have inspired Charles Perrault to write his story about Bluebeard. He was a powerful lord, a Marshal of France and the faithful companion of Joan of Arc whom he attempted to rescue from prison in Rouen; for many years he hid his criminal instincts. When he was brought before the court in Nantes and charged with alchemy, raising the devil and the massacre of children, he confessed his crimes in great detail, hesitating only about the number of his victims: a hundred, two hundred or more. On 26 October 1440 Gilles de Rais was hung between two of his accomplices.

JARZÉ
Pop 1 368

Michelin map 🔢 southwest of fold 2 or 🔢 southeast of fold 20

The countryside is measured out in pasture, crops and woodland round Jarzé-en-Baugeois which belonged to Jean Bourré *(see p 154)*. The castle, which was built in 1500 and burnt down in 1794, was restored in 19C.

Church. – This was originally a collegiate church built in the Flamboyant style on the foundations of an 11C building.
The seigneurial chapel (right) is covered with lierne and tierceron vaulting. The 16C stalls in the chancel are decorated with amusing carvings. A niche in a pillar on the right of the chancel contains a late 15C statuette of St Cyr, in robe and bonnet, holding a pear in his hand; St Cyr, the son of St Juliette of Tarsus, was martyred at the age of 3. This young child is more likely the son of Jean Bourré reminding us that his father introduced the Good Christian pear into Anjou *(see p 16)*.
At the back of the apse are traces of a beautiful early 16C **mural** of the Entombment.

EXCURSION

⊙**Chapel of Our Lady of Montplacé.** – *Round trip of 4 km - 2 1/2 miles by D 82 north towards La Flèche; take the first turning on the right. Return by D 766.*
The little chapel, standing alone on its bluff, is visible from afar. The neighbouring farm buildings add a touch of simplicity to its noble appearance; there is a fine 17C western doorway dedicated to the Virgin.
In about 1610 the previous chapel on this site was being used as a sheepfold although it still contained an ancient statue of the Virgin. One day when the shepherdess brought in her sheep the statue was illuminated. Next day the whole neighbourhood came to see; miraculous healings occurred; religious fervour grew; soon the pilgrims' offerings were such that the present chapel was built and completed towards the end of the 17C. A tradition was established of making a pilgrimage to the Protector of the Baugeois region.

Entrance by the side door.

The three large altars are in the purest 17C style. In the niche in the lefthand altar is the ancient statue venerated by the pilgrims. It is a *Pietà* carved in walnut showing traces of its original colouring. The walls are hung with many votive offerings.

★★ # LANGEAIS
Pop 4 142

Michelin map 🔢 fold 14 or 🔢 folds 34, 35 – Local map p 122 – Facilities

The town's white houses nestle below the château's walls. Facing the château there is a lovely Renaissance house decorated with pilasters; the church's tower is also Renaissance.

Louis XI's château. – It was Fulk Nerra, Count of Anjou *(p 47)*, who, at the end of the 10C, built the **keep**, the ruins of which still stand in the gardens – it is the oldest existing keep in France.
The château, now extant, was built by Louis XI from 1465-69 as a strongpoint on the road from Nantes, the route most likely to be taken by an invading Breton Army. This threat vanished after the marriage of Charles VIII and Anne of Brittany was celebrated at Langeais itself in 1491.

★★ CHÂTEAU *time: 1 hour*

⊙The château was built in one piece – a rare event – and has not been altered since – an even rarer event. It is one of the most interesting in the Loire Valley owing to the patient efforts of Mr Jacques Siegfried, the last owner, who refurnished it in the style of the 15C.
From the outside it looks like a feudal fortress: high walls, huge round towers, a crenellated and machicolated sentry walk and a draw-bridge over the moat.
The façade facing the courtyard is, however, less severe and suggests a manor house with mullioned windows and pointed dormers decorated like the doors of the stair turrets.
The buildings consist of two wings set at a right angle; on the west side of the courtyard a terraced garden rises to the tomb of Mr and Mrs Siegfried at the foot of the keep.

★★★ **The apartments.** – Well presented with contemporary period furnishings the atmosphere is more alive than in most other old castles and gives an accurate picture of aristocratic life in the 15C and early Renaissance. There are many fine tapestries mostly Flemish but with some *mille-fleurs.* Note the many examples of the girdle of the Franciscan Tertiaries and the repetition of the monogram K and A for Charles VIII and Anne of Brittany.

The guardroom, now transformed into a dining room, has a monumental chimneypiece the hood of which represents a castle with battlements manned by small figures.

(Photo Pix)

Langeais Château
Diptych of Charles VIII and Anne of Brittany

One of the first floor bedchambers has an early four-poster bed, a credence table and Gothic chest. The room where Charles VIII and Anne of Brittany celebrated their marriage is hung with a series of tapestries portraying the Nine Heroes. Charles VIII's chamber has a fine Gothic chest and a curious 17C clock. The upper great hall, rising through two storeys, has a chestnut timber roof in the form of a ship's keel. The Creation is the theme of the Renaissance tapestries hanging here. The sentry walk, a covered gallery the length of the façade, offers views of the Loire and the town's pointed roof tops.

EXCURSIONS

Cinq-Mars-la-Pile. – *5 km - 3 miles northeast by N 152. Description p 94.*

St-Étienne-de-Chigny. – *7.5 km - 4 1/2 miles northeast by N 152; fork left into D 76 and left again into D 126 towards Vieux-Bourg. Description p 163.*

Luynes. – Pop 3925. *12 km - 7 1/2 miles northeast by N 152 and then left into D 49.* The road (N 152), along the Loire embankment, offers a good view of this picturesque village on the hillside, where the cellars are hollowed out of the rock. The **market hall** *(halles)* is of wood with a high roof of flat tiles. There are several timber-framed houses; opposite the church in Rue Paul-Louis-Courier there is a house with carved beams depicting St Christopher, a *Pietà* and the Virgin.

From the road, D 49, which climbs north through the vineyards, there is a fine view south of the 13C **castle** guarding the community.

LASSAY-SUR-CROISNE   Pop 145

Michelin map 🖾 fold 18 or 🖾🖾🖾 fold 16 (11 km - 7 miles west of Romorantin)

Lassay is a village in the Sologne, a region of woods and vast pools of water.

⊙ **St Denis' Church.** – The charming little 15C church has a beautiful rose window and a slender spire.

In the left transept, above the recumbent figure of Philippe du Moulin, there is an attractive early 16C **fresco** of St Christopher; on the right the artist has painted Lassay church and on the left in the background the Château du Moulin.

★ **Château du Moulin.** – *1.5 km - 1 mile west by a track beside the River Croisne.*
⊙ The Château du Moulin stands in a rural setting its red brick walls reflected in the water of the moat.

It was built between 1480 and 1506 by **Philippe du Moulin**, an important noble devoted to the service of Charles VIII and Louis XII, who saved the life of Charles VIII at the Battle of Fornoue in 1495. It follows the square fortress plan surrounded by a curtain wall reinforced with round towers.

In 15C fashion the buildings are decorated with the diaper pattern and bands of stone; the effect is more elegant than military.

The keep or residence has large mullioned windows and is furnished in contemporary style: in the dining room there is a 15C sideboard and a chandelier both from the Sologne; there is a painted ceiling in the salon; the bedrooms contain tester beds and Flanders tapestries; 19C comfort is represented by the central heating. Near the entrance is the vaulted kitchen with its enormous chimney; the spit was turned by a dog running in the wheel.

A gourmet ... ?

If you are, look in the current ***Michelin Guide France***
for the establishments with stars.

Michelin map 🔲 fold 5 or 🔲 fold 1 – Local map p 121

The romantic ruins of this feudal fortress rise in a jagged silhouette on a rocky promontory above the village and the River Loir which is spanned by a Gothic bridge. The castle was the principal stronghold of the Counts of Vendôme in the Middle Ages and its strategic importance greatly increased as early as the 12C owing to its position between the kingdom of France under the Capets and the possessions of the Angevin kings.

In 1188 Henry II of England and his son Richard the Lionheart besieged the castle in vain.

In 1589 the troops of the League *(see p 18)* captured the castle but the following year it was besieged by Henri IV's soldiers under the Prince de Conti and surrendered. The King ordered the castle to be slighted.

SIGHTS

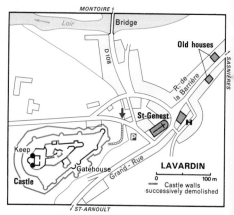

⊙ **Castle.** – The path skirting the south side of the castle offers a good view of the gatehouse and the keep. Although well worn by the weather and the passage of time, the impressive ruins give a good idea of the three lines of defence, of the gatehouse (14C) and of the rectangular 11C keep (26 m - 85 ft high) which was reinforced in the following century with towers of the same height. The innermost defensive wall is the best preserved.

⊙ **St Genest's Church.** – The church was built in an archaic Romanesque style with a square belfry porch. Low-relief sculptures have been re-used in the structure; those in the apse represent the signs of the zodiac.

Interior. – The church is divided into three parts by square piers capped by delicately carved early 12C imposts. The chancel, which is entered through a triumphal arch, ends in an oven-vaulted apse, where curious Romanesque pillars support roughly hewn capitals. The windows in the north aisle are framed by delightful twisted Romanesque colonnettes.

The numerous **mural paintings** date from the 12 to 16C. The oldest, most stylized and majestic ones are on the pillar at the entrance to the left apsidal chapel: Baptism of Christ and a Tree of Jesse. The well conserved group in the chancel and apse shows scenes from the Passion: the Washing of the Feet *(right)* and *(left)* Christ in Majesty surrounded by the symbols of the Evangelists.

In the right apsidal chapel note a St Christopher and Last Judgement (15C) where Paradise (above) and Hell are colourfully portrayed. On the pillars in the nave and aisles are 16C figures of saints venerated locally. Note the Martyrdom of St Margaret on the wall of the south aisle and the Crucifixion of St Peter on a pillar on the north side of the nave.

Old houses. – One is 15C and half-timbered while the other is Renaissance with an overhanging oratory, pilastered, mullioned dormer windows and a loggia overlooking the courtyard.

⊙ The **Town Hall** (Mairie) (**H**) contains two beautiful 11C rooms with handsome 15C vaulted ceilings; the one on the ground floor is used for exhibitions.

The 12C **bridge** over the Loir gives an attractive view of the lush green banks of the river.

*To choose a hotel, restaurant or camping site use the annual **Michelin Guides France** and **Camping Caravaning France.***

LAYON Valley

Michelin map 🔲 folds 6, 7 or 🔲 folds 31, 32

The Layon, which was canalized under Louis XVI, follows the trough which runs northwest between the Mauges schists *(p 136)* and the Saumur limestone escarpments, except between Beaulieu and St-Aubin where the river has traversed the ancient massif. In the clear air, the deeply incised meanders sometimes create an impression of a hilly terrain.

The region has a certain attraction with its vineyards, its crops sometimes interspersed with fruit trees (walnut, peach, plum, etc), its hillsides crowned with windmills, its wine growers' villages with their cemeteries planted with cypresses.

The "Coteaux du Layon". – The delicious fruity, liqueur-like white wines of the Layon vineyards are produced by the *chenin* often known as *pineau* variety of grape. They are harvested in late September when the grapes begin to be covered with a mould known as *pourriture noble.*

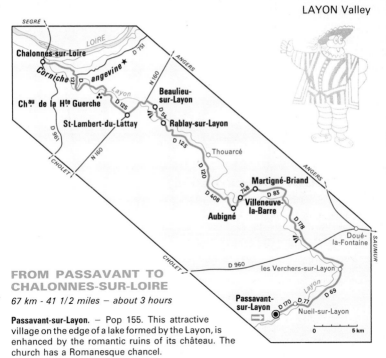

FROM PASSAVANT TO CHALONNES-SUR-LOIRE

67 km - 41 1/2 miles − about 3 hours

Passavant-sur-Layon. − Pop 155. This attractive village on the edge of a lake formed by the Layon, is enhanced by the romantic ruins of its château. The church has a Romanesque chancel.

> *Take D 170 to Neuil-sur-Layon, turn right after the church into D 77; after the bridge over the Layon bear left into D 69 towards Doué-la-Fontaine.*

The landscape at this point is still typical of the Poitou with its hedgerows, sunken roads and farmsteads roofed with Roman tiles. The vineyards are grouped on the exposed slopes and at Neuil slate roofs appear.

> *Beyond Les Verchers bear left into D 178 towards Concourson.*

The road runs parallel with the Layon through fertile country; beyond Concourson it offers an extensive view of the river valley.

> *In St-Georges-sur-Layon take the road north towards Brigné, turning left into D 83 to Martigné-Briand.*

Martigné-Briand. − Pop 1 835. This vineyard village clusters round its ruined château, which was burnt down during the Vendean War *(p 136)*.

> *Take D 748 southwest towards Aubigné, turning right into a narrow road to Villeneuve-la-Barre.*

Villeneuve-la-Barre. − Drive through this picturesque village, which is gaily decorated with flowers in season, to the **Benedictine monastery**, a handsome edifice with a courtyard. The rather austere chapel, in a former barn, has white stained glass windows with abstract motifs.

Aubigné. − Pop 258. This picturesque village has preserved several elegant town houses. Near the church stands an old fortified gateway where the remains of the portcullis and draw-bridge can be seen.

> *Leave Aubigné on D 408 to Faveraye-Mâchelles and turn right into D 120 which passes through the village. After crossing D 24 bear left into D 125 to Rablay-sur-Layon.*

Rablay-sur-Layon. − Pop 592. This is a well sheltered attractive wine village; in Grande Rue there is a brick and half-timbered house (15C) with an overhanging upper storey.

> *Take D 54 to Beaulieu.*

This road crosses the Layon, then skirts a vine covered cirque; from the plateau there is an extensive view of the valley.

Beaulieu-sur-Layon. − Pop 995. This wine grower's village *(panoramic table)* in the midst of the Layon vineyards has attractive mansard-roofed houses. The town hall building was once the residence of the steward of the Abbess of Ronceray. There are 13C frescoes in the **church**.

To the west of Beaulieu on D 55 *(right)* in a low building is a **Caveau du Vin** with a collection of old Angevin wine bottles and glasses.

> *Take N 160 south towards Chemillé.*

The road descends into the valley; its steep sides are riddled with caves and quarries. The bridge over the Layon offers an attractive view of the narrow course of the river and a ruined medieval bridge.

St-Lambert-du-Lattay. − Pop 1 203. A **Museum of the Grape and the Wine of Anjou** was established in the Coudraye cellars in 1978. It describes the ravages of phylloxera which reduced the vineyards from 45 000 ha - 174 sq miles in 1883 to 10 000 ha - 38 sq miles in 1893. Vineyard tools and barrels, illustrations and commentaries embody the living memory of a people who have always been engaged in the cultivation of the grape.

> *Take D 125 northwest towards St-Aubin-de-Luigné.*

The road winds its way up and down the slopes which produce the Quart de Chaume wine *(p 126)*.

Before entering St-Aubin turn left into D 106 and soon after turn right.

ⓧ**Château de la Haute-Guerche**. – The castle was built in the reign of Charles VII and burnt down in the Vendean wars *(p 136);* only its ruined towers now dominate the valley. Extensive view of the countryside.

Return to D 125 and continue west to Chaudefonds; turn right into D 121 which leads to Ardenay on the Angevin corniche road.

★ **Angevin Corniche Road.** – *Description p 126.*

Chalonnes-sur-Loire. – *Description p 126.*

Le LIGET Charterhouse

Michelin map 🔲 north of fold 6 or 🔲🔲🔲 fold 14 (10 km - 6 miles east of Loches)

On the eastern edge of Loches Forest, bordering the road, stands the great wall of the ⓧ**charterhouse**; the noble 18C **gateway★** is flanked by numerous outbuildings which give an idea of the size and wealth of the house just before the Revolution. The monastery was founded in 12C by Henry II of England in expiation, so it is said, of the murder of Thomas à Becket, Archbishop of Canterbury; it was sold as state property at the end of 18C and mostly demolished. Nonetheless the few traces which remain suggest how large and impressive the buildings must have been.

Walk past the outbuildings (carpenter's shop, forge, locksmith's shop, bakery, etc) and descend the central path.

In front of the house are the ruins (left) of the 12C church; behind it still stands one side of the great cloister which was built in 1787: in the cell walls are the hatches through which the monks received their meals.

ⓧ**St John's Chapel.** – *Return to the Loches road; 1 km - 1/2 mile east turn left.*
Standing alone in the middle of a field is an unusual round 12C building where the first monks of the charterhouse probably lived. The interior is decorated with some Romanesque frescoes: the Deposition and the Entombment.

La Corroirie. – Eastwards towards Montrésor, in the bottom of a small valley, behind a screen of trees (left) stands another building belonging to the charterhouse which was fortified in 15C. Clearly visible are the fortified gate and the square machicolated tower with draw-bridge.

Le LION D'ANGERS   Pop 2 775

Michelin map 🔲🔲 fold 20 or 🔲🔲🔲 fold 19 – Local map p 138

The town is picturesquely sited on the right bank of the River Oudon just north of its confluence with the Mayenne. It is a horse breeding centre, particularly of half-breeds, the horse racing and competitions held here are famous throughout Anjou.

St Martin's Church. – The tracery decoration above the door is pre-Romanesque; the nave with its wooden vaulting is Romanesque. On the left wall of the nave above the entrance door are some 16C murals showing the Devil vomiting the Seven Deadly Sins, a Crucifix and St Christopher. In a recess there is a diptych of an Ecce Homo.

★ **L'Isle-Briand National Stud.** – *1 km - 1/2 mile east of Le Lion-d'Angers.*
ⓧThe national stud at L'Isle-Briand, which was transferred from Angers in 1974, is an ultra-modern establishment; about 80 selected horses are stabled here. The tour includes the barns, the harness room, the forge and the riding school. The loose boxes are grouped according to the different types of horses: Normandy cob, Breton or Percheron draught horses, Anglo-Arabs, pure-bred Arabs, saddle horses, trotters, etc. Former champions who have won many races, are brought here to breed.

LIRÉ   Pop 2 250

Michelin map 🔲🔲 fold 18 or 🔲🔲🔲 fold 29 (3 km - 1 1/2 miles south of Ancenis) – Local map p 126

Liré, a village in the Loire Valley, owes its fame to **Joachim du Bellay** (1522-60), the poet, who was born in the vicinity. Du Bellay, like his friends the poets of the Pléiade *(p 30)*, was brought up on Greek and Latin poetry and he sought to provide the French language with literary works of the same stature as he admired in the ancient languages; he was the author of the manifesto of the group, "The Defence and Illustration of the French Language", which appeared in Paris in 1549.
He signed it I.D.B.A. which stands for Ioachim du Bellay Angevin and shows his affection for his native province. In 1553 he went to Rome with his cousin, the Cardinal, and wrote his finest work The Regrets.

ⓧ**Joachim du Bellay Museum.** – The museum occupies a 16C house *(restored)* in the middle of the town. Souvenirs of the poet are displayed on the first floor; the ground floor is devoted to local traditions and customs.

Michelin map 🗺 fold 6 or 🗺 south of fold 14 — Facilities

Loches is a small town on the south bank of the Indre; its military past is most evident in the old town, which is huddled on the slopes of a bluff above the river and still resembles a medieval fortified town with two of its original three defensive walls quite well preserved. Fine **views**★ of the castle from the public garden on the north bank.

Loches was the birthplace of the romantic poet, **Alfred de Vigny** (1797-1863), whose mother's family had been closely involved with the town's history since the Renaissance. The poet *(see p 30)* left the town when only a few months old.

A thousand-year-old Fortress. — Loches is built on a natural strong point which has been occupied since at least 6C when Gregory of Tours spoke of a fortress commanding a monastery and a small town. From 10 to 13C Loches was under the sway of the Counts of Anjou who altered the fortress by building a residence and a moated keep on the end of the promontory. Henry II of England *(p 48)* reinforced the defences during his reign. On his death in 1189 his son, Richard the Lionheart took possession of the land before leaving on the crusade with Philippe-Auguste. In the Holy Land Philippe-Auguste, an artful schemer, abandoned Richard and hurried back to France (1191) where he began an intrigue with John Lackland, Richard's brother, who agreed to give up the fortress (1193). When Richard was ransomed — he had been held captive in Austria — he hastened to Loches and captured the castle by surprise in less than three hours (1194); his exploit was celebrated in all the chronicles of the day. When Richard died, Philippe-Auguste re-captured the castle by way of revenge but less brilliantly: the siege lasted a whole year (1205). Loches was given to Dreu V and repurchased by Louis IX in 1249.

Loches became a royal residence; those who lived there included Louis IX, Philip the Fair and John the Good. In 1429, after her victory at Orléans, Joan of Arc rejoined Charles VII at Loches and insisted that he should set out for Rheims.

The Lady of Beauty (La Dame de Beauté). — **Agnès Sorel**, who was born at Fromenteau Castle in the Touraine in 1422, was the owner of Beauté Castle (at Nogent-sur-Marne) near Paris and also a great Beauty, so that her title had a double meaning. She was Charles VII's favourite; when the Dauphin, the future Louis XI, made life at court in Chinon impossible for her, she came to live in Loches. Her influence on the King was often beneficial — she cured him of his depression and encouraged him in his effort to save his kingdom, — but her taste for luxury coupled with great generosity was a heavy burden on the slender royal purse. She died on 9 February 1450 at Jumièges where she had gone to be with Charles VII who was campaigning. Her body was brought back to

(Photo Serge Chirol)

Loches Château — Recumbent figure of Agnès Sorel

Loches and buried in the collegiate church. Some years later the canons, who had benefited from her largesse, asked Louis XI to transfer her tomb to the castle. He agreed on condition that the gifts went too. The canons let the matter drop.

Louis XI's Cages (late 15C). — A tour of the castle will include the dungeons and barred cells but not the cages in which Louis XI liked to confine his prisoners; these "monuments of tyranny" were destroyed by the inhabitants of Loches in 1790. The cages were made of a wooden framework covered with iron. The more comfortable measured 2 m - 6 1/2 ft cubed but there was a shallower model in which the prisoner could only lie or sit. Legend has it that the prisoner never came out alive; it seems however that the cages were used only at night or to transport the prisoner. Cardinal Jean Balue, who is said to be the inventor of these cages, knew them well. He was greatly in favour under Louis XI who covered him with honours but he plotted secretly with the Duke of Burgundy; in 1469 he was discovered and imprisoned in Loches until 1480; he died 11 years later.

★★ **MEDIEVAL CITY** (LA CITÉ MÉDIÉVALE)

🕐 *Time: 2 hours — park the car in Mail Droulin*

★ **Royal Gate** (Porte Royale). — 13C. It had powerful defences; it was flanked by two towers in 15C; the machicolations and the slots for the draw-bridge chains are still visible.

   Go through the gateway; turn left into Rue Lansyer to reach the museums.

🕐 The **Lansyer Museum** (M) contains works by Lansyer (1835-93), a local painter who was a pupil of Gustave Courbet and a friend of Delacroix; and objects from the Far East.

🕐 Le **Terroir Museum** houses a reconstruction of a local interior and enables the visitor to see the inside of the Royal Gate. View over Loches.

★ **St-Ours' Church.** — In 1802 the old collegiate church of the Virgin became the parish church dedicated to St Ours, a local apostle in 5C. The roof of the nave rises in two octagonal pyramids and is flanked by two towers. The Angevin porch shelters a

Romanesque doorway, richly decorated with strange carved animals; the upper part (badly damaged) represents the Virgin and the Wise Men. A Gallo-Roman altar is used as a holy water stoup.

The famous pyramid vaulting in the nave was built by Prior T. Pactius in 12C.

The transept, which was designed for a chapter of 12 canons, opens into the aisles (12, 14 and 15C).

★★ **Château.** – The tour begins in the **Agnès Sorel Tower (B)** which dates from 13C and has been known since 16C as the "Beautiful Agnès Tower".

Royal Apartments (Logis Royaux). – From the terrace which provides a fine view of Loches and the Indre Valley, it is clear that the château was built at two different periods. The Vieux Logis (14C) the older, taller building is heavily fortified with four turrets linked by a sentry walk at the base of the roof. It was enlarged under Charles VIII and Louis XII by the addition of the more recent Nouveau Logis, in the manner and style of the Renaissance.

Enter the **Vieux Logis** by the room known as Charles VII's ante-chamber where a copy of the manuscript of the proceedings of Joan of Arc's trial (1431) is on display. On the wall hang a 16C tapestry narrating an allegorical depiction of music as well as a portrait of Charles VII, a copy of the painting by Jean Fouquet. Then enter the great hall with the large fireplace where on 3 and 5 June 1429 Joan of Arc came to urge Charles VII to go to Rheims. She was accompanied at the time by Robert Le Masson, Chancellor of France, who died in 1443, Dunois (p 78) and Gilles de Rais (p 110). Lovely tapestries (Verdures and Oudenaarde) adorn the walls.

The **recumbent figure of Agnès Sorel**★, placed in the Charles VIII Room, is of special interest. During the Revolution, soldiers of the Indre battalions, whose historical knowledge was not equal to their Revolutionary zeal, took the favourite of Charles VII for a saint, chopped up her statue, desecrated her grave and scattered her remains. The alabaster monument was restored in Paris under the Empire and again on the occasion of its transfer to the Nouveau Logis. Agnès is shown recumbent, with two angels supporting her lovely head and two lambs – the symbol of gentleness and her name – lying at her feet. In the same room is displayed the portrait by Fouquet of the Virgin, whose face is that of the beautiful Agnès, amidst red and blue angels (the original is in Antwerp).

Another room contains an interesting **triptych**★ from the school of Jean Fouquet (15C), which originally came from St Antony's church, with panels evoking the Crucifixion, Carrying of the Cross and Deposition. The tour ends in Anne of Brittany's oratory, a tiny room finely worked and decorated with the ermine of Brittany and the girdle of St Francis. The canopy opposite the altar originally surmounted the royal pew and the only door was the one to the right of the altar.

Return to the Church of St-Ours and by way of Rue Thomas-Pactius, make for the Mail du Donjon. Turn round, after a bend to the right, to get a view of the church.

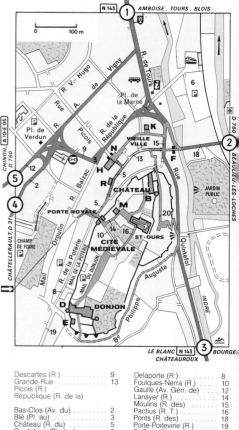

★★ **Keep** (Donjon). – The keep was built in the 11C by Fulk Nerra (p 47) to defend the fortified town from the south, its only vulnerable side. It is a powerful square construction which, together with the towers Ronde and Martelet, forms an imposing fortified group. Early in 13C the promontory was defended by a moat, a rampart and the keep which comprised a residence and its outbuildings, a collegiate church and houses for the canons.

On the outside can still be seen the putlog holes in which the timbers supporting the hoardings rested. To the left of the entrance in Philippe de Commines's dungeon, is an iron collar weighing 16 kg - 35 lb.

The floors of the three storeys have vanished but three sets of fireplaces and windows can still be seen on the walls. A staircase of 157 steps climbs to the top of the keep from which there is a fine view of the town, the Indre Valley and Loches Forest.

Round Tower (Tour Ronde — **D**). — This round tower was in fact another keep. Like the Martelet it was built in the 15C to complete the fortifications at the point where three walls met: the keep wall, the castle wall and the town wall.

Known as the Louis XI Tower, the round tower contains four rooms, one above the other. Below the torture chamber is a vaulted cell in which Cardinal La Balue is said to have been imprisoned.

Martelet (**E**). — The most impressive dungeons, occupying several floors below ground, are to be found in this building. The first was that of **Ludovico Sforza** the Moor, Duke of Milan, who was taken prisoner by Louis XII. For eight years (1500-08) at Loches, he paid for his tricks and treacheries. On the day of his release the sunlight was so bright and the excitement of freedom so great that he fell dead. Ludovico, who was Leonardo da Vinci's patron, covered the walls of his prison with paintings and inscriptions. Next to the stars, cannons and helmets, may be seen a phrase, hardly surprising in the circumstances: *celui qui n'est pas contan* (he who is not content).

Below, lit by a solitary ray of light, is the dungeon where the Bishops of Autun and Le Puy, both implicated in the Constable of France or Charles, Duke of Bourbon's change of allegiance to the Emperor Charles V, found leisure to hollow out of the wall a small altar and a symbolic Stations of the Cross. In another cell was interned the Count of St-Vallier, father of Diane de Poitiers *(p 85)*. He was sentenced to death and informed of his reprieve — on the intervention of his daughter — only when on the scaffold.

On the same underground level as the dungeons, galleries open off to quarries, which in the 13C, provided stone for the small fortified covered passageways flanking the ramparts.

Tourists who are pressed for time should turn right on leaving the Martelet to reach the Mail de la Poterie and their cars. For those with another 1/2 hour to spare, we would highly recommend a walk round the outside of the ramparts.

★ **Walk round the outside of the ramparts and the old town.** — Turn left on coming out of the Martelet.

This walk *(3/4 hour on foot)* shows one that this medieval town was in fact an entrenched camp, complete with all its own defences. The perimeter wall is more than 1 km - 3/4 mile long and is pierced by only two gateways.

Note first the three spur towers built in the 13C in front of the keep, then walk in the moat to Rue Quintefol before coming up on to the ramparts: good view of the chevet of St-Ours' Church. This section within the second perimeter wall follows Rue St-Ours around picturesque old houses.

On emerging through the perimeter wall take one of the narrow pedestrian streets opposite which leads to the late 15C **Porte des Cordeliers** (**F**), which, with the Porte Picois *(see below)* are the only two remaining gates of the town's original four. It was the main gate of the city on the road to Spain. Go through the gate to see its riverside façade with machicolations and flanked by bartizans.

Bear north to the 16C **St Antony's Tower** (Tour St-Antoine — **K**) one of the rare belfries in central France; then to the 15C **Porte Picois** (**N**) also with machicolations; it is adjacent to the **town hall★** (**H**) a dignified Renaissance building adorned with flowered balconies. Continue to the **Maison de la Chancellerie** (**R**) of the Henri II period (mid 16C), embellished with fluted columns, pilasters and wrought-iron balconies.

ADDITIONAL SIGHT

Beaulieu-lès-Loches. — *Description p 61.*

EXCURSIONS

Bridoré. — Pop 426. *14 km - 9 miles southeast by ③ on the plan.*
The late 15C **church,** dedicated to St Roch, contains a monumental 15C statue of the Saint (nave right). The legend of St Hubert *(p 45)* is evoked on a 16C low relief sculpture.
The **Castle,** which belonged to Marshal Boucicaut in 14C, was altered in 15C by Imbert de Bastarnay, Secretary to Louis XI. It is an imposing pile, bordered by towers, caponiers and a deep dry moat on three sides. The most interesting parts are the gatehouse, flanked by a machicolated round tower, and the rectangular keep with a Louis XII style dormer window and lateral bartizans with pepperpot roofs; the main apartments adjoin the keep.

★ **Indre Valley.** — Michelin maps 📖 fold 15, 16 or 📖 folds 13, 14 — *27 km - 16 miles northwest by ①, N 143 and D 17 — about 1 hour.*
From Chambourg-sur-Indre to Esvres D 17 takes a picturesque route beside the Indre which meanders lazily past a windmill or a boat moored in the reeds.

Azay-sur-Indre. — Pop 289. Azay stands in a pleasant site at the confluence of the Indre and the Indrois *(p 109)*. Adjoining is the park of the château that once belonged to La Fayette.

Reignac. — Pop 855. Visible from the bridge over the Indre (on the road to Cigogné), in a pastoral setting, is the Reignac windmill.

Cormery. — *Description p 96.*

Cross the Indre and follow N 143 towards Tours for 1 km - 1/2 mile then bear left into D 17.

The trip ends at Esvres, located in lovely surroundings.

*The layout diagram on page 3 shows the **Michelin Maps** covering the region. In the text, reference is made to the map which is the most suitable from a point of view of scale and practicality.*

★★ LOIR Valley

Michelin map 60 fold 17 and 64 folds 2 to 7

The Loir winds placidly from the Ile-de-France to Anjou through a peaceful and smiling landscape bordered by gentle hills. Green meadows, smart towns and charming villages justify the title Gentle France *(la Douce France)*.

From its source to its confluence with the Sarthe (350 km - 218 miles) the Loir has made its way through a chalky terrain, flowing under steep bluffs on the outside of its many bends. Since the Neolithic period men have hollowed caverns in these bluffs and these troglodyte dwellings are one of the charms of the valley.

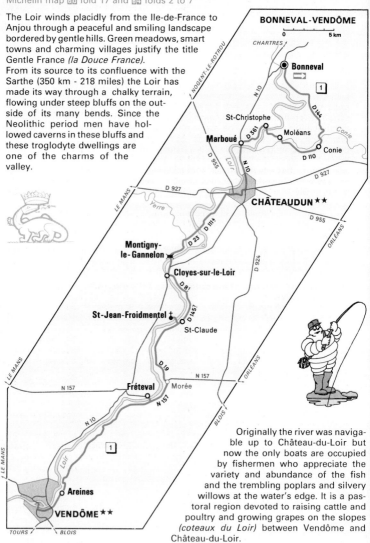

Originally the river was navigable up to Château-du-Loir but now the only boats are occupied by fishermen who appreciate the variety and abundance of the fish and the trembling poplars and silvery willows at the water's edge. It is a pastoral region devoted to raising cattle and poultry and growing grapes on the slopes *(coteaux du Loir)* between Vendôme and Château-du-Loir.

In the Middle Ages pilgrims on the road to Santiago de Compostela followed the upper reaches of the river before turning south to Tours; their religious fervour has left its mark in the priories, commanderies, churches and chapels which are often decorated with frescoes.

UPPER REACHES

1 From Bonneval to Vendôme *77 km - 47 miles — allow one day*

Bonneval. – *Description p 70. Leave Bonneval by D 144.*

Uninterrupted views as the road crosses the plateau. Before **Conie** the road crosses the river of the same name and follows it (D 110) downstream to **Moléans** with its 17C castle. In the pretty village of **St-Christophe** the road rejoins the slow waters of the Loir which it follows (D 361) to Marboué.

Marboué. – Pop 1 017. Once a Gallo-Roman settlement, the village is known for its tall 15C belltower and crocketed spire and for its bathing beach on the river.

★★ **Châteaudun.** – *Description p 78.*

Montigny-le-Gannelon. – *Description p 141.*

Cloyes-sur-le-Loir. – *Description p 95.*

Leave Cloyes by D 81 east to Bouche-d'Aigre.

A picturesque road (D 145⁷) follows the east bank of the Loir south through **St-Claude** with its pointed church on the hill.

St-Jean-Froidmentel. – Pop 418. On the west bank is the village of St-Jean-Froidmentel. Its church has an attractive Gothic-Renaissance doorway; above the basket-handle arch is an accolade and two small pediments.

Return to the east bank.

Only a row of poplars separates the road from the river. Between Morée and Fréteval there are fishing huts on the bank and a few smart houses with a flat-bottomed boat moored in the river.

Fréteval. — Pop 865. The ruins of a **medieval castle** *(1/4 hour on foot Rtn)* look down from their bluff on the east bank to Fréteval on the far bank which is a favourite rendez-vous of fishermen.

Soon the road runs further inland past elegant houses and attractive churches.

Areines. — *Description p 54.*

> *Enter Vendôme by ② on the map.*

★★ **Vendôme**. — *Description p 186. About 1 hour.*

MIDDLE REACHES

② From Vendôme to La Chartre

> *78 km - 49 miles — allow one day — Local map p 121*

★★ **Vendôme**. — *Description p 186. About 1 hour.*

> *Leave Vendôme by ⑥, D957, then bear left into D5 to Villiers.*

◯ **Villiers-sur-Loir**. — Pop 1 001. The village overlooks the sloping vineyards facing Rochambeau Castle. The church is decorated with some very attractive 16C **murals**: on the left wall of the nave there is a huge St Christopher *(p 45)* carrying the child Jesus and the Legend of the Three Living and the Three Dead *(p 39)*. 15C stalls.

> *Take the road towards Thoré. Immediately after crossing the Loir turn left.*

Rochambeau. — The road runs along the foot of the cliff through the semi-troglodyte village up to the castle where Marshal Rochambeau (1725-1807) was born; he commanded the French expeditionary force in the American War of Independence and is buried in Thoré.

> *Return to the west bank of the river and turn left into D5.*

Le Gué-du-Loir. — The hamlet was built where the Boulon joins the Loir amid lush meadows and islands ringed by reed beds, willows, alders and poplars. On leaving the hamlet the road (D5) skirts the wall of **Bonaventure Manor**, which was probably named after a chapel dedicated to St Bonaventure. In 16C it belonged to Henri IV's father, Antoine de Bourbon-Vendôme who entertained his friends there, including some of the poets of the Pléiade. Later Bonaventure came into the possession of the de Musset family. The poet, **Alfred de Musset**, whose father was born at the Manor, used to spend his holidays as a child with his godfather, Louis de Musset, at the Château de Cogners, since the Manor had by then been sold.

> *Continue west along D5 (direction Savigny); then take the second turning to the right (C13) by a wayside cross.*

A wooded valley leads to the picturesque village of **Mazangé** clustered round the pretty church with its Gothic door.

> *Return to Gué-du-Loir; turn right into D24 (direction Montoire-sur-le-Loir).*

The road cuts off a large loop in the river where, in cutting its course, the Loir had revealed a cliff face in which the inhabitants of Asnières hollowed out their troglodyte houses.

> *Turn right into D82 to Lunay.*

Lunay. — Pop 1 207. Lunay is grouped in a valley round the main square where some old houses have survived. St-Martin's **church** is huge and Flamboyant with an attractive doorway: the stones of the arch are carved with ivy and pampres; in one of the niches with decorated canopies is a charming little statue of the Virgin and Child.

> *Return to D24.*

Les Roches-l'Évêque. — Pop 256. The village is confined between the river and the cliff. The troglodyte dwellings are well known locally, festooned with wistaria and lilac.

> *Turn right across the Loir (D917); in St-Rimay turn right to Lavardin.*

★ **Lavardin**. — *Description p 112.*

> *Take the minor road along the south bank of the river to Montoire.*

Montoire-sur-le-Loir. — *Description p 141.*

> *Leave Montoire by D917 (direction Château-du-Loir).*

Soon Troo and its church appear on the sky line.

★ **Troo**. — *Description p 183.*

> *Continue westwards along D917 to Sougé; turn left into the signed tourist road to Artins.*

Vieux-Bourg d'Artins. — The village is situated right on the river bank. The **church** has Romanesque walls with Flamboyant windows and a pointed arched doorway.

> *From Artins take D10 east; then turn right to l'Isle Verte; after 100 m - 110 yards turn left into a road which runs in front of the Château du Pin.*

From the bridge opposite the château one can see **l'Ile Verte** (the Green Island) a little way upstream where the Braye joins the Loir. It was here, where the row of poplars tremble in the breeze and the willows mark the edges of the meadows, that the poet Ronsard wanted to be buried; nowhere is more evocative of his genius.

◯ **Couture-sur-Loir**. — Pop 467. The **church** has a Gothic chancel with Angevin vaulting and 17C woodwork in the Rosary Chapel (on right of chancel). The recumbent figures in the nave are Ronsard's parents; note the costume detail.

> *In Couture-sur-Loir take D57 south to La Possonnière.*

La Possonnière Manor. — *Description p 156.*

> *Return to Couture and continue north (D57) crossing the Loir below the Château de la Flotte on its wooded hill. On the north bank turn left into D305.*

Poncé-sur-le-Loir. − *Description p 156.*

Continue west on D 305. In Ruillé turn left into D 80 which crosses the Loir.

The road is very picturesque particularly south of Tréhet; the hillside is riddled with caves.

Villedieu-le-Château. − Pop 553. This village has a pleasant **setting** in a valley surrounded by slopes covered with vineyards and fruit trees interspersed with troglodyte dwellings.

The houses in their gardens, the ruined ramparts and the remains of the belfry of St John's Priory compose a charming picture.

Return to Tréhet and turn left into D 10.

La Chartre-sur-le-Loir. − Pop 1 791. Facilities.

On the north bank of the river are the Bercé Forest *(p 63)* and the Jasnières Vineyard which produces a little known mellow white wine which ages well.

LOWER REACHES

③ From La Chartre to La Flèche

74 km - 46 miles − 1/2 day − Local map p 120

La Chartre-sur-le-Loir. − *See above.*

The road from La Chartre to Marçon (well known wine) passes through quiet countryside.

In Marçon turn right into D 61 which crosses the river valley to the foot of the slope on which St Cecilia's Chapel (Chapelle de Ste-Cécile) stands. Turn left into D 64 skirting the hillside which is riddled with troglodyte dwellings.

Château-du-Loir. − *Description p 78.*

Leave Château-du-Loir by D 10 going south (direction Château-la-Vallière). After crossing the bridge in Nogent turn right immediately into C 2.

La Bruère. − Pop 279. The **church** contains *(nave)* several statues: St Fiacre holding his spade, St Roch and St Sebastian; the graceful chancel vaulting is in the Renaissance style; the windows are 16C.

Leave La Bruère by D 11 going west; turn right into D 30 going north to Vaas.

From the bridge over the Loir one sees the weir, washing places, tiny gardens, houses and a church: this is **Vaas.**

Turn left into D 305 to Le Lude.

The road passes through meadows, nursery gardens and conifer forests thick with gorse and broom.

Follow the signed tourist route, turning left into D 188 to La Chapelle-aux-Choux.

Cherré Archaeological Site. − This site had already been identified in 19C but it was aerial photography which speeded up research in the 1970s. The Gallo-Roman settlement dates from 1C and 2C AD and comprises a temple, baths, two other buildings and a theatre of pointed reddish sandstone which has been completely excavated. During the excavations a necropolis from the Hallstatt period (the protohistoric period - 8C to 5C BC) was discovered under the cavea (the seating aera).

Continue south, bearing left over the river and then turn right into D 141 which skirts the grounds of Le Lude Château.

Le Lude. − *Description p 128.*

Leave Le Lude by D 305 going northeast across the river. Turn left immediately into D 307 and then left again towards Mansigné.

Soon after the turn and before reaching La Grifferie Château there is a view over the valley which is laid out in fruit orchards, asparagus beds, potato fields and maize plantations.

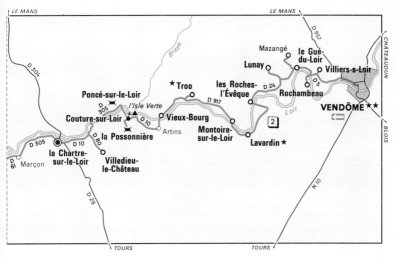

Bear left into D214 to Luché-Pringé. After crossing the River Aune, turn right into D13 to Vénevelles Manor.

Vénevelles Manor. — 15-17C. The manor is set in a quiet valley and surrounded by a broad moat.

Luché-Pringé. — Pop 1433. The exterior of the **church** (13-16C) is unusual: the many ornamented gables and the musicians sitting on the edge of the roof on either side of the façade. Above the entrance door is a low relief of St Martin *(p 176)* on horseback.
The interior contains an early 16C *Pietà* (right) carved in walnut. The wide chancel (13C) ends in a square chevet; the Angevin vaulting is supported on tall slim columns in the traditional Plantagenet style. Next to the church stands an elegant priory (13-15C) with an octagonal turret.

Pringé. — The tiny Romanesque **church** at Pringé was altered in 15C. The doorway in the façade is Romanesque. The interior is decorated with 16C murals showing St Hubert, St George and St Christopher.

Gallerande Château. — The road (D13) skirts the moat enclosing the park which is romantic and deserted; it is planted with huge trees: cedars, limes and oaks border the vast lawns. From the courtyard gate there is a fine view of the northeast façade of the château which has four machicolated round towers and an unusual octagonal keep.

Continue along D13; turn left into N23 to reach La Flèche.

★ **La Flèche.** — *Description p 101.*

★★ The LOIRE Valley

Michelin map 🅱🅳, 🅱🅴 and 🅱🅵 or 🅱🅱🅲 and 🅱🅱🅳

The Loire, so often celebrated by the poets since Ronsard and Du Bellay, for long brought life to the countryside, but today no river traffic plies the great waterway. None the less, the river still gives its character to the region and the finest landscapes are those it adorns with its long vistas and graceful curves.

GEOGRAPHICAL NOTES

The Loire, a former tributary of the Seine. — The longest river in France — 1 020 km - 634 miles — rises at the foot of the peak, Gerbier-de-Jonc on the southern edge of the Massif Central, but only its middle course is decribed in this guide.
Originally the Loire followed the course of the River Loing and flowed into the Seine but, when an arm of the Atlantic penetrated inland as far as Blois, the river abandoned its old bed and turned westwards.
North of the great loop thus formed extends the great Orleans Forest thriving on the granite sand carried down by the river from the Massif Central.

A fickle river. — The Loire with its irregular and capricious regime is sometimes furious and sometimes indolent. In summer, only a few rivulets *(luisettes)* trickle between the sand or gravel banks *(grèves)*. In these conditions it has the appearance of a "sandy river", but in autumn, during the rains, or at the end of winter, when the snow melts, it is in spate and its swirling waters then run high. It sometimes bursts the dykes, known as *levées or turcies,* built to protect the countryside from floods. The waters spread over the valley floor like a huge yellow blanket pierced here and there by tiled roofs or a few poplar trees.
Many village walls bear the tragic dates of great floods: 1846, 1856, 1866 and 1910.

Shipping on the Loire. — Up to the mid 19C, in spite of disavantages — sandbanks, whirlpools, floods, mills and tolls — the Loire and its tributaries, particularly the Cher were much used as a means of communication. As early as the 14C navigation was organised by a guild of mariners centred on Orléans who charged a toll and kept the channel clear. In 17C-18C a canal was built from the River Loing to Orléans which developed into a large port with warehousing. In addition to merchandise — wood and

(Photo Pix)

An "unexplodable" steam boat on the Loire at Amboise

coal from the Forez, pottery from Nevers, grain from the Beauce, wines from Touraine and Anjou – there was a great flow of passengers who preferred the river to the road. The journey from Orléans to Nantes by river took six days, and from ten to twenty for the return journey with a good wind. Coaches were transported on rafts.

The river traffic comprised flat bottomed barges (scows or lighters) with large square sails. **Toues,** barges without rigging, are still used today to transport hay and livestock; **sapines** with a greater capacity and rudely made of fir planks, were destroyed at the end of the voyage; **gabarres** were much larger vessels with sails up to 20 m - 66 ft high. The boats travelled in groups with a mother ship pulling two decreasingly smaller boats, one of which carried the bargee's cabin. The convoy was preceded by a wherry or punt to sound the river bed. The bargees had to be skilled on the upstream voyage to negotiate the bridges; the punt anchored beyond the bridge and the barges were hauled through with their sails lowered. At Ponts-de-Cé and Beaugency, where the current flowed obliquely through the arches, ropes from the bridge were used to guide the boats.

The "Unexplodables". – In 1832 the first steamboat service was started between Orléans and Nantes. It caused a sensation. Two days were enough for the journey, but there were accidents, for boilers exploded. Enthusiasm died down. The appearance of new steamboats nicknamed "unexplodables" restored confidence so much so that in 1843 more than 100 000 passengers were carried on the Loire and the Allier by the various steamboat companies which ran the services between Moulins and Nantes.

With the development of the railway, navigation on the Loire declined. In 1862 the last shipping company closed down.

The Boatmen. – Dressed in blue, with a red scarf and belt and gold earrings, the boatmen were a rough crew, given to frequent drinking, teasing the barmaids and using rough language. While waiting for a favourable wind the boatmen would sit round a table savouring an eel stew and a glass or two of wine before embarking on a chorus of their favourite songs.

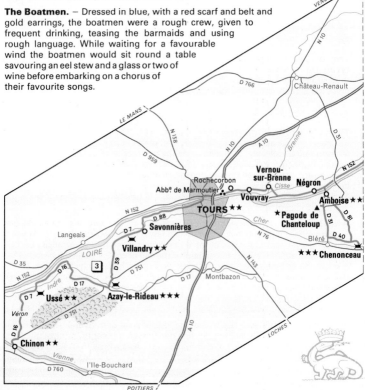

VIEWS OF THE LOIRE

The itineraries described below link the sights of prime importance with the most picturesque stretches of road. Car drivers should not allow the natural beauty of the countryside to distract them from the dangers of the winding roads.

On the **north bank**, N 152 offers only rare glimpses of the Loire before Blois but after Blois the road follows the embankment closely and lovely vistas succeed one another as far as the outskirts of Tours; between Tours and Angers the road continues along the river offering picturesque stretches of road.

On the **south bank**, D 751 wanders slightly from the Loire. Nevertheless, scenic views may be enjoyed a couple of miles downstream from Blois as well as between Amboise and Tours; also further downstream below Saumur and along the Angevin Corniche Road. The traffic-free country lanes parallel to the main road which follow the river bank more closely also offer superb views: D 88 west of Tours; D 16 downstream from Villandry; D 132 beginning at Gennes; and D 210 from Montjean-sur-Loire to St-Florent-le-Vieil.

★★★ DOWNSTREAM TO BLOIS

① From Orléans to Blois

84 km - 52 miles — about 6 hours — local map p 123

★ **Orléans.** — *Description p 146.*

> *Leave Orléans by Avenue Dauphine (south of the plan).*

Nursery gardens and rose gardens line both sides of the road as far as the Loiret which flows between wooded banks.

Olivet. — *Description p 152.*

> *In Olivet turn left into D 14 which leads to La Source Floral Park.*

★★ **La Source Floral Park.** — *Description p 152.*

> *Take D 14 westwards.*

Smart little houses with pretty gardens line the road to Cléry.

★ **Cléry-St-André.** — *Description p 94.*

★ **Meung-sur-Loire.** — *Description p 139.*

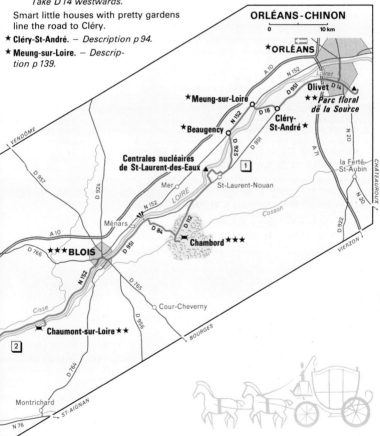

Take N 152 to Beaugency; soon the large towers of the St-Laurent Nuclear Power Station are visible on the horizon.

★ **Beaugency.** — *Description p 60.*

> *Leave by ③ or D 925 and after 6 km - 4 miles take D 951 to the right. Turn right again just before St-Laurent-Nouan.*

Ⓥ **St-Laurent-des Eaux Nuclear Power Station.** — Information centre and viewing platform.

> *After Nouan-sur-Loire the road enters the walled Chambord Estate where motorists are advised to drive slowly.*

LOIRE Valley ★★★

The sudden appearance of the stately façade of the Chambord Château on the River Cosson, makes for an unforgettable experience.

★★★ **Chambord Château.** – *Description p 74.*

Take D 84 northwest to Montlivault on the banks of the Loire.

The road which follows the embankment offers beautiful **views★** of this verdant setting: poplars, fields of asparagus, tulips and gladioli. On the north bank stand the silhouettes of Ménars Château *(p 139)*, then Blois with its basilica, cathedral and castle.

On arriving in Blois by ② cross the Loire to reach the town centre.

★★★ **Blois.** – *Description p 64. About 1/2 day.*

★★★ DOWNSTREAM TO TOURS

② From Blois to Tours

89 km - 55 miles – about 4 hours – local map p 122

★★★ **Blois.** – *Description p 64. About 1/2 day.*

Leave Blois by ⑤, N 152.

The road offers numerous views of the Loire which is strewn here with sandbanks which are a lush green in summer. The Chaumont metal bridge leads to Chaumont Château on the south bank.

★★ **Chaumont-sur-Loire.** – *Description p 84.*

Return to the north bank.

Shortly after Le Haut-Chantier Amboise Château is visible from the road.

★★ **Amboise.** – *Description p 44.*

Leave Amboise on D 81 then at Civray de Touraine bear left to Chenonceau.

★★★ **Chenonceau Château.** – *Description p 85.*

Return by D 40; at La Croix de Touraine bear right into D 31 to Amboise.

★ **Chanteloup Pagoda.** – *Description p 77.*

In Amboise cross the river and turn left into N 152 towards Tours.

Négron. – Standing below N 152 this village has a charming square overlooked by the ☉ church, a Gothic house with a Renaissance front and a 12C **barn** with fine timberwork roof.

Vernou-sur-Brenne. – *Description p 190.*

Vouvray. – *Description p 190.*

Continue west along N 152 towards Tours.

On approaching **Rochecorbon**, a small town at the foot of a bluff riddled with troglodyte dwellings, note the **lantern**, a watchtower on the top of the hill. Further on, at the end of a long wall (right) stands an imposing 13C doorway, part of **Marmoutier Abbey**, which was founded by St Martin in 372 and fortified in 13C and 14C.

Enter Tours by ④ on the plan.

★★ **Tours.** – *Description p 176. About 1/2 day.*

★★★ DOWNSTREAM VIA CHINON TO SAUMUR

③ From Tours to Chinon

61 km - 38 miles – about 5 hours – local map p 123

★★ **Tours.** – *Description p 176. About 1/2 day.*

Leave Tours by D 88 going west.

The road runs along the embankment on the south bank of the Loire passing gardens and vegetable plots and St Cosmas' Priory *(p 182)*. Fine views of the south bank of the river.

In L'Aireau-des-Bergeons turn left into D 288 to Savonnières.

Savonnières. – *Description p 169.*

★★★ **Villandry.** – *Description p 189.*

After Villandry take the road south (D 39) out of troglodyte country and into the Indres Valley.

★★★ **Azay-le-Rideau.** – *Description p 57.*

The road (D 17) runs west between Chinon Forest *(left)* and the River Indre, which divides into several channels.

In Quincay turn right into D 7, then bear left into D 119 which crosses the river; in Bréhémont turn left into D 16.

A charming but narrow road winds between hedges and spinneys with occasional glimpses of the river. A bridge spanning the Indre provides one of the best views of Ussé Château.

★★ **Ussé.** – *Description p 184.*

From Ussé take D 7 westwards and then turn south into D 16.

The road passes through Huismes village and across the **Véron**, a tongue of highly fertile alluvial soil at the confluence of the Loire and the Vienne. It yields grain, grapes and fruit in abundance; the plums used in the famous *"pruneaux de Tours"* are grown here. On the southern edge lies Chinon in the shadow of its massive ruined castle.

★★ **Chinon.** – *Description p 89. Tour : 2 hours.*

④ From Chinon to Saumur

38 km - 23 1/2 miles — about 3 hours — local map p 127

★★ Chinon. — *Description p 89. Tour : 2 hours.*

> *Leave Chinon by ③ on the plan and then turn right at the end of the avenue of plane trees into D 751 west to Saumur.*

Just before entering Candes turn right into D 7 on to the bridge over the Vienne to view the attractive **setting★** of the village at the confluence of the Loire and the Vienne.

> *Return to the south bank of the Vienne.*

★ Candes-St-Martin. — *Description p 73.*

Montsoreau. — *Description p 145.*

> *In Montsoreau turn left into D 947 south to Fontevraud.*

★★ Fontevraud-l'Abbaye. — *Description p 103.*

> *Return to Montsoreau.*

From the bridge over the Loire west of Montsoreau there is a fine view upstream of Montsoreau and Candes and downstream of Saumur castle which is just visible. The road (D 947) is bordered by troglodyte dwellings and white Renaissance houses.

Small wine villages nestle between the road and the limestone cliffs, which are riddled with caves and old quarries — some are now used for growing mushrooms. The sloping vineyards produce a dry or medium dry white wine, a Cabernet rosé called **Cabernet de Saumur**, and a red wine well known called **Champigny**.

As the road enters Saumur it passes an elegant church, Our Lady of Ardilliers *(p 169)*.

★★ Saumur. — *Description p 166. About 1 1/2 hours.*

★ DOWNSTREAM TO ANGERS

⑤ From Saumur to Angers

48 km - 30 miles — about 3 1/2 hours — local map p 127

★★ Saumur. — *Description p 166. About 1 1/2 hours.*

> *Leave Saumur by ⑤ on the plan.*

St-Hilaire-St-Florent. — *Description p 168.*

On the right extend huge meadows bordered by trees and protected by dykes.

Chênehutte-les-Tuffeaux. — Pop 668. The village **church** stands beside the road on the north side of the village. It is an attractive Romanesque building with a handsome doorway in the same style; the arch stones are carved.

Trèves-Cunault. — Pop 467. A 15C crenellated tower is all that remains of the old castle. Tucked in beside it is the little **church★** of Trèves. The beauty of its interior derives from the great arches of the broad Romanesque nave; the chancel arch frames the rood beam bearing a crucifixion. The holy water stoup by the entrance is of porphyry with primitive carvings; to the right is a recumbent figure; to the left stands a tall stone reliquary pierced with Flamboyant arches.

★★ Cunault Church. — *Description p 97.*

Les Rosiers. — *Description p 159.*

> *Re-cross the bridge and bear right immediately into D 132 along the south bank of the river.*

Le Thoureil. — Pop 359. This quiet, spruce little village was formerly a very active river port for the handling of apples. Inside the **church**, on either side of the choir there are two beautiful wooden reliquary shrines dating from the late 16C, which originally belonged to the Abbey of St-Maurus of Glanfeuil *(see below);* they are adorned with statuettes of Benedictine monks (Maurus, Roman) and saints who were popular locally (Christopher, John, Martin, James, Eloi or Eligius).

St-Maur-de-Glanfeuil Abbey. — This ruined Benedictine abbey *(now an international ecumenical centre)* is named after St Maurus, a hermit who came from Angers and founded a monastery in the 6C on the site of the Roman villa of Glanfeuil on the Loire.

Excavations in the courtyard have revealed a 4C Gallo-Roman temple (nymphaeum) dedicated to the water goddesses (Nymphs) which St Maurus converted into a chapel; the column bases are clearly visible.

On the first floor is an austere chapel (1955) which is decorated with sparkling stained glass windows. On the second floor there is a superb **Carolingian cross**; originally it was mounted on the gable of the 9C abbey church which the Normans destroyed; it was then inserted in the wall of the 11C building.

St Maurus' tomb is in St Martin's Chapel (11-13C) near the little cemetery.

> *Continue to St-Rémy-la-Varenne; turn right into D 55 and cross the river to St-Mathurin-sur-Loire; bear left into D 952.*

This is a picturesque route along the banks of the majestic river Loire.

★★ Angers. — *Description p 47. About 1/2 day.*

Plan your own itinerary by looking at the map of the principal sights (pp 4-6).

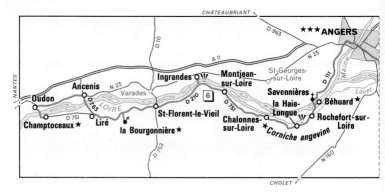

★ DOWNSTREAM TO CHAMPTOCEAUX

6 From Angers to Champtoceaux

83 km - 50 miles — about 4 hours — local map p 126

★★★ **Angers**. – *Description p 47. About 1/2 day.*

> *Leave Angers by boulevard du Bon-Pasteur going west and turn left into D 111 going south to Bouchemaine.*

Beyond La Pointe the road leaves the river bank to wind through the vineyards to Épiré and then descends into the valley of a stream which joins the Loire at Savennières.

Savennières. – Pop 1 101. The attractive village **church** has a Romanesque chevet ornamented with modillions and carved friezes; the south door is also Romanesque. The walls of the nave are of schist decorated with a fish-bone pattern in brick.

> *Cross the north arm of the river to Béhuard Island.*

★ **Béhuard**. – *Description p 62.*

Rochefort-sur-Loire. – Pop 1 819. Rochefort lies in a rural setting on the Louet, a side stream of the Loire. The neighbouring slopes produce the famous **Quart de Chaume**, a distinctive and heady white wine.
There are several old houses, with turrets or watchtowers, in the main square below the D 751.

> *Take D 751 west.*

★ **Angevin Corniche Road**. – For the next 5 miles the road along the south bank of the Loire turns and twists through many right bends cut into the cliff face. Beyond Haie-Longue there are superb views of the riverside villages lying in the broad valley.

La Haie-Longue. – In a bend in the road at the entrance to La Haie-Longue stands a chapel dedicated to **Our Lady of Loretto**, the patron saint of aviators; legend has it that her house was carried by the breeze from Nazareth to Jugoslavia and thence to Loretto on the Italian coast where it is venerated as the Holy House (Santa Casa). Opposite stands a monument in honour of René Gasnier, a pioneer in aviation. Behind the monument is a viewing table. From here there is a remarkable **view**★ of the River Loire and its side streams *(see p 17)* glinting silver in the light; the turreted manor houses set about with meadows and sloping vineyards make a charming picture. The wine from these vineyards is known as "Coteaux du Layon" *(p 112)*.

Chalonnes-sur-Loire. – Pop 5 358. Chalonnes, which was the birthplace of St Maurille, Bishop of Angers in 5C, is pleasantly situated. From the quayside on the Loire there is an attractive view of the river. The old port now harbours more pleasure craft than fishing boats.

West of Chalonnes the road (D 571) skirts the edge of the plateau from which small streams flow north to join the Loire.

Montjean-sur-Loire. – Pop 2 492. The narrow streets of Montjean are confined on a rocky promontory overlooking the Loire. From the terrace near the church there is a wide **view** of the Loire Valley, of the suspension bridge over the river and of numerous villages with their grey slate roofs.

> *From Montjean to St-Florent take D 210.*

The **road**★ along the river embankment provides views over the Loire (right) and of the slopes rising to the south of the Thau, an old side stream of the Loire (left). Beautiful **view** on reaching Ingrandes.

Ingrandes. – *Description p 109.*

> *Return to the south bank and continue west on D 210.*

St-Florent-le-Vieil. – *Description p 163.*

West of St-Florent-le-Vieil the road (D 751) winds through gently rolling hills.

★ **La Bourgonnière Chapel**. – *Description p 71.*

Liré. – *Description p 114.*

> *Take D 763 north across the Loire to Ancenis.*

Ancenis. – Pop 7 263. Town plan in the Michelin Red Guide France.
The houses of Ancenis, built of schist and roofed with slate, rise in tiers on the north bank of the Loire overlooking the suspension bridge which is 500 m - 550 yards long. The town fortifications and the castle ramparts, now in ruins, commanded the valley so that Ancenis was known as "the key to Brittany".

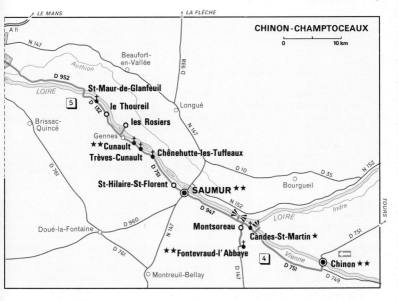

The town was once a busy port in the shipment of wine and was active in the sailcloth industry. Ancenis is now an important agricultural market and has one of the largest cooperatives in France, the CANA (Cooperative Agricole La Noêlle à Ancenis), which is involved in many different activities. The vineyards of the district are known for their **Muscadet** (white wine) and **Gamay** (rosé).

Leave Ancenis by ④ on the plan, N23 going west.

Oudon. — Pop 2 001. The dominant feature is the medieval keep, built between 1392 and ⊙ 1415. From the top of the **tower** there is a beautiful view of the valley.

★ **Champtoceaux.** — Pop 1 396. Facilities. Champtoceaux is built on an impressive **site**★ on the top of a ridge overlooking the Loire Valley. The terrace behind the church (**Promenade de Champalud★★**) is like a balcony above the Loire which divides into several channels round the islands in midstream: (viewing table). Beyond the terrace are the ruins of the fortress which was demolished in 1420 and a toll bridge over the Loire. The local white wines are to be recommended.

★ LORRIS   Pop 2 592

Michelin map 📖 fold 1 or 🔢 fold 42 or 🔢 fold 7

Lorris is famous for its charter of freedom which was granted in 1122 by Louis VI. The town was a hunting seat for the Capet kings and a place of residence for Blanche of Castille and her son Louis IX of France.
In 1215 it was the birthplace of Guillaume de Lorris, who wrote the first part of the Romance of the Rose *(Roman de la Rose) (p 139),* a poem of courtly love which influenced Chaucer in his writings.

★ **Church of Our Lady (Notre-Dame).** — The church is noteworthy not only for the purity of its architecture (12-13C) but also for its furnishings. The elegant Romanesque door leads into the luminous Gothic nave. High up in the nave are a **gallery** and the early 16C **organ loft★** carved with pilasters and medallions. The late 15C **choir stalls★** are decorated with the Prophets and Sibyls on the cheekpieces and scenes from The Golden Legend, the New Testament and everyday life on the misericords. Above the old altar hang two 18C angels. Also worth noting are the polychrome statues in the ambulatory and an alabaster Virgin (late 15C) near the baptismal font.
A **museum** about the organ and old musical instruments has been created under the eaves.

Place du Martroi. — This spacious square is the centre of the village. The 16C **town hall**, of brick with stone courses and heavily ornamented dormer windows, stands in the main street; opposite is the **market** *(halles)* covered with an oak roof (1542).

EXCURSION

Orléans Canal. — *Round trip of 14 km - 9 miles by D 44 going northwest and then a left turn into D 444.* The canal, which was finished in 1692, linked the Loire to the Loing just north of Montargis. Little engineering was required except at Grignon Locks. It is now out of service but its waters attract many fishermen.

Grignon. — The hamlet is set deep in the countryside beside the three locks.

The road passes through **Vieilles-Maisons;** the church has a timber-framed porch.

Forest Lake (Étang des Bois). — This little lake, fringed with oak, beech and chestnut trees, is very popular in the season.

★★ Le LUDE Château

Le Lude lies on the south bank of the Loir which is the border between Maine and Anjou; since the erection of the first fort, La Motte, it has seen a thousand years of history. The Son et Lumière, which was started in 1957, has proved a great attraction to visitors. The 11C fortress of the Counts of Anjou was replaced in 13-14C by a castle which withstood several assaults by the English before it fell in 1425; it was recaptured two years later by Ambroise de Loré, Beaumanoir and Gilles de Rais *(pp 110, 116)*.

In 1457 the castle was acquired by Jean de Daillon, a childhood friend of Louis XI. His son built the present château on the foundations of the earlier fortress: it kept the traditional square layout with a massive tower at each corner but the large windows and the delicate decoration make it a country house in the contemporary taste.

★★★ **Son et Lumière.** — *See Practical Information at the end of this guide.*
Skilful lighting and the fountains playing enhance the beautiful design of the château and its park on the banks of the Loir; a natural plateau provides a superb stage for the cast of 135 in scintillating costumes, who present a succession of tableaux from a Renaissance pavane to the waltzes of the Second Empire, accompanied by fireworks.

⊙**Tour.** — The U-shaped early 17C courtyard was closed off in the late 18C by an arched portico. Facing the park, to the right, is the François I Wing. Its façade is a mixture of the fortress style, with its round medieval towers, and Renaissance refinement, with its windows framed by pilasters, pedimented dormer windows, medallions and carved ornamentation. Overlooking the river, the Louis XVI Wing in white tufa stone exemplifies the Classical style: it is severe and symmetrical and the façade's central projecting part is topped by a carved pediment. The north wing *(visible from Rue du Pont which skirts the château)* is the earliest wing (early 16C); it was rearranged in the 19C when the stone balconies and equestrian statue of Jean de Daillon were added.

In the Louis XII Wing is the ballroom restored in the 15 and 16C style. The 18C building contains a fine suite of rooms, especially a splendid oval saloon in pure Louis XVI style with woodwork and mirrors. In the François I Wing the library has a 17C Gobelins tapestry; in the dining room, where the window recesses reveal the thickness of the medieval walls, there is a vast chimneypiece with a carved salamander and ermine tufts *(p 28)*, while on the walls hang three Flemish tapestries including a *Verdure* showing a red parrot.

ADDITIONAL SIGHT

⊙**Architects' House** (**Maison des Architectes**). — *3 Rue du Marché-au-Fil, on the left side of the post office near the entrance to the château.*
The house, which was built in 16C by the architects of the château, presents the ornamentation typical of the Renaissance period: mullioned windows, pilasters with Corinthian capitals, decorated with roundels and lozenges, and friezes running between the floors.

EXCURSION

Genneteil; La Boissière. — *Round trip of 28 km - 17 miles — about 1 1/2 hours. Leave Le Lude by D257 going southwest.*

Genneteil. — Pop 453. The Romanesque **church** has a 13C belltower with a stair turret and a beautiful 11C doorway; the arch stones are carved with the signs of the zodiac and human faces. The lefthand chapel is decorated with Romanesque frescoes.

Take D138 southeast.

Chigné. — Pop 296. The fortified **church** (12-15C) presents an interesting façade flanked by a tower. Above the tri-arched doorway note the line of carved brackets and the primitive carvings which have been incorporated, much altered, in the building.

Continue via les 4 Chemins to La Boissière.

La Boissière. — *Description p 69.*

Take D767 north; in La Croix-de-Beauchêne take D138 right.

Broc. — Pop 402. The attractive **church** has a squat Romanesque tower and a row of carved brackets on the chevet. The broad nave is roofed with lierne and tierceron vaulting; the Romanesque apse is decorated with 13C frescoes: Christ in Majesty (on half-dome), the Annunciation (left) and the Virgin in Majesty (right). On the nave wall is a very beautiful wooden Crucifix of the Louis XIII period.

Return to Le Lude via La Croix-de-Beauchêne and D307.

Michelin map 🔲 fold 13 or 🔲 folds 10, 22
Plan of the conurbation in the Michelin Red Guide France

Le Mans a large modern town stands on the banks of the Sarthe at its confluence with the Huisne; it is a thriving provincial capital, its calendar marked by frequent fairs: Spring Fair (end of March or early April); the Grand Exhibition called the Four-Day Fair (mid September); the Onion Fair (first Friday in September). It is also one of the most important insurance centres in France. Its industry is closely involved with the construction and racing of cars (24 hour Le Mans circuit, Bugatti circuit).

The citizens of Le Mans are fond of good food: potted pork *(rillettes)*, plump pullets *(poulardes dodues)*, capons *(chapons)* accompanied by sparkling cider and the famous Reinette apple.

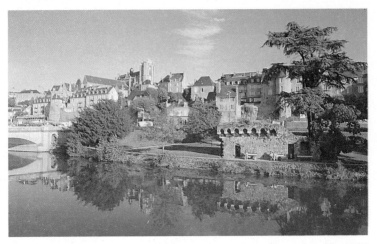

(Photo J.-P. Langeland/DIAF)

River Sarthe at Le Mans

HISTORICAL NOTES

In 4C the ancient town of Subdinnum surrounded itself with ramparts to resist the barbarian invasions; this was the period when St Julian began to convert the people of the region.

The Plantagenet Dynasty. – The Plantagenet connections with this town were beneficial. When **Geoffroy Plantagenet**, Count of Anjou, married Matilda, the grand-daughter of William the Conqueror he added Normandy and Maine to his domains. Geoffroy often resided at Le Mans and on his death in 1151 he was buried in the cathedral.

His son, who in 1154 became **Henry II** of England, was the founder of the Coëffort Hospital and it was to Le Mans, his birthplace, that he retired in his old age only to be expelled by one of his rebellious sons **Richard the Lionheart**, then in alliance with the French King.

While on the Third Crusade Richard married Queen Berengaria of Navarre and it was to her in her widowhood that Philippe-Auguste gave the county of Maine which he had reconquered from Richard's younger brother, John Lackland. Berengaria founded Epau Abbey *(p 135)* where she was buried. After her death Louis IX gave the county to his brother Charles *(p 48)*. During the Hundred Years War Le Mans was under English control until 1448.

The drama of 5 August 1392. – In the summer of 1392 King **Charles VI** of France launched an expedition against the Duke of Brittany, who supported the English. On 5 August the king left Le Mans with his troops and rode westwards. Suddenly, as they approached a leper house, an old man, disfigured and in tatters, blocked his road and cried "Don't go any further, noble king, you have been betrayed!"

Charles was deeply affected by this incident but continued on his way. A little later, when they paused to rest under the hot sun, a soldier let his lance fall against a helmet, causing a strident clang in the silence. Charles jumped. Gripped by a sudden fury and believing he was being attacked, he drew his sword and shouted out that he was being delivered to his enemies. He killed four men, let his horse have its head and galloped about wildly without anyone being able to intervene. Finally he was worn out and one of his knights was able to mount behind and bring the horse under control. They laid the king in a wagon and tied him down; then they took him back to Le Mans persuaded that he was about to die.

The terrible onset of madness in the middle of the Hundred Years War had serious consequences. Deprived of its ruler and a prey to princely rivalries, the kingdom grew weak. From time to time Charles VI would regain his reason only to sink again soon after into madness. Henry V of England took advantage of the situation: in 1420 he imposed the famous treaty of Troyes by which Charles VI disinherited his son and recognized Henry as his heir.

Charles VI died in 1422; the drama begun near Le Mans had lasted thirty years.

The Comic Novel. – The cathedral chapter in Le Mans had several members of note: Arnould Gréban, author of a Mystery of the Passion (c1450) a poem of 30 000 lines, Ronsard, who was a canon in 1560 and Jacques Pelletier, a friend of Ronsard and Paul Scarron.

Scarron (1610-60) became an unordained canon of Le Mans Cathedral and also a poet; he enjoyed excellent health, a prebend and a house attached to the cathedral.

Unfortunately for him, since he preferred the gay life of the city, he had from time to time to spend some time in Le Mans where he consoled himself with food and wine. In 1638 Scarron fell victim to a noxious drug dispensed by a charlatan and was paralysed. His hard lot was mitigated by Marie de Hautefort, a former mistress of Louis XIII who had been exiled to Le Mans and who offered her friendship, and by the Muse which inspired the Comic Novel *(Le Roman Comique),* a burlesque work relating the adventures of a troop of actors in Le Mans and its neighbourhood.

In 1652 Scarron married **Françoise d'Aubigné**, grand-daughter of the Calvinist poet Agrippa d'Aubigné, who said "I would rather marry a legless cripple than the convent". When she was widowed she was elevated to the rank of Marquise de Maintenon before her secret marriage to Louis XIV (1683) over whom she had a great influence.

In the vanguard of progress. – Before the Revolution Le Mans had several flourishing industries: candle making, tanning, making sailcloth from locally-grown hemp and weaving a coarse black woollen material used for clerics' and lawyers' gowns. A dozen merchants in the town controlled about 2 000 jobs in the district which produced 18 000 items of which two thirds were exported.

In the second half of the 19C the town entered the first rank of industrial centres when **Amédée Bollée** (1844-1917), a local bell-founder, began to take an interest in the infant motor car industry. His first car *(l'Obéissante)* was finished in 1873; it was a 12 seater break with two engines each driving one back wheel; it weighed just over 4 tonnes empty and had a maximum speed of over 40 km - 25 miles per hour. Later he built the *Mancelle* the first car to have the engine placed in front under a bonnet and to have a transmission shaft. The Austrian emperor, Franz-Joseph went for a ride in the *Mancelle.*

His son Amedée (1867-1926) devoted himself mainly to racing cars; they were fitted with Michelin tyres and reached 100 km - 62 miles per hour. After the First World War he began to produce an early form of piston rings and his factory is still engaged in this line of manufacture.

In 1908 his brother, Léon Bollée, invited **Wilbur Wright** to attempt one of his first flights in an aeroplane at Les Hunaudières. When asked how the aircraft had performed Wright replied "Like a bird".

In 1936 Louis Renault set up his first decentralized factory south of Le Mans in the Arnage plain.

Le Mans Twenty-four Hour Race. – In 1923 Gustave Singher and Georges Durand launched the first Le Mans 24 hours endurance test which was to become a sporting event of universal interest and a testing ground for car manufacturers.

The difficulties of the circuit and the duration of the race are a severe test of the quality of the machine and of the endurance of the two drivers who take turns at the wheel of each car. The track has been greatly improved since the tragic accident in 1955 when several spectators died.

Whether seen from the stands or from the fields or pine woods which surround the track, the race is an unforgettable experience: the roaring of the engines, the whining of the vehicles hurtling up the straight sections at more than 350 km - 200 miles per hour, the smell of petrol mingled with the resin of the pine trees, the glare of the headlights at night, the emotion and excitement of the motor car fanatics.

Every year there is a Le Mans 24 hour motor cycle race and every other year the Grand Prix de France motorcycle race and the Le Mans 24 hour Truck race.

Course Records. – The first 24 hour race in 1923 was won by Lagache and Léonard from Chenard and Walcker; they covered 1 109.536 km at an average of 92.064 km per hour; the fastest circuit time was achieved by Clément in a Bentley: 107.328 km per hour. The most famous names in motor racing have taken part in the 54 trials which have been held since then.

In 1971 when the track was 13.469 km long H. Marko and G. Van Lennep covered 5 335.313 km in a Porsche 917 at an average of 222.304 km per hour; Siffert drove the fastest lap, also in a Porsche 917, at an average of 243.905 km per hour.

From 1972 to 1978 the circuit was 13.640 km long; D. Pironi and J.-P. Jaussaud hold the course record with 5 044.530 km in a Renault Alpine A 442 Turbo in 1978. The circuit was altered in 1979 (13.626 km) and again in 1986 (13.528) when D. Bell, with J. Stuck and A. Holbert, won his fourth Le Mans victory in a Porsche 962.

★★ ST JULIAN'S CATHEDRAL *time: 1 hour*

⊙ This magnificent edifice, dedicated to St Julian, the first Bishop of Le Mans, rises proudly above the impressive tiered arrangement of the Gothic **chevet★★★**, amazing for its system of Y-shaped two-tiered flying buttresses. The present building comprises a Romanesque nave, Gothic chancel and Radiant or Middle Gothic transept flanked by a tower. Interior illumination.

Exterior. – Overlooking the charming Place St-Michel the south porch has a superb 12C **doorway★★** contemporary with the Royal Doorway of Chartres. A comparison of the two doorways shows that they portray the same themes: Christ in Majesty, the Apostles and a series of statue columns. The doorway is flanked by statue columns: on the jambs are Sts Peter and Paul while the figures on the splay embrasures represent Solomon and the Queen of Sheba, a Prophet, a Sibyl and the ancestors of Christ. The Apostles in serried ranks occupy the niches of the lintel with Christ the King on the tympanum, surrounded by the symbols of the Evangelists, being sprinkled with incense by the angels of the first recessed arch. The other scenes on the arches are the Annunciation, Visitation, Nativity, Presentation in the Temple, Massacre of the Innocents, Baptism of Christ, Wedding Feast at Cana.

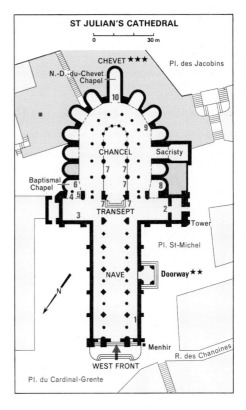

ST JULIAN'S CATHEDRAL

Looking to the right of the porch note the transept pierced by immense windows and the 12-14C tower (64 m - 210 ft high).

The west front, overlooking the Place du Cardinal-Grente, bordered by Renaissance dwellings (p 133), is in an archaic Romanesque style. One can clearly distinguish the original 11C gable embedded in the gable added the following century when the new vaulting was being built.

At the right hand corner of the west front is a pink veined sandstone menhir. Tradition has it that visitors should place their thumb in one of the holes to be sure of having visited Le Mans.

Nave. – The Romanesque main building rests on great 11C round arches which were reinforced in the following century by pointed arches. The domical vaults or Plantagenet style vaulting (p 36) springs from majestic capitals which show great finesse of detail. In the side aisles are eight Romanesque stained glass windows, the most famous one represents the Ascension (1). The great window of the west front, heavily restored in the 19C, evokes the Legend of St Julian.

Transept. – The 14-15C transept, pierced by a small columned gallery and immense windows, is striking for its ethereal quality and its bold elevation.

The south arm is dominated by the 16C organ loft (2), while the north arm is suffused with light transmitted by the beautiful 15C stained glass. Three 16C tapestry hangings (3) represent the Legend of St Julian.

At the entrance to the baptismal chapel (Chapelle des Fonts), which opens into the north arm, facing one another are two remarkable Renaissance **tombs★★**. The one on the left (4), that of Charles I of Anjou, Count of Maine, the brother of King René (p 48), is the work of Francesco Laurana. The recumbent figure lies, in the Italian style, on an antique sarcophagus and the delicacy of the facial features recall Laurana's talents as a portraitist.

On the right the magnificent monument (5) to the memory of Guillaume Du Bellay, cousin of the poet, shows the figure holding a sword and a book and reclining on one elbow in the antique manner on a sarcophagus which is adorned with an attractive frieze of aquatic divinities.

The tomb of Cardinal Grente (6) was placed here in 1965.

Chancel. – This lofty and soaring Gothic chancel (13C) is one of the finest in France – 34 m - 112 ft high (compare Notre-Dame in Paris 35 m - 115 ft); it is encircled by a double ambulatory and a crown of apsidal chapels.

The serried ranks of the tall upward sweeping columns support lancet arches showing a definite Norman influence. In the high windows of the chancel and first ambulatory and in the low windows of the chapels the 13C **stained glass★★** is a blaze of colour dominated by vivid blues and reds. Binoculars are needed to identify the rather rigid and wild figures of the Apostles, bishops, saints and donors.

Hanging above the 16C choir stalls is the famous series of **tapestries** (7) of the same period depicting the lives of Sts Gervase and Protase.

Chancel precincts. – In the first chapel on the right (8) is a moving 17C terracotta Entombment.

The sacristy door beyond was formerly part of the 17C rood screen. The beautiful 16C woodwork, in the sacristy, originally formed the high backs of the choir stalls. The 14C Canons' Doorway (9) has a tympanum with an effigy of St Julian.

The 13C chapel Notre-Dame-du-Chevet is closed by a delicate 17C wrought iron grille. The 13C stained glass windows depict the Tree of Jesse (10) and the story of Adam and Eve.

The vaulting is covered with paintings dating from 1380. The scene illustrating an Angels' Concert, displays great delicacy of draughtsmanship.

★★ THE MEDIEVAL TOWN (LE VIEUX MANS) *time: 1 hour*

Closely packed inside the Gallo-Roman ramparts (visible from the quays), the medieval town is built on a hill dominating the Sarthe. Restaurants and boutiques animate this picturesque ensemble of winding streets, cut by stepped alleys, bordered by 15C half-timbered houses, Renaissance town houses and 18C *hôtels* graced with wrought iron balconies.

From Place des Jacobins follow on foot the itinerary indicated on the plan below.

Place St-Michel. — Standing in the cathedral precincts is the Renaissance house (W) where Paul Scarron lived during his period as a member of the Chapter. The presbytery, no 1*bis,* has retained a 15C staircase turret.

During the two summer months a temporary tourist information bureau is set up in the square.

★ **Queen Berengaria's House (Maison de la Reine Bérengère** − **M²)**. − *Nos 7-9 Rue Reine-Bérengère*. This elegant house was built between 1490 and 1515 for an alderman of Le Mans; Queen Berengaria, wife of Richard the Lionheart, would not have known it since she lived in 13C. The decoration consists of an accolade above the door, historiated brackets supporting the beams and statues of St Catherine and St Barbara.

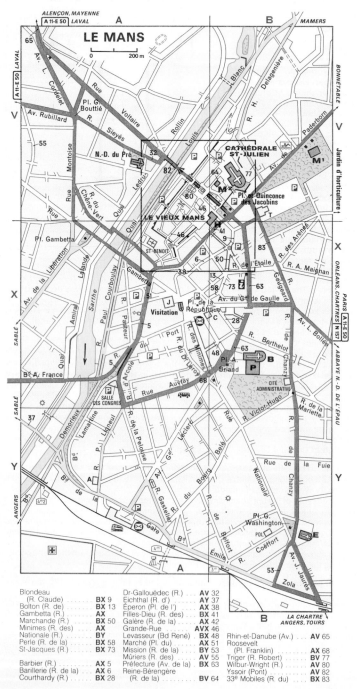

Museum of History and Ethnography. – Queen Berengaria's House is now a museum of history and ethnography. The ground floor is devoted to the history of the cathedral. The glazed pottery of the Sarthe region (Ligron, Malicorne, Prevelles...) is lively and fantastic; the astonishingly fresh colours – yellow, green and brown – are used lavishly on the statuettes, altarpieces, chafing dishes, pots, roof finials, etc. There are also paintings and drawings of old Le Mans and the Sarthe region.

House of the Two Friends (Maison des Deux-Amis – Y). – Nos 18-20. The two friends are shown supporting a coat of arms. Built in the 15C, a century later it was the home of Nicolas Denizot, the poet and painter and friend of Ronsard and Du Bellay.

On the opposite side of Rue Wilbur-Wright which was cut through the hillside to relieve traffic congestion, is the

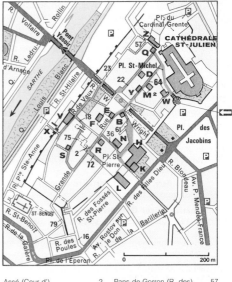

Assé (Cour d') 2	Pans-de-Gorron (R. des) ... 57
Boucheries (R.) 16	Pilier-Rouge (R. du) 61
Bouquet (R.) 18	Reine-Bérengère (R. de la) .. 64
Chanoines (R. des) 22	St-Honoré (R.) 72
Chapelains (R. des) 23	St-Pavin-de-la-Cité (R.) 75
Écrevisse (R. de l') 36	Truie-qui-file (R. de la) 79

Red Pillar House (Maison du Pilier Rouge – B), a half-timbered house containing the tourist information centre; its corner post is decorated with a death's head.

At the beginning of the Grande-Rue stands (right) the Green Pillar House (Maison du Pilier Vert – E) and further on the former 16C Hôtel d'Arcy (F).

Return to the Maison du Pilier Rouge and turn right into the street of the same name which ends on the Place St-Pierre lined with half-timbered houses.

Town Hall (Hôtel de Ville – H). – The town hall was built in 1760, on the site of the palace of the Counts of Maine. Take the staircase to the right of the building down to Rue des Filles-Dieu from where there is a view of the old town's southeast ramparts; on one side of the staircase is a 14C tower (K) and on the other the former Collegiate Church of St-Pierre-de-la-Cour (L), now an exhibition and concert hall.

Hôtel de Vignoles (N). – This late 16C mansion with tall French style roofs stands at the beginning of Rue de l'Écrevisse on the right.

Adam and Eve House (Maison d'Adam et Ève – R). – No 71 La Grande-Rue. This superb Renaissance mansion was the home of Jean de l'Épine, an astrologer and physician.

At the corner of the Rue St-Honoré (72) a column shaft is decorated with three keys, the sign of a locksmith. The street is lined with half-timbered houses. The picturesque Cour d'Assé opens opposite Rue St-Honoré. From here onwards Grande-Rue descends between noble Classical mansions. Bear right into the more popular Rue St-Pavin-de-la-Cité; on the left is the Hôtel d'Argouges (S) which has a lovely 15C doorway in its courtyard. Continue along Rue St-Pavin-de-la-Cité; after a vaulted passageway turn left into Rue Bouquet. At the corner of Rue de Vaux a 15C niche shelters a Mary Magdalene; at no 12 the Hôtel de Vaux (V), is late 16C. Further on to the left there is a view of the Great Postern staircase (X), part of the Gallo-Roman ramparts.

Return along Rue de Vaux to Rue Wilbur-Wright; cross it and climb the steps turning left into Rue des Chanoines. At no 26 stands the St-Jacques's canon's residence (D) built around 1560.

Turret House (Maison de la Tourelle – Q). – This Renaissance dwelling, with its windows and dormers decorated with delicate scrollwork, has a turret on the corner of the Pans-de-Gorron alley.

Hôtel du Grabatoire (Z). – On the other side of the staircase, facing the Romanesque doorway of the cathedral, this 16C mansion was originally the infirmary for sick canons; it is today, the episcopal palace. On its right note the Pilgrim's House (Maison du Pèlerin) decorated with cockleshells, the symbol adopted by pilgrims who had visited the shrine of St James at Compostela (see Michelin Green Guide to Spain).

INTERVENING SIGHTS

★ Tessé Museum (BV M¹). – The museum is housed in the former bishop's palace, which was built in 19C on the site of the Tessé family mansion; its fine collection of paintings, which was seized in 1793, now forms the nucleus of the museum.

Ground floor. – A small room (left) contains a superb enamelled copper plaque, called the Plantagenet enamel★, a unique piece representing Geoffroy Plantagenet, Count of Anjou and Maine from 1129 to 1151, Duke of Normandy in 1144 and father of Henry II of England; originally it adorned the tomb (no longer extant) of this powerful knight in the cathedral.

The Italian paintings include an interesting series of 14-15C altarpieces with gold backgrounds, a delicious female saint with slit eyes by Pietro Lorenzetti from Siena, two panels from a marriage chest by Pesellino of Florence (the Penitence of David and the Death of Absalom) and a very touching Virgin suckling the Infant Jesus.

In the Renaissance room there is a half relief in enamelled terracotta from the Della Robbia workshop; also two panels by the Master of Vivoin, part of an altarpiece from Vivoin Priory (Sarthe).

There are Classical paintings by Poussin, Philippe de Champaigne (the Dream of Elijah, the famous Vanity exhibited in the Tessé room), Georges de la Tour (St Francis in ecstasy) and Nicolas Tournier (the Drinking Party — in the entrance). The 18C room contains a superb bookcase attributed to Bernard Van Risenburgh.

First floor. – The Northern school of painting is represented by Van Utrecht, Kalf (Still Life with armour), several bambocciata (on peasant subjects) and landscapes. A whole room is devoted to the Comic Novel by Scarron: as well as a portrait of the author there are paintings by Coulom and engravings by Oudry and Pater illustrating burlesque adventures.

Second floor. – This floor is reserved for temporary exhibitions of other collections belonging to the museum.

Horticultural Garden (Jardin d'horticulture – BV). – This beautiful garden with its rockery and cascading stream was designed in 1851 by Alphand, the landscape gardener who was responsible for the Bois de Boulogne, Montsouris Park and Buttes-Chaumont in Paris. From The Mall on the terrace there is a pleasant view of the cathedral.

Place et quinconce des Jacobins (BV). – The square, Place des Jacobins, which is famous for its view of the chevet of the cathedral, was laid out on the site of a former Dominican convent. At the entrance to the tunnel through the old town stands a monument to Wilbur Wright and an unusual floral clock.

Directly opposite a modern concert hall has been built; the interior is decorated with a tapestry by Picart le Doux.

The Quinconce des Jacobins is a series of terraced avenues of lime trees.

Yssoir Bridge (AV 82). – View of the cathedral, the old town, the Gallo-Roman precinct and a riverside walk past traces of medieval fortifications.

Close to the bridge on the north bank is the church of Notre-Dame-du-Pré.

Church of Our Lady in the Fields (Notre-Dame-du-Pré – AV F). – In a square planted with magnolia trees stands the old abbey church of the Benedictine convent of St Julian in the Fields (St-Julien-du-Pré); the column capitals and chancel are Romanesque.

THE MODERN TOWN CENTRE *time: 1 1/2 hours*

Church of the Visitation (AX). – This church, which stands in the main square, Place de la République, at the heart of the modern town, was originally a convent chapel; it was built in about 1730. The main façade, in Rue Gambetta, is lavishly decorated with a portico of Corinthian columns sheltering a Rococo door; the interior decor, of the same date, is also Baroque.

★ **La Couture Church** (Église de la Couture – BX B). – The church, which is now in the centre of the town and next to the Préfecture, which is housed in the old convent buildings (18C), was originally the abbey church of the monastery of St-Pierre-de-la-Couture (a corruption of culture which referred to the fields which used to surround the church). The façade is 13C. The door is framed by the Apostles putting down the forces of evil; on the pediment is Christ, between the Virgin and St John, presiding over the Last Judgment; on the arch stones, making up the Heavenly Host, are rows of Angels, patriarchs, prophets (1st row), martyrs (2nd row) and Virgins (3rd row).

The wide single nave, built in the late 12C in the Plantagenet style *(p 21),* is lit by elegant twinned windows surmounted by oculi. Note the forms of the Romanesque arches of the original nave on the blind walls of the great pointed arches which support a narrow ledge below the windows. To the left on entering is a curious 11C pilaster sculptured with a Christ in Benediction. The enchanting white marble **Virgin★★** (1571), on the pillar directly opposite the pulpit, is by Germain Pilon and originally came from the now vanished retable of the high altar. The blind arcades are hung with 17C **tapestries** and 16C panels painted by one of the monks.

The massive round 11C columns of the chancel with squat capitals showing Eastern influence in the decoration, support very narrow round arches. Above, the vaulting ribs spring from fine Plantagenet style statues.

The 11C crypt, altered in 1838, has pre-Romanesque or Gallo-Roman columns and capitals; an inverted antique capital serves as a base for one of the pillars. The 6-7C shroud of St Bertrand, Bishop of Le Mans and founder in 616 of the monastery, is exposed at the entrance *(automatic time switch for lighting).* The presumed burial place of St Bertrand is marked by a reclining plaster figure in a wall alcove.

★ **Joan of Arc's Church** (Ste-Jeanne-d'Arc – BY E). – This, the former Coëffort Hospital, was founded about 1180 by Henry II of England in atonement so it is said for the murder of his former Chancellor, Archbishop Thomas à Becket in Canterbury Cathedral. The 12C great hall or ward for the sick is now the parish church. A similar institution, the former Hospital of St John in Angers was built by the same monarch. The plain façade, pierced by an arched doorway, above which are twinned windows, opens into a vast room divided into three naves of equal height. The elevation is elegant with slender columns with finely carved capitals, supporting Plantagenet vaulting. In the Middle Ages wide canopied beds for several patients at a time, were aligned down the side aisles with an altar in the central passage.

EXCURSIONS

★ **Abbey of Our Lady of L'Épau** (Notre-Dame-de-L'Épau). *− 4 km - 1 1/2 miles by Avenue Léon-Bollée* (BX)*; turn right into the ring road, cross the railways and follow the arrows.*

In 1229 a Cistercian abbey was founded on the south bank of the Huisne by Queen Berengaria, the widow of Richard the Lionheart; she spent her last days here and her tomb is in the church.

The cloister, which was destroyed in 1365 by bands of mercenaries who were ravaging Maine, was surrounded by the monastic buildings. On the right is the **refectory** wing with the arcades of the washing place (lavatorium). Opposite are the monks' quarters, including the writing room (**scriptorium** − right) and the **chapter house** (left) which has elegant ogive vaulting; the first floor consisted of the **dormitory** with wooden vaulting. On the left is the **church**, which was built in 13C and 14C and repaired after the ravages of 1365 early in 15C; this is the date of the huge chancel window which is delicately carved. The church was designed to the traditional Cistercian plan: a square east end with three chapels facing east in each arm of the transept. The south transept contains the recumbent figure of Queen Berengaria and the entrance to the sacristy with water lily leaves decorating the square capitals; in the north transept is a spiral staircase leading to the very beautiful 15C **timber roof**.

Motor racing circuits. −

To the south of Le Mans between N 138 and D 139.

24 hour circuit. *− 13.528 km - 8 1/2 miles.* The circuit begins at the Tertre Rouge bend on N 138. The road, which is about 10 m - 33 ft wide, is marked in kilometres. The double bend on the private road and the Mulsanne and Arnage hairpin bends are the most exciting hazards on the 24 hour course. In 1972 the course was realigned to provide the public with a better view.

Within the confines of the race track is Les Hunaudières race course for horses where Wilbur Wright made his first flight; commemorative stele.

From the main entrance to the track on D 139 a tunnel leads to the Bugatti circuit and the museum.

Bugatti permanent circuit. − *4.240 km - 2 1/2 miles.* Car drivers and motorcyclists may apply for permission to use this track which is linked to a school for racing drivers.

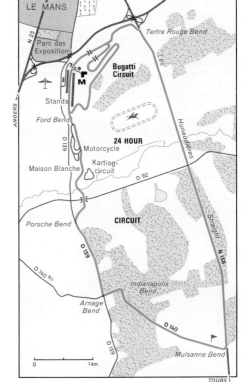

★ **Car Museum (M).** *− Access by D 139 north of D 92; enter the enclosure in front of the Automobile Club de l'Ouest and take the road to the left under the bridge.*

Over 150 vehicles trace the history of the car from the beginning; steam-driven De Dion Bouton 1885, Serpollet; Krieger electric car, Bollée petrol-driven car, racing cars, the revered veterans from 1920 to 1949 and many of the cars which took part in the 24 hour races. The cars are exhibited on a rotation basis so that there is always new interest. There is also a collection of about 60 old two-wheelers.

Montfort-le-Gesnois. − Pop 2 430. *20 km - 12 1/2 miles east of Le Mans by Avenue Léon-Bollée* (BX) *and N 23; after 16 km - 10 miles bear left.*

Just west of **Connerré** (pop 2 636), a small town which is famous for its potted pork *(rillettes),* lies the ancient commune of Pont-de-Gennes which grew on a picturesque site near the Roman bridge over the River Huisne. The present narrow hump-back **bridge** was built of sandstone in 15C and spans the expanding river where it flows between the trees. View of the 13C church of St Giles, a ruined mill covered with creepers and overshadowed by weeping willows and a little weir where the water tumbles and races.

Loudon Woods (Bois de Loudon). − *18 km - 11 miles southeast by Avenue Jean-Jaurès* (BY), *N 223 and D 304; fork left into D 145^E and turn left again into D 145.*

Woodland tracks branch off (right) D 145 into the coniferous forest; in the autumn the sandy soil is covered with a thick carpet of heather.

Spay. − Pop 1 848. *10 km - 6 miles southwest by N 23 and D 51 turning near Arnage.*

The 9C Romanesque **church** (restored) has a Baroque high altar richly decorated and a very elegant 14C Virgin and Child. The precious pyxis (1621) is part of the church's treasure.

★ **MANSE Valley**

Michelin map ▨▨▨ fold 35 or ▨▨ folds 14, 15 and ▨▨ fold 4

The River Manse flows west through quiet picturesque countryside away from the main roads to join the Vienne at L'Ile-Bouchard.

FROM L'ILE-BOUCHARD TO N10

27 km - 17 miles – about 2 hours

L'Ile-Bouchard. – *Description p 108*.

Leave L'Ile-Bouchard by D757 going north; bear right into D21 and left into D138.

Avon-les-Roches. – Pop 688. The 12-13C **church** has a stone spire over the right transept. The arches of the porch and the door are decorated with archivolts and delicately carved capitals; an inscription in the porch (left) tells of the death of Charles the Bold.

Take the road east towards Crissay; after 1 km - 1/2.mile turn left.

Roches-Tranchelion Collegiate Church. – The ruins of this Gothic collegiate church (1527) are visible from afar. *Cars may use the steep earth track which leads up to the church.* The ruins perched on a height overlooking the surrounding countryside bear witness to past greatness. Little remains of the vaulting but the elegant façade is still standing, decorated with delicate carving; note the seated figure above the great window under the triumphal arch and the Renaissance decoration of pilasters and medallions representing the local lords.

Return to the road to Crissay.

Crissay-sur-Manse. – Pop 118. The ruins of the 15C castle (left), the stone spire of the village church (right) and the several 15C houses with square turrets compose a charming picture.

St-Épain. – Pop 1 409. The village **church** (12, 13 and 15C) is capped by a 13C square tower; the **fortified gate**, adjoining it, is all that remains of the 15C curtain wall. Note the **Hôtel de la Prévôté** with its mullioned window and overhanging upper storey. Pass through the doorway to admire the hôtel's other façade, which is flanked by a round tower.

On the other side of the main street stands a house with a watch turret where the road bends southeast to Ste-Maure.

This road climbs up the verdant Manse valley.

After passing under the railway, bear left.

★ **Courtineau Road**. – This small picturesque road winds between the stream hidden amidst the trees and the cliff dotted with troglodyte dwellings. The chapel of **Notre-Dame-de-Lorette**, a small 15C oratory, has been carved into the cliff face beside a small troglodyte dwelling of the same period.

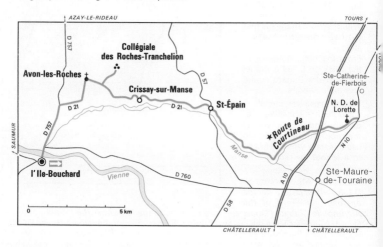

Les MAUGES

Michelin map ▨▨▨ folds 30, 31 or ▨▨ folds 18, 19 and ▨▨ folds 5, 6

The southern part of Anjou on the borders of the Vendée and Poitou, which is known as Les Mauges, is a silent secret region bordered by the Loire to the north, by the Layon valley to the east and the departments of the Vendée and Deux-Sèvres to the south and west. The terrain consists of schist rock, an extension of the Armorican massif culminating in Puy de la Garde (210 m - 689 ft); Les Mauges is a mixture of woodland and pasture used for cattle raising, where the Durham-Mancelle breed is fattened before being sold in thousands at the markets in Chemillé and Cholet.

The straight main roads, which were created during the Revolution and under the Empire for strategic reasons, are superimposed on a network of deep lanes well suited to ambushes which played a prominent part in the Vendée War; the windmills which still crown the heights were often used by the Whites to send signals.

The Vendean War (1793-96). – The execution of Louis XVI had been a shock; the persecution of the priests caused discontent; the decision of the Convention in February 1793 to impose conscription provoked a revolt. To the cry "Long live God and Long live the King" the peasants of the Vendée and Les Mauges, who were not receptive of the new ideas, rose against the Republic and banded together under the white flag of the monarchy, hence their name, the Whites. They chose leaders from their own kind — Stofflet, the gamekeeper and Cathelineau, the pedlar — or from among the nobles — Elbée, Bonchamps, La Rochejaquelein and Charette.

On 15 March they captured Cholet and soon held Les Mauges. The Blues (blue was the colour of the republican uniform) counterattacked and pushed the catholic and royalist army back to the Sèvre; but the Whites regained the advantage and captured the whole of Anjou (June 1793). Alarmed at this turn of events, the Convention sent the Mayence army under Kléber and Marceau.

At first it was beaten at Torfou (19 September 1793) but then it was victorious at Cholet (17 October) after a bloody battle in which the Vendeans were forced to retreat to St-Florent *(p 163)*. The following day 80 000 Vendeans crossed the Loire. The survivors were massacred in their thousands, shot down or drowned in the Loire. General Westermann

(Photo Lauros/Giraudon)

Cathelineau by Girodet-Trioson (1824)
(Cholet Museum)

wrote to the Convention: "The Vendée is no more, it has died under our free sword... I have crushed the children under the horses' feet and massacred the women. I have not one prisoner with which to reproach myself". At the end of January 1794 the Convention sent Turreau's **"infernal columns"** but the extermination plan failed. Insurrection rose again in Les Mauges and in the Poitou marshes; this was the period of the **Chouans.** They weakened, however, and entered into a parley under General Hoche. A treaty was signed on 17 February 1795 but the peace was precarious and often violated; the treaty finally was confirmed under the Consulate.

Memorials of the Vendean War. — Throughout the region there are monuments to the events of 1793-96. At **Maulévrier** in the grounds of Colbert Château a pyramid commemorates Stofflet, a native of that region; nearby is a martyrs' cemetery *(p 138)*.

At the crossroads on N 149 and D 753 near **Torfou** stands a column celebrating the victory of the Vendeans over the Mayence army (19 September 1793). Bonchamps was buried at **St-Florent-le-Vieil** *(p 163)*. A cross was erected on the road to Nuaillé near **Cholet** where La Rochejaquelein fell on 29 January 1794.

ROUND TRIP OF THE MAUGES

90 km - 56 miles — allow one day — local map p 137

Le Fuilet. — Pop 1 761. *8 km - 5 miles west of Montrevault.* Le Fuilet and the neighbouring hamlets — les Challonges, Bellevue, les Recoins, etc. — lie on an excellent clay soil which has given rise to the many brickworks and potteries which produce a variety of articles (ornamental, horticultural or artistic). The potteries are open to the public during working hours: preparation and shaping of the clay by hand or by machine according to the works.

Beaupréau. — Pop 6 195. *9 km - 5 miles south of Montrevault.* Beaupréau is a small town built on a steep slope on the north bank of the River Evre. In 1793 it was the headquarters of the Vendeans; their leader, d'Elbée, owned a manor at St-Martin, on the east

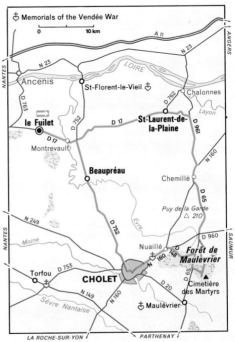

side of the town. The 15C **château** overlooking the Evre (good view from the south bank) is now a clinic. Although it was set on fire in 1793, the entrance has retained its character two large towers flanking a 17C pavilion which has a pyramidal roof flanked by two small slate cupolas.

Cholet. − *Description p 93.*

Maulévrier Forest. − *15 km - 9 miles east of Cholet.* The **Martyrs' Cemetery**, which is situated between Yzernay and Chanteloup beside D 196, is surrounded by a forest of tall oak trees. During the Vendean War, Stofflet used its inaccessibility to conceal his headquarters where the wounded were brought for treatment. On 25 March 1794, however, the Blues penetrated the forest and massacred 1 200 of the Whites; two days later the Vendeans took their revenge with a second massacre. The commemorative chapel standing alone in the forest is now a peaceful place.

St-Laurent-de-la-Plaine. − *Pop 1 203. 5 km - 3 miles southwest of Chalonnes.*
The **museum of old crafts** is housed in the 18C vicarage, one of the two houses in the village which survived the ravages of the Republicans in 1794; an annexe has recently been added in the same style. About fifty trades are illustrated with implements collected from all over France (weaving equipment from St-Étienne). Various work shops − clogmaker, oil dealer, blacksmith, wax chandler, laundry − have been reconstructed on either side of a paved street in addition to the traditional exhibition rooms (lace).

The maps and plans are orientated with north at the top.

★ MAYENNE Valley

Michelin map 🔢 folds 10, 20 or 🔢 folds 19, 31

The quiet Mayenne follows a picturesque and winding course between steep wooded banks as it flows south to join the Loire. It was made navigable in 19C when 39 locks were built between Laval and Angers and is now ideal for pleasure craft.
The valley is too steep for any villages to be built beside the river so it has been preserved in its natural state. The route described below passes through the villages of low red stone houses with slate roofs which crown the top of the slopes. There are good views of the river, some from a bridge and some from the by-roads which lead down to a picturesque site on the river bank to a mill or an isolated château.

FROM CHÂTEAU-GONTIER TO ANGERS

71 km - 44 miles − allow one day −
local map p 138

Château-Gontier. − *Description p 81.*

Daon. − Pop 430. The village and its 16C manor house is superbly sited on a slope above the Mayenne. Daon was the birthplace of Abbé Bernier who negotiated the peace between the Chouans and the Republicans.

> *In Daon turn left into D 213 towards St-Michel-de-Feins; then take the second turning on the left.*

A long avenue of lime and plane trees leads straight to the attractive 16C moated **manor house** at **l'Escoublère.**

> *Return to Daon and take D 22 southeast, bearing right into D 190 to Marigné and D 78 to Chenillé-Changé.*

Chenillé-Changé. − Pop 153. The village occupies an attractive site on the east bank of the Mayenne.

> *Take the road across the river to Chambellay and turn right into D 187.*

La Jaille-Yvon. − Pop 249. The village is perched on the cliff above the river. From the east end of the church there is an extensive view of the fields and meadows in the valley.

> *Take D 189 west and turn left into N 162 going south.*

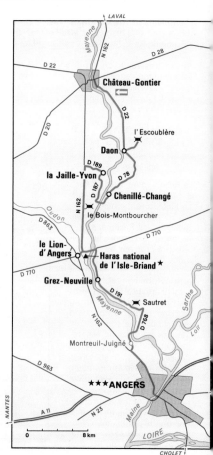

Shortly after the turning to Chambellay one sees (left) the imposing 15-17C buildings of the **Château du Bois-Montbourcher,** surrounded by lawns and woods on the edge of a vast lake.

Le Lion d'Angers. – *Description p 114.*

★ **L'Isle-Briand National Stud.** – *Description p 114.*

Grez-Neuville. – Pop 943. A charming village usually bedecked with flowers.

The road down the east bank (D 191) sometimes overhangs the river; it passes (left) **Le Sautret Château,** an impressive building with a dry moat.

In Feneu take D 768 south across the river to Montreuil-Juigné.

★ ★ **Angers.** – *Description p 47. About 1/2 day.*

★ MÉNARS Château

Michelin map ⑥④ fold 7 or ②③⑧ fold 3 (8 km - 5 miles northeast of Blois)

The 17C château on the north bank of the Loire was bought in 1760 by the Marquise de Pompadour, who had been Louis XV's mistress. She had extensive alterations carried out by the architect, Gabriel; the furniture and decoration were of the very best but the Marquise had little enjoyment of them since she died in 1764. Her brother, the Marquis of Marigny, who inherited the marquisate of Ménars, invited the architect Soumot to lay out the gardens.

The entrance court is bordered by the service **buildings** which the famous Marchioness had built; their elegance belies their humble purpose. An underground passage enabled the servants to reach the château without crossing the courtyard.

The terrace faces the Loire; in the Marchioness' time it was the entrance to the château: visitors arrived at Ménars by river in the days before the road was built. The steep slope between the château and the water is laid out in **terraces ★** decorated with statues, vases, grottoes, fountains, temples of Venus and avenues of hundred-year old trees.

★ MEUNG-SUR-LOIRE   Pop 5 659

Michelin map ⑥④ fold 8 or ②③⑧ fold 4 – Local map p 123

This picturesque fortified village extends up the slope from the Loire which laps at the roots of the tall trees in the Mall to the main road (N 152) which is up on the plateau away from the old town. From the **old market** a narrow and twisting street, **Rue Porte-d'Amont,** climbs up to an archway; little lanes skirt **les Mauves,** a stream with many channels which runs between the houses (Rue des Mauves, Rue du Trianon).

The town has raised a statue to its most famous son, **Jean de Meung.** In about 1280 he added 18 000 lines to the Romance of the Rose *(le Roman de la Rose)* which had been written some forty years earlier by Guillaume de Lorris *(p 127)* and consisted of 4 000 lines. The allegorical narrative was the greatest literary achievement of a period which did not lack readers of stamina. Chaucer translated part of the work and was much influenced by it throughout his poetic career.

The bridge at Meung was often fought over during the Hundred Years War; it was captured by the English in 1428 and retaken by Joan of Arc on 14 June 1429.

★ **St Liphard's Church.** – The plain building with its tower and spire dates from 11C and 13C; the chevet is semi-circular and the transept has unusual rounded ends. From beyond the chevet there is a good view of the church and the château.

Château. – The venerable building is a curious mixture of styles. The entrance front (13C), where there are traces of the drawbridge which spanned the dry moat, is medieval; the main entrance was created on the opposite front in 16C, when the medieval entrance was walled up, and altered in 18C. The interior owes much to the 19C. After visiting the rooms in the château the tour goes **underground** to the 12C chapel with its palm tree vaulting and the dungeons where prisoners were put to the "question".

Until 18C the château belonged to the Bishops of Orléans, who administered justice in their diocese but, being men of God, they did not have the right to put men to death. Prisoners sentenced to lifelong confinement were lowered on ropes into an underground tower, **oubliette,** with a well at the bottom; each day they received the same quantity of bread and water, however many they were, until they died of starvation or illness. François Villon *(see p 29),* who had powerful patrons, was the only one ever to come out alive; he suffered only one summer of imprisonment before Louis XI released him during a visit to Meung.

MIRÉ   Pop 1 035

Michelin map ⑥④ fold 1 or ②③② fold 20 (10 km - 6 miles north of Châteauneuf-sur-Sarthe)

The **church** is roofed with wooden keel vaulting decorated with 43 late 15C painted panels depicting the four Evangelists, angels bearing the instruments of the Passion and the Apostles presenting the Creed.

Vaux Château. – *3.5 km - 2 miles northwest by D 29 towards Bierné.*
Set back from the road (right) stands the partially ruined but picturesque château. The ruined curtain wall enclosed an elegant building with a stair turret and mullioned windows. This manor house was built at the end of 15C by Jean Bourré *(p 154),* Lord of Miré. Happy in the knowledge that he had provided the Angevin orchards with a delicious fruit, he urged his steward "above all" to "take good care of the Good Christian pears" which he was gathering.

139

Michelin map 🔢 south of folds 15, 16 and 🔢 north of folds 5, 6 or 🔢 north of folds 1, 2

Approached from the west Mondoubleau appears clustered on the east bank of the River Grenne. Perched at a crazy angle on a bluff to the south on the road to Cormenon are the ruins of a red sandstone **keep**, the remains of a fortress built at the end of the 10C by Hugues Doubleau from whom the town has taken its name. Partly hidden among the houses and trees are the remains of the curtain wall *(p 34)* which protected the keep and the several precincts of the castle.

Old houses. – 15C. On the corner of Rue du Pont de l'Horloge and the castle ramp.

Mall Walk. – Rue Gheerbrant leads to the post office and the square, Place St-Denis; go through the public garden behind the post office to reach the Grand Mall (Grand Mail), a long shady avenue providing a pleasant view of the valley.

EXCURSIONS

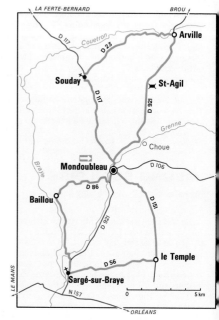

Arville. – *Round trip of 26 km - 16 miles north by D 921 – about 1 hour.*

St-Agil Château. – An interesting château encircled by a moat. The part of the building dating from the 13C was altered in 1720. The early 16C entrance pavilion is flanked by two towers decorated with a diaper pattern in red and black bricks. The machicolations guard the sentry walk and the pepperpot roofs. The main building has a dormer window with a medallion of the lord of the manor, Antoine de la Vove. The park was landscaped by Jules Hardouin-Mansart and transformed in 1872 in the English style. The splendid lime trees were planted in 1720.

Arville. – *Description p 54.*

> *Turn left into D 23 to Oigny and Souday.*

Souday. – Pop 688. The nave of the **church** is extended by an interesting 16C two-storey chancel. Two flights of stairs, with wrought-iron railing which date from 1838, lead to the upper floor which is lit by Renaissance stained glass depicting the Passion and the Resurrection of Christ. The elegant ogive vaulting in the crypt springs from columns without capitals. The south transept is decorated with 16C paintings of St Joseph, St Joachim and four scenes from the life of John-the-Baptist; on the ceiling are the symbols of the four Evangelists.

> *Return to Mondoubleau by D 117.*

Sargé. – Michelin map 🔢 north of folds 5, 6 or 🔢 north of folds 1, 2 – *Round trip of 24 km - 15 miles – about 1 hour – leave Montdoubleau by D 151 going southeast.*

Le Temple. – Pop 156. All that is left of the Templar commandery is a 13C church with a squat belltower and a square chevet nestling pleasantly by a pool.

> *Turn right into D 156.*

Sargé-sur-Braye. – Pop 974. St Martin's **church** was built in 11C and 15C. The painted wainscoting dated from 1549. The murals discovered in the nave are 16C (*Pietà*, St Martin) and in the 14C chancel (Christ in Majesty and the Labours of the Months: note the three faces of Janus symbolizing January).

Baillou. – Pop 250. The little village is picturesquely clustered below a great 16C-17C château.

The beautiful early 16C **church** stands alone on a mount. The Renaissance doorway is flanked by scrolled pilasters, surmounted by figures of Adam and Eve.
The south transept contains a carved altarpiece (1618) depicting the death of the Virgin surrounded by the Apostles and the donor, a priest called Gaultier.

> *Take D 86 back to Mondoubleau.* Fine view of the town on arrival.

★ MONTGEOFFROY Château

Michelin map 🔢 folds 11, 12 or 🔢 fold 32 (24 km - 15 miles east of Angers)

⊘ This beautiful château was designed to a regular plan — an imposing central block linked by terraced pavilions to two wings set at right angles. It was built for the Marshal de Contades in 18C but retains some traces of earlier 16C buildings: the two round towers which flank the château, the moat surrounding the courtyard and the chapel (right). Montgeoffroy has remained in the possession of one family and has therefore preserved its original furnishings signed by Gourdin, Garnier and Durand and its fine paintings by Rigaud, Drouais, Pourbus the Younger, Van Loo, Desportes etc. The whole château is a model of proportion and harmony. Each piece of furniture stands in the place for which it was designed. The hangings and tapestries have not been altered.
There is a fine 16C stained glass window in the chapel.
The stables house the different horse-drawn vehicles used by the family: from a two-seater carriage to an English mail-coach, a sort of diligence.

MONTIGNY-LE-GANNELON   Pop 334

Michelin map 🔢 south of fold 17 or 🔢 fold 38 (2 km - 1 mile north of Cloyes-sur-le-Loir) — Local map p 118

This fortress on the north bank of the Loir can be seen from afar on the N 10. The name Montigny comes from Mons-Igny meaning Signal Hill; Gannelon evokes the traitor who betrayed Roland to his enemies or more likely Saint-Avit de Châteaudun, a priest who inherited the fortress in 11C.
The small town, which lies between the river and the bluff, was once fortified; the Roland Gate (12C) still stands on the side facing away from the river.

⊘ **Château.** — A second wall with five gates enclosed the château; the composite west façade faces the approach through the park.
The Ladies' Tower (Tour des Dames) and the Clock Tower (Tour de l'Horloge) are the only remains of the Renaissance château which was rebuilt in 1495 by Jacques de Renty. The Montmorency Pavilion to the north of the Clock Tower was erected in 1834 by the Prince de Montmorency, the Duke of Laval. Many souvenirs of his embassies are on display. His grandson, Count Sigismond of Lévis-Mirepoix, asked Parent, an architect who had been a pupil of Viollet-le-Duc, to redesign the east front, which faces the Loir Valley, in the neo-Gothic style.
Hidden behind a screen of greenery is the coach house, a vast shelter on a frame of steel girders which was built at the same period as the Eiffel Tower.

MONTLOUIS-SUR-LOIRE   Pop 7 003

Michelin map 🔢 fold 15 or 🔢 fold 36 or 🔢 fold 13 — Facilities

Montlouis rises up a hillside of tufa which is riddled with caves. Its vineyards are on the plateau between the Loire and the Cher, facing south; they produce a heady and fruity white wine made from the famous Pinot de la Loire grape. Beside the church stands a Renaissance mansion (now the clergy house); the dormer windows are decorated with shells.

The Babou Family. — In 16C Montlouis was ruled by the Babous of La Bourdaisière, a turbulent family whose main residence, the Château de la Bourdaisière, lay a few miles to the south on the banks of the Cher. It was built c1520 by Philibert Babou, silversmith to François I, and lived in by Marie Babou, his wife, who was called *"la belle Babou"* and had a roving eye: she boasted of having "known", in the biblical sense of the word, François I, Charles V and many others. Gabrielle, the beautiful daughter of Antoine d'Estrées and Françoise Babou, who was born in 1573, also enjoyed the royal favour: she was the mistress of Henri IV and when she died the King turned to another Babou for consolation.

⊘ **Loire House (La Maison de la Loire).** — *Quai A. Baillet.* A permanent exhibition on the fauna and flora of the region is displayed here.

MONTOIRE-SUR-LE-LOIR   Pop 4 431

Michelin map 🔢 fold 5 or 🔢 fold 24 or 🔢 fold 1 — Local map p 121 — Facilities

Montoire developed round St Giles' Priory which was founded in 7C. In 9C Charles the Bald had a fort built to protect the country from Norman incursions.
Pilgrims making for Tours to pray at the tomb of St Martin used to stay the night in Montoire which was also on the route to Compostela in Spain. At this period leper houses were set up in Montoire and Troo.

A self-made man. — In 16C Montoire passed into the possession of the Bourbon family. Early in 18C the Regent sold the manor of Montoire to Louis Fouquet, son of the Minister of Finance, who sold it in his turn to the Count of Les Noyers de Lorme. In fact the count's name was **Amédée Delorme** and his father was an innkeeper in Blois; he went to Paris and found employment as a footman. There he met the Regent in a brothel and lent him some money. He continued to serve the Regent as a money lender and after making a tidy sum he increased it considerably speculating in Rue Quincampoix at the time of John Law *(p 185)*, a Scots financier who founded a bank in 1719 which crashed in 1720.

A momentous meeting. – In mid-October 1940 German uniforms appeared in large numbers, convoys of machine guns roved the streets, anti-aircraft batteries were set up on the hills, military patrols erected barbed wire barriers on the roads and made house to house searches, the electricity and telephones were cut off, German railwaymen replaced the staff of the SNCF, people living in houses beside the railway line were ordered to close their shutters and stay indoors, a squadron of Messerschmidts frightened the cattle in the fields, two armoured trains bristling with guns patrolled the line from Vendôme to La Chartre.

On 22 October Hitler and Pierre Laval met in Montoire Station; in the event of an attack Hitler's train could have withdrawn into the tunnel at St-Rimay to the east. The following day saw the famous meeting between Hitler and Marshal Pétain in which the German Chancellor tried to persuade the French Head of State to make war against the United Kingdom.

SIGHTS

Bridge. – Beautiful **view**★ of the Loir flowing past old houses covered with wistaria where weeping willows trail their tendrils in the water among the fishing boats moored to the banks.

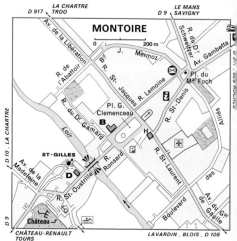

★ **St Giles' Chapel.** – At the ⊙beginning of the lane leading to the chapel stands a Renaissance house (Maison du "Jeu de Quilles" – **D**) which bears a plaque dedicated by a guild *(p 182)* to one of its members who was a native of Montoire.

The main gate opens on to the apse of a graceful Romanesque chapel which belonged to a Benedictine priory of which Ronsard was once head. He left in October 1585 to visit his other priories, St Madeleine de Croixval and St Cosmas, near Tours, where he died two months later. The chapel and the prior's lodging are pleasantly set about with lawns and yew trees.

★★ **Mural paintings.** – The paintings are to be found in the apse and transepts which are shaped like a clover leaf. Each half-dome bears a figure of Christ painted at a different date. The oldest (first quarter of 12C) in the apse shows a very majestic Christ surrounded by angels; this is the **Christ of the Apocalypse**.

In the south transept is another 12C Christ offering the keys to St Peter (missing); this figure shows Byzantine influence in the tight and symmetrical folds of the garments. The third figure in the north transept dates from 13C and shows Christ with the Apostles recalling Pentecost; the unnatural attitudes and the colours – white, ochre and the blue of the haloes – are typical of the local school *(see p 39)*. Note too the paintings on the arches of the crossing, particularly the Battle of the Virtues and Vices on the western arch.

⊙**Castle** (**Château**). – A stone and flint wall encloses the 11C square keep which stands on a spur of rock. Fine view of the Loir Valley and the keep at Lavardin.

⊙A model reconstruction of the castle is on show in the entrance hall of the **Town Hall** (**H**).

Renaissance Houses (**B**). – Two Renaissance houses stand side by side in Place Clemenceau; the larger, with mullioned windows and high dormer windows, is also the older. There are two others in Rue St-Oustrille (maison du "Jeu de Quilles") and Rue St-Laurent (Antoine-Moreau Hospital); the façade of the latter has been restored.

★ MONTPOUPON Château

Michelin map 𝟨𝟦 fold 16 or 𝟤𝟥𝟨 fold 14 (12 km - 7 1/2 miles south of Montrichard)

⊙Of the old 13C fortress only the towers remain; the main building, which has mullioned windows and Gothic style gables, was built in 15C while the entrance pavilion, which is decorated in the Renaissance style on the rear façade, is early 16C.

The **outbuildings**★ contain an excellent demonstration of the way the castle was run in the last century. The kitchen, with its oven and copper pans, was still in use in 1978; the laundry displays delicate garments, decorated with pleats and edged with lace, such as were worn in 19C. The hunting museum presents hunting costumes and hunting souvenirs and the guide demonstrates the different notes of several horns and tells the story of the Montpoupon Hunt (1873-1949). There are carriages on display in the stables and the equipment used by the owners of the château in the saddle and harness rooms.

You will find a selection of touring programmes on pp 7-9.

Plan your route with the help of the map of principal sights on pp 4-6.

★ MONTRÉSOR

Michelin map 🔲 fold south of folds 16, 17 or 🔲🔲 southeast of fold 14

The sloping site of Montrésor on the north bank of the River Indrois is reflected in the water. The old market in the town is a timber frame construction; the handsome 16C house with a watch tower in the main street is now the police station.

★ Château. – The curtain wall with its ruined towers belongs to the fortress built by Fulk Nerra *(p 47)* in 11C; within it at the centre of a charming, half-wild park stands the residence built in the early 16C by **Imbert de Bastarnay**, lord of Montrésor from 1493. This building has mullioned windows on the south front facing the river, gabled dormers and two machicolated towers. In 1849 the château was restored by **Count Xavier Branicki**, a Polish emigré who accompanied Prince Napoleon to Constantinople during the Crimean War and tried to raise a Polish regiment.

The furnishings are as they were at the time of Branicki: his shooting trophies decorate the entrance hall; military souvenirs and medals and pictures by Polish and French painters are exhibited throughout. Also worthy of note are low-reliefs in wood representing the battles of John III Sobieski of Poland (17C), a boudoir containing Italian Primitives and gold and silver plate. From the curtain wall above the river there is an attractive view of the valley and the houses of the town.

Church. – The church was built between 1519 and 1541 in the Gothic style — only the doorway is Renaissance; it was originally a collegiate foundation set up by Imbert de Bastarnay, who built the castle, to house his tomb. The **Bastarnay tomb★** in the nave consists of three recumbent figures in white marble — Imbert, his wife and son — resting on a base decorated with statues of the twelve Apostles. In the chancel chapel (left) is a painting of the Annunciation by Philippe de Champaigne (17C).

★ MONTREUIL-BELLAY

Michelin map 🔲 south of fold 12 or 🔲🔲 fold 33 — Facilities

The little town of Montreuil-Bellay possesses a very lovely **site★** beside the Thouet on the border of the Poitou and Anjou regions. From the east bank of the river and bridge there are good views of the château and church. The gardens along the west bank are an agreeable place for a stroll as is the picturesque square, Place des Ormeaux, in front of the château entrance.

Long stretches of the mediaeval wall are still standing: **St John's Gate** (Porte St-Jean), which is flanked by two large rusticated towers, dates from 15C.

Recalcitrant vassals. – In 1025 Fulk Nerra *(p 47)*, Count of Anjou, gave this stronghold to his vassal **Berlay** (distorted into Bellay), who made it into a powerful fortress. A century later, safe behind their stout walls, his successors plotted and intrigued against their overlord. In 1151, one of them, Giraud, held out for a whole year before he capitulated to Geoffroy Plantagenet, who then razed the keep which he had just reduced by means of an early incendiary bomb: a vessel full of oil was sealed, heated to incandescence and launched by a mangonel *(p 26)*.

When the Plantagenets acceded to the throne of England and thus became the main enemy of the king of France, the Berlays (who later became the du Bellays) pledged their allegiance to their immediate overlord; Philippe Auguste thereupon besieged their castle and dismantled it.

SIGHTS

★★ Château. – Imposing walls, pleasant gardens and remarkable furnishings are the main features of Montreuil Château. Behind the fortress aspect, within the fortified gateway, stands the graceful residence built by the Harcourt family in 15C. From the courtyard terrace fine views of the church, the château and the grounds which descend in great steps down to the river.

The **medieval kitchen** with its central chimney like the one at Fontevraud *(p 103)* was slightly altered in 15C and is still in perfect condition: copper pans and a kitchen range (19C) with seven fire boxes fuelled by charcoal.

The 15C **Canons' Lodge** has four stair turrets with conical roofs serving four separate sets of rooms, each consisting of living rooms over a store room, for the canons who served in the castle chapel.

The **New Château** was built in 15C; it has a beautiful stair turret decorated with mul-

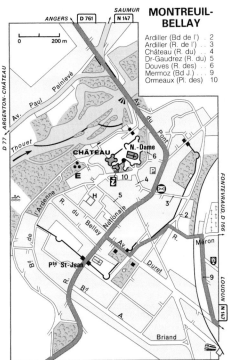

MONTREUIL-BELLAY

Ardiller (Bd de l')	2
Ardiller (R. de l')	3
Château (R. du)	4
Dr-Gaudrez (R. du)	5
Douves (R. des)	6
Mermoz (Bd J.)	9
Ormeaux (Pl. des)	10

lioned windows protected by delicately carved mock balustrades. The loggia with its ogee arch is 19C; on its right stands a 12-13C tower. Under the Angevin vaulting in the **cellar** the brotherhood of the Sacavins holds its meetings; it was founded in 1904 by the then owner of the castle, Georges de Grandmaison, to advertise Anjou wine. The winepress, into which the grapes were poured directly from the courtyard through a trap door, was still in use at the beginning of this century.

The rooms in the château are 7 m - 23 ft high and fully furnished. The dining-room (49 m² - 527 sq ft) has painted ceiling beams; the little **oratory** decorated with frescoes is late 15C: the angelic musicians on the vaulting are playing a motet of which the guide plays a recording. Visitors see the bedroom of the Duchess of Longueville, Condé's sister, who was the prime mover behind the Fronde *(p 107)* and was exiled by Louis XIV to Montreuil where she lived in brilliant style. In the Great Salon a Brussels tapestry hangs above a German marquetry cupboard; in the small music salon there is a superb bureau made by the famous cabinet maker, Boulle (1642-1732), inlaid with copper and tortoise-shell.

Church of Our Lady (Notre-Dame). – It was built as the seigneurial chapel between 1472 and 1484 and has astonishingly strong walls and buttresses. Note the black mourning band *(p 34)* in the nave and the private oratory for the owner of the castle.

Les Nobis (E). – Deep in the vegetation beside the Thouet are the ruins of St Peter's Church which was burnt down by the Huguenots in 16C; the Romanesque apse is decorated with carved capitals. Nearby are two wings of a 17C cloister.

EXCURSION

Asnières Abbey. – *7.5 km - 5 miles northwest by D 761; after 5.5 km - 3 miles turn right.*

On the northern edge of Cizay Forest are the romantic ruins of what was once an important monastery founded in 12C. The tall and graceful **chancel★** with its delicately ribbed vaulting is, like the chancel of St Sergius' Church in Angers, the most perfect specimen of Angevin Gothic art *(see p 36)*. The Abbot's chapel, which was added in 15C, has a pointed recess decorated with trefoils and festoons and 14C crucifix.

★ MONTRICHARD   Pop 3 786

Michelin map 64 folds 16, 17 or 238 fold 14 – Facilities

From the south bank of the river and the bridge over the Cher there is a good **view** of the town and its medieval houses clustered around the church below the crumbling keep.

The north bank above the town is pitted with quarries (**Bourré** is a village 3 km - 2 miles to the east, its stone has been used for the construction of the nearby châteaux) which have been transformed into troglodyte dwellings or converted into caves for growing mushrooms or maturing wine by the **Champagne method.**

SIGHTS

★ Keep. – The square keep which stands on the edge of the plateau above the River Cher is enclosed by the remains of its curtain wall *(p 34)* and by a complex system of ramparts which protected the entrance. It was built *c*1010 by Fulk Nerra *(p 47)*, reinforced with a second wall in 1109 and then with a third in 1250. Despite being reduced in height by 4 m - 13 ft on the orders of Henri IV in 1589 for being in the possession of the Leaguers *(see p 64)*, the keep recalls the distant past. From the top (tiny platform: 4 people only) there is a panoramic **view★★** of the town and the Cher Valley.

St Cross Church. – The church which was originally the castle chapel stands below the keep at the top of the Great St Cross Steps (Grands Degrés Ste-Croix). The façade is decorated with elegant Romanesque arches; the arches of the porch are ornamented with a twisted torus. The elegant doorway is also Romanesque.

Jeanne de France, the daughter of Louis XI, and her young cousin, the Duke of Orleans, were married in this chapel in 1476.

The bride, who was 12, was ugly and deformed and had no attraction for Louis d'Orléans who had been forced into the marriage by the king. Knowing that his daughter could not bear a child, Louis XI hoped in this way to bring to an end the Orleans line, which was a junior branch of the Valois family which chafed at the royal authority. Events however, took a different course. In 1498 Louis XI's son, Charles VIII, died accidentally at Amboise *(see p 44)* leaving no heir since his sons had died in infancy. As the king's nearest relative Louis d'Orléans acceded to the throne as Louis XII. In his will Charles VIII had stipulated that the new king should marry his widow, Anne of Brittany. Jeanne was repudiated and devoted herself to a life of good works; she retired to Bourges where she founded a religious order.

Old houses. – There are several picturesque old façades up by the keep. **Hôtel d'Effiat** in Rue Porte-au-Roi, which was built in the late 15-early 16C, has a Gothic décor with a few Renaissance elements; in 16C it was the residence of Jacques de Beaune, Treasurer to Anne of Brittany and then to Louise de Savoie, the mother of François I; the mansion has retained the name of its last owner, the Marquis d'Effiat, who at his death (1719) presented it to the town to be converted into an old people's home.

There are two old timber-framed houses in the square, Place Barthélemy-Gilbert, and on the corner of Rue du Pont stands **Ave Maria House** (16C) which has three gables and finely carved beams. Opposite are the Lower St Cross Steps (Petits Degrés Ste-Croix) which lead to some troglodyte dwellings.

Further on, on the corner of Rue du Prêche, stands the 11C stone façade of the Sermon House (**Maison du Prêche**).

Nanteuil Church. – *On the road to Amboise (D 115)*. The church is a tall Gothic building with a Flamboyant doorway but the apses are Romanesque decorated with carved capitals. The tall and narrow nave is roofed with Angevin vaulting.

Above the entrance porch is a chapel built by Louis XI; it is approached by two sets of stairs, one from the interior of the church and the other outside.

There is a long-established tradition of a pilgrimage to the Virgin of Nanteuil on Whit-Monday.

EXCURSION

Thésée. – *10 km - 6 miles east by the road on the north bank or by N 76*. 1 km - 1/2 mile east of Thésée on the north side of the road are the ruins of Tasciaca, which was built by the Romans as a staging post and warehouse on the Roman road from Bourges to Tours. The riverbank to the east of Thésée is riddled with troglodyte dwellings.

MONTSOREAU   Pop 454

Michelin map 〽 folds 12, 13 or 〽〽 fold 33 – Local map p 127 – Facilities

Montsoreau is famed for its castle which dominates the confluence of the Loire and the Vienne *(boat trips, see p 92)*.

Castle. – The castle was built in 15C by a member of the Chambes family which produced bold warriors and enterprising women. One of the ladies of Montsoreau seduced the Duke of Berry, brother of Louis XI and through him formed the League for the Public Good (Ligue du Bien Public) which the king defeated only by the assassination of the pretender and his mistress. A century later one of the most active executioners in the massacre of the Huguenots on St Bartholomew's Day was a Chambes. An event in the history of the family and the castle was used by Alexander Dumas in one of his novels, *La Dame de Montsoreau*. The heroine was forced by her jealous husband to meet her lover, Bussy d'Amboise, at the Château de la Coutancière (on the north bank of the Loire) where he was assassinated. After this outburst, husband and wife lived in perfect harmony until they died forty years later.

The river front, which was once at the water's edge, is an impressive example of military architecture.

The castle houses a **Goum Museum** about the conquest of Morocco, Marshal Lyautey and the history of the cavalry regiments *(goums)* recruited in Morocco. The collections, formerly in Rabat, were brought to France in 1956 when Morocco became independent.

(Photo G. Sioen/C.E.D.R.I.)

Montsoreau

★★**Panorama.** – *1 km - 1/2 mile by the road to the right of the castle up the hill; signposts.*

There is a belvedere in the vineyards on the cliff top: view downstream of the town, the castle and the Loire Valley, upstream of the tree-lined confluence of the Loire and the Vienne.

La Herpinière Windmill. – *1.5 km - 1 mile southwest by V 3.*

There used to be a number of windmills on the plateau; this one in the commune of Turquant dates from 15C. The milling chamber is hollowed out of the tufa below ground level. The miller's house (now an artists' studio: sculpture, weaving) and its outbuildings (forge, winepress) are also underground.

MOULIHERNE

Michelin map fold 12, 13 or fold 33

Mouliherne stands on a rock on the north bank of the quiet Riverolle.

Church. – The church, which is built on a mound, has a beautiful square 13C belltower with splayed windows and a twisting spire typical of the Baugé region.
The interior vaulting demonstrates the evolution of the Angevin style *(see p 36):* in the chancel barrel vaulting; in the south transept an early example of quadripartite vaulting; in the north transept and on the transept crossing a more elaborate version of the former supported on beautiful Romanesque capitals decorated with water lily leaves and fantastic animals; in the nave, wide and soaring Gothic vaulting (12-13C), which was repaired in 15C near the transepts.
Behind the high altar in the nave are some 9-10C Carolingian sarcophagi made of shell stone but undecorated.

EXCURSION

Linières-Bouton. – Pop 97. *5 km - 3 miles east by D 62.*
This is a quiet village just off the main road. The **church** has a beautiful **chancel** built in the Plantagenet style; there is a painting of the Annunciation (1677), a huge Baroque cross in wood gilt and a sculpture of the Holy Family, probably 17C.

MULSANS

Michelin map fold 7 or fold 3 (14 km - 9 miles northeast of Blois)

Mulsans is a small farming village on the edge of the Beauce with the traditional walled-in farmyards of the region. The charming **church** has Flamboyant windows and a fine Romanesque belltower decorated with blind arcades and twin bays. There is a Renaissance gallery supported on carved wood columns extending the full width of the nave and incorporating the porch; this is a regional feature known as a *"caquetoire"* where people pause to talk after church.

★ ORLÉANS

Michelin map fold 9 or fold 40 or fold 5 – Local map p 123
Plan of the conurbation in the Michelin Red Guide France

Orléans has always been an active business centre, trading in the wheat of the Beauce, the honey, poultry and potatoes of the Gâtinais, the game of the Sologne and the wines of the Loire Valley; the town has several industrial zones such as Fleury-les-Aubrais, St-Jean-de-la-Ruelle and Chapelle-St-Mesmin where Michelin built a tyre factory in 1951; in between there is an unbroken network of garden centres, nursery gardens and market gardens which have made Orléans the "city of roses" and one of the poles of the "garden of France" as the Loire Valley is called; in the past the traditional activities included vinegar-making and the production of sweets *(cotignacs).*
Orléans is the capital of the Central region of France (an economic division) and an important administrative and university town. These activities are mostly concentrated in the **Orléans-la-Source** district where a new town has been built on the northern edge of the Sologne Forest; it includes a sorting office for postal cheques, the National Centre for Scientific Research, the Bureau for Geological and Mineral Research, a university teaching hospital and the university campus.

(Photo Berne/Photogram-Stone)

Orléans Cathedral

HISTORICAL NOTES

Orléans is proud of its rich past but many wars have left few visible traces or monuments. After the Hundred Years War and the Wars of Religion, the bombing raids of 1940 demolished half the town. There are, however, a few medieval or Renaissance façades which give the old town its charm.
The **Festivals of Joan of Arc** (mainly on 29 April, 7 and 8 May) go back to 1435; every year with great rejoicing the inhabitants celebrate their deliverance from the English. Orléans is also the birthplace of the writer Charles Péguy.

From the Carnutes to Joan of Arc. – The Gauls considered the country of the Carnutes to be the centre of their territory, Gaul; each year the Druids held their great assembly there and it was at Cenabum (Orléans) that the signal was given to revolt against Caesar in 52 BC; the population rose and massacred the Roman merchants. By way of reprisal the legions set fire to the town.
A Gallo-Roman city soon rose from the Gaulish ruins but, despite recent archaeological discoveries, its appearance is an enigma. In 3C the town was called Aurelianum and was the seat of a bishop. In June 451 it was besieged by Attila the Hun. St Aignan, the bishop, encouraged the citizens to resist while waiting for help. The town walls shook under the pounding of the battering rams but help arrived at last and Aetius, the patrician, repulsed the invaders who withdrew to the east.
Orléans then sank into relative obscurity. Clovis subdued the town in 498 and in 511 the first Council of France was held there. Under the Carolingians the bishop was **Theodulf** *(p 106),* a brilliant churchman in Charlemagne's entourage. Orléans did not escape the depredations of the Normans.
In 10C and 11C Orléans was one of the focal points of the Capet monarchy; the others were Paris and Chartres. In 996 Robert the Pious, son of Hugh Capet held his coronation in the cathedral. The city then enjoyed a burst of prosperity and in 1137 declared itself emancipated and set up a commune which Louis VII hastened to repress. In 13C Orléans was a busy city of about 15 000 inhabitants earning their living from agriculture and trade, particularly through the river port. In 1305 Clement V issued a papal bull founding the university and thus confirming the intellectual status of the city where Roman law had been taught since 1235. In 14C Orléans continued to grow until there were about 25 000 inhabitants. In 1344 Philippe VI de Valois created the Duchy of Orléans for his second son Philippe: thereafter it became the custom that the Duchy be granted to the cadet branch of the royal family.
The long period of prosperity came to an end with the Hundred Years War. Orléans declared for the Armagnacs and the "king of Bourges" and thus assumed a strategic importance for the English who invested the city in the autumn of 1428.

SIEGE OF ORLÉANS
0   500m
St Loup Fort
Burgundy Gate
St Loup Island
ORLÉANS
Notre-Dame Tower
St Antony's Fort
LOIRE
St Aignan Island
Les Tourelles Fort
Augustinian Monastery
Bridge of boats
St-Jean-le-Blanc Fort

The Siege of 1428-29. – This memorable siege was one of the great episodes in the history of France; it marks the rebirth of a country and a people which was sinking into despair.

The forces engaged. – From the beginning of 15C the defence of Orléans had been organised to repulse an English attack. The city wall was composed of two parts *(see plan);* on the east side was the old square wall of the Gallo-Roman camp and on the west a longer wall, enclosing more ground, which was built in 14C. There were 34 towers and the wall was divided into six sections each defended by 50 men. All the inhabitants took part in the defence of the city whether as soldiers or by maintaining the walls and ditches. In all about 10 000 men were involved under the orders of the Governor of Orléans, Raoul de **Gaucourt,** and his captains.
During the summer of 1428 the commander of the English army, the **Earl of Salisbury,** had destroyed the French strongholds along the Loire and gained control of the river downstream from Orléans thus preventing the city from being relieved from the west. After the fall of Beaugency on 25 September he began to march on Orléans. His army consisted of 400 men-at-arms, 2 250 archers, together with 400 lancers and 1 200 archers recruited in France, in all over 4 000 men.
The struggle began on 17 October when the English pounded the city with bombards and heavy cannon; their chief aim however was to cut the city off from any contact with the surrounding contryside. On the south side of the town there was a bridge spanning the Loire which was defended at its southern end by Les Tourelles Fort. The people of Orléans had earlier demolished all the building in this district to make the enemy's approach more difficult. On 24 October, however, the English captured Les Tourelles Fort but, as Salisbury was inspecting the ground he was killed by a cannon ball fired, it was thought, from the tower of Notre-Dame Church. The French defenders blew up an arch and built a hasty wooden outwork in front of St Antony's Fort on an island in the river. By way of counteraction the besiegers demolished two arches in front of Les Tourelles Fort and raised a high earth bank.
Orléans was now cut off from the rest of the French Kingdom. On 8 November the majority of the English forces withdrew to Meung-sur-Loire and the French took the opportunity to raze the other suburbs to prevent the English from re-establishing themselves there. The besiegers were not, however, inactive. They surrounded the

town with a series of trenches commanded by small forts but their lines were not impenetrable particularly in the northeastern sector where sorties were still possible. Dunois (also known as the Bastard of Orléans), who had arrived with his troops on 25 October, looked down from the top of the walls on the English forts without being able to intervene.

The two sides settled down to a war of attrition punctuated by skirmishes outside the gates. From time to time feats of arms raised the morale of the besieged. The prowess and cunning of Master-Gunner Jean de Montesclerc became famous: he killed many English soldiers and would often pretend to die so that when he re-appeared the dismay and alarm of the English were redoubled. Two bombards called Rifflart and Montargis rose to fame owing to their fire power and their range which caused great damage on the south bank of the Loire.

The months of misery and waiting seemed, however, to grow longer and longer; food grew scarce and in February 1429 part of the garrison left. The English were close to victory. Dunois, however, remained optimistic.

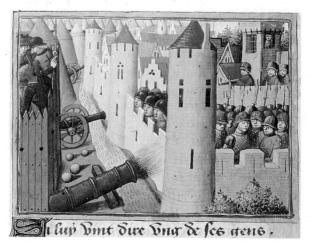

The Siege of Orléans

The Arrival of Joan of Arc. — In April 1429 Joan of Arc persuaded the future **Charles VII** to rescue Orléans. She left Blois with the royal army, crossed the river and approached Orléans by the south bank so as to take the English by surprise but the river was too high and the army had to return to the bridge at Blois. In the meanwhile Joan and a few companions crossed by boat a few miles upstream of Orléans at Checy and entered the town on 29 April by the Burgundy Gate (Porte de Bourgogne). She was greeted by an enthusiastic crowd and issued her famous ultimatum to the English, that they should surrender the keys of all the good French towns that they had captured and violated to her the Maid who had been sent by God to boot them out of France.

The Orléanais rallied and prepared for battle while Joan confronted the hostility of the captains and the Governor.

On 4 May the royal army, which Dunois had rejoined, attacked St-Loup Fort without warning Joan. When she learned of it she made a sortie, raising her banner, and the French were victorious. The following day Joan, who was excluded from the captains' council, suggested pressing forward the attack against Les Tourelles Fort and on the morning of the 6 May, although efforts were made to fault her, Joan herself led the attack against the Augustinian monastery. A second time her forceful intervention upset the English who were engaged in pursuing the retreating French troops. This second victory increased her popularity and made the captains look ridiculous. The English troops grew alarmed. Joan called on them again to withdraw and when they refused she went on the offensive again on 7 May against the advice of the Governor who tried to bar her way. While fighting in the front line outside Les Tourelles Fort she was wounded in the shoulder by a crossbow bolt. The English thought she was done for and Dunois suggested postponing the attack to the following day but, after having the wound dressed and praying to the saints, Joan returned to the attack bearing her standard. With renewed vigour the French hurled themselves against the English and the remaining French made a sortie from the town on to the bridge. The English garrison in the fort were caught in the crossfire; they were forced to abandon the fort and surrendered.

On Sunday 8 May the English withdrew from the last forts and lifted the siege: Joan received a triumph in Orléans for her victory.

This check to the English advance had enormous repercussions. Not only did it upset the invader's plans and weaken the position of the Duke of Bedford, the regent in England, but it gave new confidence to the Dauphin and his army. On 18 June the French forces won the Battle of Patay.

Since 1435 the town of Orléans has celebrated the victory of 8 May with a procession during the Joan of Arc Festival *(p 147)*. The first monument to the glory of the Maid was erected in 1502.

SIGHTS

★ **St Cross Cathedral (Ste-Croix — EFY).** — The Cathedral of the Holy Cross was begun in
the 13C and its building went on until the 16C, but it was partly destroyed by the
Protestants in 1568. Henri IV, the first Bourbon King, being grateful to the town for
having supported him, undertook to rebuild the cathedral, not in the style of the 17C, but
in the Gothic style so as to preserve its architectural unity.
The work went on throughout the 18 and 19C ending under Charles X. The old
Romanesque towers still standing before the Wars of Religion (1562-98), gave place to
pseudo-Gothic towers.

Façade. — The three large doorways with three rose windows above them are crowned
by a gallery with openwork design. Note the fine workmanship — the stone becomes
lacework at the uppermost level of the towers. At the base of the two towers admire the
delicacy of the spiral staircases, also with openwork design, at each of the four
corners.
It is only on reaching the vast **doorway** that one realizes that this is not a typical medieval
façade; contrary to the very detailed carved scenes usually found covering a doorway, at
Ste-Croix there are but four gigantic statues; they are the Evangelists.

Interior. — The vast main body of the cathedral comprises five aisles enhanced by the
pure lines of the elegant pillars. On the north side of the chancel, in the Chapel of St Joan
of Arc, is the statue of Cardinal Touchet (1894-1926), who made incessant efforts to
propagate the cult of the Maid. In the central chapel of the apse is a fine marble Virgin by
Michel Bourdin (early 17C), a sculptor born in Orléans. In the side aisles of the central
nave are late 19C stained glass windows, representing the life of Joan of Arc.
Splendid early 18C **woodwork**★★ adorns the chancel. It was made to the designs of
Mansart, Gabriel and Lebrun by Jules Degoullons, one of the decorators of Versailles
and designer of the stalls in Notre-Dame, Paris.
In the **crypt** are traces of the three buildings which preceded the present cathedral and
two sarcophagi; one belonged to Bishop Robert de Courtenay (13C). It was he who
collected the most precious items in the **Treasury**; it includes two gold medallions (11C)
magnificently decorated with cloisonné enamel in the Byzantine manner which used to
decorate the gloves worn by the Bishop of Orléans for ceremonies and processions; 13C
gold and silverware; a tree of Jesse (late 15C Flemish work) and interesting 17C
paintings: Christ bearing the Cross by Zurbaran.

North Side and East End. — Go round the cathedral. On the north side, note in the centre of
the rose window the sun rays — Louis XIV's emblem. At the base are excavations, which
have revealed the old Gallo-Roman walls and part of a tower.
The **east end** is clearly visible from the gardens of the former episcopal palace (FY **Q**), an
18C building which now houses the municipal library. Admire the openwork of the flying
buttresses and the pinnacles surmounting the piers.

Campo Santo (EY). — To the left of the ultra-modern Regional Fine Arts School (École
Régionale des Beaux-Arts) is a graceful Renaissance portal and on the west side of this
same building is a garden edged with an arcaded gallery. The garden was a cemetery
outside the walls in the 12C, the galleries were added in the 16C. Now it is a pleasant
place for outdoor exhibitions.

★★ **Fine Arts Museum (Musée des Beaux-Arts — EY M¹).** — The new museum's arcaded
façade harmonises with that of the Préfecture building to the south of Place
Ste-Croix.

> *Start on the second floor.*

In the gallery devoted to the primitives is an outstanding 15C painting from the Sienese
school, a Virgin and Child with two angels by Matteo di Giovanni. The 14-16C sculptures
include a marble Virgin and Child (1370) and a fine bust of Cardinal Morvillier by
Germain Pilon. The Italian, Flemish and Dutch schools are represented by works by
Correggio *(Holy Family),* Tintoretto *(Portrait of a Venetian),* A. Carracci *(Adoration of the
Shepherds),* Pourbus the Younger *(Anne of Austria),* Van Goyen *(Skaters)* and Van de
Velde *(Battle of the North Sea).* Velasquez's remarkable *St Thomas (c*1620) dates from
the period the artist spent in Seville.
On the first floor is displayed the 17-18C French school: vast religious paintings inspired
by the Counter-Reformation, *St Charles Borromeo* by P. de Champaigne, *Triumph of
St Ignatius* by Claude Vignon. The chiaroscuro technique is exemplified in *St Sebastian*
from G. de La Tour's studio. Among 17C canvases are *Bacchus and Ariadne,* a rare
mythological work by Le Nain, and a good portrait of *Le Nôtre* from Claude Lefevre's
studio. Masterpieces from Richelieu's château include the graceful *The Four Elements*
by Deruet and *Louis XIV as a child.*
The remarkable collection of 18C portraits shows the evolution of portraiture as formal
likeness gradually gave way to character study: Mme de Pompadour by Drouais;
Moyreau, the engraver by Nonotte; the Marquis of Lucker by L. Tocqué. Paintings by
H. Robert *(Landscape with ruined tower, The Wash House)* and Boucher *(The Dovecote)*
are noteworthy.
In the Pastel Gallery there are precious 18C portraits including works by Perronneau and
Nattier as well as expressive busts by Pigalle and Houdon and French ceramics and
medallions.
The 19C is represented by artists such as Gros, Cogniet, Courbet *(The Wave),* Boudin,
Antigna, a native of Orléans, and Gauguin *(Fête Gloanec).*
20C art is illustrated by works by Soutine, Gromaire, Max Jacob and sculptures by
Bourdelle, Maillol, Zadkine, Charles Malfray and Gaudier-Breszka.

Hôtel Groslot (EY H). — Built in 1550 by the bailiff Jacques Groslot, this large
Renaissance mansion in red brick with diapering in black was subject to extensive
remodelling in the 19C. Admire the delicate scrollwork on the staircase pillars and the

ORLÉANS

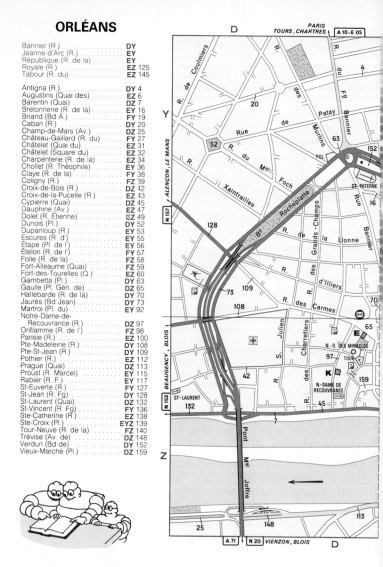

two main entrances flanked by caryatids. This was the king's residence in Orléans: François II, who died here after opening in 1560 the States-General, Charles IX, Henri III and Henri IV all stayed here.

Cross the building. On the other side in the **garden** the façade of the former chapel of St-Jacques (15C) has been set up.

On the other side of the road stand the elegant **Pavillons d'Escures (EY N)**. These bourgeois town houses in brick with stone courses date from the early 17C.

Place Ste-Croix (EY 139), a vast symmetrical esplanade, bordered by Classical façades and arcades, was laid out c1840 when Rue Jeanne-d'Arc was opened up opposite the west front of the cathedral; the north and south sides were completed recently with the construction of the Fine Arts Museum and the Prefecture, stone-faced buildings which, with their arcades and balusters, harmonise with the older buildings. On the south side of the square there is a bronze statue of the Loire in the guise of a pleasant young woman holding the fruits of the river valley in the folds of her dress; facing it on the north side of the square is a nude figure symbolizing the Beauce. The 15C **Hôtel des Créneaux (EZ R)** was the town hall from 16C to 1790.

★ Historical Museum (EZ M²). — It is housed in an elegant little mansion, **Hôtel Cabu** ⊙ (1550), beside another Renaissance façade re-erected in the square after the demolitions caused by the Second World War.

On the ground floor is the astonishing **Gallo-Roman treasure★** from Neuvy-en-Sullias (31 km - 19 miles east of Orléans) which consists of a series of expressive statues, a horse and a wild boar in bronze and statuettes from a pagan temple.

The first floor is devoted to the Middle Ages: delicate carved **ivories★** (12-16C), ceramics and souvenirs of Joan of Arc (15C German tapestry, 17C standard from the Joan of Arc Festival). The second floor is occupied by local folklore, gold and silverware and clocks. The courtyard has retained its elegant gallery and well.

Place du Martroi (EY 92). — The square is not only the geographical but also the historical centre of the town owing to the statue of Joan of Arc by Foyatier (1855). The name is derived from the Latin word martyretum which was used to refer to the 6C Christian cemetery. On the west corner of Rue Royale stands the old Chancellery Pavillion (**Pavillon de la Chancellerie**) which was built in 1759 by the Duke of Orléans to house his archives.

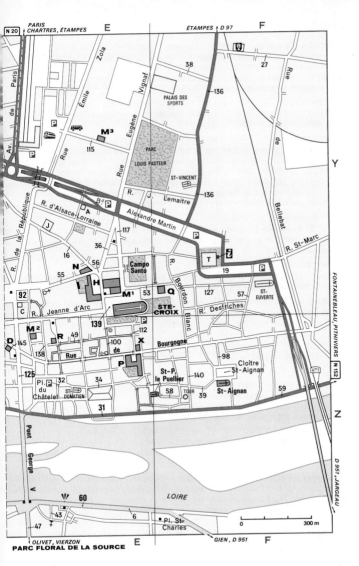

PALAIS DES
SPORTS

38

136

27

M³

115

PARC
LOUIS PASTEUR

ST-VINCENT

Y

R. d'Alsace-Lorraine

B⁴

R. J. Lemaitre

136

Alexandre Martin

R. St-Marc

117

36

16

56

N

55

Campo
Santo

T

19

I

H

92

M¹

53

Q

127

57

ST-
EUVERTE

R. St-Marc

C

R. Jeanne d'Arc

STE-
CROIX

R. Destriches

M²

R

49

139

100
de

112

X

Bourgogne

D

145

138

Rue

P

98

Cloître
St-Aignan

125

32

34

St-P.
le Puellier

140

N 152

Pl.
du
Châtelet

ST-
DONATIEN

58

TOUR

39

St-Aignan

59

31

Z

Pont
George
V

60

LOIRE

43

47

6

Pl. St.
Charles

0   300 m

N

FONTAINEBLEAU, PITHIVIERS

D 951, JARGEAU

D 951, JARGEAU

Rue Royale (EZ 125). – This broad street, lined with arcades, was opened up *c*1755 when the Royal Bridge (**Pont George V**) was built to replace the old medieval bridge which had stood 100 m - 100 yds upstream in line with St Catherine Street, the old north-south axis of the city.

⊙**Charles Péguy Centre** (EZ D). – The centre is housed in the old **Hôtel Euverte Hatte**, which is also known as Agnès Sorel House, perhaps because Charles VII's favourite lived there as a child; the present building was erected later in the reign of Louis XII. The rectangular windows are framed with Gothic friezes; the Renaissance arcade in the courtyard was added in the reign of François I.

The centre traces the life and career of **Charles Péguy** (1873-1914), poet and campaigner, who was born in Orléans and died on 5 September 1914 at the beginning of the Battle of the Marne. His writings reflect the causes he adopted and defended with intransigeance: Dreyfus, socialism, patriotism, Catholicism. He wrote about the life of Joan of Arc: a long play in 1897 and a series of mysteries in 1911-12. On the first floor there is a library devoted to Péguy, his work and literary, political and social environment; a whole room is given to the Dreyfus affair. The Péguy museum on the second floor contains manuscripts and souvenirs.

★**Joan of Arc House** (DZ E). – The tall timber-framed façade contrasts with the
⊙modernity of the square, Place du Général-de-Gaulle, which was badly bombed in 1940. The building is a faithful reconstruction of the house of Jacques Boucher, Treasurer to the Duke of Orléans, where Joan stayed in 1429. An audiovisual show on the first floor recounts Joan of Arc's entry into Orléans on 8 May 1429; there are period costumes and weapons of war.

Beyond the house and the two adjacent Renaissance façades on the right there is an arch leading into Jacques Boucher Square. Standing alone in the garden is the **Pavillon Colas des Francs**, an elegant little Renaissance building, where Boucher's grandson conducted his business; the ground floor housed the records while the silver was kept upstairs.

⊙**Hôtel Toutin** (DZ K). – The house was built in 1540 for Toutin, François I's son's manservant. The porch leads into a small courtyard: on the left is a double Renaissance arcade covered in Virginia creeper; on the right a statue of François I seated against a wall of ivy.

Quai Fort-des-Tourelles (EZ 60). − Opposite a statue of Joan of Arc standing in a small square is a commemorative cross and an inscription on the low wall beside the Loire which mark the site of the southern end of the medieval bridge and the Tourelles Fort in 15C; its capture by Joan of Arc led to the defeat of the English and the lifting of the siege. Fine view★ of the whole town.

Quai du Châtelet (EZ 31) provides a quiet shady walk beside the river; in 19C, however, when the Loire was an important means of transport, it was one of the busiest parts of the town with boats unloading to supply the markets.

Rue de Bourgogne (EF Z). − This was the main east-west axis of the old Gallo-Roman city. Now reserved largely for pedestrians, it is ideal for window shopping. There are several old façades: no 261 is a 15C stone house with a half-timbered gable.

Along the street is the **Prefecture** (EZ **P**), housed in a 17C Benedictine convent. Opposite in Rue Pothier is the façade of the old Thesis Hall **(Salle des Thèses)** (EZ **X**), a 15C library, which is the only remnant of the University of Orléans which in the Middle Ages had between 4 000 and 5 000 students. Jean Calvin, the religious reformer, studied law there in 1528.

Church of St-Pierre-le-Puellier (EFZ). − The 12C Romanesque church, which has been deconsecrated, is at the heart of an old district of half-timbered houses and pedestrian streets.

Church of St-Aignan (FZ). − The nave of this huge Gothic church, which was consecrated in 1509, was burnt down during the Wars of Religion leaving only the choir and the transepts which make a church of moderate size.

Natural Science Museum (EY M³). − Dioramas present animals and birds in their natural habitat. There are aquariums on the ground floor; the display on the third floor explains the variations in the level of water in the Loire and the source of the Loiret.

ADDITIONAL SIGHTS

Olivet. − Pop 14 489. Facilities. Like the southern suburbs of Orléans between the Loiret and the Loire, the greater part of Olivet is given over to growing flowers, roses and ornamental plants. It is also a pleasant summer resort on the south bank of the Loiret, composed of elegant houses and old water mills, where people come for the fishing and canoeing (embarkation near the river bridge).

Mill Walk. − *Round trip of 5 km - 3 miles from the bridge by the side road along the north bank of the Loiret going west and returning by D 14 going east.*
Two old mills straddle the river over their mill races between the wooded banks of the Loiret; ducks and swans glide up and down on the quiet stream.

★ ★ **La Source Floral Park.** − The huge park (30 ha - 74 acres) is divided into a great variety of styles of planting: symmetrical beds, rock gardens, wooded parkland, evergreen and flowering shrubs. The spectacle changes with the seasons: in spring − tulips and daffodils followed by irises, rhododendrons and azaleas; from mid-June to mid-July − roses; in July and August − summer flowers; in September − before the dahlias a second flowering of the roses; at the end of the season − chrysanthemums in the exhibition hall.

The park is a delight to the eye of everyone, very instructive to the amateur gardener and a showcase for the local horticulture. From the **mirror★**, a semi-circular pool, there is a fine view of the château and the delicate "Louis XIII embroidery" which decorates the lawns.

The **Loiret Spring★** which bubbles up from the ground is supplied by water which branches off from the Loire at St-Benoît-sur-Loire, some 36 miles upstream and flows underground to re-emerge in the park.

Throughout the year flamingoes stalk by the Loiret while flocks of cranes and emus and herds of deer roam the park.

Le PERCHE-GOUËT

Michelin map ▦▦ folds 15, 16 − Local map p 153

Le Perche-Gouët, which is sometimes known as Lower Perche, was named in 11C after William Gouët who owned five baronnies within the jurisdiction of the Bishop of Chartres: Alluyes la Belle, Brou la Noble, La Bazoche, la Gaillarde, Authon la Gueuse and Montmirail la Superbe. Before the Revolution the administration of Le Perche-Gouët was divided between the authority in the Orléans district and that of the Upper Maine. Le Perche-Gouët describes a sort of crescent between the Loir and the Huisne; the soil is composed of chalk marl and banks of sand or clay. Much of the immense forest which once covered the land has been replaced by fields and orchards.

The eastern part of Le Perche-Gouët is very similar to the Beauce but is distinguished by its scattered farms and the abundance of hedges and trees. The western border is marked by a range of wooded hills, only 250 m - 820 ft high, indented by a network of alluvial valleys and agricultural villages. Most of the streams − Ozanne, Yerre, Braye − flow east into the Loir; only the Rhône drains north-west into the Huisne at Nogent-le-Rotrou.

The farms which are hidden in the deep lanes were originally built of wattle and daub or within a brick framework. Their owners raise cattle, particularly dairy herds, which have replaced the breeding of the Percheron draught horses, their coats dappled grey, roan or black.

Maize is the modern crop grown for cattle fodder; its tall stems provide excellent cover for the game which used to shelter in the hedges before they were grubbed up to the alarm of the hunting fraternity.

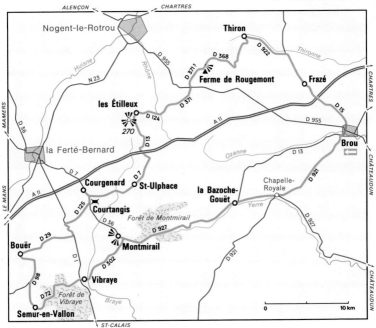

ROUND TRIP STARTING FROM BROU

97 km - 60 miles − about 1/2 day

Brou. − *Description p 73.*

> *Take D 15 northwest.*

Frazé. − *Description p 105.*

Thiron. − Pop 854. The village has grown up on the south bank of the Thironne which flows out of the Monks' Pool (Etang des Moines) near the old abbey founded by St Bernard in 1114 and dedicated to the Holy Trinity. Tiron Abbey (it was spelt without an h in those days) was especially thriving in 12 and 13C. Among the abbots in 16C were Charles de Ronsard, the poet's brother, and Philippe Desportes, himself a poet. In 1629 the Benedictines of St-Maur moved in. The **abbey church** is still a huge building even though the chancel collapsed in 1817. Near the entrance (left) is the tombstone of John II of Chartres, Abbot of Tiron in 13C; the old monks' stalls in the nave are 14C; the woodwork and stalls in the present chancel date from 1740. A few buildings from the 17C college still exist.

Rougemont Farm. − From the road (D 371³) passing the farm there is an extensive **view** of the Ozanne river valley.

Les Étilleux. − Pop 200. South of the village near a small farm on the D 13 take the path (signpost) which climbs to the top of a mound (270 m - 886 ft; radio relay station): beautiful **views** of the Ozanne Valley, the hills of Perche and the Huisne Valley.

St-Ulphace. − Pop 288. Half way up the slope stands the **church** (15-16C); its powerful façade is flanked by a tower; Renaissance doorway.

Courgenard. − Pop 412. The **church** door is carved in low relief statues in the Renaissance style. The right wall of the nave is decorated with 16C murals depicting Hell and the Legend of the Three Living and the Three Dead; Baroque altarpiece.

Courtangis Château. − Among the tall trees (beech, oak and ash) in an idyllically isolated valley are the turrets, dormers and French roofs of a graceful early 16C manor house.

Bouër. − Pop 204. Bouër is a tiny little village hidden in the hills overlooking the Huisne Valley. The slate spire of the **church** is joined to the belltower by scrolls. There are two attractive wooden altars in front of the chancel.
From the terrace a fine view of the Huisne Valley.

Semur-en-Vallon. − Pop 413. An attractive village by a man-made lake. In the valley on the western edge of Vibraye Forest stands a 15C moated and turreted **castle**; the entrance front, which is flanked by round towers with lanterns, was altered in 17C; steep French roofs. A Decauville **train** for tourists runs on a 1.5 km - 1 mile long circuit.

Vibraye. − Pop 2 391. Facilities.

Montmirail. − Pop 451. The small town of Montmirail was the capital of the five baronnies of Le Perche-Gouët. It was built on an excellent defensive site and was once strongly fortified. In 15C the Count of Anjou built a **castle** on the top of the medieval mound. The present buildings were altered in 18C by the Princesse de Conti when the rooms were decorated in the Louis XV style: three storeys of huge rooms and dungeons dating from 14C and 15C. **Panoramic view★** of Le Perche-Gouët.
The **church** (12-16C) has a 16C stained glass window in the chancel and an early 17C painted sepulchre in the left aisle. Opposite is a carved stone which, until the Revolution, contained a reliquary.

A picturesque road (D 927) runs through Montmirail Forest.

La Bazoche-Gouët. – Pop 1 451. The **church**, 12 or 13C, was altered early in 16C by the addition of Flamboyant windows in the side aisles: the one on the south side is remarkable; fine doorway with niches resting on spiral columns. Inside one sees the square tower supporting the 16C belltower. The Renaissance windows in the chancel were the gift of the Bourbons-Conti, who owned the estate; the detail and realistic expressions are remarkable; the subject is the Passion copied from German engravings.

Return to Brou via Chapelle-Royale and D 921.

PITHIVIERS
Pop 9812

Michelin map 🔟 fold 20 or 🔟 fold 41
Town plan in Michelin Red Guide France

Pithiviers is situated on the border between the Beauce and the Gâtinais. Its main activities are related to the local products – cereals and sugar beet (sugar refinery at Pithiviers-le-Vieil) – but other industries are being introduced.
The rectangle containing the old town is enclosed on four sides by a shady Mall; it is pleasant to wander in the quiet old streets which radiate from Place du Martroi, an irregular triangle of open space in the shadow of the great tower of St Salomon's church.

Pithiviers Steam Train and Transport Museum. – The railway museum was founded by amateurs in the old terminus of a line which until 1951 used to deliver sugar beet to the refineries and carry passengers between Pithiviers and Toury 32 km - 20 miles to the west; the track is 0.60 m - approximately 2 ft wide, the same gauge as the prefabricated light railway developed by Decauville. The museum contains several locomotives, some in working order, and various items of narrow gauge rolling stock from a minute 2-axle machine built in 1870 (3 tonnes unloaded weight) to a powerful locomotive (1895) from the regional railway which was 1 m - over 3 ft gauge. There are many reproductions on display as well as items of equipment and uniform, old tickets, lamps, etc.
The visit ends with a train ride (4 km - 2 1/2 miles).

Museum. – Local souvenirs are attractively displayed on the first floor; the first room on the South Sea Islands adds a touch of the exotic. Another room is devoted to famous local people, to the more or less legendary origins of the culinary specialities of Pithiviers and to saffron, an aromatic colouring agent derived from the crocus; the west Gâtinais was the first place in Europe to cultivate it.

★ Le PLESSIS-BOURRÉ Château

Michelin map 🔟 fold 20 or 🔟 fold 19 (20 km - 12 miles north of Angers)

Le Plessis-Bourré stands far away at the end of a vista of meadowland, a white building beneath blue grey slate roofs, bringing to the mind's eye the seigneurial life of the 15C.
Born in Château-Gontier **Jean Bourré** (1424-1506) first entered royal service under the dauphin Louis, the son of Charles VII, whom he served faithfully. When Louis XI assumed the crown in 1461, Bourré was appointed Financial Secretary and Treasurer of France. In addition to building several châteaux – Jarzé *(p 110)* and Vaux *(p 139)* among others – he bought the estate of Plessis-le-Vent and in 1468 ordered work to begin on the new château. The design was inspired by the château at Langeais which he had supervised during its construction, and has a magnificent unity of style.

(Photo Hervé Boulé)

Le Plessis-Bourré Château

Among the many illustrious guests that Bourré welcomed to his new residence were Pierre de Rohan (p 188), Louis XI and Charles VIII.

Le Plessis, isolated by a wide moat spanned by a many arched bridge 43 m - 47 yd long looks, from outside, like a fortress protected by a gatehouse with a double draw-bridge and four flanking towers. The largest of these is battlemented and served as a keep. A platform 3 m - 10 ft wide at the base of the wall provided for artillery crossfire.

The chapel's slender spire rises above the roof to the left of the gatehouse.

Beyond the entrance archway, Le Plessis is transformed into a country mansion with a spacious courtyard, low wings, an arcaded gallery, turret staircases and high dormer windows of the seigneurial wing.

On the ground floor the visitor will see the Chapel Ste-Anne and the Hall of Justice before visiting the richly furnished and decorated state apartments, which have a charming view of the gentle countryside.

The first floor has among other rooms a great vaulted chamber with a fireplace. The guardroom has a coffered wooden **ceiling**★★★ painted at the end of the 15C with such allegorical figures as Fortune, Truth, Chastity (a unicorn) and Lust, the Musician Ass, etc. Humorous and moral scenes depict the unskilled barber at work on a patient, the overweening man trying to wring the neck of an eel, a woman sewing up a chicken's crop, etc. There is a large collection of fans in the library.

The cellars and attics are also open to the visitors. The palm tree ceiling of the tower staircase rests on carvings inspired by alchemy more truculent than the paintings on the first floor. The attic under the beautiful chestnut keel roof gives access to the sentry walk.

EXCURSION

La Hamonnière Manor. — *9 km - 5 1/2 miles north towards Champigné by D 508, D 74 west and in Écueillé D 107 north.*

The architecture of the manor house, which was built between 1420 and 1575, shows the evolution of the Renaissance style. The buildings round the courtyard consist of a plain residential block (right) with a stair turret, a Henri III section (left) with a window bay framed by pilasters and capitals following the Classical progression of the orders, and at a right angle a low wing with two twisted columns supporting the dormer. To the rear stands the keep, probably the last addition made in 16C; it has a stair turret running from top to bottom and round arched windows.

GREEN TOURIST GUIDES

Picturesque scenery, buildings
Attractive routes
Touring programmes
Plans of towns and buildings.

Le PLESSIS-MACÉ Château

Michelin 🔢 fold 20 or 🔢🔢 fold 19 (13 km - 8 miles northwest of Angers)

Hidden amidst greenery this château is surrounded by a wide moat. Started in the 11C by a certain Macé, the château became the property in the mid-15C of Louis de Beaumont, the Chamberlain and favourite of Louis XI, who transformed it into a residence fit to accommodate his royal master. The year 1510 saw the beginning of a 168-year-old ownership by the Du Bellay family.

From the exterior Le Plessis still has the appearance of a fortress with its tower-studded wall and rectangular keep, dismantled but still battlemented and surrounded by a moat.

Once inside the great courtyard the country residence becomes apparent: the decorative elements in white tufa stone enhance the grey of the schists, while windows let in the light.

To the right are the outbuildings housing the stables and guard-room. To the left are the chapel, an unusual staircase turret, and the main dwelling surmounted by pointed gables. In the angle of the main dwelling is a charming **bal-cony** where the ladies watched the

(after photo Chrétien, Angers)

Le Plessis-Macé — Balcony

jousting tournaments and other entertainments. The balcony opposite, in the outbuildings, was reserved for the servants.

One can visit the dining room, the large banqueting hall, several bedrooms, one of which was the king's, and the **chapel**, which has kept its rare Gothic panelling of the 15C and forms two floors of galleries, the first reserved for the Lord and his Squires, the second for the servants.

PONCÉ-SUR-LE-LOIR

Pop 426

Michelin map 📖 fold 5 or 📖📖 fold 23 — Local map p 121

Beside the road (D 917) leading into Poncé from the east stands a Renaissance château. On the west side of the town, south of the main road and the railway line, is the **Craft Centre** "Les Grès du Loir". It is housed in the 18C buildings of the old Paillard paper mill on the river bank and consists of the studios of several independent craftsmen: pottery, glassware, ironwork, weaving, woodwork and candle making.

Château. — It originally consisted of two pavilions flanking the central staircase tower, one of which was destroyed in the 18C and replaced by a characterless wing. Ionic pilasters flanking the windows and pronounced horizontal cornices give a balanced but geometrically severe aspect to the façade. The north front, formerly the entrance front, has an elegant Italian style arcade which forms a terrace at first floor level.

The stone **Renaissance staircase★★** is one of the most remarkable in France; in front of it are the remains of a former loggia. The coffered ceilings of the six flights are sumptuously sculptured, with a delicacy, fantasy and art of perspective rarely attained. Over 130 motifs portray realistic, allegorical and mythological subjects.

One can also stroll in the well-kept **gardens**, with their highly effective symmetrical layout: on the edge of the square lawn, the tree covered walk makes a long vaulted path on one side, and on the other is a labyrinth conducive to tranquillity and meditation; overlooking the entire scene runs a terrace with a mall of lime trees.

The dovecot remains with its 1 800 holes and revolving ladders for gathering the eggs. The outbuildings house a **museum of Sarthe folklore.**

PONTLEVOY

Pop 1 700

Michelin map 📖 fold 17 or 📖📖 folds 14, 15

A small town situated in the agricultural region to the north of Montrichard, Pontlevoy still has some charming old houses.

Old Abbey. — The former abbey is mainly interesting for its noble 18C buildings and a 15C Gothic church. The foundation dates from 1034, when Gelduin de Chaumont, vassal of the Count of Blois, established a Benedictine community here as a token of gratitude to the Virgin for surviving a shipwreck.

In the 17C, when a reform of monastic life became essential, the abbey was entrusted to the Benedictines of Saint-Maur and the Abbot Pierre de Bérule who opened an educational establishment in 1644 which made Pontlevoy famous until the 19C.

Proclaimed the École Royale Militaire in 1776, the college added to its secular teaching, the military training of scholars chosen by the king from among the gentry.

In keeping with this scholastic tradition, the former abbey today undertakes technical teaching with respect to road transport.

The former **abbey church**, rebuilt in the 2nd half of the 15C after being damaged during the Hundred Years War, consists of only the chancel of the imposing edifice which was planned but never completed. In 1651 two large stone retables with marble columns were added to the high altar and to the axial chapel where Gelduin and his first descendants are buried.

In the 18C **conventual buildings** one can see the refectory decorated with a monumental stove of Delftware, one of four which the Maréchal de Saxe had commissioned for Chambord (p 74), the remarkable staircase leading to the upper floor and the majestic façade giving on to the gardens, with emblazoned pediments at regular intervals.

Road Transport Museum. — Some 20 vehicles built between 1900 and 1960 are displayed in the old riding school.

Local Museum. — This museum, which is housed in the west wing, is devoted to the history of Pontlevoy and its site.

The first rooms to be opened present one of the earliest advertising men, **Auguste Poulain**, who was born in Pontlevoy in 1825 and founded the famous chocolate factory in Blois: old advertisements, chromolithographs etc. dating from late last century.

Another room displays about a hundred photographs made on plates which illustrate village life from 1902.

The museum possesses a collection of 10 000 plates, a photographic record of Pontlevoy, made by Louis Clergeau, a clock-maker with a passion for photography, and by his daughter Marcelle.

La POSSONNIÈRE Manor

Michelin map 📖 fold 5 or 📖📖 west of fold 24 (1 km - 1/2 mile south of Couture-sur-Loir) — Local map p 121

When Louis de Ronsard, soldier and man of letters, returned from Italy in the early 16C he undertook to rebuild his country seat in the new Italian style; he created La Possonnière and the profusion of mottoes engraved on the walls.

The Prince of Poets. — In 1524 **Pierre de Ronsard**, Louis' son, was born at the manor. He was destined for a brilliant future in the army or the diplomatic service and at 12 became a page at the court of François I. An illness, however, left him half deaf at 15 and he had to relinquish his ambitions. He took holy orders and turned to poetry and the study of the ancient authors; Pindar in Greek and Horace in Latin became his models. He excelled in composing sonnets in which he described the beauty of Cassandra Salviati (p 175) and Marie (p 71). He was the leader of the Pléiade group of poets (p 30) and in 1558 was appointed Poet Laureate but, afflicted with gout, he withdrew to his priories at Ste-Madeleine de Croixval (6 km - 4 miles southeast of la Possonnière) and at St-Cosme-lès-Tours (p 182) where he died in 1585 leaving a considerable body of work.

Manor. — The manor house is built against the hillside on the northern fringes of the Gâtines Forest and enclosed with a wall. The name comes from the word *posson* (*poinçon*, a measure of volume) and has sometimes been altered to Poissonnière under the influence of the family coat of arms.

The main façade has mullioned windows in the style of Louis XII on the ground floor but the windows on the first floor are flanked by pilasters with médallions, clearly in the Renaissance style.

Projecting from the rear façade is a graceful stair turret; the elegant doorway is capped by a pediment adorned with a bust. The pediment dormer at the top of the turret bears the arms of the Ronsard family, three silver fishes on a blue ground.

POUANCÉ   Pop 3410

Michelin map 63 fold 8 or 232 fold 17

Pouancé in its protective ring of lakes is on the border between Anjou and Brittany. In the Middle Ages it played an important economic role owing to its iron foundries which were supplied with ore from the Segré basin. The surrounding woods provided shelter for the Chouans during the Revolution. The main road through the town (N 171) passes at the foot of the ruined **castle** (13-15C). The towers and curtain wall of dark schist are impressive and reinforced by a firing caponier linked to the keep by a postern.

EXCURSIONS

Pierre Frite Menhir. — *5 km - 3 miles south by D 878, bearing left into D 6 in La Previère and then a track to the right (signpost).* This menhir is 6 m - 20 ft high.

La Motte-Glain Château. — *17 km - 10 1/2 miles south.*
The château was built late in 15C by **Pierre de Rohan** (p 188), Counsellor to Louis XI and then one of the commanding officers of the armies of Charles VIII and Louis XII in Italy. The main interest is the exterior of red stone with its strong lines and gatehouse flanked by two round towers. The decoration on the front overlooking the courtyard — scallop shells and pilgrims' staffs — are a reminder that the château is on the road from Mont-St-Michel to Compostela in Spain (p 38).

Le PUY-NOTRE-DAME   Pop 1497

Michelin map 64 fold 12 or 232 fold 32 (7 km - 4 miles west of Montreuil-Bellay)

★ **Church.** — The church is a remarkable example of Angevin architecture and was built in 13C. The tower with its stone spire above the south transept is decorated with mouldings forming a recess containing a very beautiful statue of the Virgin (16C). On the north side of the church, enclosed in a cylindrical building, is the well from which the town takes its name. In the Middle Ages people came from all over France to venerate the Virgin's Girdle, a relic brought from Jerusalem in 12C, which is kept in the church. The tall, slim nave and aisles lend majesty to the interior; the vaulting in the chancel is rich with lierne and tierceron ribs. The carved stalls beyond the high altar are 16C.

★ **RIVAU Castle**

Map 67 fold 10 or 232 fold 34 (11 km - 7 miles north of Richelieu) — Local map p 92

The 13C castle was fortified in 15C by Pierre de Beauvau, Charles VII's chamberlain. Joan of Arc found horses for her soldiers here on her way to the siege of Orléans. Rivau is mentioned by Rabelais; Gargantua gave the castle to one of his knights after the Picrocholean War. The draw-bridge in the keep leads into the main courtyard.

The **interior** is paved with white tufa; the elegant rooms contain Gothic and Renaissance furniture: there is a fine 15C Gothic credence table bearing the royal arms in the Guardroom (huge fireplace) and the bedroom next to the oratory contains a tester bed with Renaissance columns. Exhibition of contemporary paintings by Pierre-Laurent Brenot.

La ROCHE-RACAN Château

Michelin map 64 fold 4 or 232 fold 23 (2 km - 1 mile southeast of St-Paterne-Racan)

The Château de la Roche-Racan stands perched on a rock (*roche* in French) overlooking the Escotais Valley which together with the nearby Loir, were a constant source of inspiration to the first owner and poet, **Racan** (1589-1670).

Born at Champmarin near Aubigné, Honorat de Bueil, marquis de Racan (1589-1670), was a member of the well known local family, the Bueils (p 169). Little inclined to the life of a soldier and unlucky in love, Racan retired to his country seat for the last forty years of his life, a period described in his work, *Stances à la retraite*.

There he strolled by his fountains or hunted hare or deer or visited Denis de la Grelière, the Abbé of la Clarté-Dieu, who invited him to put the Psalms into verse. He brought up his children, pursued his law suits, grew beans and rebuilt his château.

Château. — In 1634 Racan commissioned a local master mason, Jacques Gabriel, a member of a long established family of architects, to build this château. The main building was originally flanked by two pavilions only one of which remains standing today, pedimented and adorned with a corner turret and caryatids. Long balustured terraces, above mask-decorated arcades, overlook the park and Escotais Valley.

Michelin map 🔲 fold 18 or 🔲 fold 16 – Facilities

The point where the River Sauldre divided into several arms was the site of the former capital of the Sologne. Always an important market town, Romorantin-Lanthenay has gained a new impetus from modern industries such as electronics, refrigeration plants and cameras and other activities such as flour-milling and sheet-iron and steel-plate rolling. In 1968 a Matra factory was opened on the east side of the town for the production of plastic car bodies and the mass production of saloon cars.

Royal associations. – In the 15C Romorantin was the fief of the Valois-Angoulême branch of the French royal family and it was here that François d'Angoulême, later **François I**, spent his turbulent childhood and where his wife to be, Claude of France, the daughter of Louis XII was born in 1499. The king loved Romorantin and in 1517 he commissioned Leonardo da Vinci, then at Amboise *(p 46)*, to draw up plans for a palace destined for his mother Louise de Savoie. Leonardo envisaged a palace astride the Sauldre, to be built with prefabricated units, but the death of Louise put an end to the project. Da Vinci also studied the possibility of creating a canal to link Romorantin to the Loire.

In France, the Feast of the Epiphany *(la Fête des Rois)* is celebrated by eating a cake *(la Galette des Rois)* which contains a bean. The finder of this bean is the bean king of Twelfth Night. On 6 January, Epiphany, 1521, François I led a mock attack on the Hôtel St-Pol, where a bean king reigned. The occupants of the house were defending themselves by hurling snowballs, apples and eggs from the windows when some ill advised person threw out a glowing log which landed on the royal cranium. To dress the wound the doctors shaved his head; the King then grew a beard. His courtiers followed suit.

ROMORANTIN-LANTHENAY

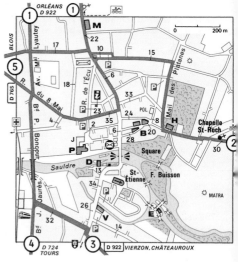

SIGHTS

★ **Old Houses (B)**. – On the corner of Rue de la Résistance and Rue du Milieu stands **La Chancellerie**, a corbelled Renaissance house, of brick and half timber construction, where the royal seals were kept when the King stayed in the town. The corner post portrays a coat of arms and a musician playing an instrument similar to the bagpipes. Opposite stands **Hôtel St-Pol**, built of stone and glazed bricks with window mouldings.

⊘ Standing at the junction of Rue du Milieu and Rue de la Pierre is the charming **Maison du Carroir d'Orée** (archaelogical museum) whith its remarkable carved corner posts showing the Annunciation *(left)* and St George killing the Dragon *(right)*.

★ **The Sologne Museum (H)**. – The collections are presented in an attractive setting in ⊘ the Town Hall. They deal with the ethnography and folklore of the Sologne region. Every aspect of the local way of life – soil, housing, crafts and costume – is treated in turn. Remarkable reconstruction of the living room of a country cottage and a clog maker's workshop.

★ **View from the bridges**. – The bridges over the Sauldre provide some attractive views. From the north branch of the river there is a **view** of the Chapter Mill (**Moulin du Chapitre** – **D**) opposite the old Royal Château (**Château royal** – **P**) which dates from 15 and 16C and now houses the sub-Prefecture.
The narrow southern branch presents a row of attractive half-timbered houses (**V**).

Public Garden (**Square Ferdinand-Buisson**). – A pleasant park with tall trees and footbridges over the river; views of the river banks including the fulling mill (**E**).

⊘ **St Stephen's Church** (**St-Etienne**). – Over the transept crossing rises a Romanesque tower with delicate sculptures. Beyond the nave with its Angevin vaulting is the sombre chancel which is also roofed with Angevin vaulting springing from powerful Romanesque pillars; each rib of the apsidal vault supports the statue of an evangelist.

St Roch Chapel. – At the entrance to the St-Roch district. The graceful building is flanked by turrets with round arched windows typical of the neo-Renaissance.

⊘ **Car Racing Museum (M)**. – Exhibition of Matra racing cars, including the Formula 1 car which was world champion in 1969, and a series of show cases tracing the technical developments in car construction. There is also a specialist library.

Les ROSIERS

Michelin map 64 fold 12 or 232 folds 32, 33 — Local map p 127

Les Rosiers is a village on the north bank of the Loire opposite Gennes. The **church,** which has a Renaissance tower, is the work of the Angevin architect Jean de l'Espine; the windows of the stair turret are flanked by pilasters. The statue in front of the church is of Jeanne de Laval, the second wife of King René of Anjou *(p 48).*

EXCURSION

Le Prieuré. — *7.5 km - 5 miles west by the bridge into Gennes, right into D 751 and left in Le Sale-Village.*
At the centre of the hamlet is the charming priory screened by handsome cedar and elm trees said to have come from Sully. The 12-13C **church** has a beautiful Romanesque square tower and a fine 17C painted wooden altar.

SABLÉ-SUR-SARTHE

Michelin map 64 fold 1 or 232 fold 21 — Local map p 167 — Facilities
Town plan in the Michelin Red Guide France

Situated at a point where two tributaries, the Vaige and Erve, flow into the Sarthe, Sablé is dominated by the austere façade of its château, which once belonged to the Colbert family and is now used by a department of the National Library. The town's name is famous since it also refers to the shortbread biscuits made in the local factory.
In the 17C the fief belonged to Laval-Boisdauphin, marquis de Sablé. In 1711 Colbert de Torcy, the nephew of the great Jean-Baptiste Colbert, Louis XIV's Minister, rebuilt the château and radically changed the aspect of the town: many houses and the hospital date from this period.
The town was once renowned for a black marble veined with white, which was extracted from the quarries on the north bank of the Sarthe, upstream from the town. It was much used at Versailles and also in the Marble Salon at La Lorie Castle *(p 169).*
The small port on the canalized part of the Sarthe used to receive sand laden barges from the Loire. Secondary metallurgical industries such as wire drawing, screw cutting, smelting, bolt and nut works and the production of foodstuffs (milk, cheese and biscuits) are the main sources of employment today.

EXCURSIONS

Solesmes. — *3 km - 2 miles northeast by D 138. Description p 171.*

★ **Asnières-sur-Vègre.** — *10 km - 6 miles northeast by D 138 and D 22. Description p 55.*

Auvers-le-Hamon. — *Pop 1 201. 8.5 km - 5 miles north by D 24.*
The **church's** nave is ornamented with 15-16C **mural paintings** depicting a series of local saints: to the right St Mamès holding his intestines, St Martin on horseback, St Cénéré as a Cardinal, St Eutropius, St Andrew on his cross, St Luke riding a bull, the Nativity and the Flight into Egypt. To the left a macabre dance, St Avertin, St Apollonia whose teeth were pulled out by her torturers, St James and the Sacrifice of Isaac.

La Chapelle-du-Chêne. — *6 km - 4 miles southeast by D 306. In Les Nœuds turn left.*
The basilica is the object of pilgrimages to Notre-Dame-du-Chêne (Our Lady of the Oak), represented by a 15C terracotta statue. In the park there is a small scale model of the Holy Sepulchre and the Stations of the Cross.

St-Denis d'Anjou. — *Pop 1 279. 10.5 km - 6 1/2 miles southwest by D 309.*
The village, which is covered with flowers in season, has a 12C **fortified church** with keel vaulting and 12 and 15C **frescoes** which were discovered in 1947 and have been gradually restored: St Christopher (west wall); the martyrdom of John the Baptist, the legends of St Nicolas, St Giles and St Hubert on two levels. Opposite the church, which belonged to the Chapter of Angers, stands the 15C canons' house, which is now the Town Hall, and the 16C market, which has a very steep slate roof under which wine was bought and sold.

Varennes-Bourreau Chapel. — *6 km - 4 miles southeast of St-Denis d'Anjou (D 615).*
The chapel nestles in the lush vegetation beside the River Sarthe; it is decorated with beautiful 12 and 15C frescoes: a mandorla of Christ his hand raised in blessing. The village of Varennes was formerly a small port engaged in the transport of wine to Angers before the vines were destroyed by phylloxera.

SACHÉ

Michelin map 64 fold 14 or 232 fold 35 (6.5 km - 4 miles east of Azay-le-Rideau)

Saché is well known because **Balzac** *(see p 30)* often went to stay there. A more recent famous resident was the American sculptor, **Alexander Calder** (1898-1976), who created mobiles and stabiles in abstract forms; one of his mobiles is displayed in the main square of Saché which bears his name.

Saché Château. — The 16 and 18C château is set in a pleasant park. In the last century it belonged to M. de Margonne, a friend of Balzac who loved to escape to Saché from the bustle of Paris and the dunning of his creditors; in the peaceful surroundings of the château he wrote easily and the action of one of his novels, *Le Lys dans la Vallée,* is set in the Indre Valley between Saché and Pont-de-Ruan. The room where Balzac worked remains as it was in his lifetime. Other rooms in the château contain portraits, manuscripts, first editions and souvenirs of the 1850s.

★ ST-AIGNAN

Pop 3690

Michelin map 🆖 fold 17 or 🔢 fold 15 − Facilities

St-Aignan stands on the south bank of the Cher at the heart of a region of woods and vineyards: Coteaux du Cher is the wine produced in Seigy and Couffy.
There is a picturesque view of the little town on its sloping site from the bridge or from the north bank on D 675 north of Noyers. Both the church and the château are interesting; so too is Rue Constant-Ragot which contains two Gothic houses and provides the best view of the chevet of the church. A stroll in the narrow streets and neighbouring square will reveal some 15C carved stone or half-timbered houses.

★ **St Aignan's Church.** − The collegiate church is a Romanesque building dating from 11 and 12C with an impressive tower over the transept. A spacious tower-porch with delicately carved capitals leads into the high light nave; the capitals are finely carved into acanthus leaves and fantastic animals; the chancel and ambulatory have historiated capitals showings the Flight into Egypt *(north ambulatory)*, the Sacrifice of Isaac and King David *(south side)*.

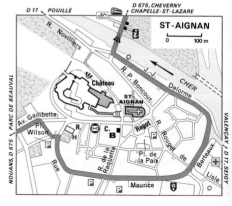

★★ **Crypt.** − *Entrance in left transept.* Known formerly as St John's or the Church of the Grottoes, it was probably the early Romanesque church which was used as a stable or store during the Revolution. It is similar in plan to the chancel and decorated with **frescoes** (from 12 to 15C): St John the Evangelist (15C) in the central chapel of the ambulatory, the legend of St Giles in the south chapel. A great Christ in Majesty in a double mandorla (1200) fills the half dome of the chancel and spreads his blessing through the mediation of St Peter and St James to the sick who are prostrate; the vault over the transept crossing shows the figure of Christ in Judgment resting on a rainbow.

Château. − A great flight of steps starting from the church porch leads up to the château courtyard; pleasant view of the roofs of the town, one or two of slate amongst the tiles. The château consists of two buildings at right angles, mostly built in 16C and backing on to the remains of the medieval fortifications on the east side of the courtyard. The elegant Renaissance dwelling has pilasters flanking the windows, carved dormer gables and a handsome stair in an octagonal turret terminating in a lantern. The terrace overlooks the turbulent waters of the Cher passing under the bridge.

Provost's House (Maison de la Prévôté). − *On leaving the church cross the main street, Rue Constant-Ragot.* The 15C building is used for temporary exhibitions.

EXCURSIONS

St Lazarus' Chapel (Chapelle St-Lazare). − *2 km - 1 mile northeast; cross the river and turn right into N 76.* On the north side of the road stands a chapel with a gable belfry which was once part of a leper house.

Beauval Ornithological Park. − *4 km - 2 1/2 miles south by D 675.*
There is a fine view of the vineyards as the road descends to Beauval Park in the valley. The park is essentially a breeding station dedicated to the preservation of species threatened with extinction. The great aviaries interspersed among the flowers and trees house an exceptional collection of exotic birds. Around the ducks' lake are mandarin ducks, Barbary ducks, Canada geese, flamingoes, crested cranes, etc.; further on are aviaries for parrots, budgerigars and toucans.

Chémery Château. − *13 km - 8 miles northeast by D 675 bearing right in St-Romain-sur-Cher into D 63.* The château (15 and 16C) is a mixture of medieval and Renaissance architecture. It was raised on the site of a 12C fortress. In summer it is the setting for a **Son et Lumière** spectacle entitled "the Death of Orion".

★★ ST-BENOÎT-SUR-LOIRE

Pop 1925

Michelin map 🆖 fold 10 or 🔢 fold 6 (10 km - 6 miles southeast of Châteauneuf)

The basilica of St Benedict on Loire (St-Benoît-sur-Loire) is one of the most famous Romanesque buildings in France.

Foundation (7C). − According to Celtic tradition St-Benoît-sur-Loire was the place where the local Carnute druids assembled *(p 147)*.
In 645 or 651 a group of Benedictine monks led by an abbot from Orléans came to this spot and founded a monastery which very soon gained the favour of the great as is shown by the gift of a shrine by Mumma. In about 672 the Abbot of **Fleury**, as the monastery was called, learned that the body of St Benedict, the father of western monasticism who died in 547, was buried beneath the ruins of the Abbey of Monte Cassino in Italy; he gave orders for the precious relic, a source of miracles and cures, to be transported to the banks of the Loire where it attracted great crowds of people and brought increasing success to the monastery.

Theodulf, Odo, Abbo and Gauzlin. — Charlemagne gave Fleury to his adviser and friend, **Theodulf** *(p 106)*, the brilliant bishop of Orléans, who founded two famous monastic schools, an external one for secular priests and an internal one for postulant monks. The scriptorium produced some beautiful work.

The death of Theodulf and the Norman invasions upset the courses of study and the smooth running of the monastery; discipline suffered.

In 10C a spectacular change took place. In 930 **Odo**, a monk from the Touraine, became Abbot of Cluny; he imposed the Cluniac rule at Fleury and reopened the abbey school. St Benedict's regained its prosperity: students flocked to the school, particularly from England, and the French king and princes offered gifts and patronage. The Archbishop of Canterbury, Oda, received the Benedictine habit from Fleury.

The late 10C is dominated by **Abbo**, a famous scholar and teacher, who enjoyed the favour of the Capets. He entered Fleury as a child, studied in Paris and Rheims where he was under the celebrated Gerbert, who had himself been at Fleury, and then returned *c*975 to Fleury as head of studies. He added to the already extensive library and extended the area of study; in his reign as Abbot (from 988) the Abbey was at the forefront of western intellectual life with a particularly strong influence in England and the west of France. He was also a very able organizer of the monastic life of the Abbey.

Abbo was very influential with Robert II and commissioned a monk called Aimoin to write a **History of the Franks,** which became the official chronicle expounding the "ideology" of the Capet monarchy. Abbo was assassinated in 1004 in a revolt.

The reign of Abbot **Gauzlin**, the future Archbishop of Bourges, early in 11C is marked by the production of the so-called Gaignières **Evangelistary,** an illuminated manuscript — gold and silver lettering on purple parchment — which is the work of a Lombard painter, and by the construction of the handsome porch belfry.

The present church (crypt, chancel, transept) was built between 1067 and 1108; the nave was not completed until the end of 12C.

Modern times. — In 15C St-Benoît passed *in commendam:* this meant that the revenues of the abbey were granted by the monarch to "commendatory abbots", often laymen, who were simply beneficiaries and took no active part in the religious life of the community.

The monks did not always make such abbots welcome. Under François I they refused to receive Cardinal Duprat and shut themselves up in the tower of the porch. The King had to come in person, at the head of an armed force, to make them submit.

During the Wars of Religion (1562-98) one of these abbots, Odet de Châtillon-Coligny, the brother of the Protestant leader Admiral Coligny, was himself converted to Protestantism. He had St-Benoît looted by Condé's Huguenot troops. The treasure was melted down — the gold casket containing the relics of the Saint alone weighed 17.5 kg - 39 lb — the marvellous library was sold and its precious manuscripts, about 2 000 in number, were scattered to the four corners of Europe. Some are now to be found in Berne, Rome, Leyden, Oxford and Moscow.

The celebrated Congregation of St-Maur, introduced to St-Benoît in 1627 by Cardinal Richelieu, restored its spiritual and intellectual life. The abbey was closed at the Revolution, its archives transferred to Orléans and its property dispersed. At the beginning of the First Empire the monastic buildings were destroyed *(1)* and the church fell into disrepair. In 1835 it was registered as an historical monument, and it was restored on various occasions between 1836 and 1923. Monastic life was revived there in 1944.

The poet and artist Max Jacob (1876-1944) retired to the abbey in St-Benoit-sur-Loire, before he was arrested in 1944.

★★ THE BASILICA

time: 3/4 hour

ⓥ This imposing edifice was built between 1067 and 1218. The towers were originally much taller.

★★ **Belfry Porch.** — The belfry originally stood by itself, and is one of the finest examples of Romanesque art. The richly carved capitals are worthy of attention: abaci and corbels delicately carved in the beautiful golden stone. Stylised plants and, particularly, flowing acanthus leaves alternate with fantastic animals, scenes from the Apocalypse, and events in the life of Christ and the Virgin Mary. On the porch (second column from the left), one of the capitals is signed *Umbertus me fecit.*

Nave. — It was completed in 1218 in the transitional Romanesque style. It is very luminous with its white stonework and high vaulting which let in plenty of light. The organ loft was added about 1700.

(Photo Serge Chirol)

Basilica of St-Benoit-sur-Loire — The porch

(1) Only a small façade belonging to the former students' chapel, remains. It is in the village opposite the war memorial in Place de l'Université.

Transept. – Like the chancel, this was finished in 1108. The dome, built on superimposed squinches, carries the central bell tower. Under the dome are the stalls dated 1413, and the remains of a choir screen in carved wood presented in 1635 by Richelieu, when he was Commendatory Abbot of St-Benoît.

In the north transept is the precious 14C alabaster statue of Notre-Dame-de-Fleury. A plaque on the right recalls that the poet Max Jacob, who used to pray before this statue, lies in the village cemetery.

★★ **Chancel.** – The very long Romanesque chancel was built between 1065 and 1108; note
⊙ the decor of blind arcades with sculptured capitals forming a triforium. The ambulatory with radiating chapels is typical of a church built for crowds and processions; this plan can be found in most Benedictine churches.

The floor is paved with a Roman mosaic brought from Italy in 1531 by Cardinal Duprat; it is similar to the style popular in the eastern part of the Roman Empire. The recumbent figure is that of Philippe I, the fourth Capet King, who died in 1108.

★ **Crypt.** – An impressive masterpiece of the second half of the 11C, it has kept its original appearance. Large round columns form a double ambulatory with radiating chapels round the large central pillar containing the modern shrine of St Benedict, whose relics have been venerated here since the 8C.

ST-CALAIS   Pop 4779

Michelin map 64 fold 5 or 238 fold 1

St-Calais on the border between Maine and the Vendôme region, is a market town dominated by the ruins of a medieval château. A few old gables still look down on the narrow streets.

Five bridges span the River Anille. The district on the west bank grew up round the Benedictine abbey which was founded in the reign of Childebert (6C) by Calais, a coenobite monk from the Auvergne. The monastery was destroyed during the Revolution but the few 17C buildings which survived are now occupied by the Town Hall, the theatre and the museum.

Apple Turnover Festival (Fête du chausson aux pommes). – This great festival has taken place every year since 1581 (first Saturday and Sunday in September) to commemorate the end of the plague.

SIGHTS

⊙ **Notre Dame Church.** – Construction began in 1425 with the chancel; the building is a mixture of the Flamboyant and the Renaissance styles. The bell-tower is surmounted by a crocketed stone steeple.

The Italian **façade★** was finished in 1549 and is typical of the second Renaissance. The carved panels of the twin doors portray scenes from the life of the Virgin; above in the transom are two horns of plenty framed by a semicircular arch. The whole doorway is flanked by two Ionic pilasters. The charming side doors are surmounted by curvilinear pediments and niches. A pedimented window and an oculus are set in the upper part of the gable which is surmounted by five pinnacles ornamented with statues.

The first three bays of the interior are Renaissance; the vaulting with pendentives springs from majestic columns with Ionic capitals. The 17C organ loft came from the abbey and the organ case is of the same date. A Baroque retable adorns

ST-CALAIS

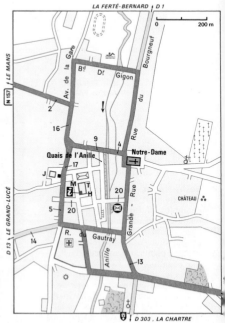

Coursimault (R.)	2
Dauphin (R. du)	4
Dr-Olivier (R. du)	5
Guichet (R. du)	9
Image (R. de l')	13
Lucé (R. de)	14
Mans (R. du)	16
Maubert (R. H.)	17
Sadi-Carnot (R.)	20

the high altar; a strong cupboard to the right of the chancel contains the "Shroud of St-Calais" which is made of Sassanid (6C Persian) material.

Riverside (Quais de l'Anille). – Pleasant views of the riverside wash houses now covered in moss and gardens of flowers against a background of picturesque roofs.

For a peaceful night
the Michelin Red Guide France revises annually its choice
of pleasant, quiet and well situated hotels.

ST-ÉTIENNE-DE-CHIGNY
Pop 846

Michelin map 🅶🅴 fold 14 or 🅶🅶🅶 fold 35 (13 km - 8 miles northeast of Langeais)

Set back from the village which is on the Loire embankment is the **Vieux Bourg** nestling in the Bresme Valley; there are several old houses with steep gables.

★ **Church.** – The church was built in 1542 by Jean Binet, major domo to François I and
🕐 Mayor of Tours, whose arms appear both within and without in the form of a mourning band *(p 34)*. The nave is covered by a remarkable **hammerbeam roof**; the tie beams are carved with enormous grotesque masks and, in the chancel, Jonah in the belly of the whale. The 16C **stained glass window** in the chevet shows the Crucifixion flanked by the figures of the donors, Jean Binet and his wife, Jeanne de la Lande. In the north transept hangs a 16C painting of the Virgin and Child by the French school; there is also a mural of a bishop. The font dates from 16C.

ST-FLORENT-LE-VIEIL
Pop 1560

Michelin map 🅶🅶 fold 19 or 🅶🅶🅶 fold 30 – Local map p 126

The hill on which St-Florent is built is visible from a distance. From the bridge over the Loire there is a good **view** of the town and of the schist houses descending to the riverside; on the top of the hill stands the church surrounded by trees.

The Mercy of Bonchamps. – The revolt of the Vendée *(p 136)* began in St-Florent on 12 March 1793. The Whites were defeated at Cholet and retreated to St-Florent on 18 October with their prisoners and their wounded, including **Bonchamps** who was near to death. Incensed by the atrocities committed by Westermann and the Mayence Army, the Whites prepared to avenge their leader by massacring the Republicans imprisoned in the church. Hearing by chance of their impending fate, Bonchamps begged his cousin, Autichamps to obtain a reprieve for the prisoners. Autichamps therefore ran to the church shouting that Bonchamps wanted the prisoners to be spared and they were spared. Among their number was the father of David d'Angers, the sculptor, who created the moving monument in the church.

Church. – The church stands on the top of Mount Glonne; in a chapel *(left)* stands the white marble **tomb**★ of Bonchamps presented by David d'Angers as a hero of old.

Esplanade. – The tree-lined esplanade near the church ends in a column which was erected in honour of the Duchess of Angoulême, daughter of Louis XVI.
From the terrace there is an extensive **view**★ of the Loire Valley.

Join us in our never ending task of keeping up to date.
Send us your comments and suggestions, please.

Michelin Tyre Public Limited Company
Tourism Department
Davy House — Lyon Road — HARROW — Middlesex HA1 2DQ

ST-GEORGES-SUR-LOIRE
Pop 3015

Michelin map 🅶🅶 folds 19, 20 or 🅶🅶🅶 fold 31 – Local map p 126

St-Georges on the north bank of the Loire is situated not far from a famous vineyard, "La Coulée de Serrant" where some of Anjou's finest white wines are produced.

Old Abbey. – The Abbey was founded in 1158 by the Augustinian Order. In 1790 it was occupied by a scholarly community which emerged in 1635 as the result of an effort to bring together the different Augustinian communities: the Genovefans were regular canons belonging to the Abbey of St Geneviève in Paris.
The handsome building, which dates from 1684 and is occupied by the Town Hall, contains a grand staircase with a remarkable wrought iron banister and the chapter house with its original wainscoting where temporary exhibitions are held.

EXCURSION

★★ **Serrant Château.** – *2 km - 1 mile northeast by N23 towards Angers. Description p 171.*

ST-PATERNE-RACAN
Pop 1508

Michelin map 🅶🅴 south of fold 4 or 🅶🅶🅶 fold 23

St-Paterne stretches out along the Escotais, which is bordered by riverside wash houses and weeping willows.

Church. – The church contains interesting works of art, some of which came from the nearby Abbey of La Clarté-Dieu. The 16C terracotta group to the left of the high altar portrays the Adoration of the Magi; at the centre is a charming **Virgin and Child**★.
In the nave, 18C polychrome statues represent the four great Latin Doctors of the Church – Ambrose, Augustine, Jerome and Gregory the Great – while in the south chapel a large retable (the Virgin of the Rosary) of the same period is accompanied by a 16C terracotta group of St Anne and the Virgin.

EXCURSIONS

La-Roche-Racan Château. – *2 km - 1 mile south by D 28. Description p 157.*

St-Christophe-sur-le-Nais. – Pop 877. *2.5 km - 1 1/2 miles north by D 6.* Also in the Escotais Valley this village is the scene of a pilgrimage to St Christopher (second last Sunday in July). The **church** is in reality composed of two separate buildings, a former 11-14C priory chapel and the parish church with its 16C nave and belfry.

On the threshold of the nave a gigantic St Christopher welcomes the visitor. To the right in a recess is a reliquary bust of the Saint.

To the left of the chancel, the door leading to the Prior's oratory is surmounted by a fine 14C statue of the Virgin and Child. Two Renaissance medallions decorate the church's wooden roof.

Neuvy-le-Roi. – Pop 1 052. *9 km - 6 miles east by D 54.* The **church** which dates from the 12 and 16C has a Romanesque chancel and a nave covered with Angevin vaulting *(p 36);* note in the north aisle the complex pattern of vaulting with projecting keystones (16C), and to the south of the chancel the elegant seigneurial chapel, also with projecting keystones.

On the outside of the north aisle there are many lateral gable ends, frequently to be seen in the region.

ST-VIÂTRE
Pop 1 162

Michelin map **64** north of fold 19 or **238** fold 17

This smart little town in the Sologne was formerly a place of pilgrimage containing the relics of St Viâtre, a hermit who retired to the spot in 6C and, so the legend says, made himself a coffin from the trunk of an aspen tree.

Church. – The 15C transept gable is built of brick with a black diaper pattern and edged with spiral rosettes. The belltower porch shelters the 14C door.

At the chancel step stands a remarkable carved wood desk (18C) of surprising size. In the right transept are four **painted panels★** dating from the early 16C: a realistic evocation of the life of Christ and of St Viâtre.

St-Viâtre Wayside Altar. – A brick building (15C) at the north entrance to the village.

STE-CATHERINE-DE-FIERBOIS
Pop 484

Michelin map **64** southwest of fold 15 or **232** fold 35

The spirit of Joan of Arc hovers over this village which lies east of the N 10 grouped round the steep roofs and handsome slate belltower of the church which is visible to travellers and pilgrims from afar.

Church. – On 23 April 1428, following instructions given by Joan of Arc, a sword was found here, marked with five crosses; Charles Martel was supposed to have placed it there after his victory over the Saracens at Poitiers in 732. The chapel was rebuilt in 1479 and completed in the reign of Charles VIII, whose arms together with those of Anne of Brittany appear on the building. It is in the Flamboyant style with a spire 41 m - 135 ft high and an interesting door beneath a pierced pediment; it was restored in 1859.

The interior vaulting springs directly from the piers. Hanging under a glass cover on the north wall of the nave is a small but very realistic 15C Entombment. The south transept contains an unusual 15C altar; on it stands a 15C statue of St Catherine whose image is also carved on the front. Opposite is a rare confessional in the Flamboyant style, very delicately carved.

Dauphin's House (Maison du Dauphin). – 1415. The door of the house to the left of the church is flanked by two sphinxes. Charming carving on the lip of the well in the courtyard.

Boucicault Almonry. – 1415. *On the opposite side of the street to the Dauphin's House.*

Once a guest house with dormitories and a chapel dedicated to St James for pilgrims on the way to Compostela in Spain, the building is now a **museum** of local history.

STE-MAURE-DE-TOURAINE
Pop 4 016

Michelin map **68** north of folds 4, 5 or **232** fold 35

This small town occupies a sunny site on a knoll commanding the Manse Valley. Roman in origin, the settlement developed in the 6C round the tombs of St Bridget and St Maurus, then round the keep built by Fulk Nerra. The Rohan-Montbazon family were the overlords from 1492 to the Revolution.

The town is known for its busy poultry markets and its local goats' milk cheeses. A national Cheese Fair is held annually in June.

Church. – The church dates from the 11C but its original appearance was altered when it was restored in 1866. A chapel to the right of the chancel has an attractive 16C white marble Virgin by the Italian school. In the central apse there are two painted panels, one depicting the Last Supper (16C), and the other, Christ on a gold background; the relics of St Maurus are venerated here. The crypt (11C and 12C) has a curious series of archaic Romanesque arcades and a small lapidary museum.

Covered market. – The 17C covered market at the top of the town was built by the Rohan family.

STE-MAURE PLATEAU

Round trip starting from Ste-Maure *56 km - 35 miles − about 1 hour*

The plateau is dissected by the green valleys of two rivers − the Manse and the Esves − and bordered by three others − the Indre (north), the Vienne (west) and the Creuse (south). It is composed of lacustrine limestone which is easily eroded by running water; in the south there are bands of sand and shell, deposited during the Tertiary era by the Falun Sea and formerly used to improve the soil.

Ste-Maure. − See p 164.

   Leave Ste-Maure by D 59 going southeast.

The line of the road running through the valleys between limestone bluffs is often marked by a row of poplars.

Bournan. − Pop 231. The village **church** is Romanesque; it has a beautiful apse and a tower over the side chapel topped by a facetted spire.

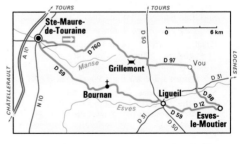

Ligueil. − Pop 2426. Ligueil is a small town built of white stone and an important dairy centre. There are a few old houses. The decorated wooden washing place, now restored, is on the edge of the town on the road to Loches (D 31).

Esves-le-Moutier. − Pop 161. The village, which lies on the south bank of the Esves, takes its name from a priory which was surrounded by a wall; the **church** (10-12C) has a massive square tower with bartizans. The interior contains a 17C wooden gilt altarpiece.

Grillemont Château. − The huge white château stands half way up a slope overlooking an attractive **valley**★ of meadows round a lake; the slopes are capped by stands of oak and pine. The huge round towers of the castle with their pepperpot roofs were built in the reign of Charles VII for Lescoet, the governor of Loches Castle; in 1765 the 15C curtain wall was replaced by magnificent Classical buildings.

SARTHE Valley

Michelin map 64 folds 1 to 3 or 232 folds 20 to 22

The River Sarthe flows slowly southwest through the beautiful Maine countryside, describing its meanders in the soft soil of the Upper Cretaceous rocks. Around Sablé the water had to make its way through a granite outcrop. The river is navigable as far Le Mans with lateral canals running parallel. Woodland alternates with meadows and fields of cereals, potatoes and cabbages.

FROM LE MANS TO SABLÉ *73 km - 45 miles − about 3 hours*

★★ **Le Mans.** − Description p 129. About 6 hours.

   Leave Le Mans by N 23.

Spay. − Description p 135. Take D 51 to Fillé.

Fillé. − Pop 744. The village is on the north bank of the Sarthe; the **church,** which was rebuilt after 1944, contains a large statue of the Virgin in glazed terracotta (late 16C).

La-Suze-sur-Sarthe. − Pop 3709. The bridge over the Sarthe provides a good view of the river, the remains of the castle (15C) and the church.

   Leave La-Suze by the D 79 going west through woods towards Fercé.

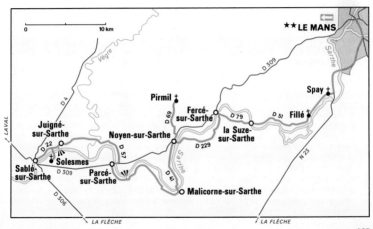

Fercé-sur-Sarthe. − Pop 458. Attractive views from the bridge and from the road up to the church.

Return across the river and turn right into V5 to St-Jean-du-Bois; turn right into D229.

The road passes a troubadour style castle (left) and provides several glimpses of the Sarthe before reaching Noyen.

Noyen-sur-Sarthe. − Pop 2029. Noyen is built in terraces on the sloping north bank overlooking the canal which at this point runs parallel to the broad Sarthe. From the bridge there is an attractive **view** of a weir, a mill, an island of poplars, a jumble of roofs and little gardens, the beach and another island.

Take D69 north to Pirmil.

Pirmil. − Pop 401. The **church**, a Romanesque building with buttresses, dates from 1165. The capitals are finely carved. The springers of the ogive vaulting are decorated with a series of figures: St Stephen, St Michael, a bishop, a priest and a grotesque head.

Return south through Noyen taking D41 to Malicorne-sur-Sarthe.

Malicorne-sur-Sarthe. − Pop 1773. Malicorne is pleasantly situated at the water's edge. From the bridge there is a pretty view of a mill and the poplars along the bank.

On the eastern side of the town, on the D133 to Mézeray, there is a working **pottery** which produces pieces in the perforated Malicorne style and also reproductions of period pieces.

The 11C **church** contains a recumbent figure of one of the lords of Chaources (chapel on the right of the nave), a *Pietà* (right transept) and an attractive 16C piscina (left wall on the nave).

Downstream, set back from the south bank of the river in a beautiful park stands the 17C **château** (altered) where Madame de Sevigné liked to stay, which belonged to the Marquise de Lavardin. The château has turrets and Mansard roofs and is surrounded by a moat which is spanned by a charming hump-back bridge.

Take D8 west towards Parcé, making a detour (V1) to the right via Dureil, which provides attractive glimpses of the River Sarthe before rejoining D8.

Parcé-sur-Sarthe. − Pop 1432. Parcé is a charming little village grouped round a Romanesque tower with a mill on the river. The old cemetery at the entrance to the village with its slim cypress trees makes a peaceful setting for the chapel with its gable belfry.

After crossing the river and the canal, turn left into D57. In Avoise take V4 to Juigné which crosses the River Vègre before joining D22; bear left.

Juigné-sur-Sarthe. − Pop 816. Juigné is a pleasant village set on a promontory which juts south across the valley. There are 16 and 17C houses and the 18C château which belonged to the Marquis of Juigné. From the church square there is a view of the river below and of Solesmes Abbey dowstream.

Solesmes − *Description p 171.*

Take D22 beside the canal and the old marble quarries to Sablé.

Sablé. − *Description p 159.*

Respect the life of the countryside
Go carefully on country roads
Protect wildlife, plants and trees.

★★ **SAUMUR**　　　　　　　　　　　　　　　　Pop 33953

Michelin map 64 fold 12 or 232 fold 33 − Local map p 127 − Facilities

Saumur is famous for its cavalry school, its wines − especially its sparkling *(mousseux)* wines − and its mushrooms; local production of mushrooms represents 70% of the national figure. These activities have been joined by the manufacture of toys and knitwear and mechanical and electrical firms. Saumur also has the largest factory making carnival masks in Europe.

Each year a tattoo using horses and motor transport is given by the Cadre Noir on the vast Place du Chardonnet *(see p 194)*. Repeat performances are given in the Riding School of the National Equitation Centre in Terrefort *(p 169)*.

An eventful history. − Charles the Bald built a fortified monastery in 9C to house the relics of St Florent who converted the region to Christianity in 4C; it was soon destroyed by the Normans. In 11C Saumur was the subject of numerous conflicts between the Count of Blois and the Count of Anjou. In 1203 the town was captured by Philippe Auguste. On several occasions the castle was destroyed and then restored or rebuilt. From the time of Louis IX (13C) Saumur shared the destiny of the House of Anjou *(see p 48)*.

In the late 16C and early 17C the town enjoyed its greatest glory. It was one of the great centres of Protestantism. Henri III gave it as a stronghold to the King of Navarre. The future Henri IV appointed as Governor Duplessis-Mornay, a great soldier, great scholar and fervent Reformer, who was known by the Roman Catholics as the Huguenot Pope. He founded a protestant academy which gained great renown. In 1611 a general assembly of the protestant churches was held there to confirm their organisation following the death of Henri IV and the departure of Sully. Louis XIII grew alarmed at the protestant danger and ordered the town walls to be demolished in 1623. The Revocation of the Edict of Nantes in 1685 dealt Saumur a fatal blow; many of the inhabitants emigrated; the temple was demolished.

Armoured Corps and Cavalry Academy (Ecole d'application de l'Arme blindée et de la Cavalerie) (AY). – In 1763 the Carabiniers Regiment, a crack corps recruited from the best horsemen in the army, was sent to Saumur. The present central building was constructed between 1767 and 1770 as their barracks. It now houses the Cavalry School which trains the elite of the French cavalry and took its modern title in 1943. Distinct from the military school is the **National Equitation Centre** (Ecole Nationale d'Equitation) which was formed in 1972 to train civilian riding instructors. The **Cadre Noir** (Black Squad) belongs to this school

(after photo J. Bénazet/Pix)

Rider of the Cadre Noir performing a croupade

which is situated at St-Hilaire-St-Florent on the Terrefort plateau near Saumur.

Saumur Cadets. – In June 1940 the officers and cadets of the Cavalry School made it a point of honour to defend the passage of the Loire. For three days, from 18 to 20 June, although inferior in number and having only training equipment they performed many heroic feats and succeeded in holding the Germans in check on a 20 km - 12 miles front between Gennes and Montsoreau.

★★ CHÂTEAU (BZ) *Time: 1 1/2 hours*

The château is compact and massive but the vertical lines of its pointed and ribbed towers lend it grace. Despite being a fortress it is decorated as if it were a country house with sculptured machicolations and balustrades at the windows overlooking the courtyard. It stands high above the Loire Valley on a sort of pedestal created by the star shaped 16C fortifications.

A succession of fortresses has been built on the promontory. The present building, which succeeds Louis IX's castle, was rebuilt at the end of 14C by Louis I, Duke of Anjou and completed by Louis II. The interior was altered in 15C by René d'Anjou and external fortifications were added at the end of 16C by Duplessis-Mornay. Under Louis XIV and Louis XV it was the residence of the Governor of Saumur; afterwards it became a prison and then barracks; now it houses two museums. From the top of the watchtower *(tour du guet)* there is a fine **panorama**★ of the town and the valleys of the Thouet (south) and the Loire (east, west).

★★ **Museum of Decorative Arts (Musée d'Arts décoratifs).** – The exhibits, which include the Lair Collection, form a fine display of works of art from the Middle Ages and the Renaissance period: Limoges enamels, alabaster and wooden sculptures, tapestries, furniture, paintings, church ornaments and a collection of faience and French porcelain (17 and 18C) together with furniture and tapestries from the same period. The 15 and 16C tapestries include the Return from the Hunt, the Coronation of Vespasian and the Capture of Jerusalem; the last two are part of the History of Titus.

★ **Equine Museum (Musée du Cheval).** – The museum depicts the history of the saddle horse and equitation in different countries down the years: collections of saddles, bits, stirrups and spurs, fine engravings referring to the Saumur Cavalry School, horse racing and famous thorough-breds (mainly from the work of George Stubbs).

ADDITIONAL SIGHTS

★ **Old town (BY).** – The narrow twisting streets between the castle and the bridge still follow their original line; in some areas the old houses have been preserved while in others new constructions have been built in the medieval style or are resolutely modern but full of surprises (south of St Peter's Church).

Along the main shopping street, Rue St-Jean, and in the square, **Place St-Pierre,** half-timbered houses and 18C mansions with wrought-iron balconies stand side by side. The new market in the town (1982) blends with the older styles.

★ **St Peter's Church (St-Pierre – BY).** – The church is Romanesque except for the west front which collapsed in 17C and was rebuilt. The beautiful Romanesque door *(illustration p 36)* in the south transept lead into the interior which is hung with two series of 16C **tapestries**★ depicting the life of St Peter and the life of St Florent (starting on the left side of the nave). Regular concerts of organ music.

★ **Town Hall (BY H).** – Only the lefthand section of the building is old (16C). Originally the Loire flowed past the foundations and the building was a bridge head and part of the town walls, hence its military aspect. The façade facing the courtyard, however, is not at all military; it is in the Gothic-Renaissance transitional style with some fine carving.

★ **Church of Our Lady of Nantilly (BZ).** – This is a fine Romanesque building. Louis XI, who had a great devotion to the Virgin, added the right aisle; his oratory is used as a baptismal chapel. A pillar on the left in the same aisle, bears an epitaph composed by King René d'Anjou for his nurse Tiphaine. Opposite stands the enamelled cross which belonged to Giles, Archbishop of Tyre and Keeper of the Seals under Louis IX.

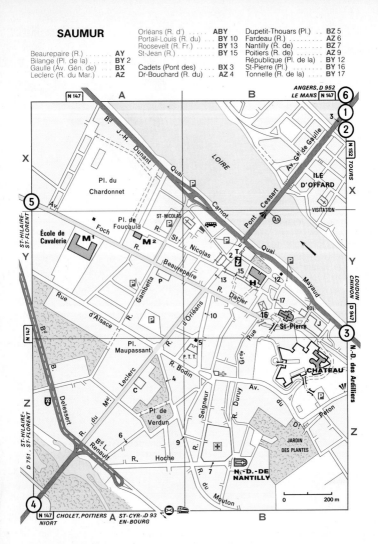

SAUMUR

Beaurepaire (R.) ...... **AY**	Orléans (R. d') ..... **ABY**	Dupetit-Thouars (Pl.) .. **BZ** 5
Bilange (Pl. de la) ..... **BY** 2	Portail-Louis (R. du) ... **BY** 10	Fardeau (R.) .... **AZ** 6
Gaulle (Av. Gén. de) .. **BX**	Roosevelt (R. Fr.) .... **BY** 13	Nantilly (R. de) ...... **BZ** 7
Leclerc (R. du Mar.) .... **AZ**	St-Jean (R.) .... **BY** 15	Poitiers (R. de) ...... **AZ** 9
		République (Pl. de la) . **BY** 12
	Cadets (Pont des) .... **BX** 3	St-Pierre (Pl.) .... **BY** 16
	Dr-Bouchard (R. du) .. **AZ** 4	Tonnelle (R. de la) .... **BY** 17

The 12C painted wooden statue of Our Lady of Nantilly was placed in the apse on the right of the chancel.

There are fine **tapestries**★★ dating from 15 and 16C except for eight in the nave which were made at Aubusson in 17C and show scenes from the life of Christ and the Virgin. There is a Tree of Jesse in the left transept and the eighteen capitals are of interest. The organ case, which is supported by telamones, dates from 1690.

★ Cavalry Museum (AY M¹). – Entrance in Avenue Foch.

The very rich collection of souvenirs traces the history of the school and the heroic deeds of the French cavalry and the armoured corps since 18C.

The exhibits include ornamental swords inlaid with mother-of-pearl, ebony or tortoiseshell and incised sabres which belonged to Egyptian Mamelukes or to marshals and generals of the French Empire: two damascened sabres which were the property of Kellermann, pistols which belonged to Augereau and Daumesnil, the baton of Brune and various items of equipment used by Kléber and Bertrand.

The uniforms of Napoleon's Grand Army and the Imperial Guard are illustrated by a collection of Sèvres and Meissen porcelain figures and a series of helmets, cuirasses and sabres which were used by dragoons and hussars.

It is interesting to note the names of some of those men who served in the cavalry of the African Army between 1830 and 1962: Bugeaud, Gallieni, Charles de Foucault, who was an officer before he became a missionary, Lyautey, de Lattre de Tassigny.

Finally the history of the French cavalry is traced from 1870 through the two world wars and the Indo-Chinese and Algerian campaigns.

★ Museum of the Armoured Corps (Musée des Blindés – AY M²).

It contains over 150 vehicles showing the development of the Armoured Corps, the modern cavalry, since 1918.

The lefthand gallery presents French equipment including one of the first light tanks to appear on the battle field, the 1918 Renault tank, surrounded by American armoured vehicles used in the liberation of Europe.

The righthand gallery contains foreign equipment: British tanks, type T34 Soviet tanks and German 1939-45 Panzers.

St-Hilaire-St-Florent. – 2 km - 1 mile northwest by ⑤ on the plan, D 751.

The village consists of one long street straggling at the foot of the hill beside the River Thouet. It is a suburb of Saumur devoted to the production of a famous sparkling white wine made by the Champagne method; on either side of the road there is one cellar after another (all the famous makes are open to visitors for tasting).

★ National Equitation Centre. — The centre was opened in 1972 on the Terrefort plateau; it consists of several units each comprising a granary where foodstuffs are stored, a large airy riding school and stabling for 450 horses with harness rooms and showers. The system is highly automated.

In 1984 the **Cadre Noir** (Black Squad) was established here. The great riding school can hold 1 200 seated spectators.

Mushroom Museum. — *On the western edge of the city, 2 km - 1 mile beyond the wine cellars.*

The ancient tufa quarries which pit the hillsides round Saumur are extensively used for cultivating mushrooms which need humidity and a constant temperature (between 11% and 14%C). Muhsrooms have been grown in the quarries since the time of Napoleon I; production is now on an industrial scale and occupies 800 km - 497 miles of galleries yielding some 120 000 tonnes per annum.

The various methods of culture are presented in a working environment; the oldest method in mushroom beds is being replaced more and more by more modern techniques in wooden crates or plastic bags.

Church of Our Lady of Ardilliers. — *On the eastern edge of the city, Quai L.-Mayaud by ③ on the plan, D 947.*

This beautiful 17C building is one of the most popular places of pilgrimage in France. Devotion to Our Lady of Ardilliers began to develop in the reign of François I owing to the discovery of a miraculous statue on this spot by a farm labourer in the last century but it reached its height in 17C when the number of pilgrims exceeded 10 000 a year.

EXCURSIONS

★ Boumois Château. — *7 km - 4 1/2 miles northwest by ⑥ on the plan. Description p 71.*

Bagneux Dolmen. — *2 km - 1 mile south by ④ on the plan, N 147; in front of Bagneux Church turn left into D 160.*

The Great Dolmen is situated in the village itself. It is one of the most remarkable megalithic monuments in Europe. It measures 20 m - 22 yds long and 7 m - 8 yds wide and consists of 16 vertical stones forming a passage and supporting a roof 3 m - 12 ft high which is composed of four capstones; one of them is broken and is held up by an interior prop.

St-Cyr-en-Bourg. — Pop 1772. *8 km - 5 miles south by D 93.*

The vine growers of Saumur **(les Vignerons de Saumur)** conduct the whole wine-making process, from the grape to the finished product, in a series of underground galleries reaching 25 m - 82 ft below the ground; a motorised vehicle circulates in the galleries. There is a commentary and wine tasting in a special chamber.

SAVONNIÈRES
Pop 1813

Michelin map 64 fold 14 or 232 fold 35 (2.5 km - 1 1/2 miles east of Villandry — Local map p 122

The church has a beautiful Romanesque doorway decorated with animals and doves.

Petrifying Caves. — *On the western edge of the town on the road to Villandry, D 7.*

The caves were formed in the Secondary Era. In 12C they were used as quarries and then partially flooded with water. The continuing infiltration of water saturated with limestone is slowly creating stalactites, pools and curtains. There is a reconstruction of the prehistoric fauna and a **museum of petrification** with lithographic stones and 19C copper matrices.

Wine tasting takes place in the caves.

SEGRÉ
Pop 7 416

Michelin map 63 south of fold 9 or 232 fold 18

The schist houses of Segré cascade down the slope to the river which is bordered by quays and spanned by picturesque bridges.

The town is the capital of the Segréen, a region of woods and meadows devoted to mixed farming — crops and livestock, and has given its name to a high grade iron ore.

Old Bridge. — The arch describes a hump back over the River Oudon. Attractive views of the old parts of the town.

St Joseph's Chapel. — Views of the old town and the Oudon Valley.

EXCURSIONS

★ La Lorie Château. — *2 km - 1 mile southeast; signpost on the road to Angers.*

La Lorie is an imposing 18C château approached by a long avenue of trees which meet overhead and surrounded by formal French gardens.

A dry moat surrounds a square courtyard which is bordered on three side by ranges of buildings with white tufa ties; a statue of Minerva "the Bearer of Peace" adorns the central range, which was built in 17C by René Le Pelletier, Provost General of Anjou; the château's imposing dimensions are due to the additioh of the two wings and the symmetrical outbuildings.

The same nobility of line and form is to be found in the interior: the great gallery decorated with beautiful Chinese vases, the late 18C marble saloon, the adjoining chapel and the 18C woodwork in the dining room. The great Salon is the most unusual; it is sumptuously decorated with Sablé marble and was designed by Italian artists in 1779; the musicians played in the overhead rotunda.

Le Bourg d'Iré; Nyoiseau. – *Round trip of 21 km - 13 miles – leave Segré by D 923 going southwest towards Candé; beyond the level crossing turn right into D 181.*

Le Bourg d'Iré. – Pop 911. *8 km - 5 miles west.* From the bridge there is a most attractive **view** of the River Verzée.

> *Return to the northern edge of the village and take D 219 north to Noyant-la-Gravoyère, a mining town; turn right into D 775; after 1 km - 1/2 mile turn left to Nyoiseau.*

The road runs through a schist gorge, partially flooded by small lakes which make this the most picturesque section of the excursion. The land surrounding the two lakes – St-Blaise and La Corbinière – has been laid out as a **leisure park.**

Nyoiseau. – Pop 1 562. The village – its name is a corruption of Niosellum meaning little nest – is perched on the slopes of the Oudon Valley. Down by the river are the remains of a Benedictine Abbey for women.

> *Return to Segré by D 71 and D 775.*

Raguin Château. – *8.5 km - 5 miles southwest by D 923; in St-Gemmes-d'Andigné bear left into D 183.*

The old 15C castle was replaced c1600 by Guy du Bellay, son of Pierre du Bellay (cousin of the poet), with a Renaissance style building.

Although a marshal in the king's army, du Bellay had a taste for luxury and he made Raguin a luxurious and elegant château. When his son, Antoine, married in 1648, he had the first floor salon and another room fitted with wainscots and had the walls and ceiling entirely redecorated; in the second room, "Chambre des Amours", the cherubs play with the initials of the newly-wed couple.

After the death of his father and then of his wife in 1666, Antoine du Bellay sold the château which changed hands several times.

SELLES-SUR-CHER   Pop 4656

Michelin map 🔢 fold 18 or 🔢 fold 16

Selles-sur-Cher is prettily situated in a bend of the River Cher; the towers of its castle are reflected in the river. The town developed round the abbey which was founded by St Eusice a hermit who lived in that spot. Only the abbey church now remains.

SIGHTS

St Eusice' Church. – The church, which dated from 12 and 15C, was burned by Coligny in 1562; it was partially restored in 17C and then more thoroughly in the last century. The façade, which is almost entirely Romanesque, has re-used the columns and capitals from an earlier church which was destroyed by the Normans in about 903.

The **chevet,** which is well built, is ornamented with two friezes of figures; those below the windows are rough, simple and heavy but those above are better proportioned and more elegant. The lower frieze depicts scenes from the New Testament; the upper one illustrates the life of St Eusice.

Near the north wall are low relief sculptures of the Labours of the Months; higher up and further to the right there is a beautiful Visitation, protected by the transept chapel. It is however all very worn.

In the north wall, which was built late in 13C, there is a charming door decorated with carved capitals supporting tori separated by a strand of flowers and wild rose leaves.

The crypt contains the tomb of St Eusice (6C).

Castle. – Hidden on the south bank of the Cher are the remains of an austere 13C fortress, within a rectangular moated enclosure, approached by four bridges. In contrast, framing the present entrance on the east side are two light 17C buildings joined together by a long arcaded wall, which is pierced by oculi and topped by a parapet walk. These were built by **Philippe de Béthune,** Sully's brother *(see p 174)* who bought the castle in 1604.

Beyond the magnificent cedar and mulberry trees of the inner park, in the old part on the west side, is the gilded pavilion **(Pavillon Doré),** an elegant building, decorated in the Italian Renaissance style, which Philippe de Béthune introduced into the old 13C fortress. It has magnificent gilded chimneys, wall paintings and coloured coffered ceilings; all have retained their lustre. Also on view are the study containing souvenirs of the Count of Chambord (1820-83), pretender to the French throne after the death of Charles X, the little oratory and the bedroom. While living in the gilded pavilion, Philippe de Béthune had a new château built in the contemporary style in red brick outlined in white stone. Here grandeur and generous proportions replace the intimate charm of the gilded pavilion. The tour includes the Guard room with its great chimney, the bedroom of Maria Sobieska, the queen of Poland, in which the bed with its twisted columns stands on a dais, and the attractive games room.

Local History and Folklore Museum. – The exhibits are varied: documents about Selles' past, tools used by vine growers, basket makers, coopers and watermen, and an interesting section on the preparation of gunflint, a thriving industry in the region from the middle of 18C until the invention of the percussion cap *(see also Meusnes p 171 and Luçay-le-Mâle p 185).*

EXCURSIONS

Châtillon-sur-Cher. – Pop 1 293. *5 km - 3 miles west by N 75 towards St-Aignan and a turning to the left.*
The little village stands on the north slope of the Cher Valley. **St Blaise's Church** contains (left wall of chancel) a **panel★** by the school of Leonardo da Vinci showing St Catherine between two cherubs: the treatment of the hands, a little mannered but very attractive, and the facial expression are typical of da Vinci's style.
A statue of St Vincent, patron of vine-growers, is surrounded by the batons of their brotherhood which are carried in their processions.

Meusnes. – Pop 1 017. *6.5 km - 4 miles southwest by D 956 briefly towards Valençay and then D 17 west.*
The **church** is in the pure Romanesque style. There is a triumphal arch in the transept surmounted by three charming openwork arcatures. Several beautiful 15 and 16C statues have been reinstated.
A small **gunflint museum,** housed in the town hall, describes this industry which flourished in the region for three hundred years.

Chabris. – Pop 2 589. *8 km - 5 miles southeast by D 51.*
Chabris, which is Roman in origin, is set on the south bank of the River Cher; it produces good wine and goat cheese.
The **church,** which is dedicated to St Phalier, a 5C hermit who died in Chabris, is a very old place of pilgrimage (feast day third Sunday in September).
The chevet is decorated with unusual primitive sculptures of fantastic animals, the Annunciation and sections of stone laid in a diaper pattern which come from an earlier church which was rebuilt in 15C. The porch, which has a double arcade and gallery, shelters a Gothic door with carved panels. The chancel contains two naive panels depicting the life and miracles of St Phalier who was thought to help women conceive.
The **crypt,** which is probably 11C, contains the sarcophagus of the saint; it takes the form of a confessio opening off a passage to enable the faithful to venerate the relics.

★★ SERRANT Château

Michelin map 🔲 fold 20 or 🔲🔲🔲 fold 31 (2 km - 1 mile northeast of St-Georges-sur-Loire)

Although built over a period of three centuries, 16 to 18C, this sumptuous moated mansion has great unity of style. Its massive domed towers and the contrast between the dark schist and the white tufa give it considerable character.
Serrant Château was begun in 1546 by Charles de Brie, bought by Hercule de Rohan, Duke of Montbazon, in 1596, and sold in 1636 to Guillaume Bautru whose granddaughter married the Marquis of Vaubrun, Lieutenant-General of the king's army. On the death of her husband, who was killed beside Turenne at the Battle of Altenheim, the Marchioness continue the building work until 1705. She commissioned J. Hardouin-Mansart to build the beautiful chapel to the memory of her husband and Coysevox to design the white marble mausoleum. In 1749 her daughter, the Duchess of Estrées, sold the estate to an Irishman, Francis Walsh, who was made Count of Serrant in 1755 by Louis XV as a reward for his family's support for the Stuart cause; they provided the ship which carried Bonnie Prince Charlie to Moidart in 1745. Two generations earlier another Walsh had enabled James II to flee to exile in France. The château has remained in the family and now belongs to Prince Jean-Charles de Ligne.

Tour. – The **apartments** are magnificently furnished. Sumptuous Flemish tapestries hang in the dining room. Of particular note are the great staircase, the coffered ceilings on the first floor, the library with its ten thousand volumes and the state rooms where both Louis XIV and Napoleon have been received. There are many works of art: Flemish and Brussels tapestries, a very beautiful Italian cabinet, a bust of the Empress Marie-Louise by Canova, portraits.

SOLESMES   Pop 1 224

Michelin map 🔲 folds 1, 2 or 🔲🔲🔲 fold 20 – Local map p 165

A few miles upstream from Sablé lies Solesmes which has achieved fame through the Benedictine Order. From the north bank of the Sarthe and from the bridge there is an impressive **view★** of the north front of the abbey, a dark wall, about 50 m - 164 ft high, which was built at the end of 19C in the Romanesque-Gothic style and is reflected in the stream. Next to it stands the 18C building of the earlier priory.

Under the Rule of St Benedict. – The Benedictine priory of Solesmes was founded in 1010 by the Lord of Sablé and served by monks from St-Pierre-la-Couture in Le Mans *(p 134).* It grew rapidly and by the early 16C was very rich; in 17C it fell into decline and was taken over by the monks of St-Maur.
The Revolution brought ruin but a new community was established in 1833 by a priest from Sablé, Dom Guéranger, and in 1837 the abbey became the headquarters of the Benedictine Order in France. In 1901 a law was passed expelling all religious orders from France but they returned when it was repealed twenty years later.
Since then the name of Solesmes has been linked with the restoration of the liturgy and the revival of the Gregorian chant in France.
The abbey **services** to which the public is admitted demonstrate the beauty of the liturgy celebrated in Benedictine monasteries.

St Peter's Abbey. — *Only the abbey church (in the main courtyard) is open to the public.*

The **church★** comprises the nave and transept which date from 11 and 15C and the domical vaulted chancel which was added in 1865. The famous groups of sculpture, which are known as the **"saints of Solesmes"★★**, are to be found in the transept.

The works in the right transept were commissioned by Prior Guillaume Cheminart: a monumental Entombment (1496) with a beautiful representation of Mary Magdalene at prayer; on the left a terracotta *Pietà* from an earlier period.

The works in the left transept, which is dedicated to the Virgin, were commissioned by Prior Jean Bougler between 1530 and 1556; the composition is rather crowded but the detail is interesting. The main scene is the Entombment of the Virgin; Jean Bougler is shown holding one end of the shroud; overhead are the four Fathers of the Church and the Assumption. On the sides are Jesus among the Doctors (left) and scenes from the life of the Virgin (right).

MICHELIN GUIDES

The Red Guides (hotels and restaurants)

    Benelux — Deutschland — España Portugal — main cities Europe — France — Great Britain and Ireland — Italia

The Green Guides (beautiful scenery, buildings and scenic routes)

    Austria — Canada — England : The West Country — Germany — Greece — Italy — New England — Portugal — Scotland — Spain — Switzerland London — New York City — Paris — Rome

    ...and 6 guides on France.

The SOLOGNE

Michelin map 64 folds 8, 9, 18, 19 or 238 folds 4, 5, 16, 17

The Sologne is a paradise for hunters and fishermen, an immense flat tract of land (504 000 ha - 1 946 sq miles) extending to the horizon and composed of heathland, forests (40% of the whole area) and many solitary pools.

The Sologne, which lies between the Loire and the Cher, is bordered to the east by the Sancerre Hills and to the west by a curved line running north from Romorantin via Mur-de-Sologne, Cheverny and Chambord to La Ferté-St-Cyr.

The Sologne terrain, which is composed of clay and sand, slopes very gently westwards as can be deduced from the direction in which the main rivers — Cosson, Beuvron and Sauldre — flow.

Development. — In the past the region was a desolate waste ravaged by fevers which arose from the stagnant water of the huge lake but it changed radically in the reign of Napoleon III who had acquired the Lamotte-Beuvron estate and instigated improvements. The Sologne Central Committee started to plant birch and Norway pine trees, to dig canals, to construct roads, to clear and drain the pools and to improve the soil.

The fevers disappeared, the population increased: the Sologne acquired something like its present appearance.

The Sologne countryside. — The area under cultivation is about 200 000 ha - 772 sq miles. Maize is an excellent crop because it feeds the livestock and provides good cover for the game thus reconciling the interests of both farmers and hunters. The fodder produced feeds 50 000 cattle and 10 000 sheep. Many farms have taken up pheasant rearing or other activities connected with the provision of game. Wherever the farmer has been able to drain the land, one finds fruit orchards and also farms involved in the intensive rearing of cattle, sheep and goats.

The region round Contres produces vegetables and fruit which are sold locally or sent to the central markets or to the canneries. More asparagus is grown in the Sologne and in the Loire Valley near Blois than anywhere else in France; the cultivation of strawberries has become very specialised leading to an increase in production. Along the Cher Valley and in the neighbourhood of Blois the production of wine has improved owing to the introduction of the Sauvignon grape. Markets are held in certain small towns such as Gien and Sully and Lamotte-Beuvron which is the geographical centre of the Sologne.

The traditional local industries (sawmills, packaging materials) have been joined by other manufactures: porcelain at Lamotte-Beuvron, armaments at La Ferté-St-Aubin and Salbris, sports cars at Romorantin, poultry farming at Theillay and the cultivation of dahlias on a vast scale at Villeherviers.

The **forests** are also a source of revenue in the Sologne producing wood, mushrooms, bees and game: ducks on the open water; partridge, pheasant and hare in the copses and on the fallow land. The Sologne is well described by Maurice Genevoix in *Raboliot,* the story of a poacher.

(Photo M. Varin/Pitch)

Woodcock in the Sologne

TOWNS AND SIGHTS

The Sologne is at its most attractive in the early autumn when the russet of the falling leaves mingles with the evergreen of the Norway pines above a carpet of bracken and purple heather broken by the occasional melancholy pool. The bursts of firing which announce the hunting season can detract a little from the charm of the region. The nature of the Sologne is best appreciated by taking a walk.

Owing to the many enclosures, prohibited areas and animal traps it is best to keep to the marked paths such as the GR31 and the GR3c *(see p 10)*. Another picturesque trip in the Sologne is the **train** which runs between Romorantin and Salbris on a metric railway operated by the "Compagnie du Blanc Argent".

The "Sologne Scenic Route", the D922 between Romorantin and La Ferté-St-Aubin, passes through typical Sologne landscapes.

Argent-sur-Sauldre. – *Description p 54.*

Aubigny-sur-Nère. – *Description p 55.*

★ **Blancafort.** – *Description p 63.*

Bracieux. – Pop 1 150. Bracieux is a smart village on the border of the Sologne and the region round Blois. The houses are grouped round the 16C market on the south bank of the Beuvron which is spanned by a picturesque bridge.

Cerdon. – *Description p 54.*

★★ **Chambord Château.** – *Description p 74.*

Chaumont-sur-Tharonne. – Pop 905. The line of the former ramparts can be traced in the lay-out of the town which is picturesquely situated round its 15-16C church on a bluff in the centre of the Sologne region.

★★ **Cheverny Château.** – *Description p 88.*

La Ferté-St-Aubin. – *Description p 101.*

Fontaines-en-Sologne. – Pop 568. The **church,** which dates for the most part from 12C, shows how widespread was the Angevin style *(see p 36):* flat chevet, nave with remarkable domed vaulting. It was fortified in 17C. Beside the church there are half-timbered houses with roofs of small flat tiles, commonly found in the region.

Gy-en-Sologne. – Pop 444. Tour of a typical Sologne cottage, the **Locature de la Straize** (16C).

Lanthenay Church. – The church contains a painting of the Virgin between John the Baptist and St Sebastian, dating from 1523 and attributed to Timoteo Viti from Urbino who influenced Raphael in his early days. 17C canvas of the dead Christ with the Virgin and St John. 16C wooden painted statues of St Francis and St Claire.

Lassay-sur-Croisne. – *Description p 111.*

★ **Le Moulin Château.** – *Description p 111.*

Neuvy. – Pop 279. Neuvy stands on the southern edge of the Boulogne Forest on the north bank of the River Beuvron. The **church** stands on its own in its graveyard near a farm built of half timber and half brick on the opposite bank. It was partially rebuilt in 1525. The rood beam supports 15C statues; in the right transept there is a 17C painting of the dead Christ supported by two angels.

★ **Romorantin-Lanthenay.** – *Description p 158.*

St-Viâtre. – *Description p 164.*

Salbris. – Pop 6 134. Facilities. Salbris on the south bank of the Sauldre, is a busy crossroads and a good centre for excursions into the forest. **St George's Church** was built of stone and brick in 15 and 16C; the furnishings are 17C. The centre of the retable on the high altar is occupied by a *Pietà* (16C). The transept chapels are remarkable for the coats of arms of the donors on the key stones of the vault and the attractive pendant sculptures representing the Three Wise Men and the Virgin and Child (south) and the symbols of the Evangelists (north).

Selles-St-Denis. – Pop 1 172. The village lies on the north bank of the Sauldre. The **church,** which dates from 12 and 15C and has side chapels and an apse in the Flamboyant style, is decorated with 14C murals of the life of St Genoulph to whom it is dedicated.

Villeherviers. – Pop 342. The village is set among vineyards and asparagus fields in the broad valley of the Sauldre. There is Plantagenet vaulting in the 13C **church.**

Villesavin Château. – *Description p 189.*

SUÈVRES

The ancient Gallo-Roman city of Sodobrium hides its picturesque façades below the noisy main road (N 152) on the north bank of the Loire. **St Christopher's Church** beside the road is entered through a huge porch *(caquetoire)* where the parishioners could pause to engage in conversation. The stonework is decorated with various fishbone and chevron patterns characteristic of the Merovingian period.

The houses at n° 9 and n° 14b in Rue Pierre-Pouteau date from 15C. Turn right into a picturesque dead-end, Rue des Moulins, running beside the stream which is spanned by many footbridges and reflects the tamarisk and weeping willow trees. *Go back to the turning and cross the stone bridge.* The washing place is at the corner of Rue St-Simon; on either side of the street are traces of an old fortified gate. Further on through the trees (left) one sees the two-storey Romanesque tower of **St Lubin's Church** with its attractive south door (15C).

★ SULLY-SUR-LOIRE

Sully Castle commanded one of the Loire crossings. Its history is dominated by four great names: Maurice de Sully, Bishop of Paris who commissioned the building of Notre-Dame, Joan of Arc, Sully and Voltaire.

The Determination of Joan of Arc. — In 1429 Sully belonged to Georges de la Trémoille, a favourite of Charles VII. The King was living in the castle when Joan of Arc defeated the English at Patay and captured their leader, the famous Talbot, Earl of Shrewsbury. Joan hastened to Sully and at last persuaded the indolent monarch to be crowned at Rheims. She returned to the castle in 1430 after her check before Paris, and there felt the jealousy and hostility of La Trémoille gaining influence over the King. She was detained almost as if a prisoner but escaped to continue the struggle.

Sully's capacity for work. — In 1602 Maximilien de Béthune, the Lord of Rosny, bought the château and the barony for 330 000 *livres*. Henri IV made him Duke of Sully and it was under this name that the great Minister passed into history.

Sully had begun to serve his King at the age of twelve. He was a great soldier, the best artilleryman of his time and a consummate administrator. He was active in all the departments of State: Finance, Agriculture, Industry and Public Works.

A glutton for work, Sully began his day at 3am and kept four secretaries busy writing his memoirs. He entitled them: *Wise and Royal Economies of State.* Fearing indiscretions he had a printing press set up in one of the towers of the château and the work was printed on the spot, although it bore the address of a printer in Amsterdam. The old Duke had a mania for orderly accounts. Every tree to be planted, every table to be made, every ditch to be cleaned was the subject of a legal contract.

Sully had an awkward character and he often went to law, especially with the Bishop of Orléans. Since the Middle Ages it had been the custom for the Lord of Sully to carry the Bishop's chair on the day of his entry into Orléans. The former Minister, very much the ducal peer and a Protestant into the bargain, refused to comply with this custom. Finally he obtained permission to be represented at the ceremony.

Sully embellished his castle. The building originally stood on the Loire itself. He separated it from the river by an embankment, dug moats which he filled by deflecting a nearby river, laid out the park and enlarged the buildings.

Sully's career came to an end with the assassination of Henri IV in 1610. The Minister retired but he assured Louis XIII of his loyalty and encouraged his co-religionists to do the same. Richelieu made him a Marshal of France.

The spirit of Voltaire (18C). — Exiled from Paris by the Regent for his biting epigrams, Voltaire spent several seasons with the Duke of Sully who surrounded himself with philosophers and free thinkers. Voltaire was 22. His gaiety and wit made him the life and soul of the castle. In the shade of the park among the trees which he described as "carved upon by urchins and lovers" young François-Marie-Arouet (he had not then adopted his pen name) indulged in flirtations which he transferred to the stage. A theatre was built for him in the castle where he produced his tragedies and comedies with his friends playing the roles.

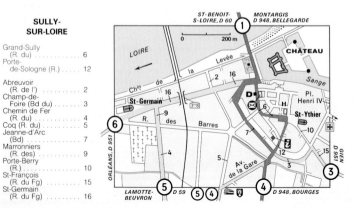

★ CASTLE (CHÂTEAU) *time: 3/4 hour*

The castle is an imposing feudal fortress dating largely from before 1360. The keep (early 15C), which faces the Loire is rectangular, with round towers at the four corners. The wing added to the living quarters by Sully was begun in late 15C and remodelled in the following centuries.

One can visit several apartments in the 14C keep, notably the large guardroom on the ground floor, another immense hall (portraits of the Dukes of Sully) on the first floor where Voltaire's plays were performed and the oratory in which there is an excellent copy of the funerary group showing Sully and his wife (original at Nogent-le-Rotrou). Finally, on the second floor, there is the unique chamber with its famous timber roof. The apartment, unfortunately, is cut in two by the chimneystack. The visit ends with a tour of the sentry walk facing the Loire.

★ ★ **The timber roof.** — The upper hall of the keep has one of the finest timber roofs that have come down to us from the Middle Ages. Dating from 1363 and keel shaped it is as good as new. There are no woodworms, no rot to attract flies and, therefore, no cobwebs. This is due to the type of wood, chestnut, and the great care taken by the carpenters of the day. Trees aged fifty to a hundred years were chosen, stripped of their bark while still standing, felled in winter when the moon is on the wane and squared off and sawn up into logs. The beams were then stored in a damp place or weathered under water for several years to wash out the sap, dried under cover in the open air for several more years, blackened with smoke and coated with disinfectant to make them rot-proof and finally assembled in such a way that air could circulate freely.

Renaissance pavilion. — This contains Sully's study and, on the first floor, the great saloon with its painted ceiling which was the Minister's bedroom.

ADDITIONAL SIGHTS

Collegiate Church of St-Ythier (Collégiale de St-Ythier). — Built in 1529, the Chapel of Notre-Dame-de-Pitié was enlarged in 1605; it then became the Collegiate Church of St-Ythier. There are two 16C **stained glass windows**: the one at the end of the south aisle shows pilgrims on their way to St James's shrine in Santiago de Compostela; the second showing the Tree of Jesse with the Virgin and Child Jesus is in the central apse. In the north aisle is a 16C *Pietà* above the high altar.

Renaissance House (D). — Above the façade decorated with medallions and pilasters, the dormer windows in the roof with twin bays are surrounded by caryatids.

St-Germain. — The 13C church has been destroyed several times over the centuries and was last restored in 1944. Its remarkable fine spire, 38 m - 125 ft high, has been re-erected in 1960.

★ TALCY   Pop 241

Michelin map 64 fold 7 or 238 fold 3

Talcy is a remote village in the Beauce; the road south to Mer on the Loire is bordered here and there with rose trees.

★ **Castle.** — The castle is austere in appearance but interesting for its literary associations, for its furniture and, on a more humble level, for two little masterpieces: the dovecot and the wine press.

This 13C manorial dwelling was bought in 1571 by a rich Florentine, Bernardo Salviati, a cousin of Catherine de' Medici. The Salviati family so famous in literary history retained the estate until 1667. Bernardo was the father of Cassandra, to whom **Ronsard** *(see p 158)* dedicated so many sonnets, and of Giovanni Salviati, whose daughter, Diana, similarly inspired the young Agrippa d'Aubigné. Cassandra's daughter married Guillaume de Musset and one of her direct descendants was the great poet Alfred de Musset (1810-57).

Fine furniture (16-18C) and Gothic tapestries soften the severity of the feudal halls which are roofed in the French style with fine Renaissance beams. The 15C keep with its double doorway (postern and carriage gate) has two corner turrets and a crenelated sentry walk which looks medieval but dates from 1520. The fenestration at the first floor level was modified in the 18C.

The first courtyard owes its charm to a graceful gallery and an attractive well. In the second courtyard is a large 16C **dovecot**; its 1 500 pigeon holes are admirably preserved.

The old **wine press** is still in working order after 400 years of use. The carefully balanced mechanism enables two men to obtain ten barrels of juice at a single pressing.

Times and charges for admission to sights described in the guide are listed at the end of the guide.

The sights are listed alphabetically in this section either under the place — town, village or area — in which they are situated or under their proper name.

Every sight for which there are times and charges is indicated by the symbol ⊘ in the margin in the main part of the guide.

Michelin map 🆖 fold 15 or 🔲🔲 folds 35, 36 and 🔲🔲 fold 13 — Local map p 122

Tours, the capital of Touraine, is traditionally a centre for excursions into the châteaux country but it has many attractions of its own: its clear light, the orderly street plan, the squares and gardens, the churches, monasteries and museums.

HISTORICAL NOTES

Gallo-Roman Metropolis. — During the Roman period the settlement known as Turons became a prosperous and free city with the name Caesarodunum (Caesar's Hill) and extended over the plain (100 ha - 250 acres). Late in 3C however invasions obliged the inhabitants to take refuge in the present cathedral district which was the administrative and economic centre containing the baths and the arena. A wall was built to enclose the city and traces of it can still be seen near the castle and in the nearby street, Rue des Ursulines.

In 375 the town, which had reverted to its former name Turones, became the seat of government of the third Lyonnaise, a province comprising Touraine, Maine, Anjou and Armorica.

St Martin's City (4C). — The man who became the greatest bishop of the Gauls started as a legionary in the Roman army. At the gates of Amiens the young soldier met a beggar shivering in the cold wind. He cut his cloak in two with his sword and gave half to the poor man. The following night in a dream he saw Christ wearing half his cloak; he was baptised and began his mission. At Ligugé in Poitou he founded the first monastery on Gallic soil. His faith and charity spread his fame far afield. In 372 the people of Tours begged him to become their bishop. Although Christianity had arrived in Gaul a century earlier, paganism was still rife. St Martin fought it with vigour; idols, statues and temples were systematically destroyed. The iconoclast was, however, also a builder and he covered Touraine with churches and chapels. The monastery of Marmoutier was built at the gates of Tours.

St Martin died in Candes in 397. The monks of Ligugé and Marmoutier quarrelled over his body; while the men of Poitou slept, the men of Tours transferred the saint's body to a boat and rowed hard upstream for home. Then a miracle occurred; although it was November, the trees turned green, the plants burst into flower and the birds sang — a St Martin's summer. In 471 a basilica was built over his tomb; it measures 50 m × 20 m - 164 ft × 66 ft and has 120 columns and 32 windows.

A popular pilgrimage — In 496 or 498 **Clovis** came to St Martin's Basilica to meditate and promised to be baptised if he defeated the Alamanni. He returned in 507 during the war against the Visigoths and commanded his army not to despoil the territory of Tours out of respect for St Martin. After his victory at Vouillé, near Poitiers, he did not forget to visit the basilica on which he bestowed many presents in thanksgiving. For the occasion he wore the insignia of the consulship which the Emperor of the East had conferred on him. These visits of Clovis' were the beginning of the special protection which the Merovingians accorded to the prestigious sanctuary.

In 563 a young deacon in poor health, who was heir to a noble Gallo-Roman family in the Arverne (later Auvergne), visited St Martin's tomb. His name was Gregory. He was cured and settled in Tours. Owing to his piety and probity, coupled with the renown of several of his relatives (he was the great nephew of St Nizier of Lyons) he was elected bishop in 573. **Gregory of Tours** produced many written works, especially the **History of the Franks** which has been the main source of information about the Merovingian period; he also wrote eight Books of Miracles and the Lives of the Fathers. Under his enlightened direction the town developed and an abbey grew up round St Martin's Basilica. Gregory died in 594.

For many years pilgrims had been flocking to Tours for cure or counsel. The shrine of St Martin at Tours acquired a great reputation which was assisted by skilful propaganda about the numerous miracles which had taken place round his tomb. Among the ordinary pilgrims in search of the supernatural were kings and princes and powerful lords seeking absolution for their many crimes and abuses. The sanctuary was also a place of asylum, an inviolable refuge for both the persecuted and the criminal.

The popularity of the cult of St Martin brought the abbey great riches; its estates, the result of many donations, extended as far as Berry and Bordelais.

Royal favour was expressed in the abbey being granted the right to mint money.

Abbot Alcuin. — While remaining a great religious centre, at the end of 8C Tours became an intellectual and artistic centre also under the influence of Alcuin, a monk of Anglo-Saxon origin, originally from York in England, who had met **Charlemagne** in Italy and accompanied him back to France. The French king wanted to raise the level of learning in his kingdom and he opened a large number of schools to train a well-informed clergy capable in its turn of instructing the population. At his palace in Aix-la-Chapelle he organised a meeting of a group of scholars led by the great figure of Alcuin, the inspirer of the Carolingian Renaissance. After serving energetically at court Alcuin decided to retire; Charlemagne offered to appoint him abbot of St Martin of Tours (796). Although the community counted over 200 monks, it was not very active. Alcuin undertook to renew its prestige. He reformed the abbey school creating two cycles of study: one was elementary, the other consisted of the seven "liberal arts" (grammar, rhetoric, logic, arithmetic, geometry, music and astronomy). Students came from all over Europe. He revived the scriptorium where the copyists designed a new calligraphy for the illuminated manuscripts. He also produced a revised version of the **Vulgate** bible which became the authorised text throughout the kingdom. He remained in close touch with **Charlemagne** who sought his advice and visited him just before his coronation in December 800. Alcuin died on Whitsunday 804 at about 75 years of age.

For fifty years after his death Tours continued to be a brilliant cultural centre. In 813 a council met in Tours and ordained that the clergy should comment on the Bible in French rather than Latin.

In the 840s the **scriptorium** of St Martin's Abbey produced some splendid masterpieces: the so-called Alcuin Bible, the so-called Moutier-Grandval Bible and the famous Bible of Charles the Bald. Artists from Aix-la-Chapelle and Rheims renewed and enriched the illustrative technique of the abbey scriptorium.

From the early Capets to Louis XI. — The Norman invasions reached Tours in 853: the cathedral, the abbeys and the churches were set on fire and destroyed. The relics of St Martin were removed and hidden in the Auvergne. The ancient abbey fell into decline and passed to the Robertians who were lay priests. In 903, after further attacks, the abbey was surrounded by a wall and a new town grew up to the west of the old city; it was called Châteauneuf or Martinopolis.

The Robertians in charge of St Martin's Abbey held immense temporal power and the opportunity to pursue ecclesiastical careers; abbots, bishops and archbishops were appointed from among the 200 canons attached to the abbey. The surname "**Capet**" by which King Hugh was known at the end of 10C comes from an allusion to the "cappa' (cloak) of St Martin, thus proving that the success of the new royal dynasty owed much to the famous monastery. One of Hugh Capet's vassals, Eudes I, Count of Blois and Tours, obtained from his king c984 the neighbouring Abbey of Marmoutier which was to acquire greater importance in 11C.

In 997 a huge fire destroyed Châteauneuf and St Martin's Abbey which had to be completely rebuilt, including the basilica which dated from 471. The rivalry in 11C between the houses of Blois and Anjou, whose domains met in Touraine, ended with the Angevins victorious.

When Pope Alexander III held a great council in Tours in 1163, Touraine belonged to the Plantagenets but in 1205 **Philippe Auguste** captured the town which then remained French.

The 13C was a period of peace and prosperity; Louis IX adopted the **livre tournois,** the money minted in Tours, in preference to the livre parisis as the official currency. Early in 13C a monk from Marmoutier, John, author of the History of the Counts of Anjou and of the Life of Geoffroi le Bel, painted a very flattering portrait in his *In Praise of Touraine* of the citizens of Touraine and their wives. "They are always celebrating and their meals are of the very best; they drink from gold and silver cups and spend their time playing at dice and hunting. The women are astonishingly beautiful, they make up their faces and wear magnificent clothes. Their eyes kindle passion but they are respected for their chastity".

In 1308 Tours played host to the Etats Généraux (French Parliament). Less welcome events soon followed; the arrival of the **Black Death** (1351) and the beginning of the Hundred Years War forced the citizens to build a new wall in 1354 enclosing Tours and Châteauneuf. Touraine, which had been coveted by the great royal vassals, was raised to a Duchy for the future Charles VII and he solemnly entered the town of Tours in 1417. In 1429 Joan of Arc stayed in Tours while her armour was being made. Charles VII settled in Tours in 1444 and on 28 May he signed the Treaty of Tours with Henry VI of England.

Under **Louis XI** Tours was very much in favour; the city acted as the capital of the kingdom and a mayor was appointed in 1462. The king liked the region and lived at Plessis Château *(p 182).* Once again life became pleasant and the presence of the court attracted a number of artists of which the most famous was **Jean Fouquet** (born in Tours c1415) who painted the magnificent miniatures in the Great Chronicle of France and Jewish Antiquities.

The Abbey once again enjoyed the royal favour and recovered some of its former prestige. Louis XI died in 1483 at Plessis; the court moved to Amboise.

Silk weaving and Wars of Religion. — Louis XI had promoted the weaving of silk and cloth of gold in Lyons but the project had not met with much enthusiasm so the weavers and their looms were moved to Touraine. The industry reached its highest output in the middle of 17C when 11 000 looms were at work and there were two fairs each year. In 1680 decline set in under the effect of competition from Lyons; in 1789 only 1 000 looms were at work in Tours. The silk industry has experienced a modest recovery in 20C *(see p 178).*

In this world of craftsmen, intellectuals and artists, the **Reformation** found its first supporters and Tours, like Lyons or Nimes, became one of the most active centres of the new religion. In 1562 the Calvinists caused great disorder, particularly in St Martin's Abbey. The Roman Catholics were merciless in their revenge; ten years before Paris Tours had its own St Bartholomew's massacre: 200 to 300 Huguenots were drowned in the Loire. In May 1589 Henri III and the Parliament retreated from Paris to Tours which once again resumed its role as the royal capital.

By contrast in 17 and 18C Tours lost its political and economic importance and in 1801 the population had dropped to only 20 000 inhabitants, less than Angers and Orléans. In 19C development was slow; there was some building and improvement but little industry. The railway acted as a stimulant and the station at St-Pierre-des-Corps was the focus of renewed activity. In 1921 Tours had overtaken Orléans with 75 000 inhabitants.

The Wars. — Owing to its communications facilities Tours was chosen in 1870 as the **seat of the Government for the National Defence** but three months later, in the face of the Prussian advance, the government withdrew to Bordeaux. In June 1940 the same chain of events took place but at greater speed. The town was bombed and burned for three days from 19 to 21 September. In 1944 the bombardments began again: 136 people were killed on 20 May. In all, between 1940 and 1944, 1 543 buildings were destroyed and 7 960 were damaged; the town centre and the districts on the banks of the Loire were the most afflicted.

LIFE IN TOURS

Tours has now overflowed from its original site between the Loire and the Cher and consists of a huge conurbation (250 000 ha - 965 sq miles). The course of the Cher has been straightened and canalised for 7 km - 4 1/2 miles to provide two residential areas, an artificial lake (25 ha - 62 acres) and water sports facilities.

Tours has many light industries: processing, pharmaceutical laboratories, printing works. A factory making tyres has been built by Michelin in Joué-lès-Tours on the southwest edge of the city. Tours has not abandoned its traditional livelihood; Jacquard still has 100 looms producing silk and velvet cloth, which is exported throughout the world or used to restore the many châteaux and houses in France.

Tours is an important rail and road junction; it is also the economic centre for the west central region of France and a market for the wine and agricultural products of the area; there are two fairs in May and September. In July on St Anne's day the picturesque garlic and basil fair is held.

The varied cultural and intellectual life of the city is supported by the university, which includes a Centre for Advanced Studies of the Renaissance, a National Conservatory of Music, a Regional School of Fine Arts and various specialist institutes of higher education, which together with the other Faculties are distributed about the town and accommodate 12 000 students.

TOURS

	Churchill (Bd Winston) . . **V** 26	Proudhon (Av.) . . . . **V** 73
	Delaroche (R.) . . . . **U** 32	République (Av. de la) . . **X** 75
	Eiffel (Av. Gustave) . . . . **U** 36	St-Avertin (Rte de) . . . . . **X** 77
Alouette (Av. de l') . . . . . **X** 2	Grammont (Av. de) . . . . . **V** 39	St-Cosme (Égl.) . . . . **V E**
Bordeaux (Av. de) . . . . . **X** 6	Jaurès	St-Jean (Égl.) . . . . **X** 81
Bordiers (R. des) . . . . . . **U** 10	(Bd et R. Jean) . . . . . **V** 48	St-Symphorien (Égl.) . . . **U** 85
Brulon (R. Léon) . . . . **X** 17	Larçay (R. de) . . . . **X** 53	Ste-Radegonde (Égl.) . . . **U** 87
Chantepie (R. de) . . . . . . **X** 21	Moulin (R. Jean) . . . . **V** 59	Ste-Thérèse (Égl.) . . . . . **V** 88
Chanterie (R. de la) . . . . **U** 23	N.-D. de la Paix (Égl.) . . . **X** 61	Savonnières (Rte de) . . . **X** 89
Chevalerie (R. de la) . . . **U** 24	Paul-Bert (Quai) . . . . **U** 64	Tranchée (Av. de la) . . . . **U** 95
Christ-Roi (Égl.) . . . . **U** 25	Portillon (Quai de) . . . . . **U** 72	Wagner (Bd Richard) . . . . **V** 98

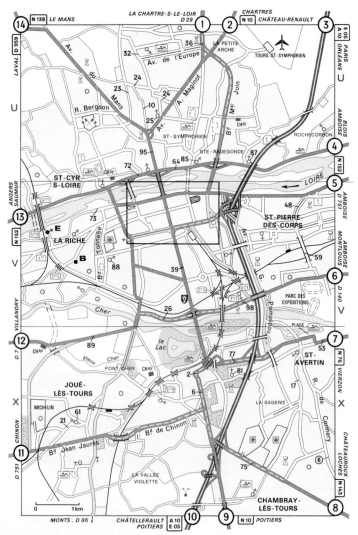

If you are puzzled
by an abbreviation or a symbol in the text or on the maps,
look at the key on p 42.

★★ OLD TOURS

time: 1 1/2 hours

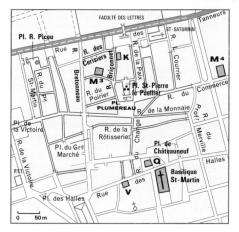

The vast restoration work begun about 1970 around Place Plumereau and the building of the Faculty of Letters beside the Loire have brought the old quarter to life; its narrow streets, often pedestrian precincts, have attracted shops and craftsmen, and the whole quarter, near the university, with its numerous restaurants becomes one of the animated centres of the town at the end of the day.

★ **Place Plumereau.** – This picturesque and animated square, formerly the hat market (Carroi aux Chapeaux), is lined with fine 15C timber-framed houses alternating with stone façades. On the corner of Rue du Change and Rue de la Monnaie there is a lovely house with two slate-hung gables with posts decorated whith sculptures; close attention to the corner post will reveal a representation of the circumcision (16C). Continue to the corner of Rue de la Rôtisserie where there is an old façade with wooden lattice work.

To the north of the square a vaulted passageway opens on to the attractive little **Place St-Pierre-le-Puellier,** with its pleasant gardens; excavations have uncovered a Gallo-Roman and medieval cemetery and the foundations of the old church after which the square is named. Part of the nave is still visible on one side of the square and from the Rue Briçonnet. To the north, a large ogive vaulted porch opens on to a small square where four centuries of architecture are harmoniously represented together.

★ **Rue Briçonnet.** – This charming street is bordered by houses showing a rich variety of local styles: from the Romanesque façade to the 18C mansion. No 35 by the narrow Rue du Poirier has a Romanesque façade, no 31 has a Gothic façade (late 13C); opposite (no 32) is a Renaissance house with lovely wooden statues. Not far away an elegant staircase tower marks the entrance to Place St-Pierre-le-Puellier. Further north on the left, nos 23 and 21 have Classical façades. Opposite (no 16) is **Tristan's House** (Maison de Tristan – **K**), a remarkable brick and stone construction with a late 15C pierced gable, which houses the Language Study Centre; one of the window lintels in the courtyard bears the inscription *Priez Dieu Pur,* an anagram of the name of Pierre du Puiz, who built the mansion.

Gemmail Museum (Musée du Gemmail - M³). – A beautiful Restoration building with columns, **Hôtel Raimbault** (1835), contains an exhibition of non-leaded stained glass windows which have the luminosity of ordinary stained glass and the brilliance of precious stones *(see p 39).* The 58 pieces on display are the work of master craftsmen whose art is that of a colorist working from a cartoon; a studio has been reconstructed in the old stables.

Rue Bretonneau. – No 33 is a 16C mansion with a fine décor of Renaissance foliage; the north wing was added about 1875.

Rue des Cerisiers. – To the west of Rue Bretonneau, no 21 is a 15C house with a Gothic façade.

Petit-St-Martin District. – In this pedestrian zone, round Rue du Petit-St-Martin, there are numerous art and craft workshops, particularly around the charming **Place Robert-Picou,** formerly the Herb market (Carroi aux herbes).

Place de Châteauneuf. – There is a fine view of the **Charlemagne Tower (Q),** and the remains of the **old Basilica of St-Martin** built in the 11 and 13C over the tomb of the great Bishop of Tours, after the Normans had destroyed the 5C sanctuary.

The new building was as famous as the old for its size and splendour. Sacked by the Huguenots in 1562 it fell into disrepair during the Revolution and its vaulting collapsed. The nave was pulled down in 1802 to make way for the Rue des Halles.

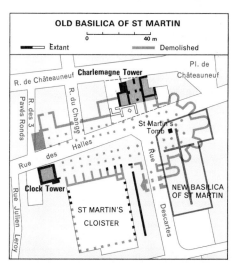

OLD BASILICA OF ST MARTIN

TOURS ★★

Charlemagne Tower which dominated the north transept, isolated since that time, partially collapsed in 1928, but carefully restored, still has its noble appearance. From the Rue des Halles, note a fine sculptured capital dating from the 12C. At the top of the tower a low-relief dating from the restoration work depicts St Martin sharing his mantle.

Further along Rue des Halles stands the **Clock Tower** (Tour de l'Horloge − **V**) marking the façade of the basilica; in the 19C it was crowned with a dome.

The **new Basilica of St-Martin**, built between 1887 and 1924, has the shrine of St Martin in the crypt; it is still the object of pilgrimages.

★ **Hôtel Gouin (M⁴)**. − This mansion, a perfect example of living accommodation during the Renaissance, is one of the most interesting in Tours. Burnt out in 1940, the north façade with the staircase tower and the **south façade**★ with finely sculpted Renaissance foliage scrolls were, however, spared.

It houses the **museum** of the Touraine Archaeological Society which has a very varied collection of exhibits from the Prehistoric era through the Gallo-Roman, medieval and Renaissance periods to the 19C.

Acquisitions during the last ten years include a medecine chest made for Jean-Jacques Rousseau and his pupil Dupin de Francueil, from Chenonceau Château *(p 85)*.

Other items in the artistic display are an Archimedes' screw, an inclined plane, a vacuum pump etc.

★★ CATHEDRAL DISTRICT   *time: 2 hours*

★★ **St Gatien's Cathedral (CY)**. − The cathedral was begun early in 13C and completed in 16C. It demonstrates the complete evolution of the French Gothic style; the chevet is typical of the early phase, the transept and nave of the development and the Flamboyant west front belongs to the final phase. The first traces of the Renaissance are visible in the tops of the towers.

Despite the mixture of styles the soaring **west front** is a harmonious whole. Monotony is avoided by the slight asymmetry of detail. The foundations of the towers are a Gallo-Roman wall; the solid buttresses show that the bases are Romanesque. The rich Flamboyant decoration was added to the west front in 15C: pierced tympana, festooned archivolts, ornamented gables over the doorways; the buttresses, which reach to the base of the belfries, were decorated at the same period with niches and crocketed pinnacles.

The 15C superstructure of the north tower is surmounted by an elegant lantern dome in the early Renaissance style. The south belfry which was built in 16C on the Romanesque tower, is also surmounted by a lantern dome in the late Renaissance style.

The **interior** of the cathedral is striking for the purity of its lines. The 14 and 15C nave blends perfectly with the **chancel** which is older, one of the most beautiful works of 13C. The **stained glass windows**★★ are the pride of the cathedral. Those in the chancel with their warm colours are 13C. The rose windows in the transept are 14C; the south window is slightly diamond-shaped and the north one is divided by a supporting rib. The windows in the third chapel in the south aisle and the great rose window in the nave are 15C.

The chapel which opens into the south transept contains the **tomb**★ of the children of Charles VIII, a graceful work by the school of Michel Colombe (16C) mounted on a base carved by Jerome de Fiesole *(p 30)*.

★ **The Psalette (Cathedral Cloister − CY F)**. − This is an elegant Gothic-Renaissance building where the canons and choir master met, hence the name Psalette − where the psalms were sung. The cloisters, which are on the north side of the cathedral, have three ranges: the west range (1460) supports the first floor library while the north and east ranges (1508-24) are almost completely covered by terraces. A graceful Renaissance

TOURS

Bordeaux (R. de)	**BZ**	Marceau (R.)	**ABYZ**
Commerce (R. du)	**AY** 8	Nationale (R.)	**BYZ**
Grammont (Av. de)	**BZ**	Scellerie (R. de la)	**BY**
Halles (Pl. et R.)	**AY**	Bretonneau (R.)	**AY** 2
		Briçonnet (R.)	**AY** 3
		Carmes (Pl. des)	**AY** 4

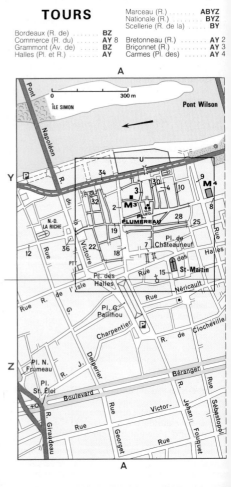

spiral stair leads up to the tiny archive room (1520) next to the library, a beautiful room with ogive vaulting containing an exhibition of the 13-14C frescoes from the church in Beaumont-Village.

★ **Place Grégoire de Tours (CY 20)**. — Fine view of the east end of the cathedral and the Gothic flying buttresses; to the left is the medieval gable of the **archbishop's palace** (now the Fine Arts Museum): the decisions of the ecclesiastical court were read out from the Renaissance gallery. In Rue Manceau there is a 15C canon's house with two gabled dormers and at the beginning of Rue Racine, a tufa building with a 15C pointed roof which housed the Justice-les-Bains — the seat of jurisdiction of the metropolitan chapter, which had been built on the site of the Gallo-Roman baths.

★★ **Fine Arts Museum (Musée des Beaux-Arts – CY M²)**. — The museum is housed in the old archbishop's palace (17-18C); a gigantic cedar, of perfect shape, was planted in the main courtyard in 1804. The round tower (left) is recognizable as part of the Gallo-Roman wall from its alternate bands of brick and stone. From the formal garden there is a good **view** of the front of the museum and the cathedral.

The rooms, which are decorated with Louis XVI panelling and silks made in Tours, make a perfect setting for the works of art, some of which used to adorn the châteaux of Richelieu and Chanteloup (now demolished) and the abbeys of Touraine: the Duke of Choiseul's desk, lacquer commode, paintings by Boucher, portraits by Largillière, Tocque, Perronneau and Vestier, sculptures by Le Moyne and Houdon, 17C Flemish and Dutch paintings including a famous ex-voto by Rubens and a *Flight into Egypt* by Rembrandt.

Among the 14 and 15C paintings on the ground floor are some Italian primitives and the museum's masterpieces: two paintings by **Mantegna**, Christ in the Garden of Olives and the Resurrection. There is also a room devoted to Greek and Etruscan ceramics.

The second floor is devoted to 19 and 20C work: Delacroix, Chasseriau, Boulanger's portrait of Balzac, impressionnist canvasses and works by Calder *(p 159);* one room is devoted to the contemporary painter Olivier Debré. There is also a display of **ceramics** by Avisseau (19C), a native of Touraine: plates decorated with motifs in relief in the style of Bernard Palissy.

Castle (BCY). — A tree-lined walk beside the Loire skirts the heterogeneous buildings of the castle, reminders of past ages. The Guise Tower **(Tour de Guise)**, with machicolations and a pepperpot roof, was part of the 11C fortress; it owes its name to the young Duke of Guise who was imprisoned in the castle after the assassination of his father *(pp 64 and 66)* and then escaped. Next to it stands the **Mars Pavilion**, which was built in the reign of Louis XVI and is flanked on the south side by a 13C round tower.

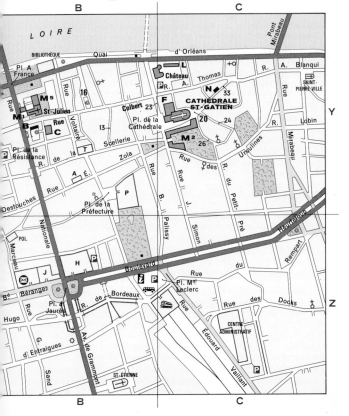

★ **Historical Museum** (Historial de Touraine). – The museum, which is housed in the rooms
of the Mars Pavilion and the Guise Tower, recalls the great moments in the history of
Touraine in some 30 waxwork tableaux with 165 figures in rich apparel. The most
spectacular scenes show the marriage of Charles VIII and Anne of Brittany, the workshop
of Jean Chapillon and his companion smiths, a ball at the court of the Valois etc.
A tropical **aquarium** presents over 150 varieties of tropical fish from both freshwater and
seawater.
On the quay stands the **Governors' Lodging (CY L)**, a 15C building with gable dormers. At its
base and running towards the Guise Tower is the Gallo-Roman wall, composed of
courses of brick alternating with small stones, typical of the period. The fine room on the
second floor contains a permanent exhibition about living in Tours **(Vivre à Tours)** which
presents the development of Tours through models and archaeological information.
This is an excellent introduction to any visit to the city.

Take Rue des Maures and then Rue Albert-Thomas.

Nearby in Rue Racine is the contemporary arts centre (**Centre de Création Contemporaine** –
(CY N) which organises temporary exhibitions of all forms of contemporary art.

★ **ST JULIEN DISTRICT** (BY) *time: 1 hour*

The streets near the bridge over the Loire suffered considerable bomb damage in the
Second World War; behind the regular modern façades in Rue Nationale some
picturesque little squares have still survived.

Wilson bridge (AY). – The stone bridge was built in 18C when the route from Paris to
Spain passed through Tours rather than Amboise.

St Julian's Church (BY). – The 11C belfry porch is set back from the street in front of the
13C church; the sobre Gothic interior is lit by windows (1960) by Max Ingrand and
Le Chevalier. Originally it had an adjoining cloister (now a garden) and conventual
buildings. The Gothic chapter house still exists and **St Julian's Cellars** (12C), a huge
vaulted chamber which now houses the **Museum of Touraine Wine** (BY M¹).

★ ★ **Trade Guild museum** (Musée du Compagnonnage – BY M⁵). – *Entrance through a porch,
8 Rue Nationale, and a footbridge.*
The museum is housed in the Guest Room (11C) and the **monks' dormitory** (16C) above the
Chapter house of St Julian's Abbey. It traces the history, customs and skills of the trade
guilds which provided training for their members and protected their interests. Both
current and obsolete trades are represented through their tools, historical documents
and the many **masterpieces** which the **companions** (derived from *cum panis* and meaning
someone with whom one shares one's bread) had to produce to become mastercrafts-
men.

★ **Beaune-Semblançay Garden** (BY B). – *Entrance through a porch, 28 Rue Nationale.*
The Hôtel de Beaune-Semblançay belonged to the unfortunate Minister of Finance
under François I who was hanged in Montfaucon. Bombs destroyed most of the
Renaissance mansion except for an arcaded gallery supporting a chapel, a beautiful
façade decorated with pilasters and surrounded by plants and the charming and finely
carved **Beaune Fountain**.

In Rue Jules-Favre stands the sobre and elegant façade of the chamber of commerce
(**Palais du Commerce** – BY C) which was built in 18C for the merchants of Tours; the
courtyard is more elaborately decorated.

Rue Colbert (BY). – Before Wilson Bridge was built, this street together with its
extension, Rue du Commerce, was the main axis of the city. The half-timbered house at
no 41 bears the sign "A la Pucelle armée" (The Armed Maid); Joan of Arc's armour was
made by the craftsman living here in April 1429. Rue Colbert and Rue de la Scellerie,
which is reached via Rue du Cygne, are full of antique dealers.

Place Foire-le-Roi (BY 16). – This was the site of the free fairs established by François I;
it was also the stage for the mystery plays which were performed when the kings visited
Tours. The north side is lined by 15C gabled houses. The beautiful Renaissance mansion
(no 8) belonged to Philibert Babou de la Bourdaisière *(see p 141)*. On the west side a side
street leads into the narrow and winding "Passage du Cœur-Navré" (Broken-Heart
Passage) which leads into Rue Colbert.

EXCURSIONS *plan p 178*

★ **St Cosmas' Priory; Plessis-lès-Tours.** – *3 km - 2 miles west by Quai du Pont-Neuf
and its continuation Avenue Proudhon, before finally following the embankment to the
priory (signpost).*

★ **St Cosmas' Priory** (V E). – The priory, not much more than a ruin, is situated in a peaceful
place in the middle of well cared for gardens; there remain a few traces of the church at
ground level, as well as the chevet wall, the chancel and the ambulatory (11 and 12C); the
poet **Ronsard** *(p 156)* was buried here in 1585. He was Prior of St-Cosmas' from 1565 until
his death; a stone slab with a flowering rose tree covers his tomb. In the monks'
refectory, a large 12C building, note the reader's pulpit decorated with columns and
sculptured capitals. The **Prior's lodging**, where Ronsard lived and died, is a charming small
15C house; in Ronsard's time an outside staircase led to the first floor of the residence,
which only had one great room on each level; this staircase was pulled down in the 17C
when the inside staircase was built. The "lodging" now houses a small **lapidary museum**
and a collection of drawings, plans, photos and engravings evoking Ronsard's life.

Plessis-lès-Tours Château (V B). – This modest brick building is only a small part of the
château built by Louis XI in the 15C which consisted of three wings in an U-shape. The
visit includes the room where Louis XI died, surrounded by linenfold panelling, frequent
in the 15C; various other rooms evoke the memory of Louis XI.

Son of Charles VII and Marie of Anjou, **Louis XI** was born in Bourges in 1423 and acceded to the throne in 1461. He spent a lot of time at Plessis-lès-Tours. Anxious to encourage the economic expansion of his kingdom after the ravages of the Hundred Years War, he developed industry and trade. His struggle with the Duke of Burgundy, Charles the Bold, who had designs on the crown, ended in the defeat and death of the Duke in 1477, and annexation of part of the Duchy in 1482. Louis XI's last years were clouded; fearing an attack on his life and imagining that he had leprosy, he lived in a fog of mistrust and superstition. The betrayal of Cardinal **Jean Balue** appeared in this context; a favourite of Louis XI who showered him with honours, the cardinal secretly conspired with the Duke of Burgundy; he was unmasked in 1469 and imprisoned at Loches until 1480, but lived another 11 years after his release.

On the first floor there are paintings and sculptures recalling the memory of St Francis of Paola, a Calabrian hermit, whom Louis XI called to his side at the end of his life. St Francis was the founder of the ascetic Minim Order; he established his first French community on the royal estate at Plessis.

★ **Meslay Tithe Barn (Grange de Meslay).** — *10 km - 7 miles northeast by ② on the plan, N 10 and a road to the right.*

This former fortified farm belonging to Marmoutier Abbey has a beautiful porch, the remains of a perimeter wall and a remarkable **tithe barn**. The barn is a very good example of a 13C agricultural building. The rounded main door is set in a pointed gable and the roof is 15C chestnut timberwork. Touraine music concerts *(see p 194)* and art exhibitions are held in this barn.

Montbazon. — Pop 3011. Facilities. *9 km - 5 1/2 miles south by ⑨ on the plan.*

Montbazon is one of the twenty fortresses built by Fulk Nerra *(p 47)*. Those who enjoy a good view will walk up to the ruined **keep** which dominates the village. Take Rue des Moulins on the left of the Town Hall and a path to the right beyond the old gateway.

Mettray Dolmen. — *12 km - 8 miles northwest by ⑭ on the plan, N 138 turning right into D 76 to Mettray.*

About 2 km - 1 mile north of Mettray on the right bank of the Choisille, in a spinney *(access by a stone path: signpost)* stands the beautiful dolmen of the "Fairy Grotto". It is one of the most skilfully constructed megalithic monuments in France; it is 11 m - 37 ft long and 3.7 m - 12 ft high and consists of twelve evenly cut stone slabs.

★ **TROO**   Pop 337

Michelin map 🔢 fold 5 or 🔢 fold 24 or 🔢 fold 1 — Local map p 121

Troo, which perches on a steeply rising slope and is distinguished from afar by its belfry tower, still has numerous troglodyte dwellings. The houses rising in tiers, one above the other, are linked by narrow alleys, stairways and mysterious passages. A labyrinth of galleries, called *caforts* (short for *caves fortes*), exists underground in the white tufa rock. In times of war these *caforts* served as hideouts.

SIGHTS

★ **The "Butt" (Butte).** — This is a feudal motte or a Gaulish burial mound which provides a splendid **panorama** (viewing table and telescope) of the sinuous course of the River Loir and of the small church of St-Jacques-des-Guérets on the opposite bank.

Old Collegiate Church of St Martin. — The collegiate church was built in 1050 and altered a century later. It is dominated by a remarkable square tower pierced by openings; the splays are ornamented with small columns in characteristic Angevin style. The windows in the Romanesque apse are Gothic. The nave and chancel are covered by a convex vault. The historiated capitals at the

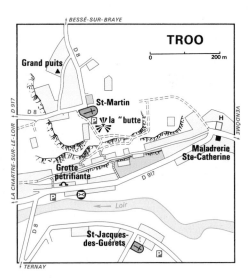

transept crossing are Romanesque. The choir stalls and communion table are 15C. The 16C wooden statue is of St Mamès who is invoked against all stomach ailments.

Great Well (Grand puits). — It is known also as the talking well because of its excellent echo; it is 45 m - 148 ft deep and covered by a wooden shingle roof.

St Catherine's Leper-house (Maladrerie Ste-Catherine). — On the eastern edge of the town on the south side of D 917 stands a 12C building with fine Romanesque blind arcades. Originally it was a hospice for sick pilgrims travelling to Tours or Compostela; there was also a leper-house to the west of Troo. When the latter disappeared the hospice took over its goods and its name.

Limestone Cave (Grotte pétrifiante). — The cave which continually streams with water contains stalactites and lime encrusted objects.

Church of St-Jacques-des-Guérets. — The services in this church were conducted by the Augustinians from the abbey of St George in the Wood (St-Georges-des-Bois) southeast of Troo.

The **murals** ★ were painted between 1130 and 1170; they show Byzantine influence; the drawing and the freshness of the colours are particular attractive. The most beautiful are in the apse: the Crucifixion, in which the half-figures represent the sun and the moon, and the Resurrection of the Dead (left); Christ in Majesty, surrounded by the symbols of the Evangelists; and the Last Supper (right). Statues of St Augustine and St George adorn the embrasure of the central window. On the right side of the apse appears the martyrdom of St James, beheaded by Herod, with Paradise above: the elect shelter in niches like pigeonholes. High up on the south wall of the nave is St Nicholas performing a miracle: the saint is throwing three gold pieces to three sisters whose father was about to sell them; below is the Resurrection of Lazarus. Further on is a vast composition representing the Descent into Hell: Jesus, majestic, delivers Adam and Eve. The left wall of the church was painted at different times from 12 to 15C: Nativity and Massacre of the Innocents. In the church are two painted wooden statues (16C): in a niche (left) St James on a base which bears the arms of Savoy; in the chancel (left) St Peter.

★★ USSÉ Château

Michelin map ▨▧ fold 13 or ▨▨▨ fold 34 (14 km - 8 miles northeast of Chinon) — Local map p 122

The château stands with its back to a cliff on the edge of Chinon Forest and looks down over its terraced gardens to the River Indre. Its impressive bulk and fortified towers contrast with the white stone, the myriad roofs, the turrets, dormers and chimneys which rise against a green background. The best places for a good view are on the bridge, some 200 m - 220 yds from the château, or on the Loire embankment. According to tradition, when Perrault, the great writer of fairy tales, was looking for a setting for the Sleeping Beauty, he took Ussé as his model. This story is illustrated by waxwork tableaux in the attics *(access by the sentry walk)*.

From the Bueils to the Blacas. — Ussé is a very old fortress; in 15C it became the property of a great family from Touraine, the Bueils who had distinguished themselves in the Hundred Years War (1337-1453). In 1485, Antoine de Bueil, who had married one of the daughters of Charles VII and Agnès Sorel, sold Ussé to the Espinays, a Breton family who had been chamberlains and cup bearers to the Duke of Brittany, Louis XI and Charles VIII. It was they who built the courtyard ranges and the chapel in the park. The château often changed hands. Among its owners was Vauban's son-in-law; the great engineer often stayed at Ussé. The estate now belongs to the Marquis of Blacas.

⊘**TOUR** *time: 3/4 hour*

The outside walls (15C) have a military aspect while the buildings overlooking the courtyard are more welcoming and some even have a touch of the Renaissance style; they have been much restored. The courtyard is enclosed by three ranges: the east wing is Gothic, the south is partly Gothic and partly Classical, the west is Renaissance; the north wing was removed in 17C to open up the view of the Loire and Indre Valleys from the terrace. The west wing is prolonged by a 17C pavilion.

The interior has several fine features: a 17C *trompe-l'œil* ceiling; the kitchens which now house a collection of oriental arms; the grand staircase (17C); an ante-chamber containing a beautiful 16C Italian ebony cabinet inlaid in the interior with ivory and mother-of-pearl; the State Bedchamber (chambre du roi) with its 18C furniture and hangings; the great gallery on the ground floor hung with Flemish tapestries; the great gallery on the first floor hung with paintings. There is also an **exhibition of historic costumes** belonging to the Galliera Museum.

(Photo Pix)

Ussé Château
Flemish tapestry after Teniers the Younger

The **chapel**, which stands alone in the park, was built between 1520 and 1538. It is a pure Renaissance building; the west façade is the most remarkable. The letters C and L, which appear elsewhere and are one of the decorative elements, are the initials of Charles d'Espinay, who built the chapel, and of his wife, Lucrèce de Pons. The light and soaring interior is decorated with a beautiful pendant keystone and 16C carved stalls in the chancel and an attractive Virgin in enamelled earthenware by Luca della Robbia in the south chapel which has ogive vaulting.

Geographically Valençay is in the Berry region but the château belongs to the Loire Valley by the period of its construction and its huge size in which it resembles Chambord.

A Financier's Château. – Valençay was built *c*1540 by Jacques d'Estampes, the owner of the castle then existing. He had married the daughter of a financier, who brought him a large dowry, and he wanted a residence worthy of his new fortune. The 12C castle was demolished and in its place rose the present sumptuous building which is in fact incomplete. Finance has often been involved in the history of Valençay; among its owners were several Farmers-General and even the famous **John Law** *(p 141)* whose dizzy banking career was an early and masterly example of inflation.

Talleyrand, who had begun his career under Louis XVI as Bishop of Autun, was Minister for External Relations when he bought Valençay in 1803 at the request of Napoleon so that he would have somewhere to receive important foreign visitors. Talleyrand managed his own career so skilfully that he did not finally retire until 1834.

VALENÇAY

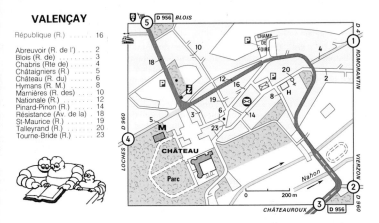

République (R.) 16

Abreuvoir (R. de l') 2
Blois (R. de) 3
Chabris (Rte de) 4
Châtaigniers (R.) 5
Château (R. du) 6
Hymans (R. M.) 8
Marnières (R. des) 10
Nationale (R.) 12
Pinard-Pinon (R.) 14
Résistance (Av. de la) . 18
St-Maurice (R.) 19
Talleyrand (R.) 20
Tourne-Bride (R.) 23

⊙**TOUR** *time: 1 hour*

Son et Lumière. – *See Practical Information at the end of the guide.*
The entrance pavilion is a huge building, designed like a keep but for show not defence with many windows, harmless turrets and fancy machicolations. The steep roof is pierced with high dormer windows and surmounted by monumental chimneys. This sort of architecture is also found in the Renaissance châteaux of the Loire Valley but here there are also the first signs of the Classical style: superimposed pilasters with Doric (ground floor), Ionic (first floor) and Corinthian (second foor) capitals. The Classical style is even more evident in the roofs of the huge corner towers: domes take the place of the pepperpot roofs which were the rule on the banks of the Loire in 16C.

West Wing. – This wing was added in 17C and altered in 18C. At roof level Mansard windows alternate with ox eyes (circular apertures). The tour of the ground floor includes the great Louis XVI vestibule; the gallery devoted to the Talleyrand-Périgord family; the Grand Salon and the Blue Salon which contain many works of art and sumptuous Empire furniture including the famous "Congress of Vienna" table; the apartments of the Duchess of Dino. On the first floor the bedroom of Prince Talleyrand is followed by the room occupied by Ferdinand VII, King of Spain, when he was confined to Valençay by Napoleon from 1808 to 1814; the apartments of the Duke of Dino and those of Mme de Bénévent; the great gallery and the great staircase. The rooms are brought to life by wax figures.

⊙**Park.** – Black swans, ducks and peacocks strut freely in the formal gardens near the château. Under the great trees in the park one sees deer, llamas, zebra, dromedary camels and kangaroos in vast enclosures.

⊙**Car Museum (Musée de l'Automobile du Centre – M).** – The museum is concealed in the park; it contains the collection of the Guignard brothers, the grandsons of a coach-builder from Vatan (Indre). There are over 60 old cars (dating from 1898, perfectly maintained in working order; there are also road documents from the early days of motoring, old Michelin maps and guides from before 1914.

EXCURSION

Luçay-le-Mâle. – Pop 2334. *10 km - 6 miles southwest by ④ on the plan, D960.*
⊙This quiet village contains an interesting **Gunflint Museum.** Like Selles-sur-Cher and Meusnes *(p 171),* Luçay contributed for many years to the local production of gunflint which came from a deposit of high quality flint. The museum displays documents on the extraction of gunflint, the processing and sale from 17 to 19C when the percussion cap was invented. The way of life of the craftsmen is shown, their tools and techniques, the sale price and the export market of the product.

To find a hotel, restaurant, garage or car dealer
look in the current **Michelin Guide France.**

Michelin map 🔢 fold 6 or 🔢🔢🔢 fold 2 – Local maps pp 118 and 121 – Facilities
Town plan in the Michelin Red Guide France

At the foot of a steep bluff, which is crowned by a castle, the River Loir divides into
several channels which flow slowly under the many bridges of Vendôme. The belfries,
gables and steep slate roofs of the old town huddle on the islands in the river while the
more recent districts now extend to the bluff. The traditional glove making which started
in the Renaissance period has been joined by printing, the manufacture of car
components, machine and aircraft controls and plastics.

A troubled history. – Although the origins of Vendôme go back to the neolithic and
Gaulish periods and the town received its name, Vindocenum, in the Gallo-Roman
period, it only began to acquire importance under the Counts, first the Bouchard family,
who were faithful supporters of the Capet dynasty, and particularly under the son of Fulk
Nerra *(p 48)*, Geoffrey Martel (11C), who founded Holy Trinity Abbey.
Since the Count of Vendôme was a vassal of the Plantagenets, his domain was involved
in the Hundred Years War: its position on the border between the French and English
possessions made it particularly vulnerable. In 1371 the royal house of Bourbon
inherited Vendôme and in 1515 François I raised it to a duchy. In 1589 the town sided with
the League but was captured by its overlord, Henri IV, and suffered for its disloyalty; the
town was sacked and only Holy Trinity church was left standing.

Henri IV's son, César. – Henri IV gave Vendôme to César, his son by Gabrielle
d'Estrées. César de Vendôme often lived in his domain during his years of conspiracy,
first during the minority of Louis XIII and then against Richelieu. For four years he was
imprisoned at Vincennes before being exiled. Finally he lent his support to Mazarin and
died in 1655.

Balzac's schooldays. – On 22 June 1807 the College of the Oratorians in Vendôme
registered the entry of an eight year old boy, Honoré de Balzac. The future novelist was
an absent-minded and undisciplined pupil. In those days the college discipline was
severe as Balzac himself recalled: "once entered the pupils did not leave until the end of
their studies... the traditional leather ferula still played its terrible role... letters to parents
were obligatory on certain days, so was confession."
Balzac had little aptitude for riding the hobby-horse, the forerunner of the modern
bicycle, and was laughed at by his fellow-pupils. He regularly got put into detention in
order to read in peace. Such a regime undermined his health and his parents had to take
him away. When he returned home his grandmother exclaimed in consternation: "look
how the college returns the pretty children we send there".

★ **HOLY TRINITY ABBEY** **(LA TRINITÉ)** *time: 1 hour*

One summer night, Geoffrey Martel, Count of Anjou, saw three fiery spears plunge into a
fountain and decided to found a monastery which was dedicated on 31 May 1040 to the
Holy Trinity. Under the Benedictine Order the abbey grew considerably so that
eventually the abbot was automatically made a cardinal also; in 12C this office was held
by the famous Geoffrey of Vendôme who was a friend of Pope Urban II, a native of
Champagne.
Until the Revolution pilgrims flocked to Holy Trinity to venerate the Holy Tear which
Christ had shed on Lazarus' tomb and which Geoffrey Martel had brought back from
Constantinople. The knights of Vendôme would rally to the cry of the "Holy Tear of
Vendôme" and "Lazarus' Friday". The curative powers of the relic were invoked in the
case of eye diseases; this explains the repeated use of the theme of the resurrection of
Lazarus in the decoration of the church.

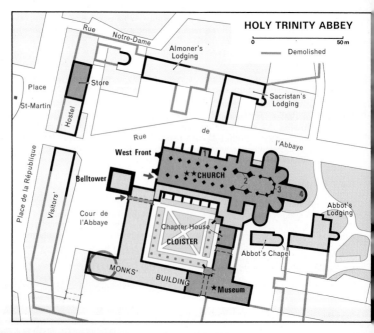

★★ Abbey Church. — The church is a remarkable example of Flamboyant Gothic architecture. The entrance to the abbey precinct is in Rue de l'Abbaye. On either side of the wall stand the Romanesque arcades of the Abbey granary which have been incorporated into more modern buildings; in fact from 14C onwards the monks allowed the citizens to build their shops against the abbey walls.

Romanesque Belltower. — Standing alone (right) is the 12C belltower, 80 m - 262 ft high, which served as a model for the Old Belltower of Notre-Dame de Chartres. The bays and arcades, which are blind at ground level, grow larger as the embrasures also increase in size. The transition from a square to an octagonal tower is made by means of mini-belltowers at the corners. The base of the first storey is decorated with grinning masks and animals.

West Front. — The astonishing Flamboyant west front, which is accentuated by a great incised gable, was built early in 16C by Jean de Beauce, who designed the New Belltower of Chartres Cathedral; the decorative openwork is like a piece of lace and contrasts with the plainer Romanesque tower.

Interior. — The nave, which was started at the transept end in the middle of 14C was not completed until after the Hundred Years War; the transept, all that is left of the 11C building, leads to the apse with radiating chapels.

The nave is remarkable for the width of the triforium and the height of the windows. The transition from the 14C to 15C phase of construction is achieved without spoiling the unity of conception: the capitals cease, the design of the frieze changes as does the decoration of the triforium and the ribs. The baptismal chapel (1) in the north aisle contains a beautiful Renaissance font in white marble supported by a carved foot from the gardens of Blois Château.

The primitive capitals of the transept crossing are surmounted by polychrome statues (13C) of the Virgin and the Archangel Gabriel at the Annunciation, St Peter and St Eutropius who was venerated in the abbey church.

The transept vaulting with its historiated keystones was altered in 14C in the Angevin style *(see p 36)*; in the left transept are statues of John The Baptist (14C) and the Virgin (16C).

The 14C chancel, which is lit by windows of the same date, is decorated with beautiful late 15C stalls (2). The choir screen (3) enclosing the chancel shows Italian influence. To the left of the high altar is the base, decorated with tears, of the famous monument of the Holy Tear with a small aperture through which the relic was exposed by one of the monks.

The chapels radiating from the ambulatory are decorated with 16C stained glass which has been much restored: the best section, which shows the meal in Simon's house, taken from a German engraving, is in the first chapel to the left of the axial chapel which contains the famous **window** dating from 1140 depicting the Virgin and Child (4).

Conventual buildings. — Only the east side of the 14C cloisters exists in its entirety. The chapter house has been cleared and restored. The Classical style buildings now house a museum *(see below)*.

Take the passage through the south range of buildings to admire the monumental south front which was built between 1732 and 1742; the pediments bear the royal fleur de lys, the device (Pax) and the emblem (Lamb) of the Order of St Benedict.

★ Museum (M). — The collections are displayed in the monastic buildings of Holy Trinity Abbey and reached by a majestic stairway.

The most interesting rooms on the **ground floor★** are devoted to mural painting in the Loir Valley and religious art in Vendôme during the Middle Ages and the Renaissance: remains of the tomb (16C) of François de Bourbon-Vendôme and of Marie de Luxembourg, keystone from the cloister vaults, font from the abbey church, etc.

On the upper floors are the sections on prehistory and antiquity. Some rooms have been devoted to paintings, furniture and porcelain from 16 to 18C: a superb harp made by Nadermann (late 18C), Marie-Antoinette's instrument maker. Another room displays the tools used in the old local crafts and a reconstruction of a Vendôme rural interior.

ADDITIONAL SIGHTS

Public Garden (Jardin Public). — The gardens descend to the water's edge by the River Loir and offer a good view of Vendôme, Holy Trinity Abbey and the 15C Water Gate (**Porte d'Eau** or Arche des Grands Prés — **B**). The open space on the opposite bank, **Place de la Liberté**, an extension of the gardens, provides another view of the Water Gate from a different angle.

Ronsard Park. — Round this shady open space are the Lycée Ronsard (formerly the College of the Oratorians where Balzac was a pupil and now occupied by the offices of the Town hall), the tourist information office, which is housed in the 15C Hôtel du Saillant (also called Hôtel du Bellay), and the modern municipal **library** which contains an important collection of old books including 11 incunabula. "The Fallen Warrior", on the lawn, is a bronze by Louis Leygue, a contemporary sculptor from Vendôme.

From Rue St-Jacques turn right into Rue du Change, a pedestrian zone lined with shops. On the corner is St James'Chapel (**Chapelle St-Jacques**), formerly a place of rest on the road to Compostela which now houses temporary exhibitions.

Church of Mary Magdalene (La Madeleine). — 1474. The belltower is surmounted by an elegant crocketed spire.

Place St-Martin (19). — Until 19C St Martin's Church (15-16C) stood here; only the belltower remains.

St George's Gate (**E**). – This gate was the entrance to the town from the River Loir; it is flanked by towers which were mostly built in 14C although the front facing the bridge is decorated with machicolations and carvings of dolphins and Renaissance medallions which were added early in 16C by Marie de Luxembourg, Duchess of Vendôme.

ⓥ**Castle.** – Access by car via St-Lubin district and the Temple, a hamlet which grew up round a Templar commandery (p 54). The ruined castle is set on the top of "the Mountain" (la Montagne) which overlooks the Loir; it consists of an earth wall and ramparts with 13 and 14C machicolated round towers at intervals; the great Poitiers Tower (**F**) on the east side was reconstructed in 15C.

The early 17C Beauce Gate (**K**) leads into the precinct which is now a huge garden. There are traces of the Collegiate Church of St George which was founded by Agnès of Burgundy and where the Counts of Vendôme were buried: Antoine de Bourbon and Jeanne d'Albret, the parents of Henri IV were buried here.

VENDÔME

Change (R. du)	5	Béguines (R.)	3
Poterie (R.)		Bourbon (R. A.)	4
République (Pl. de la)	14	Chartrain (Fg)	6
St-Martin (Pl.)	19	Chevallier (R.)	7
Saulnerie (R.)	22	Gaulle (R. de)	8
		Grève (R.)	9
Abbaye (R. de l')	2	Guesnault (R.)	12
		St-Bié (R.)	15
		St-Jacques (R.)	18
		Verdun (Av. de)	23

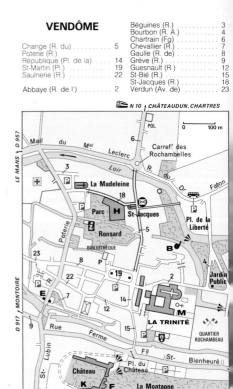

The Mountain Walk (**Promenade de la Montagne**). – From the terraces there are picturesque **views★** of Vendôme and the Loir Valley.

EXCURSIONS

Areines. – 3 km - 2 miles east by D 917 and the first turning left. Description p 54.

Nourray. – Pop 135. 11 km - 7 miles south by N 10 and the third road on the left.
ⓥThe little **church** which stands alone in the square has a row of Romanesque arcades beneath carved corbels on the chevet; note the polylobed arch which ornaments the central window.
In the interior the apse is surrounded by arcading with carved capitals.

Rhodon. – Pop 98. 19 km - 12 miles southeast by D 917 (direction Beaugency); in Villetrun turn right to Selommes (D 111) and then left (D 161)
ⓥThe internal walls and Gothic vaulting of the **church** bear traces of 14 and 15C mural paintings: Christ in Majesty in the apse and the Months of the Year on one of the transverse arches of the nave.

Villemardy. – Pop 233. 14 km - 9 miles southeast by D 957; turn left to Périgny and bear right to Villemardy.
The **church** dates from 12C; the simple nave ends in a Gothic chancel. The interior decoration in carved oak is remarkably uniform; the high altar and tabernacle, which are surmounted by an altarpiece, are in the Classical style, as are the two small symmetrical altars in the nave. The left wall of the chancel is decorated with a fresco (16C), the Adoration of the Magi, which is flanked by columns and a pediment in trompe l'œil; note the Virgin's headdress which helps to determine the date of the work.

VERGER Château

Michelin map 🔢 south of fold 1 or 🔢🔢 fold 20 (3 km - 2 miles north of Seiches)

A great moat, flint towers with dressings and machicolations in white tufa, a gatehouse and imposing outbuildings recall the huge residence which **Pierre de Rohan-Guémenée**, Marshal of Gié, started to build in 1482 and where he received Charles VIII whose life he had saved at Fornoue.
Pierre de Rohan was a marshal of France at 25 and Louis XII's head of Council. In 1506 he had the effrontery to intercept the luggage of Anne of Brittany at the Loire because he suspected it of containing goods belonging to the crown; the king was thought to be on his death bed. The queen had de Rohan exiled to Verger.
In 1776 Cardinal de Rohan ordered the château to be demolished; the precious works of art which it contained were dispersed.

---

*With this guide use the **Michelin Maps** (scale 1:200 000) shown on p 3.*

★★ VILLANDRY Château

Michelin map 🔢 fold 14 or 🔢🔢🔢 fold 35 — Local map p 124

Villandry is one of the most original châteaux in Touraine owing to the arrangement of the esplanade, the terraces, the moat, the canals and particularly the famous gardens.

★★ GARDENS *time: 1/2 hour*

In 19C, when the English landscaped garden was the fashion, the owners of Villandry re-designed the grounds. When Dr Carvallo, the founder of the French Historic Houses Association (Demeure Historique), bought the château in 1906 he patiently reconstructed the 16C French gardens. There are no other such gardens in France.

There are three terraces one above the other; the highest is the water garden with its fine stretch of water (7 000 m² - 75 350 sq ft); below is the ornamental garden where each border contains a different arrangement of heart shapes, the symbol of love (in the section behind the château); on the lowest level is the kitchen garden; between the latter and the church a herb garden has been laid out. The geometric flowerbeds are outlined with clipped yew and box hedges. Canals, fountains, vine covered pergolas create a variety of effects. The best overall view is from the terraces behind the château.

The formal arrangement is due to the influence of the Italian gardeners whom Charles VIII brought back to France but the French tradition is to be found in many small points (*see p 37*). The flowers, shrubs and fruit trees known in 16C were more or less those which are current today. Among the vegetables only the potato was missing (it was introduced in 18C by Parmentier). The art of gardening was already advanced: pruning, grafting, the use of greenhouses and the raising of early vegetables. The old Romanesque church of Villandry makes a charming background to the whole scene.

The orchard on the south-facing slope was planted according to the plans of Androuet du Cerceau; it overlooks the whole property and the valley.

TOUR OF THE CHÂTEAU *time: 1/2 hour*

Nothing remains of the early fortress except the keep, a square tower incorporated in the present structure which was built in 16C by Jean Le Breton, Secretary of State to François I. Three ranges of buildings enclose the courtyard which is open on the north side overlooking the Cher and the Loire in the valley.

Joachim de Carvallo, a Spaniard, furnished the château with Spanish furniture and an interesting collection of paintings (16, 17 and 18C Spanish schools). The great salon and the dining room on the ground floor have Louis XV panelling. The grand staircase with its wrought-iron banister leads to the picture gallery and to the room with the 13C **Mudejar ceiling** which came from Toledo; the coffers are painted and gilded with typical Moorish motifs, an unexpected sight under northern skies; there are two 16C Italian paintings on wood (St Paul and St John) in lively colours and a portrait of the Infanta by the Velasquez school.

An audiovisual display in the picture gallery shows the astonishingly varied aspect of the gardens according to the season and the time of day.

Numerous camping sites have:
shops, licensed premises, laundries, games rooms,
mini-golf, play grounds, paddling
and swimming pools.

*Consult the **Michelin Guide, Camping Caravaning France.***

VILLESAVIN Château

Michelin map 🔢 fold 18 or 🔢🔢🔢 folds 15, 16 (3 km - 2 miles west of Bracieux)

Villesavin derives from Villa Sabinus, the name of a Roman villa which stood beside the Roman road built by Hadrian which passed through Ponts d'Arian.(Hadrian's Bridges) on the south side of the River Beuvron. The villa's existence is attested by the number of sarcophagi which have been found on the land; one is displayed in the château.

The château was built in 1537 by Jean Le Breton, Lord of Villandry and superintendent of works at Chambord. It is a charming Renaissance building with certain Classical tendencies and consists of a central block flanked by symmetrical pavilions. The handsome dormer windows in the attics and the inscription on the rear façade add to the beauty of the harmonious proportions. The 16C Italian **basin** in the courtyard, which is made of white marble, is a very fine example of Renaissance decorative sculpture.

Pewterware — plates, jugs, etc. — is on display in some of the furnished rooms.

There are some vintage cars in the outbuildings.

To the left of the château stands a large 16C **dovecot** with 1 500 pigeonholes; it is well preserved including the revolving ladder.

The right to keep pigeons was one of the privileges that disappeared with the Revolution.

The size of the dovecot depended on the extent of the estate: there was one pigeonhole containing a couple of birds for each acre of land.

It is thought that the practice of keeping pigeons was brought back by the Crusaders from the Middle East where the land has always been fertilized with pigeon manure.

VOUVRAY

Pop 2 598

Michelin map 64 fold 15 or 232 fold 36 or 238 fold 13 — Local map p 122

At the heart of the famous vineyard is the village of Vouvray which is set on the south facing slopes of the hills which dominate the north bank of the Loire above Tours. There are one or two old troglodyte houses. The still or sparkling white wines are some of the most famous produced in Touraine.

The cellars (**caves**) of the wine producers and wine merchants are open the public.
In Vouvray there stands a statue of the famous Gaudissart, the travelling salesman whom Balzac *(p 30)* described in one of his novels. **Balzac** was born in Tours and often visited friends in Vouvray. The atmosphere and characters of 1830 have gone but the charm of the landscape described in his novels is still alive.

EXCURSION

Vernou-sur-Brenne. —Pop 2 050. *4 km - 2 1/2 miles east by D 46.*
The picturesque old houses of the village are surrounded by the Vouvray vineyard and backed by a hillside which is riddled with caves.

YÈVRE-LE-CHÂTEL

Pop 210

Michelin map 60 fold 20 or 237 fold 41 (6 km - 4 miles east of Pithiviers)

The position of Yèvre — on a promontory of the Beauce plateau overlooking the natural trench of the Rimarde, a tributary of the River Essone — cries out for a castle. The present ruins, the kernel of a fortified town, seem to belong to a royal castle built in 13C by Philippe Auguste.
A fortified gate under the elm trees in the main square opens into the outer bailey of the castle.

Fortress. — The fortress is diamond-shaped with a round tower at each corner containing hexagonal rooms with ogive vaulting.

The unprotected sentry walk linking the towers is dangerous.

Platforms in the northwest and south towers provide a **view** of the Beauce (**W**) and the Gâtinais (**E**). On a clear day the spire of Pithiviers church is visible. To the south the treetops in Orléans Forest darken the horizon.

St Lubin's Church. — On the south side of the village among the tombstones stands the stone shell of a huge Gothic church. Its vast size seems to have been dictated by the need for a place of refuge rather than a place of worship. The church's great elegance and the speed of its construction (the first quarter of 13C) suggest the intervention of a royal hand.

Practical Information

The French Government Tourist Offices at 178 Piccadilly, London WIV OAL, ☎ (01) 499-6911 (recorded message) or 491-7622 for urgent queries and 610 and 628 Fifth Avenue, New York, ☎ (212) 757-1125 will provide information and literature.

How to get there. – You can go directly by scheduled national airlines, by commercial and package tour flights, possibly with a rail or coach link-up or you can go by cross-Channel ferry or hovercraft and on by car or train.
Enquire at any good travel agent and remember if you are going during the holiday season or at Christmas, Easter or Whitsun, to book well in advance.

CUSTOMS AND OTHER FORMALITIES

Visa for U.S. citizens. – An **entry visa** is required for all U.S. citizens visiting France in accordance with a French security measure.
Apply at the French Consulate (visa issued same day; delay if submitted by mail).

Papers and other documents. – A valid national **passport** (or in the case of the British, a Visitor's Passport) is all that is required.
For the car a valid **driving licence, international driving permit, car registration papers** (log-book) and a **nationality plate** of the approved size. Insurance cover is compulsory and although the Green Card is no longer a legal requirement for France, it is the most effective form of proof of insurance cover and is internationally recognized by the police.
There are no customs formalities for holidaymakers importing their caravans into France for a stay of less than 6 months. No customs document is necessary for pleasure boats or outboard motors for a stay of less than 6 months but you should have the registration certificate on board.

Motoring regulations. – The minimum driving age is 18 years old. Certain motoring organizations run accident insurance and breakdown service schemes for their members. Enquire before leaving. A **red warning triangle** or hazard warning lights are obligatory in case of a breakdown.
In France it is compulsory for the front passengers to wear **seat belts.** Children under ten should be on the back seat.
The **speed limits,** although liable to modification, are : motorways 130 kph - 80 mph (110 kph when raining); national trunk roads 110 kph - 68 mph; other roads 90 kph - 56 mph (80 kph - 50 mph when raining) and in towns 60kph - 47mph. The regulation on speeding and drinking and driving are strictly interpreted – usually by an on-the-spot fine and / or confiscation of the vehicle. Remember to **cede priority** to vehicles joining from the right. There are tolls on the motorways.

Medical treatment. – For EEC countries it is necessary to have Form E III which testifies to your entitlement to medical benefits from the Department of Health and Social Security. With this you can obtain medical treatment in an emergency and after the necessary steps, a refund of part of the costs of treatment from the local Social Security offices (Caisse Primaire d'Assurance Maladie). It is, however, still advisable to take out comprehensive insurance cover.
Nationals of non-EEC countries should make enquiries before leaving.

Currency. – There are no restrictions on what you can take into France in the way of currency. To facilitate export of foreign notes in excess of the given allocation, visitors are advised to complete a currency declaration form on arrival.
Your passport is necessary as identification when cashing cheques in banks. Commission charges vary with hotels charging more highly than banks when "obliging" non-residents on holidays or at weekends.

DULY ARRIVED

Consulates: British – 6 rue La Fayette, 44000 Nantes; ☎ 40 48 57 47.

Embassy: British – 35 rue du Faubourg-St-Honoré, 75008 Paris; ☎ 42 66 91 42.
American – 2 avenue Gabriel, 75008 Paris; ☎ 42 96 12 02.

Tourist Information Centres or *Syndicats d'Initiative* 🛈 are to be found in most large towns and many tourist resorts. They can supply large scale town plans, timetables and information on entertainment facilities, sports and sightseeing.

Poste Restante. – Name, Poste restante, Poste Centrale, *departement's* postal code number, followed by the town's name, France. The Michelin Red Guide France gives local postal code numbers.
Postage via air mail to: UK letter 2.50F; postcard 1.90F
US aerogramme 3.90F; letter (20 g) 6F; postcard 3.35F.

Where to stay. – In the Michelin Red Guide France you will find a selection of hotels at various prices in all areas. It will also list local restaurants again with prices. If camping or caravanning consult the Michelin Guide Camping Caravaning France.

Electric current. — The electric current is 220 volts. European circular two pin plugs are the rule — remember an electrical adaptor.

Public holidays in France. — National museums and art galleries are closed on Tuesdays. The following are days when museums and other monuments may be closed or may vary their hours of admission:

New Year's Day
Easter Sunday and Monday
May Day (1 May)
Fête de la Libération (8 May)
Ascension Day
Whit Sunday and Monday

France's National Day (14 July)
The Assumption (15 August)
All Saints' Day (1 November)
Armistice Day (11 November)
Christmas Day

In addition to the usual school holidays at Christmas, Easter and in the summer, there are week-long breaks in February and late October-early November.

OUTDOOR ACTIVITIES

Walking

Comité National des Sentiers de Grande Randonnée, 8 avenue Marceau, 75008 Paris, ℡ 47 23 62 32.
Comité de Touraine pour la Randonnée pédestre, place de la Gare, 37000 Tours.
Topo-guides are published by the Fédération Française de la Randonnée pédestre *(address above)* and are available from the Centre d'Information, 64 rue de Gergovie, 75014 Paris, ℡ 45 45 31 02.

Riding and Pony Trekking

A.R.T.E. Val de Loire-Océan: 5 rue de Santeuil, 44000 Nantes, ℡ 40 73 57 19 (Wednesdays and Thursdays from 10am).
A.R.T.E. Val de Loire-Centre: Mr. Legrand-Sourdillon, 66 rue Devildé, 37000 Tours, ℡ 47 54 51 23.
A.N.T.E.: 15 rue de Bruxelles, 75009 Paris, ℡ 42 81 42 82.

Cruising

Syndicat interdépartemental du bassin Maine-Mayenne-Oudon-Sarthe, Maine-réservations, place du Président-Kennedy, B.P. 2207, 49022 Angers Cedex, ℡ 44 88 99 38.
Tourisme-Accueil-Loiret, Service de réservation, 3 rue de la Bretonnerie, 45000 Orléans, ℡ 38 62 04 88.

Air trips

Aérodrome d'Amboise-Dierre, ℡ 47 57 91 93.
Air Centre Tourisme, Tours St-Symphorien et Blois-le-Breuil, ℡ 47 41 40 40.
Aéro-Club de Loudun, ℡ 49 98 12 81.
Orléans, information, ℡ 38 62 04 88.

Fishing

Current brochures: folding map "Fishing in France" (Pêche en France) published and distributed by the Conseil supérieur de la pêche, 134 avenue de Malakoff, 75016 Paris; also available from the departmental fishing societies.
For information about the regulations contact the Tourist Information Centres or the offices of Water and Forest Authority (Eaux et Forêts).
Fédération de Pêche: 25 rue Charles-Gille, 37000 Tours, ℡ 47 05 33 77.

Hunting

St-Hubert Club de France, 10 rue de Lisbonne, 75008 Paris, ℡ 45 22 38 90.
Secretariats of the Departmental Hunting Federations.

Cycling

Fédération Française de Cyclotourisme, 8 rue Jean-Marie-Jego, 75013 Paris, ℡ 45 80 30 21, and its local representatives.
IGN 1/50 000 map, "1 000 km by bicycle round Orléans" (1 000 km à vélo autour d'Orléans).
Lists of cycle hire businesses are usually available from the Tourist Information Centres. The main railway stations also hire out cycles which can be returned at a different station.

Tourist routes

Tourist Office in Tours, place du Maréchal-Leclerc, ℡ 47 05 58 08.
Tourist Office in Chinon, 12 rue Voltaire, ℡ 47 93 17 85.
Comité régional du Tourisme et des Loisirs Centre Val de Loire *(see p 193)*.

Evening tours

Organised in the season by coach to Amboise, Azay-le-Rideau, Chenonceau and Le Lude: apply to the Tourist Office in Tours, ℡ 47 05 58 08.

Lecture tours and guided tours

Apply to the Tourist Office or the Tourist Information Centre.
During the tourist season: at Amboise, Angers, Beaugency, Blois, Chinon, Le Mans, Loches, Orléans, Romorantin-Lanthenay, Saumur, Tours, Vendôme.

Wine Cellar tours

Comité Interprofessionnel des Vins de Touraine, 19 square Prosper-Mérimée, 37000 Tours, ℡ 47 05 40 01.
Tourist Information Centres, especially in Amboise, Bourgueil, Chinon, Montlouis-sur-Loire, Vouvray.

USEFUL ADDRESSES

Regional Tourist Committees:

Pays de Loire: 3 place St-Pierre, 44000 Nantes, ☎ 40 48 24 30.
Centre-Val de Loire: 9 rue St-Pierre-Lentin, 45041 Orléans Cedex 1, ☎ 38 54 95 42

Departmental Tourist Committees:

Indre: Bus station (gare routière), rue Bourdillon, 36000 Châteauroux, ☎ 54 22 91 20.
Indre-et-Loire: Hôtel du Département, place de la Préfecture, B.P. 3217, 37032 Tours Cedex, ☎ 47 61 61 23, ext 2160 or 2161.
Loiret: 3 rue Bretonnerie, 45000 Orléans, ☎ 38 66 24 10.
Loir-et-Cher: 11 place du Château, 41000 Blois, ☎ 54 78 55 50.
Maine-et-Loire: place du Président-Kennedy, 49000 Angers, ☎ 41 88 23 85.
Mayenne: 84 avenue Robert-Buron, 53000 Laval, ☎ 43 53 18 18.
Sarthe: Hôtel du Département, 72000 Le Mans, ☎ 43 84 96 00.

Tourism for the handicapped

Some of the sights described in this guide are accessible to handicapped people. They are listed in the publication "Touristes quand même! Promenades en France pour les voyageurs handicapés" produced by the Comité National Français de Liaison pour la Réadaptation des Handicapés (38 boulevard Raspail, 75007 Paris). This booklet covers nearly 90 towns in France and provides a wealth of practical information for people who suffer from reduced mobility or visual impairment or are hard of hearing.
The **Michelin Red Guide France** and the **Michelin Camping Caravaning France** indicate rooms and facilities suitable for physically handicapped people.

Accommodation for young people

Youth Hostels: apply to the regional or departmental tourist committees (addresses above).
Farm lodgings (gîtes ruraux): Maison des gîtes de France, 35 rue Godot-de-Mauroy, 75009 Paris, ☎ 47 42 25 43.

Bed and breakfast

Château Accueil, c/o Visafrance, 19 rue de la Salle, 78100 St-Germain-en-Laye, ☎ 39 73 11 14.
Étapes François-Cœur, 172 Grande-Rue, 92380 Garches, ☎ 47 95 05 47.

BOOKS TO READ

Companion Guide to the Loire by Richard Wade (Collins — 1984)
Loire Valley by J. J. and J. Wailing (Thomas Nelson Ltd — 1982)
The Loire by S. Jennett (Batsford — 1975)
Eleanor of Aquitaine and the Four Kings by Amy Kelly (Harvard University Press — 1974)
Joan of Arc by Marina Warner (Penguin — 1983)
Access in the Loire (Holiday guide for the disabled). Obtainable from Pauline Hephaistos, Survey Project, 39 Bradley Gardens, West Ealing, London W13.

The books mentioned below can be obtained through public libraries:

Valley of the Loire by G. Pillement translated by A. Rosin (Johnson — 1965)
Loire and its Châteaux by Philippe and Gouvion (Thames & Hudson — 1986)
The Châteaux of France by Ralph Dutton (Batsford — 1957)
The Châteaux of the Loire by Ian Dunlop (Hamish Hamilton — 1969)
The Cathedral's Crusade, The Rise of the Gothic style in France by Ian Dunlop (Hamish Hamilton — 1982)
Châteaux of the Loire by Jacques Levron (Nicholas Kaye)
The Loire Valley by Henry Myhill (Faber & Faber — 1978)

The following novels have settings in the area:

Honoré de Balzac: Eugénie Grandet, Le Curé de Tours, La Femme de Trente Ans, l'Illustre Gaudissart, Le Lys dans la Vallée.
René Benjamin: La Vie Tourangelle
Alain-Fournier (Henri-Alban Fournier): le Grand Meaulnes
Maurice Genevoix: Raboliot
Émile Zola: Earth
Marcel Proust: A la Recherche du temps perdu, Jean Santeuil
Charles Péguy: Jeanne d'Arc
François Rabelais: Gargantua and Pantagruel comprising Pantagruel, Gargantua, Tiers Livre, Quart Livre

Easter Sunday

St-Benoît-sur Loire ..   Great Easter festival (10pm).

Easter Sunday

Solesmes ....   Easter ceremonies.

End April/early May

Le Mans ....   24 hour race:
motorcycle racing on the Bugatti Circuit *(p 135)*.

7 and 8 May

Orléans ....   Joan of Arc Festival:
Cathedral illuminations on 7; religious ceremony in the cathedral, procession, military parade on 8.

End May

Tours ....   Procession of floral floats.

Whitsun (week preceding)

Châteauneuf-sur-Loire   Rhododendron Festival.

Mid-June to end June

Le Mans ....   24 hour race:
car racing on the 24 hour Circuit *(p 135)*.

Last two weekends in June

Tours (Meslay Tithe Barn)   Touraine Music Festival
with the participation of international artists.

July

Anjou ....   Anjou Festival throughout Maine-et-Loire:
theatre, music, dance, plastic and lyric arts.

First weekend in July

Le Mans ....   Medieval Festival in Old Le Mans.

July (Fridays, Saturdays and Sundays)

Sully-sur-Loire ......   Music Festival: classical, jazz, dance.

Mid-July

Doué-la-Fontaine ....   Rose Show in the arena *(p 99)*.

End July (penultimate Thursday; last Saturday and Monday afternoon; last Sunday morning)

Saumur ....   Equestrian and motorised tattoo:
demonstrations by the "Black Squad" (Cadre Noir) *(p 169)*.

Last weekend in July

Le Ménitré map 🆖 fold 3   Headdress Parade which brings together all the regional folklore groups.
Many young women wear traditional costumes and headdresses. (☏ 41 45 63 63).

First weekend in August

Chinon ....   Medieval market:
reconstruction of Chinon in the Middle Ages;
period costumes, entertainers, puppets, old crafts, tasting of old fashioned cookery, dancing, concerts, choral singing, traditional art (admission: 20F).

15 August

Molineuf map 🆖 fold 7   Bric-à-brac Fair;
in attendance are antiquaries,
amateurs and customers.

24 December

Anjou ....   The Naulets Mass
(in a small country church, a different one each year).
Traditional Angevin groups sing Christmas carols in local dialect (Angers Tourist Information Centre: ☏ 41 88 69 93).

St-Benoît-sur-Loire ..   Christmas Eve vigil and mass (10.30pm).

Solesmes ....   Midnight mass.

---

(1) The map and fold number are given for places not described in this guide.

SON ET LUMIÈRE PERFORMANCES

This type of show was inaugurated at Chambord in 1952 by Mr. P. Robert-Houdin. The history of the châteaux and their owners is presented in an original manner. *Programme details are available from the Tourist Information Centres in Blois (☎ 54 74 06 49) or Le Lude (☎ 43 94 62 20). See illustrations on pp 7 to 9.*

Amboise: A la cour du Roy François (At the court of King Francis I)

Performance (1 1/2 hrs) at 10.30pm on 24 June and the last Wednesday and Saturday in June and Wednesdays and Saturdays in July; at 10pm on Wednesdays, Fridays (except the last) and Saturdays in August. Admission: 40F. Information:☎ 47 57 09 28.

★★ **Azay-le-Rideau: Puisque de vous n'avons autre visage**

Performance (3/4 hr) every evening at 10pm or 10.30pm from end May to end September. Admission: 30F. Information: ☎ 47 61 61 23 ext 3162.
The show, which focuses on the château, is animated by people from the Renaissance period and evokes Philippa Lesbahy, the soul of the château.

Blois: Les esprits aiment la nuit (Spirits prefer the night)

Performance (3/4 hr) at 9.30, 10 or 10.30pm according to the season from mid-March to mid-September. For details contact the Tourist Office. Information: ☎ 54 74 06 49. Admission: 14F.
Evocation of several women who lived or stayed at the château: Joan of Arc, Anne of Brittany, Claude of France and Catherine de' Medici.

★ **Chambord: Le combat du jour et de la nuit** (The conflict between night and day)

Performance (35 mins) between 9.30 and 10.45pm according to the season on Fridays, Saturdays, Sundays and holidays from mid-April to end May; every evening from early June to end September. Admission: 22F. Information: ☎ Paris (1) 42 74 22 22; Blois 54 78 67 68; Chambord 54 20 31 32.
Compelling show set in the silence of the forest on the bank of the Cosson.

Chenonceau: Au temps des Dames de Chenonceau (The Ladies of Chenonceau)

Performance (3/4 hr) at 10pm and 10.45pm on Fridays and Whitsunday and every evening from mid-June to mid-September. Admission: 25F. Information: ☎ 47 23 90 07.
Under the influence of six women Chenonceau evolved from a fortified mill into an elegant residence where sumptuous festivities were held.

Cheverny: A la lueur des flambeaux (By the light of flaming torches)

Performance (1 1/4 hrs) at 10pm on the last three Saturdays in July and three Saturdays in August. Admission: 36F. Information: ☎ 54 79 96 29.
Evening show on the theme of hunting.

Chinon: Charles VII, l'enfant maudit (Charles VII, the accursed child)

Performance (1 hr) at 10.30pm on Fridays and Saturdays in July and at 10pm in August. Price and supplementary information from the Tourist Office: ☎ 47 93 17 85.

★★★ **Le Lude: Les glorieuses et fastueuses soirées au bord du Loir** (Sumptuous nights on the banks of the Loir)

Performance (1 3/4 hrs) from mid-June to early September: at 10.30pm on Fridays and Saturdays in June and July; at 10pm on Fridays, Saturdays and certain Thursdays in August; at 9.30pm on Fridays and Saturdays in September. Fireworks. Admission: 45 to 65F. Information ☎ 43 94 62 20.

Valençay: la Reine Margot (Queen Margot)

Performance (2 hrs) at 10pm or 9.30pm on Fridays and Saturdays from end July to end August. Admission: 45 or 50F. Information: ☎ 54 00 04 42.
Evocation of the period of the Wars of Religion after the novel by Alexandre Dumas.
Knights and musicians in Renaissance costumes.

Times and charges for admission

As times and charges for admission are liable to alteration, the information below is given for guidance only.

The information applies to individual adults. Special conditions regarding times and charges for parties are, however, common and arrangements should be made in advance. In some cases admission is free on certain days, eg Wednesdays, Sundays or public holidays.

Churches do not admit visitors during services and are usually closed from noon to 2pm. Tourists should refrain from visiting when services are being held. Admission times are indicated if the interior is of special interest. Visitors to chapels are accompanied by the person who keeps the keys. A donation is welcome.

Lecture tours are given regularly during the tourist season in the major towns in the region. Apply to the tourist information centre.

When guided tours are indicated, the departure time of the last tour of the morning or afternoon will be up to an hour before the actual closing time. Most tours are conducted by French speaking guides but in some cases the term ''guided tours'' may cover group visiting with recorded commentaries. Some of the larger and more frequented sights may offer guided tours in other languages. Enquire at the ticket office or book stall. Other aids for the foreign tourist are notes, pamphlets or audio guides.

Enquire at the tourist information centre for local religious holidays, market days etc.

Every sight for which times and charges are listed is indicated by the symbol ⊙ in the margin in the main part of the guide.

a

ALLUYES

Church. – Apply to Mrs. Legrand, 35 Rue Robertet, ☏ 37 47 28 00.

AMBOISE

Château. – Guided tour (3/4 hour) mornings and afternoons; all day in July and August. Closed 25 December and 1 January. 23F. ☏ 47 57 00 98.

Clos-Lucé. – Mornings and afternoons; all day from early July to end September. Closed 25 December and in January. 23F. ☏ 47 57 62 88.

Postal Museum. – Mornings and afternoons. Closed Monday, 1 January, 1 May, Ascension Day, 1 November, 25 December. 7F. ☏ 47 57 00 11.

Town Hall Museum. – Guided tour (3/4 hour) mornings and afternoons. Closed Saturday afternoons, Sundays and holidays. 3F. ☏ 47 57 02 21.

ANGERS

Château. – Free entry to park; guided tour of chapel and royal apartments, mornings and afternoons (all day in July and August). Closed 1 January, 1 May, 1 and 11 November, 25 December. 22F (10F out of season). ☏ 41 87 43 47.

Cathedral Treasury. – Guided tour (1/2 hour) mornings and afternoons. Closed Sundays, Mondays and in October; also 1 January, 1 May, 1 and 11 November, 25 December. 12F (7F out of season). ☏ 41 88 88 97.

David of Angers Gallery. – Mornings and afternoons. Closed Mondays (except in July and August), 1 January, 14 July, 1 and 8 November, 25 December. 5F. ☏ 41 88 64 65.

Logis Barrault (Fine Arts Museum). – Mornings and afternoons. Closed Mondays, 1 January, 14 July, 1 and 8 November, 25 December. 1F. ☏ 41 88 64 65.

Prefecture. – Mondays to Fridays. Apply to reception. ☏ 41 88 74 51.

Hôtel Pincé. – All year, daily. Closed Mondays, 1 January, 14 July, 1 and 8 November, 25 December. 1F. ☏ 41 88 64 65.

St Sergius' Church. – All year, weekdays; Sunday afternoons in July and August only.

Lurçat Museum of Contemporary Tapestry. – Mornings and afternoons. Closed Monday (except in July and August), 1 January, 14 July, 1 and 8 November, 25 December. 10F. ☏ 41 88 64 65.

ASNIÈRES

Abbey. – Guided tour (1/2 hour) mornings and afternoons, July and August. Closed Tuesdays. 5F.

AUBIGNY-SUR-NÈRE

St Martin's Church. – Weekdays usually; closed Sunday afternoons.

AVOINE-CHINON

Nuclear power station and museum. – Guided tour (1 1/2 hours for the museum, 3 hours for the power station including audiovisual film) to be arranged in advance by telephone: 47 98 97 07; 2 days' notice for the museum, several days' notice for the power station. Proof of identify with a photograph must be deposited with the management during the visit. Museum tours: daily, except holidays, at 9 and 10.30am, 2pm (2.30 Saturdays and Sundays) and 3.30pm (4pm Saturdays and Sundays). Power station tours: dates and times obtainable by telephone; closed Saturdays, Sundays and holidays.

AZAY-LE-RIDEAU

Château. – Guided tour (3/4 hour) mornings and afternoons. Closed 1 January, 1 May, 1 and 11 November. 16F (9F in winter). ☏ 47 45 42 04.

BAGNEUX

Dolmen. – Daily. 5.50F. ☏ 41 50 23 02.

BAILLOU

Church. – Apply to Mr. Gilbert Touchard. ☏ 54 80 80 94.

BAUGÉ

Château. – Guided tour (1/2 hour) mid-June to mid-September, mornings and afternoons; otherwise apply to the Town Hall (Mairie), ☏ 41 89 12 12. Closed Tuesdays. 5F.

Chapel of the Daughters of the Heart of Mary. – Guided tour weekdays, except Thursdays and Sunday afternoons. ☏ 41 89 12 20.

St Joseph's Hospital. – Guided tour (1/4 hour) all year, weekday mornings and afternoons, Sunday and holiday afternoons only. 5F.

St Laurent's Church. – Closed Sunday afternoons.

BAZOUGES-SUR-LOIR

Château. – Guided tour (3/4 hour) early July to mid-September, Tuesday and Friday mornings, Thursday and Saturday afternoons; also Easter Saturday and Monday, Whit Saturday and Monday, 1 May, Ascension Day. 12F.

BEAUGENCY

Orléans District Museum (Château Dunois). – Guided tour (3/4 hour) mornings and afternoons. Closed Tuesdays from early October to end December; also 1 January, 1 May, 25 December and at the discretion of the local authority: for information ☏ 38 44 55 23. 10F.

Town Hall. – Guided tour (1/2 hour) late Monday and Saturday mornings, early Wednesday afternoons. 2F. ☏ 38 44 50 01.

BEAULIEU-LÈS-LOCHES

Abbey church. – Guided tour: July, August and September, apply to the Town Hall (Mairie); otherwise apply to Mrs. Alibrant, Rue St-Laurent.

BEAUREGARD

Château. – Guided tour (1/2 hour) mornings and afternoons; all day in July and August. Closed Wednesdays, November to April and 25 December; also in January (except 1) and early February. 15F.

BEAUVAL

Ornithological Park. – Daily all day. 26F, children 14F. ☏ 54 75 05 56.

BÉHUARD

Notre-Dame Church. – Guided tour on request. ☏ 41 72 21 15.

Times and charges

BLANCAFORT

Château. – Guided tour (3/4 hour) of the interior, free entry to gardens, mid-March to early January, mornings and afternoons. Closed Tuesdays. 17F.

BLOIS

Château. – Daily, all day mid-April to end August, otherwise mornings and afternoons; guided tour (3/4 hour) in winter only. Closed 1 January and 25 December. 20F (ticket also valid for St Saturnin Cloisters). ☏ 54 78 06 62.

Archaeological Museum. – Audiovisual presentation (1/4 hour) in tourist season only; entrance at the foot of the stairs.

Fine Arts Museum. – Same terms and ticket as for the château.

Anne of Brittany Pavillon. – Closed Sundays and holidays October to March and also 1 January, 1 and 11 November, 24 (afternoon), 25 (all day) and 31 (afternoon) December. ☏ 54 74 06 49.

Museum of Religious Art. – Afternoons. Closed Mondays.

Museum of Natural History. – Guided tour (1 hour) mornings and afternoons daily (except Mondays), June to August. Otherwise closed Mondays, Tuesdays, Thursdays, Fridays and Sunday mornings. ☏ 54 74 13 89.

Hôtel d'Alluye courtyard. – Afternoons, Tuesdays to Fridays. Apply at reception. ☏ 54 78 39 80.

Cathedral Crypt. – Apply at the Sacristy.

St Saturnin Cloisters. – Mornings and afternoons. Closed Mondays and Tuesdays, all year; also Thursdays and Fridays, early November to mid-March; also 1 January and 25 December. The ticket for the Château is also valid for the Cloisters. ☏ 54 74 16 06.

Our Lady of the Trinity Basilica. – Carillon concerts are no longer held regularly.

Poulain Chocolate Factory. – Guided tour (1 1/4 hour) Mondays to Thursdays at 8.45, 10am, 1.30 and 2.45pm, Fridays at 8.45 and 10am; book in advance on ☏ 54 78 39 21.3F.

Le BOIS-MONTBOURCHER

Château. – Not open to the public.

La BOISSIÈRE

Abbey. – Guided tour (1/4 hour) mornings and afternoons during the school holidays (Easter, summer and Christmas). Closed 14 July and 15 August. 8F.

BONNEVAL

Church of Our Lady. – Closed Sunday and holiday afternoons.

BOUËR

Church. – Closed temporarily.

BOUMOIS

Château. – Guided tour (3/4 hour) from Palm Sunday to early November, mornings and afternoons. Closed Tuesdays except in July and August. 20F. ☏ 41 38 43 16.

BOURGONNIÈRE

St Saviour's Chapel. – Enter through the park and ring the bell at the top of the steps. Mornings and afternoons. 10F. ☏ 40 98 10 18.

BOURGUEIL

Parish Church. – Closed Sunday afternoons and holidays all day.

Abbey. – Guided tour (1 hour) Sunday and holiday afternoons from early April to end October and also Mondays, Thursdays, Fridays and Saturdays in July and August. 10F. ☏ 47 97 72 04.

Blue Windmill. – Early April to end September, afternoons (from 3pm). ☏ 47 97 71 41.

Cave touristique de la Dive Bouteille. – Guided tour (1/2 hour) mornings and afternoons, early February to end November. 9.50F. ☏ 47 97 72 01.

BOURNAN

Church. – Enquire at the Café de la Mairie.

BRAIN-SUR-ALLONNES

Medieval Museum. – Afternoons. Closed Mondays and holidays. 5F. Guided tour of the archaeological site Saturdays and Sundays at 4.30pm by appointment. ☏ 41 52 03 54 (Mr. Y. Boucher) or 41 52 07 64 (Mr. M. Boucher). 5F.

BREIL

Le Lathan Château. — For permission to visit apply to ☎ 41 89 55 06 (family) or 41 89 55 18 (Town Hall - Mairie).

BRIDORÉ

Château. — Not open to the public.

BRISSAC

Château. — Guided tour (1 hour) at set times, mornings and afternoons, early April to early November. Closed Tuesdays except in July and August. 22F. ☎ 41 91 23 43.

C

CHAMBORD

Château. — Mornings and afternoons, all day in July and August. Closed 1 January, 1 May, 1 and 11 November, 25 December. 22F (10F early October to end March). ☎ 54 20 32 20. Early July to early September lecture tour and guided tour of first floor. Early May to end September audio-guided tour.

CHAMPIGNY-SUR-VEUDE

Sainte Chapelle. — Guided tour (1/2 hour) early April to early October, mornings and afternoons. 12F.

CHANTELOUP

Pagoda. — Closed Mondays. 6F.

CHÂTEAU-DU-LOIR

St Guingalois' Church. — For guided tour apply to the vicarage (presbytère), ☎ 43 44 01 28.

CHÂTEAUDUN

Château. — Guided tour (3/4 hour) mornings and afternoons. Closed 1 January, 1 May, 1 and 11 November, 25 December. 16F (10F early October to end March). ☎ 37 45 22 70.

Grottes du Foulon. — Mornings and afternoons early May to end September; otherwise afternoons only. Closed Mondays, except in July and August. 13F. ☎ 37 45 19 60.

Museum. — Mornings and afternoons. Closed Tuesdays and holidays and also mid-October to mid-November. 7F. ☎ 37 45 55 36.

Church of St John of the Chain. — Apply to the parish priest (le curé), 39 Rue Gambetta.

CHÂTEAU-GONTIER

Museum. — Free or guided tour (1/2 hour) mid-June to mid-September, afternoons. Closed Tuesdays, Sundays and holidays.

CHÂTEAUNEUF-SUR-LOIRE

Loire Nautical Museum. — April and May, Saturdays, Sundays and holidays, mornings and afternoons; June, weekdays — afternoons only, weekends and holidays — mornings and afternoons; July and August, mornings and afternoons daily; September, weekdays — afternoons only, weekends and holidays — mornings and afternoons. Closed Tuesdays. 5.20F. ☎ 38 58 41 18.

CHÂTEAU-RENAULT

Leather and Tanning Museum. — Mid-May to mid-September, Wednesday (guided tour) and Saturday afternoons. 10F. ☎ 47 56 91 35 (Town Hall - Mairie)

Château. — Not open to the public.

CHAUMONT-SUR-LOIRE

Château (stables). — Guided tour mornings and afternoons. Closed 1 January, 1 May, 1 and 11 November, 25 December. 22F. (9F out of season). ☎ 54 20 98 03.

CHEMAZÉ

Château de St-Ouen. — Not open to the public.

CHÉMERY

Château. — Daily, all day. 16F. ☎ 54 71 82 77. In summer open evenings for son et lumière (historical panorama, exhibition of costume designs from 4C to 19C).

Times and charges

CHENONCEAU

Château. – Daily, all day; Mid-November to mid-February, mornings and afternoons; 25F. Refreshments. In July and August: creche, electric train, boat trips on the Cher. ☎ 47 23 90 07. Each visitor receives a pamphlet.

Waxworks Museum. – Same conditions as for the château. 5F.

CHEVERNY

Château. – Mornings and afternoons; early June to mid-September, all day. 19F. ☎ 54 79 96 29. Feeding time at the kennels: early April to mid-September, 5pm except Sundays and holidays; otherwise, 3pm except Tuesdays, Saturdays, Sundays and holidays.

CHINON

Wine and Cooperage Museum. – Guided tour (1/2 hour) early April to end September, mornings and afternoons. Closed Thursdays. 12F. ☎ 47 93 25 63.

St Maurice's Church. – Closed temporarily.

Museum of Old Chinon. – All day. Closed Tuesdays and in February. 10F. ☎ 47 93 18 12.

Castle. – Early February to end November, mornings and afternoons; July and August, all day. Closed Wednesdays early October to mid-March. 15F (guided tour on request). ☎ 47 93 13 45.

Royal Apartments. – Guided tour only, as part of castle tour.

St Mexme's Church. – Closed temporarily; work in progress.

St Radegund's Chapel. – Guided tour (1 hour) Easter to end September, daily all day. 10F. Apply to the Société des Amis du Vieux Chinon. ☎ 47 93 18 12.

Boat trips. – April to October. Single ticket: 95F; return ticket: 120F. Information available from Val de Loire Croisières, 86540 Thuré. ☎ 49 93 89 46.

CHOLET

History and Vendean War Museum. – Mornings and afternoons. Closed Tuesdays and holidays. ☎ 41 62 21 46.

Fine Arts Museum. – Same conditions as for the museum above.

CHOUZÉ-SUR-LOIRE

Nautical Museum. – Sunday and holiday afternoons, early May to end August and also Thursdays, Fridays and Saturdays in July and August. ☎ 47 95 10 10 (Town Hall - Mairie).

CINQ-MARS-LA-PILE

Château. – Daily, all day. 7F. ☎ 47 96 40 49.

Le CIRAN

Domain. – Mornings and afternoons. Closed Tuesdays. 10F. ☎ 38 76 90 93.

CLÉRY-ST-ANDRÉ

Basilica. – Daily, all day. Donation.

CLOS

Futaie. – Guided tour (4 km) by the National Office of Forests, mid-July to mid-August, daily except Tuesdays, 9.30am to 3pm. Assembly point in the car park by the Boppe oak.

COMBREUX

Valley Lake. – Bathing facilities. Boats and pedalos for hire.

CORMERY

Notre-Dame-du-Fougeray. – Mid-June to mid-September. Apply to the Tourist Information Office. ☎ 47 43 30 84.

COUDRAY-MONTBAULT

Château. – Mornings and afternoons, early July to early September. 10F. ☎ 41 64 80 87.

COURGENARD

Church. – Apply to the Town Hall (Mairie).

COURTANVAUX

Château. – Guided tour (1 hour), early May to end September, hourly from 10am to 6pm (except between noon and 1pm). Closed Tuesdays. Otherwise, Sundays and holidays at the same times. 6F. ☎ 43 35 34 43.

COUTURE-SUR-LOIR

Church. – Apply to Mrs. Lenoir, café-tabac, for information.

CRAON

Château. – Afternoons; free access to the park from early April to early November; guided tour (3/4 hour) of the château in July and August only. Closed Tuesdays. 10F (château and park). ☎ 43 06 11 02.

CUNAULT

Church. – Gregorian Chant at 11 o'clock mass on Sundays and feast days. ☎ 41 67 92 44.

d - e

DAMPIERRE-EN-BURLY

Nuclear Power Station. – Guided tour (3 hours) daily, except Sundays and holidays, at 9am or 2pm; book in advance. ☎ 38 29 70 04.

DANGEAU

St Peter's Church. – For guided tour apply to Miss Arthur. ☎ 37 98 97 34.

DENEZÉ-SOUS-DOUÉ

Sculptured Cavern. – Guided tour (1/2 hour), Easter to All Saints Day; daily, all day, July and August; otherwise afternoons only. 12F. ☎ 41 59 08 80 or 41 59 15 40.

DESCARTES

Museum. – All year; afternoons. Closed Tuesdays. 5F. ☎ 47 59 79 19.

La DEVINIÈRE

Early February to end November, mornings and afternoons. Closed Sundays and holidays; also Wednesdays, early October to Mid-March. 12F. ☎ 47 95 91 18.

DOUÉ-LA-FONTAINE

Zoo. – Mornings and afternoons; all day, mid-April to mid-September. 32F, children under 10: 16F. ☎ 41 59 18 58.

Arena. – Guided tour (1/2 hour) mornings and afternoons. Closed Tuesdays. 3.50F

DURTAL

Château. – Guided tour (1/2 hour) July and August, mornings and afternoons. Closed Tuesdays all day and Sunday mornings. 10F. ☎ 41 76 30 24 (Tourist Information Centre at the Town Hall).

ESVES-LE-MOUTIER

Church. – Afernoons.

f

La FERTÉ-BERNARD

Church of Our Lady of the Marshes. – When closed, apply to the Town Hall (Mairie) or the Leroy bookshop (librairie), 37 Rue d'Huisne.

Regional Museum. – Guided tour afternoons, daily, early June to end September; Saturdays, Sundays and holidays only from Easter Sunday to end May and from early October to 11 November. 10F. ☎ 43 93 13 79.

La FERTÉ-ST-AUBIN

Château. – Daily, all day, end March to mid-November. Guided tour of ground floor (20 mins); unaccompanied tour of the rest of the château and of the Horse Museum. 22F.

La FLÈCHE

Military College. – Unaccompanied or guided tour (1 1/2 hours) on request (☎ 43 94 03 96), mornings and afternoons. Proof of identity is required at entrance. For reasons of security the Commander of the School reserves the right to cancel tours.

FONTAINE-GUÉRIN

Church. – Apply to the bakery (boulangerie).

FONTAINES-EN-SOLOGNE

Church. – Usually open Sundays. Information on ☎ 54 46 42 22.

Times and charges

FONTEVRAUD-L'ABBAYE

Centre Culturel de Rencontre. – Programme information: ☎ 41 51 73 52.

Abbey. – Mornings and afternoons; all day, early July to end September. Closed 1 January, 1 May, 1 and 11 November, 25 December. Admission charge not published. ☎ 41 51 71 41.

La FOSSE

Troglodyte hamlet. – Mornings and afternoons, mid-March to mid-October; all day in July and August. Closed Mondays, except from early June to end September. Early February to mid-March and mid-October to end November, Saturdays and Sundays only. 15F. ☎ 41 59 00 32.

FOURGÈRES-SUR-BIÈVRE

Château. – Guided tour (1/2 hour) mornings and afternoons. Closed Tuesdays and Wednesdays, 1 January, 1 May, 1 and 11 November, 25 December. 11F (6F early October to end March). ☎ 54 20 27 18.

FRAZÉ

Château. – Park only, Easter to mid-September, Sunday and holiday afternoons. 7F. ☎ 37 29 56 76.

La FRÉNOUSE

Robert-Tatin Museum. – Mornings and afternoons. Closed 24 and 25 December. 7F. ☎ 43 98 80 89.

GALLERANDE

Château. – Not open to the public but one may walk up to the courtyard gate.

GERMIGNY-DES-PRÈS

Church. – Mornings and afternoons. Guided tour on request. Pamphlets available in English. Donation. No visiting during services and from 11am to 2pm on Sundays and holidays.

GIEN

International Hunting Museum. – Mornings and afternoons. 11.65F. ☎ 38 67 00 01, ext. 17 18.

Faience Factory. – Museum: mornings and afternoons. Closed 1 January, 1 and 11 November, 25 December. 10F. Factory: weekdays and by appointment. ☎ 38 67 00 05.

GIZEUX

Church. – In the case of closure (fairly frequent) apply to the parish priest (le curé) who lives in Bourgueil (his other parish). For information ☎ 47 97 71 49.

La GOUBAUDIÈRE

Rural Museum. – Afternoons. Closed Tuesday and holidays. ☎ 41 58 00 83.

GUÉ-PÉAN

Château. – Guided tour (1/2 hour) daily, all day. 20F. ☎ 54 71 43 01.

GY-EN-SOLOGNE

Locature de la Straize. – Guided tour (1 hour), mid-March to end October, weekends and holidays (except Palm Sunday and All Saints'Days), mornings and afternoons. 8F. Information : ☎ 54 83 82 89.

La HAMONNIÈRE

Manor. – Guided tour (20mins) early July to mid-September, afternoons. 7F.

La HAUTE GUERCHE

Château. – July and August, daily all day.

La HERPINIÈRE

Windmill. – Guided tour (1 hour) Easter to end September, mornings and afternoons. Closed Mondays (except holiday Mondays and in July and August). 15F. ☎ 41 51 75 22.

L'ÎLE-BOUCHARD

St Leonard's Priory. – Apply to Mrs. Berton, 4 Rue de la-Vallée-aux-Nains.

St Maurice's Church. – Apply to Mr. Loicadan, 23, Rue St-Léonard.

ILLIERS-COMBRAY

Aunt Léonie's House. – Guided tour (3/4 hour) at 3 and 4pm. Closed Tuesdays, 1 January, 1 May, 14 July, 25 December. 10F. ☏ 37 24 30 97.

ISLE-BRIAND

National Stud. – All year, daily: mornings unaccompanied, afternoons guided tour (2 hours). Stallion numbers are at full strength only from mid-July to mid-February. Presentation of stallions and harness first Wednesday of each month at 2.30pm from early October to end February. ☏ 41 95 82 46.

LANGEAIS

Château. – Guided tour (3/4 hour) mornings and afternoons (all day in July and August). Closed Mondays, early November to mid-March; also 25 December. 14 F. ☏ 47 96 72 60.

LANTHENAY

Church. – Apply to the parish priest (l'Abbé Nouvellon), 6 Place Jeanne-d'Arc in Romorantin. ☏ 54 76 21 04.

LASSAY-SUR-CROISNE

St Denis' Church. – Apply to the Town Hall (Mairie): ☏ 54 83 86 22.

Château du Moulin. – Guided tour (1/2 hour) mornings and afternoons, early March to mid-November. 16F. ☏ 54 83 83 51.

LAVARDIN

Castle. – Closed temporarily, for security reasons, until work is completed.

St Genest's Church. – Guided tour available; apply to Mr. Motheron, 16 Avenue de la République, 41800 Montoire, or to the Tourist Information Centre in Montoire.

Town Hall. – Mondays to Fridays, during office hours.

LEUGNY

Château. – Guided tour (1/2 hour) afternoons in August. 15F. ☏ 47 50 41 10. Early April to end July and early September to end November, groups only; book in advance – Mr. or Mrs. Darrasse, Château de Leugny, Azay-sur-Cher, 37270 Montlouis.

LIGET

Charterhouse and St John's Chapel. – Apply to the house at the end of the courtyard, lefthand door.

LINIÈRES-BOUTON

Church. – Apply to Mr. or Mrs. Gaugain at the Station.

LIRÉ

Joachim du Bellay Museum. – Mornings and afternoons, mid-February to end December. Closed Mondays and Fridays. 10F. ☏ 40 83 24 13.

LOCHES

Medieval city. – Tour by night, early July to mid-September, starting every evening at 9pm from the Tourist Pavilion. 20F.

Lansyer and Le Terroir Museums. – Guided tour (1 1/4 hours) mornings and afternoons, end January to end November. Closed Fridays. 5.90F. ☏ 47 59 05 45.

Castle. – Early February to end November, mornings and afternoons; all day in July and August. Closed Wednesdays, early October to mid-March. 15F. ☏ 47 59 01 32.

Keep. – Same ticket and same times and charges as for the Castle. ☏ 47 59 07 86.

Times and charges

La LORIE

Château. – Guided tour (1/2 hour) afternoons, early July to end September. Closed Tuesdays. 16F. ☎ 41 92 10 04.

LUÇAY-LE-MÂLE

Gunflint Museum. – Guided tour (1/2 hour) afternoons, early July to end September, or by appointment: ☎ 54 40 43 97.

Le LUDE

Château. – Guided tour (3/4 hour) afternoons, early April to end September. 18F. The gardens are open in the mornings also. 12F. ☎ 43 94 60 09.

Architects' House. – Not open to the public.

LUTZ-EN-DUNOIS

Church. – When closed, apply to Mr. and Mrs. Ison.

MALICORNE-SUR-SARTHE

Pottery. – Guided tour (1 1/4 hours) mornings and afternoons, Easter to end September. Closed Sunday and holiday mornings, Mondays all day. 12F. ☎ 43 94 81 18.

Le MANS

St Julian's Cathedral. – Interior illuminations, 9.30pm to 11 pm, Saturdays in July and August. Visitors are requested not to walk about during services; information ☎ 43 28 28 98.

Museum of History and Ethnography. – Mornings and afternoons. Closed 1 January, Easter Day, 1 and 8 May, 14 July, 11 November, 24 and 25 December. ☎ 43 84 97 97.

Red Pillar House. – Not open to visitors.

Tessé Museum. – Same times as for the Historical and Ethnographical Museum.

Church of Our Lady in the Fields. – Sunday mornings only, between services, and late afternoons. Apply to the vicarage (presbytère). ☎ 43 28 52 69.

Church of the Visitation. – Weekdays only. ☎ 43 28 28 98.

Joan of Arc's Church. – Closed Sunday afternoons.

Abbey of Our Lady of L'Épau. – Mornings and afternoons. Closed Thursdays mid-September to mid-April. 5F. Closing time is earlier during concerts etc. Access to the roof by the spiral staircase is restricted to advance group bookings. ☎ 43 84 22 29.

Bugatti permanent circuit. – Guided tour available: information from ☎ 43 72 50 25 (Monday to Friday). Unaccompanied tour daily.

Car Museum. – Mornings and afternoons. Closed Tuesdays, mid-October to Easter. 20F. ☎ 43 72 50 66.

La MAROUTIÈRE

Château. – Guided tour (1/4 hour) for groups (minimum 10 people): apply in advance to Mme de Serrant at the château. 7F. Horse shows: mid-May and mid-September; during these shows tour of the château possible by appointment made through the Tourist Information Centre in Château-Gontier. ☎ 43 07 07 10.

MAULÉVRIER

Oriental Park. – Afternoons. Closed Mondays, 1 January and 25 December. 5F (10F for a guided tour). ☎ 41 55 50 14.

MAVES

Windmill. – Guided tour (1/2 hour), early April to end October, Sunday afternoons. To visit during the week telephone 54 87 31 35.

MÉNARS

Château. – Not open to the public.

MESLAY

Tithe Barn. – Easter to All Saints' Day, Saturday, Sunday and holiday afternoons. 10F. ☎ 47 51 31 21.

MEUNG-SUR-LOIRE

St Liphard's Church. – Closed on 11 November.

Château. – Guided tour (1 hour), Easter to All Saints' Day, daily; otherwise, Saturdays, Sundays and holidays only, mornings and afternoons. 9F for the château, 6F of the vaults.

MEUSNES

Gunflint Museum. – Unaccompanied tour mornings; guided tour (1/4 hour) afternoons; book 2 weeks in advance on ☏ 54 71 00 23. Closed Sundays, Mondays and holidays except by prior arrangement. 3F.

MONTBAZON

Keep. – Not open to the public.

MONTGEOFFROY

Château. – End of March to All Saints' Day, mornings and afternoons. 22F. ☏ 41 80 60 02.

MONTIGNY-LE-GANNELON

Château. – Guided tour (3/4 hour) Easter to All Saints' Days, Saturday, Sunday and holiday afternoons (daily in July and August). 15F. The park is open daily, all day, from Easter to All Saints' Day. 3F. ☏ 37 98 30 03.

MONTLOUIS-SUR-LOIRE

Loire House. – Early April to end August, daily all day; otherwise afternoons only. Closed Tuesdays and holidays. 7F. ☏ 47 50 97 52.

MONTMIRAIL

Château. – Guided tour (3/4 hour) Sunday and holiday afternoons, early March to end October; also daily (except Tuesday) in the afternoon, early July to early September. 15F. ☏ 43 93 65 01. Photography forbidden inside. Display in the basement.

Church. – Closed Sunday and feast day afternoons.

MONTOIRE-SUR-LOIR

St Giles' Chapel. – Apply to "Le Petit-St-Gilles Crêperie" on the corner by the bridge. 5F.

Château. – Closed temporarily.

Town Hall. – Monday to Saturday morning. Apply at reception.

MONTPLACÉ

Notre-Dame Chapel. – Closed temporarily; restoration work in progress. Re-opening in 1990.

MONTPOUPON

Château. – Guided tour (1/2 hour) early April to mid-June and in October, Saturdays, Sundays and holidays, mornings and afternoons; Mid-June to end September, mornings daily, afternoons weekdays, all day Saturdays, Sundays and holidays. 12F. ☏ 47 94 30 77.

MONTRÉSOR

Château. – Unaccompanied tour of the remparts; guided tour (1/2 hour) of the interior, early April to end October, mornings and afternoons. 19F; exterior only 10F. ☏ 47 92 60 04.

MONTREUIL-BELLAY

Castle. – Guided tour (3/4 hour) early April to early November, mornings and afternoons. Closed Tuesdays (mornings only in July and August). 22F. ☏ 41 52 33 06.

MONTRICHARD

Wine cellars. – Guided tour (3/4 hour) mornings and afternoons. Closed Saturdays, Sundays and holidays from All Saints' Day to Palm Sunday. 5F. ☏ 54 32 07 04.

Keep. – Recorded commentary. Mornings and afternoons, daily, mid-June to early September; Saturdays, Sundays and holidays only from Palm Sunday to mid-June and the last three weeks of September. 5F. ☏ 54 32 05 10.

MONTSOREAU

Castle. – Guided tour (1 hour) mornings and afternoons. Closed Tuesdays and 2 weeks in March and 2 weeks in November. 15F. ☏ 41 51 70 25.

MORTIERCROLLES

Château. – Guided tour of the precinct and chapel (3/4 hour) mid-July to end August at 3, 4 and 5pm. Closed Tuesdays. 7F.

La MOTTE-GLAIN

Château. – Guided tour (1/2 hour) mid-June to mid-September, mornings and afternoons. Closed Tuesdays. 15F. ☏ 40 55 52 23.

NÉGRON

Barn. – During exhibitions in July and August. Apply to the Town Hall (Mairie). ☎ 47 57 22 11.

NEUVY

Church. – Apply to Mr. David André opposite the church. ☎ 54 46 42 38.

NEUVY-LE-ROI

Church. – Closed Saturday and Sunday afternoons.

NOURRAY

Church. – Apply to Mr. Geyer opposite.

ORLÉANS

St Cross Cathedral. – Daily, mornings (except Sunday from 2 November to first Sunday in May) and afternoons. Pamphlets available in English. Guided tour of crypt and treasure afternoons. 7F.

Fine Arts Museum. – Mornings and afternoons. Closed Tuesdays, 1 January, 1 and 8 May, 1 November, 25 December. 10F (free Wednesdays and Sunday mornings). ☎ 38 53 39 22.

Historical Museum. – Same times as for the Fine Arts Museum. 5F.

Charles Péguy Centre. – Afternoons, early January to mid-July and early September to mid-December. Closed Saturdays, Sundays and holidays. ☎ 38 53 20 23.

Joan of Arc House. – Guided tour (3/4 hour) mornings and afternoons, early May to early November; otherwise afternoons only. Closed Mondays, 1 January, 1 May, 1 November, 25 December. 4F. ☎ 38 42 25 45.

Hôtel Toutin. – Courtyard only accessible, mornings and afternoons. Closed Sundays, Mondays and holidays and also in August. ☎ 38 62 70 61.

St Aignan's Church. – Apply to the Tourist Information Centre. ☎ 38 53 05 95.

Natural Science Museum. – Mornings and afternoons, Wednesdays and Sundays; afternoons only, Mondays, Tuesdays, Thursdays and Fridays. Closed 1 January, 1 and 8 May, 1 November, 25 December. ☎ 38 42 25 58.

La Source Floral Park. – Early April to mid-November, daily, all day; otherwise, afternoons only. 13F. ☎ 38 63 33 17.

OUDON

Tower. – Early June to mid-September, mornings and afternoons. 2.50F. ☎ 40 83 60 17 (town hall).

PARÇAY-SUR-VIENNE

Church. – Apply to the vicarage (presbytère). ☎ 47 58 54 85.

PITHIVIERS

Steam Train and Transport Museum. – Train operational, Sunday and holiday afternoons, early May to mid-October. 1 1/2 hours. 20F. ☎ 38 30 50 02 (Tourist Information Office, closed mornings except Saturday, Sunday and Monday).

Museum. – Mornings and afternoons. Closed Tuesdays. 2F.

Le PLESSIS-BOURRÉ

Château. – Guided tour (1 hour) mornings and afternoons. Closed Wednesdays, Thursday mornings and from mid-November to mid-December. 21F. ☎ 41 32 06 01.

PLESSIS-LÈS-TOURS

Château. – Guided tour (3/4 hour) mornings and afternoons. Closed Tuesdays, 1 May, 14 July, 1 and 11 November, 25 December and in January. 5F. ☎ 47 37 22 80.

Le PLESSIS-MACÉ

Château. – Guided tour (1 hour approximately) afternoons, early March to end November; mornings also, early July to end September. Closed Tuesdays. 15F. ☎ 41 32 67 93.

PONCÉ-SUR-LE-LOIR

Craft Centre "Les Grès du Loir". – Mornings, except Sundays and holidays, and afternoons. ☎ 43 44 45 31.

Château. – Mornings, except Sundays and holidays, and afternoons, early April to end September. 14F. ☎ 43 44 45 39.

PONTLEVOY

Old Abbey. – Guided tour (1/2 hour) end March to end September, mornings and afternoons; all day in July and August. Closed Mondays except in July and August. 16F (ticket valid for the Road Transport Museum and the Local Museum). ☎ 54 32 60 80.

Road Transport Museum and Local Museum. – Guided tour (1/4 hour) on the same days and at the same times as the Old Abbey. Same ticket.

La POSSONNIÈRE

Manor. – By appointment with the owner: Couture-sur-Loir, 41800 Montoire-sur-le-Loir.

POUANCÉ

Castle. – Guided tour (1/2 hour) mornings and afternoons (all day in July and August). Closed Sunday mornings, Easter school holidays, 1 January, 1 and 11 November, 25 December. 10F. ☎ 41 92 45 86.

Le PRIEURÉ

Church. – Sundays only.

PRINGÉ

Church. – Apply to Mr. and Mrs. Herteloup, first house on the right, Route de St-Jean-de-la-Motte.

r

RAGUIN

Castle. – Guided tour (1/2 hour) mornings and afternoons, Easter to end October. ☎ 41 61 40 20.

Les RÉAUX

Château. – Not open to the public. Literary exhibition "The Loire and its Poets". 10F. ☎ 47 95 14 40.

RESTIGNÉ

Church. – Saturdays only.

RHODON

Church. – Apply to Mrs. Albert Rentien.

RIVAU

Château. – Guided tour (1 hour) mornings and afternoons, mid-March to early November. 22F. ☎ 42 00 20 99.

ROCHEMENIER

Troglotyte Village. – Mornings and afternoons, early April to mid-October; otherwise irregular. Enquire in advance. ☎ 41 59 18 15. Closed Mondays except in July and August. 10F.

La ROCHE-RACAN

Château. – Guided tour (1/2 hour) mornings and afternoons, early August to mid-September. 10F.

ROMORANTIN-LANTHENAY

Maison du Carroir d'Orée (Archaeological Museum). – Mornings and afternoons, July and August. Closed Tuesdays. 6F. ☎ 54 76 22 06 (mornings).

The Sologne Museum. – Mornings and afternoons. Closed Mondays and Sunday mornings; also 1 January, 1 May, 25 December. 6.50F. ☎ 54 76 07 06.

St Stephen's Church. – Closed Sunday afternoons.

Car Racing Museum. – Mid-March to early November, mornings and afternoons. Closed Tuesdays, Sunday mornings and 1 May. 6.50F. ☎ 54 76 07 06.

ROUJOUX

Leisure Park. – Mid-April to end May, weekends, holidays and Wednesdays, 11am to 8pm; early June to end September, daily, 11am to 8pm. 30F. Mini-restaurant, crêperie, picnic area under cover and in the park. ☎ 54 79 53 39 or 54 79 53 55.

S

SACHÉ

Château. – Guided tour mornings and afternoons. Closed Wednesdays, early October to mid-March. 15F. ☎ 47 26 86 50.

ST-AGIL

Château. – Exterior only.

ST-AIGNAN

Church. – Recorded commentary in six languages. Daily except Sunday mornings. Belfry open certain days in July and August; information on ☎ 54 75 01 33.

Château. – Not open to the public except for the main courtyard.

Provost's House. – Not open except for exhibitions; information from the Town Hall (Mairie).

ST-BENOÎT-SUR-LOIRE

Basilica. – Unaccompanied tour all day. Guided tour on request (10 people minimum) in 4 languages, weekdays 11am to 3pm, Sundays and holidays at 3.15 and 4.30pm. Donation. No visiting during services and Holy Week.

Services. – Gregorian chant: discreet attendance requested. Community mass at 12 noon on weekdays, 11am Sundays and feast days. Vespers at 6.15pm daily.

ST-CALAIS

Church. – To view the shroud telephone 43 35 01 90.

ST-COSME

Priory. – Early February to end November, mornings and afternoons; all day in July and August. Closed Wednesdays, early October to mid-March. 15F. ☎ 47 37 32 70.

ST-CYR-EN-BOURG

Wine-makers' Cellar. – Guided tour (1 hour) mornings and afternoons, early May to end September. 5F. ☎ 41 51 61 09.

ST-ÉTIENNE-DE-CHIGNY

Church. – Apply to Mr. Baillet, Le Portail, St-Étienne-de-Chigny, 37230 Luynes.

ST-LAMBERT-DU-LATTAY

Museum of the Grape and the Wine of Anjou. – Mornings and afternoons, early April to end October. 10F. ☎ 41 78 42 75.

ST-LAURENT-DE-LA-PLAINE

Museum of Old Crafts. – Mornings and afternoons, early April to early November. 18F. ☎ 41 78 24 08. Live display on the first Sunday in September.

ST-LAURENT-DES-EAUX

Nuclear Power Station. – Viewing platform open daily all day. Guided tour (2 1/2 hours approximately) Mondays to Saturdays by prior appointment. ☎ 54 87 75 66. Proof of identity obligatory. Film and commentary.

ST-ULPHACE

Church. – Apply to Mrs. Peyron, the grocer (épicière).

ST-VIÂTRE

Church. – Closed holidays and Sunday afternoons. ℡ 54 88 93 26.

STE-CATHERINE-DE-FIERBOIS

Church. – Apply to the Town Hall (Mairie).

Boucicault Almonry. – Guided tour (1/4 hour) Easter to end September. Closed Sundays and holidays except 14 July. ℡ 47 65 65 36.

STE-MAURE-DE-TOURAINE

Church. – When closed apply to the vicarage (presbytère), 8 Rue de l'Église.

SALBRIS

Church. – Weekdays only.

SARGÉ-SUR-BRAYE

Church. – Enquire at the bakery (boulangerie); on closing day the church is manned by the bailiff (garde-champêtre).

SAUMUR

Castle. – Guided tour (1 1/2 hours) mornings and afternoons; all day from early July to end September; evenings in July and August. Closed Tuesdays from early November to end March; also 1 January and 25 December. 16F, museums included. ℡ 41 51 30 46.

St Peter's Church. – For a guided tour apply to the Tourist Information Centre. ℡ 41 51 03 06.

Cavalry Museum. – Guided tour (1 hour) weekday afternoons, Sunday and holiday mornings and afternoons. Closed Mondays, 1 and 8 May, 11 November, from 20 December to 5 January and in August. ℡ 41 51 05 43, ext 306.

Armoured Corps Museum. – Mornings and afternoons. 15F. ℡ 41 51 02 45.

National Equitation Centre. – Guided tour (1 hour) mornings and afternoons, early April to end October. Closed Saturday, Sunday, Monday and holiday mornings. 10F. ℡ 41 50 21 35.

Mushroom Museum. – Guided tour (3/4 hour) mornings and afternoons, mid-March to mid-November. 13F. ℡ 41 50 25 01.

SAVONNIÈRES

Petrifying Caves. – Guided tour (1 hour) mid-February to mid-December, mornings and afternoons; all day, early April to mid-October. Closed Thursdays in February, March, October, November and December. 16F. ℡ 47 50 00 09.

SELLES-SUR-CHER

Castle. – Guided tour (1/2 hour) mid-March to end October, mornings and afternoons. Closed Sunday mornings. 17F. ℡ 54 97 59 10. The animal park is open all year.

Local History and Folklore Museum. – July and August, Tuesday and Thursday afternoons, Saturday and Sunday mornings and afternoons. 5F. ℡ 54 97 40 19 (town hall).

SEMUR-EN-VALLON

Castle. – Not open to the public.

Train. – Early May to end September, Sunday and holiday afternoons; weekdays on request to the Chairman. ℡ 43 71 30 37 (at meal times). 5F.

SERRANT

Château. – Guided tour (3/4 hour) end March to early November, mornings and afternoons. Closed Tuesdays except in July and August. ℡ 41 39 13 01.

SOLESMES

Services. – Mass at 10am on Sundays, at 9.45am on weekdays. Vespers at 5pm (4pm Thursdays), Compline at 8.30pm. To visit apply in advance to the Father in charge of hospitality (Père Hôtelier).

SOLOGNE

Train rides. – For all information about timetables and fares apply to the Compagnie du Blanc Argent, Romorantin-Lanthenay Station. ℡ 54 76 06 51.

SULLY-SUR-LOIRE

Castle. – Guided tour (3/4 hour) mornings and afternoons, early March to end November. Closed penultimate Saturday in June. ℡ 38 36 25 60.

Times and charges

t

TALCY

Castle. – Guided tour (1/2 hour) mornings and afternoons. Closed Tuesday and 1 January, 1 May, 1 November, 25 December. 16F (9F out of season). ☎ 54 81 03 01.

TAVANT

Church. – Guided tour (3/4 hour) early March to end November, mornings and afternoons 6F. ☎ 47 58 58 06.

TERTRE ROUGE

Zoo. – All year. 31F; children 18F. Information: ☎ 43 94 04 55.

TOURS

Tristan's House. – The courtyard is accessible to visitors during school hours from Monday to Saturday morning except on holidays.

Gemmail Museum. – End March to mid-October, mornings and afternoons. Closed Mondays. 18F. ☎ 47 61 01 19.

Hôtel Gouin. – Early February to end November, mornings and afternoons. Closed Fridays. 10F. ☎ 47 66 22 32.

St Gatien's Cathedral. – Guided tour; apply to the clergy house (presbytère) several days in advance. ☎ 47 05 05 54.

La Psalette. – Guided tour (1/4 hour) mornings and afternoons. Closed 1 January, 1 May, 1 and 11 November, 25 December. No visiting during services on Sundays. 11F (6F out of season). ☎ 47 05 63 37.

Fine Arts Museum. – Mornings and afternoons. Closed Tuesdays, 1 January, 1 May, 14 July, 1 and 11 November, 25 December. 10F. ☎ 47 05 68 73.

Historical Museum. – Mornings and afternoons; all day from Mid-June to mid-September. 26F. ☎ 47 61 02 95.

Contemporary Arts Centre. – Afternoons, all year in accordance with the programme of exhibitions. Wednesday evenings. Closed Monday. 15F. ☎ 47 66 50 00.

St Julian's Church. – Afternoons only.

Touraine Wine Museum. – Guided tour (3/4 hour) – request in writing to the Trade Guild Museum – mornings and afternoons. Closed Tuesdays, 1 January, 1 May, 14 July, 1 and 11 November, 25 December. 5F. ☎ 47 61 07 93.

Trade Guild Museum. – Same times and charges as the Touraine Wine Museum.

TRÉLAZÉ

Slate Museum. – Guided tour (2 hours) early July to end September, afternoons daily except Mondays, otherwise Sunday and holiday afternoons only.

TROO

Limestone Cave. – Early April to end September, daily all day. 4F. ☎ 54 85 35 83.

TROUSSAY

Château. – Guided tour (1/2 hour) mornings and afternoons, mid-April to end September; daily during the Easter school holidays and from early June to end August; Sundays and holidays only in May and September. 15F. ☎ 54 44 29 07.

u - v

USSÉ

Château. – Unaccompanied tour of the exterior. Guided tour (3/4 hour) of the interior, mornings and afternoons, mid-March to mid-November. 30F. ☎ 47 95 54 05.

VALENÇAY

Château. – Guided tour (3/4 hour) mid-March to mid-November, mornings and afternoons; all day in July and August. 25F: ticket valid for the park and the Car Museum. ☎ 54 00 10 66.

Park. – Same dates and times as for the château but closed on holiday afternoons. 7F.

Car Museum. – Same dates and times and ticket as for the château.

VARENNES-BOURREAU

Chapel. – Apply to the Town Hall (Mairie) in St-Denis-d'Anjou. ☎ 43 70 52 19.

VAUJOURS

Château. – Not open to the public.

VAUX

Château. – Restoration work in progress; re-opening for tour of the moat in summer 1988.

VENDÔME

Holy Trinity Abbey. – Enquire at the museum to see the frescoes in the Chapter House.

Museum. – Mornings and afternoons. Closed Tuesdays, 1 January, 1 May, 25 December. 7.90F. ☎ 54 77 26 13.

Library. – Closed all day Sundays and Saturday and Monday mornings.

Castle. – Guided tour (1/2 hour) of the interior (unaccompanied tour of the park) mornings and afternoons, early April to end October. 5.70F. ☎ 54 77 01 33.

VENEVELLES

Manor. – Not open to the public.

VERDELLES

Château. – Not open to the public.

VERNANTES

Church. – Apply to the Secretariat at the Town Hall (Mairie). ☎ 41 51 50 12.

La VERRERIE

Château. – Guided tour (3/4 hour) from mid-February to mid-November, mornings and afternoons. 15F. ☎ 48 58 06 91.

Le VIEIL-BAUGÉ

St Symphorien's Church. – Closed Sundays and holidays.

VIEUX BOURG DE CRAVANT

Church. – Afternoons. Closed Tuesdays. 6F. ☎ 47 93 12 40.

VILLAINES-LES-ROCHERS

Cooperative. – Mornings and afternoons. Closed 1 January, 25 December and Sunday mornings from early October to Easter. ☎ 47 45 43 03.

VILLANDRY

Gardens. – Daily all day. 16F. ☎ 47 50 02 09.

Château. – Guided tour (3/4 hour) daily all day from mid-March to mid-November. 22F (gardens included). ☎ 47 50 02 09.

VILLEHERVIERS

Church. – Open during services only.

VILLESAVIN

Château. – Unaccompanied tour of exterior. Guided tour (3/4 hour) of interior from early March to mid-December; mornings and afternoons until end April, all day from early May to end September; otherwise afternoons only. 16F (exterior: 6F). ☎ 54 46 42 88.

VILLIERS-SUR-LOIR

Church. – Apply to the Town Hall (Mairie).

VOUVRAY

Wine Cellars. – Wine Fair end of January and 15 August; Wine Festival at Whitsuntide.

YÈVRE-LE-CHATEL

Fortress. – Afternoons from early April to early November and also mornings from early June to end August. Closed Tuesdays. 5F. ☎ 38 34 25 91.

YÈVRES

Church. – Apply to the parish priest (curé) of Brou. ☎ 37 47 02 70, or to Mrs. Boisserie in Yèvres.

Index

215

MANUFACTURE FRANÇAISE DES PNEUMATIQUES MICHELIN
Société en commandite par actions au capital de 875 000 000 de francs
Place des Carmes-Déchaux - 63 Clermont-Ferrand (France)
R.C.S. Clermont-Fd B 855 200 507
© Michelin et Cie, Propriétaires-Éditeurs 1988
Dépôt légal 4ᵉ trim. 88 – ISBN 2.06.013.221-5 – ISSN 0763-1383

Printed in France - 09.88.30
Photocomposition : BLANCHARD, Le Plessis-Robinson - Impression : ISTRA, Strasbourg, n° 811960